Learning Disabilities

Learning Disabilities

A Practical Approach to Foundations, Assessment, Diagnosis, and Teaching

ROGER PIERANGELO
Long Island University

GEORGE GIULIANI
Hofstra University

PEARSON

Boston   New York   San Francisco
Mexico City   Montreal   Toronto   London   Madrid   Munich   Paris
Hong Kong   Singapore   Tokyo   Cape Town   Sydney

Executive Editor: *Virginia Lanigan*
Editorial Assistant: *Scott Blaszak*
Senior Marketing Manager: *Kris Ellis-Levy*
Editorial Production Service: *Omegatype Typography, Inc.*
Composition and Manufacturing Buyer: *Andrew Turso*
Electronic Composition: *Omegatype Typography, Inc.*
Cover Administrator: *Linda Knowles*

For related titles and support materials, visit our online catalog at
www.ablongman.com.

Between the time website information is gathered and then published, it is not unusual
for some sites to have closed. Also, the transcription of URLs can result in typographical
errors. The publisher would appreciate notification where these errors occur so that they
may be corrected in subsequent editions.

Library of Congress Cataloging-in-Publication Data

Pierangelo, Roger.
 Learning disabilities: a practical approach to foundations, assessment, diagnosis, and
teaching / Roger Pierangelo, George Giuliani.
   p.   cm.
 Includes bibliographical references and index.
 ISBN 0-205-45964-1 (paperbound)
  1. Learning disabled children—Education—United States. 2. Learning disabilities—United
States. 3. Educational tests and measurements—United States. I. Giuliani, George A. II. Title.
 LC4705.P49 2006
 371.9'0973—dc22

                                                                              2005053481

Printed in the United States of America

10 9 8 7 6 5 4 3 2 1   10 09 08 07 06 05

Contents

3 Characteristics of Children with Learning Disabilities   33

6 Diagnosing a Learning Disability   110

7 Eligibility Procedures and IEP Development   120

8 Transition Services for Students with Learning Disabilities   138

PART III Teaching Students with Learning Disabilities   159

9 Overview of Learning Strategies   161

10 Strategies and Instructional Practices for Students with Learning Disabilities in Reading   177

11   Strategies and Instructional Practices for Students with Learning Disabilities in Mathematics   221

12   Strategies and Instructional Practices for Students with Learning Disabilities in Written Expression   245

13 Strategies and Instructional Practices for Students with Attention-Deficit Hyperactivity Disorder   261

16 Interim Stage: October–March 332

17 Culmination Stage: April–June 348

Preface

Learning Disabilities: A Practical Approach to Foundations, Assessment, Diagnosis, and Teaching represents a new and unique direction in college textbooks. This book is the result of several years of marketing analysis and experience. The format for this text is based on your needs as a student to have a practical, user-friendly, useful, and easily understood textbook that also can be used as a reference once you enter the workplace.

In our market research with undergraduate and graduate students, we found that

- 91% of those interviewed felt that most college texts were very difficult to read,
- 87% found them difficult to understand,
- 74% felt that most texts contained irrelevant and useless charts and tables,
- 93% indicated that they could not see using the book as a practical reference tool after the course was over,
- 71% felt that the formats were overwhelming,
- 98% felt that most texts contained too much theory and not enough "practical information," and
- 90% normally sold back their textbooks at the end of the semester because they had no practical value and would "just sit on a shelf."

This book is divided into four distinct parts:

Part I: Foundational Issues in Learning Disabilities. Part I focuses on the basic foundations of learning disabilities. Topics covered include an overview of learning disabilities, causes, and characteristics of students with learning disabilities.

Part II: Identifying a Student with a Learning Disability. Part II focuses on the process of identifying a student with a learning disability. This part includes topics covering the referral process, assessment, diagnosis, eligibility procedures for services, IEP development, and transition services.

Part III: Teaching Students with Learning Disabilities. Part III focuses on teaching students with learning disabilities. Areas covered include learning strategies, instructional strategies and practices for students with reading disabilities, instructional strategies and practices for students with math disabilities, and instructional strategies and practices for students with written expression disabilities.

Part IV: Practical Considerations for Teachers of Students with Learning Disabilities. Part IV is unique to all previous and current textbooks in the field of learning disabilities. Part IV covers a typical school year divided into four sections. Each section provides the practical roles and responsibilities, teaching strategies, classroom management, and all other necessary information for you to have as a teacher when working with students with learning disabilities. It will provide a step-by-step guide from before the first day of school begins to the end of the school term.

We have tried to provide you with a "real-world story" in order to understand, assess, diagnose, and teach students with learning disabilities. We have tried to create for you a story that has a beginning, a middle, and an end.

Many texts we have reviewed on learning disabilities have approximately fifteen or more chapters that are not connected, but rather offer students separate pieces that never show clearly the overall process in a straight line. In this text, we provide you with the practical tools necessary to understand students with learning disabilities in schools and to learn how to "put it all together."

Acknowledgments

In the course of writing this book, we have encountered many professional and outstanding sites. It has been our experience that those resources have contributed and continue to contribute enormous information, support, guidance, and education to parents, students, and professionals in the area of special education. Although we have accessed many worthwhile sites, we would especially like to thank and acknowledge the National Dissemination Center for Children and Youths with Disabilities (NICHCY).

Dr. Roger Pierangelo extends thanks to the following: the faculty, administration, and staff in the Department of Graduate Special Education and Literacy at Long Island University; the students and parents of the Herricks Public Schools he has worked with and known over the past twenty-eight years; the late Bill Smyth, a truly gifted and "extraordinary ordinary" man; Helen Firestone, for her influence on his career and tireless support of him; and Ollie Simmons, for her friendship, loyalty, and great personality.

Dr. Giuliani extends sincere thanks to all of his colleagues at Hofstra University in the School of Education and Allied Human Services. He is especially grateful to those who have made his transition to Hofstra University such a smooth one, including Dr. James R. Johnson (Dean), Dr. Penelope J. Haile (Associate Dean), Dr. Daniel Sciarra (Chairperson), Dr. Frank Bowe, Dr. Diane Schwartz (Graduate Program Director of Special Education), Dr. Darra Pace, Dr. Vance Austin, Dr. Gloria Wilson, Dr. Laurie Johnson, Dr. Joan Bloomgarden, Dr. Tai Chang, Dr. Jamie Mitus, Dr. Estelle Gellman, Dr. Joseph Lechowicz, Dr. Ron McLean, Adele Piombino, Marjorie Butler, Eve Byrne, Sherrie Basile, and Linda Cappa.

Dr. Giuliani would also like to thank his brother and sister, Roger and Claudia; mother-in-law, Ursula Jenkeleit; sisters-in-law Karen and Cindy; brothers-in-law Robert and Bob; and grandfather, all of whom have provided him with encouragement and reinforcement in all of his personal and professional endeavors.

We would like to thank Virginia Lanigan, our Allyn and Bacon editor, whose outstanding guidance, support, and words of encouragement made writing this book a very worthwhile and enjoyable experience. We would also like to thank Scott Blaszak, our Editorial Assistant, for always helping us attain any materials or information necessary to complete this textbook.

We would also like to thank the following reviewers for their comments on the manuscript: Bea Babbitt, University of Nevada, Las Vegas; Judy L. Bell, Furman University; Robin Castle, Montana State University–Northern; Laurie U. deBettencourt, University of Virginia; Andrew Dowling, Manhattanville College; Jean C. Faieta, Edinboro University of Pennsylvania; David James Hunter, Georgia Southwestern State University; Veda Jairrels, Clark Atlanta University; Marilyn Kaff, Kansas State University; Belinda Karge, California State University, Fullerton; Maribeth Montgomery Kasik, Governors State University; Kathryn A. Lund, Arizona State University; Maurice Miller, Indiana State University; Sheila Saravanabhavan, Virginia State University; Dale E. Smith, Alvernia College; John W. Somers, University of Indianapolis; Sandra Wanner, University of Mary Hardin-Baylor; Silvana Watson, Old Dominion University; and Nina Yssel, Ball State University.

We would also like to thank the following for their research contributions to this book: David Geary, Professor of Psychology at the University of Missouri at Columbia, Robin H. Lock at The University of Texas at Austin, and Beatrice C. Babbit, Associate Professor of Special Education at The University of Nevada, Las Vegas, for their contributions to Chapter 11, and Regina G. Richards, MA, an educational therapist in Riverside California, for her contributions to Chapter 12.

For over two years, the National Reading Panel (NRP) reviewed research-based knowledge on reading instruction and held open panel meetings in Washington, D.C., and regional meetings across the United States. The National Institute of Child Health and Human Development (NICHD) has formed a partnership with the National Institute for Literacy (NIFL) and the U.S. Department of Education (ED) to work on continued dissemination and implementation efforts of the NRP Report, as part of NIFL's overall mission to disseminate and implement research-based reading practices. Many organizations are turning to the NRP Report to highlight important findings that impact specific audiences such as parents, teachers, and school administrators. Such organizations are creating tools that will enable specific audiences to use the NRP findings best suited for them. We thank them for their research and writings in the field of reading disabilities and literacy.

I Foundational Issues in Learning Disabilities

Learning disabilities are disorders that affect the ability to understand or use spoken or written language, do mathematical calculations, coordinate movements, or direct attention. Although learning disabilities occur in very young children, the disorders are usually not recognized until the child reaches school age.

Children with learning disabilities are a heterogeneous group. These children are a diverse group of individuals, exhibiting potential difficulties in many different areas. For example, one child with a learning disability may experience significant reading problems, while another may experience no reading problems whatsoever, but has significant difficulties with written expression.

Learning disabilities may be mild, moderate, or severe. Students also differ in their coping skills. They can be lifelong conditions. In some students, several overlapping learning disabilities may be apparent. Other students may have a single, isolated learning problem that has little impact on their lives.

The most common "treatment" for learning disabilities is special education. Specially trained educators may perform a diagnostic educational evaluation assessing the child's academic and intellectual potential and level of academic performance. Once the evaluation is complete, the basic approach is to teach learning skills by building on the child's abilities and strengths while correcting and compensating for disabilities and weaknesses. Other professionals such as speech and language therapists may also be involved. Some medications may be effective in helping the child learn by enhancing attention and concentration. Psychological therapies may also be used.

Interestingly, there is no clear and widely accepted definition of "learning disabilities." Because of the multidisciplinary nature of the field, there is ongoing debate on the issue of definition, and there are currently at least twelve definitions that appear in the professional literature

Part I of this text focuses on understanding the basic foundational principles of learning disabilities. Topics covered include overview of learning disabilities (Chapter 1), causes of learning disabilities (Chapter 2), and characteristics of students with learning disabilities (Chapter 3).

CHAPTER

1 Introduction to Learning Disabilities

Definition of Learning Disabilities

Learning disability (LD) is a general term that describes specific kinds of learning problems. A learning disability can cause a person to have trouble learning and using certain skills. The skills most often affected are reading, writing, listening, speaking, reasoning, and doing math. Learning disabilities vary from person to person. One person with LD may not have the same kind of learning problems as another person with LD. One person may have trouble with reading and writing. Another person with LD may have problems understanding math. Still another person may have trouble in each of these areas, as well as with understanding what people are saying (National Dissemination Center for Children and Youth with Disabilities [NICHCY], 2004).

LD is a group of disorders that affects people's ability to either interpret what they see and hear or to link information from different parts of the brain. These limitations can show up in many ways: as specific difficulties with spoken and written language, coordination, self-control, or attention. Such difficulties extend to schoolwork and can impede learning to read, write, or do math.

A learning disability is a neurological disorder that affects the brain's ability to receive, process, store, and respond to information. The term learning disability is used to describe the seemingly unexplained difficulty a person of at least average intelligence has in acquiring basic academic skills. These skills are essential for success at school and work, and for coping with life in general. "LD" does not stand for a single disorder. It is a term that refers to a group of disorders.

Interestingly, there is no clear and widely accepted definition of learning disabilities. Because of the multidisciplinary nature of the field, there is ongoing debate on the issue of definition, and currently at least twelve definitions appear in the professional literature. There are several technical definitions offered by various health and education sources. Overall, most experts agree on the following descriptions.

- Individuals with LD have difficulties with academic achievement and progress.
- Discrepancies exist between a person's potential for learning and what that person actually learns.
- Individuals with LD show an uneven pattern of development (language development, physical development, academic development, and/or perceptual development).
- Learning problems are not due to environmental disadvantage.
- Learning problems are not due to mental retardation or emotional disturbance.
- Learning disabilities can affect one's ability to read, write, speak, spell, compute math, and reason. They also can affect a person's attention, memory, coordination, social skills, and emotional maturity.
- Individuals with LD have normal intelligence, or are sometimes even intellectually gifted.
- Individuals with LD have differing capabilities, with difficulties in certain academic areas but not in others.
- Learning disabilities have an effect on either input (the brain's ability to process incoming information) or output (the person's ability to use information in practical skills, such as reading, math, spelling, etc.).

Research suggests that learning disabilities are caused by differences in how a person's brain works and how it processes information. Children with LD are not stupid or lazy. In fact, they usually have average or above average intelligence, but their brains process information differently. (See Box 1.1 for more myths about LD.) A learning disability affects the way kids of average to above average intelligence receive, process, or express information. Even if the person learns to compensate and, in effect, overcomes the disorder, the difference in brain processing lasts throughout life.

IMPORTANT POINT TO NOTE

Knowing that a child has a learning disability tells you only that the child is experiencing some difficulty processing information. You must learn much more about the child before you can determine how much difficulty, the type of difficulties, and/or the impact the disability has on specific academic subjects or tasks.

History of the Field

Definitions of learning disabilities have evolved over time. These definitions have been attempts at describing a condition that had been labeled, among other terms, aphasia, neurologically impaired, Strauss Syndrome, and minimal brain dysfunction.

History suggests that the term learning disabilities originated with and became popularized by Dr. Samuel Kirk based on his writings in the early 1960s and

BOX 1.1

Myth vs. Reality about Learning Disabilities

Myth 1.   People with LD are not very smart.

Reality.   Kids with learning disabilities are just as smart as other kids. Intelligence has nothing to do with LD. In fact, people with LD have average to above average intelligence. Many have intellectual, artistic, or other abilities that permit them to be defined as gifted. Studies indicate that as many as 33% of students with LD are gifted.

Myth 2.   LD is just an excuse for irresponsible, unmotivated, or lazy people.

Reality.   LD is caused by neurological impairments, not character flaws. For some people with LD, the effort required to get through a day can be exhausting in and of itself. The motivation required to do what others take for granted is enormous. Learning disabilities are problems in processing words or information, causing otherwise bright and capable children to have difficulty learning. The disabilities involve language—reading, writing, speaking, and/or listening.

Myth 3.   LD only affects children. Adults grow out of the disorders.

Reality.   It is now known that the effects of LD continue throughout the individual's lifespan and "may even intensify in adulthood as tasks and environmental demands change" (Michaels, 1994). Sadly, many adults, especially older adults, have never been formally diagnosed with LD. Learning disabilities cannot be outgrown, but they can be identified reliably in kindergarten or first-grade children, or even earlier. Research clearly demonstrates that the earlier a child is given appropriate help for a learning disability, the more successful the outcome.

Myth 4.   The terms *dyslexia* and *learning disability* are the same thing.

Reality.   Dyslexia is a type of learning disability. It is not another term for learning disability. It is a specific language-based disorder affecting a person's ability to read, write, and verbally express him or herself. Unfortunately, careless use of the term dyslexia has expanded so that it has become, for some people, an equivalent for LD. Four out of five children identified with a learning disability are diagnosed with a reading disability (or dyslexia). They have trouble learning how spoken language translates into written text. Since every subject—including math—requires reading and writing, a reading disability affects all of a person's school-based learning.

Myth 5.   Learning disabilities are only academic in nature. They do not affect other areas of a person's life.

Reality.   Some people with learning disabilities have isolated difficulties in reading, writing, or mathematics. However, most people with learning disabilities have more than one area of difficulty. Dr. Larry Silver asserts that "learning disabilities are life disabilities." He writes, "the same disabilities that interfere with reading, writing, and arithmetic also will interfere with sports and other activities, family life, and getting along with friends." (Silver, 1998) Some children have good verbal (language) skills but weaknesses in visual and spatial perception, motor skills and, most significantly, social skills—affecting their ability to grasp the main idea, "see the whole picture," or understand cause-and-effect relationships. Many children with LD struggle with organization, attention, and memory. One-third of them may also have an attention deficit disorder—difficulty in regulating attention effectively, paying attention as needed, and shifting attention to another task, when required. Children with LD are creative and resourceful, and can frequently be characterized as gifted and as alternative thinkers. They are often very smart, and typically have strengths and talents that differ from the skills emphasized in school. With recognition of their difficulties,

(continued)

BOX 1.1

Myth vs. Reality about Learning Disabilities *(continued)*

appropriate help, and the development of their interests and talents, children with LD can learn to succeed both in school and beyond.

Myth 6.   Adults with LD cannot succeed in higher education.

Reality.   More and more adults with LD are going to college or university and succeeding. With the proper accommodations and support, adults with learning disabilities can be successful at higher education.

Myth 7.   Children with LD are identified in kindergarten and first grade.

Reality.   Learning disabilities often go unrecognized for years; most are not identified

until third grade. Bright children can "mask" their difficulties, and some kinds of learning problems may not surface until middle school, high school, or even college.

Myth 8.   More boys than girls have learning disabilities.

Reality.   Although three times more boys than girls are identified by schools as having learning disabilities, research studies show that, in fact, equal numbers of boys and girls have the most common form of learning problem—difficulty with reading. Many girls' learning difficulties are neither identified nor treated.

comments that were made at the April 6, 1963 Conference on Exploration into Problems of the Perceptually Handicapped Child. His proposed label was "enthusiastically received and helped to unite the participants into an organization known as the Association for Children with Learning Disabilities, the forerunner of today's Learning Disabilities Association" (Lerner, 2000).

> I have used the term "learning disabilities" to describe "a group of children who have disorders in development in language, speech, reading, and associated communication skills needed for social interaction. In this group I do not include children who have sensory handicaps such as blindness or deafness, because we have methods of managing and training the deaf and the blind. I also exclude from this group children who have generalized mental retardation. (Kirk, 1963, p. 2)

During the latter part of the 1960s, there became greater awareness about learning disabilities, both from the general public and Congress. In response, the U.S. Office of Education was charged with creating a federal definition for what constituted a learning disability. Samuel Kirk chaired this committee. In 1968, the first annual report of the National Advisory Committee on Handicapped Children, headed by Dr. Kirk, wrote:

> Children with special learning disabilities exhibit a disorder in one or more of the basic, psychological processes involved in understanding or in using spoken or written languages. These may be manifested in disorders of listening, thinking,

talking, reading, writing, spelling, or arithmetic. They include conditions which have been referred to as perceptual handicaps, brain injury, minimal brain dysfunction, dyslexia, developmental aphasia, etc. They do not include learning problems which are due primarily to visual, hearing, or motor handicaps, to mental retardation, emotional disturbance, or to environmental disadvantage. (*Special Education for Handicapped Children*, 1968)

By the end of 1968, "specific learning disability" (abbreviated SLD or LD) became a federally designated category of special education (U.S. Office of Education, 1968), and in 1969, the Specific Learning Disabilities Act was enacted, Public Law 91-230. In 1975, Congress enacted P.L. 94-142, the Education for All Handicapped Children's Act. Here, the definition of a learning disability was formalized for children in special education. Under P.L. 94-142, a specific learning disability was defined as follows.

. . . a disorder in one or more of the basic psychological processes involved in understanding or in using language, spoken or written, that may manifest itself in an imperfect ability to listen, think, speak, read, write, spell, or do mathematical calculations, including conditions such as perceptual disabilities, brain injury, minimal brain dysfunction, dyslexia, and developmental aphasia.

However, learning disabilities do not include, ". . . learning problems that are primarily the result of visual, hearing, or motor disabilities, of mental retardation, of emotional disturbance, or of environmental, cultural, or economic disadvantage.

The continuance of the P.L. 94-142 definition in federal law prompted further analysis. In the 1980s, a coalition of parent and professional organizations, described as the National Joint Committee on Learning Disabilities (NJCLD), criticized the definition under P.L. 94-142 for including concepts that were unclear or difficult to use to identify children with learning disabilities. In response to the criticisms, the NJCLD proposed an alternative definition.

Learning disabilities is a general term that refers to a heterogeneous group of disorders manifested by significant difficulties in the acquisition and use of listening, speaking, reading, writing, reasoning, or mathematical abilities. These disorders are intrinsic to the individual and presumed to be due to central nervous system dysfunction, and may occur across the lifespan. Problems in self-regulatory behaviors, social perception, and social interaction may exist with learning disabilities but do not by themselves constitute a learning disability. Although learning disabilities may occur concomitantly with other handicapping conditions or with extrinsic influences, they are not the direct result of those conditions or influences. (NJCLD, 1994)

Today, children in special education are protected under Public Law 108-446, The Individuals with Disabilities Education Improvement Act (IDEA 2004). The definition under IDEA has not changed in its criteria and guidelines for what constitutes a learning disability. Under current federal law the following language was established.

IN GENERAL:—The term "specific learning disability" means a disorder in 1 or more of the basic psychological processes involved in understanding or in using language, spoken or written, which disorder may manifest itself in the imperfect ability to listen, think, speak, read, write, spell, or do mathematical calculations.

DISORDERS INCLUDED.—Such term includes such conditions as perceptual disabilities, brain injury, minimal brain dysfunction, dyslexia, and developmental aphasia.

DISORDERS NOT INCLUDED.—Such term does not include a learning problem that is primarily the result of visual, hearing, or motor disabilities, of mental retardation, of emotional disturbance, or of environmental, cultural, or economic disadvantage.

As can be seen when comparing the definitions set forth by P.L. 94-142 (now IDEA) and the NJCLD, both view central nervous system dysfunction as a potential cause; both specify that speaking, listening, reading, writing, and math can be affected; and both exclude learning problems due primarily to other conditions, such as mental retardation, emotional disturbance, and cultural differences (Hallahan & Kauffman, 2003).

The key differences between the definition set forth by IDEA and the definition established by the NJCLD are listed below.

- The federal definition is older and has a medical orientation.
- The NJCLD definition allows for coexisting disabilities (e.g., learning disabilities and visual disabilities).
- The NJCLD definition acknowledges problems many of these individuals have with social skills (Smith, 2004).
- The NJCLD does not use the phrase "basic psychological processes," which has been so controversial, and does not mention perceptual handicaps, dyslexia, or minimal brain dysfunction, which have been so difficult to define.
- The NJCLD definition clearly states that a learning disability may be a lifelong condition.

As noted above, the current IDEA definition of LD remains the same as that incorporated in P.L. 94-142. The focus of IDEA is on student-age recipients of public education. However, nonacademic services to persons with developmental disabilities are provided by the Department of Developmental Disabilities (DDD) after high school. Because of DDD's requirement that a person demonstrate a "substantial disability" to qualify for services, caseworkers need to determine a substantial level of severity affecting daily living. Without a separate definition of learning disabilities, caseworkers must qualify adults for DDD services based on some criterion. Bender (1992) advises, "A practitioner in the developmental disabilities is well advised to use the definition provided by the state in which he or she practices. Generally, the state's Department of Education can provide a set of rules and regulations for special education services that includes the state definition of learning disability" (p. 82).

Finally, IDEA was reauthorized in 2004 (IDEA 2004), and its official name is the Individuals with Disabilities Education Improvement Act (Public Law 108-446). As stated by Bowe (2004),

> . . . IDEA will no longer require local education agencies (school districts) to use discrepancy in determining whether or not a given child has a learning disability. You should check with your state's department of education to see if a discrepancy requirement continues to be in effect. The new amendments to IDEA also call for a process that determines if a child responds to "scientific, research-based intervention." If a student does, the school district may rule that there is no specific learning disability, but rather a prior failure to provide adequate instruction. (p. 69)

For a historical overview of the various definitions of learning disabilities see Box 1.2.

"Discrepancy" in Diagnosing a Learning Disability

According to Ortiz (2004),

> Perhaps the most controversial aspect of the definition of LD is that the observed academic problems are greater than what might be expected based on the child's intellectual ability. This would appear to be an assumption that would be rarely questioned because it seems to make the most sense. As noted previously, LD is generally not diagnosed in individuals who have mental retardation because it is *expected* that people with low cognitive ability will have problems learning to read, write, or do math. On the other hand, there is an assumption implicit in most definitions of LD that a child would be able to perform at a normal or average level *consistent with his/her ability level* were it not for the presence of LD. That is, children with LD are performing *below* their ability, intelligence, or potential.
>
> Under the provisions of IDEA, decisions regarding the presence or absence of any disability, as well as the provision of special education services, are determined by a multidisciplinary team which, by law, must include the parents, a regular education teacher, an administrator, and all professional staff who have evaluated the child. The notion of discrepancy is reflected in IDEA, which states that "a team may determine that a child has a specific learning disability" if two conditions are met: (1) "the child does not achieve commensurate with his or her age and ability levels . . . if provided with learning experiences appropriate for the child's age and ability levels"; and (2) "the team finds that a child has a *severe discrepancy* between achievement and intellectual ability" in one or more areas of academic skills. The real problem in using this approach involves defining exactly what it means to be *below* one's *expected* level of performance.

BOX 1.2

History of the Definitions of Learning Disabilities

The definition of learning disabilities has been discussed pretty much since the time when parents and professionals began to use the term. Here are some (but not all) definitions that have been proposed in those discussions.

Among the precursors (1947): A brain-injured child is a child who before, during, or after birth has received an injury to, or suffered an infection of, the brain. As a result of such organic impairment, defects of the neuromuscular system may be present or absent, however such a child may show disturbances in perception, thinking, and emotional behavior, either separately or in combination. These disturbances can be demonstrated by specific tests. These disturbances prevent or impede a normal learning process.

A. A. Strauss, & L. Lehtinen. (1947). Psychopathology of the brain-injured child. New York: Grune & Stratton, p. 4.

An early textbook (1962): A learning disability refers to a retardation, disorder, or delayed development in one or more of the processes of speech, language, reading, spelling, writing, or arithmetic resulting from a possible cerebral dysfunction and/or emotional or behavioral disturbance and not from mental retardation, sensory deprivation, or cultural or instruction factors.

Kirk, S. A. (1962). Educating exceptional children. Boston: Houghton Mifflin, p. 261.

An early educational view (1965): Children who have learning disorders are those who manifest an educationally significant discrepancy between their estimated intellectual potential and actual level of performance related to basic disorders in the learning processes, which may or may not be accompanied by demonstrable central nervous system dysfunction, and which are not secondary to generalized disturbance or sensory loss.

Bateman, B. (1965). An educator's view of a diagnostic approach to learning disorders. In J. Hellmuth (Ed.), Learning disorders (Vol. 1, 217–239). Seattle: Special Child.

National Advisory Committee of Handicapped Children, headed by S. A. Kirk (1968): Children with special learning disabilities exhibit a disorder in one or more of the basic psychological processes involved in understanding or in using spoken or written language. These may be manifested in disorders of listening, thinking, talking, reading, writing, spelling, or arithmetic. They include conditions which have been referred to as perceptual handicaps, brain injury, minimal brain dysfunction, dyslexia, developmental aphasia, etc. They do not include learning problems which are due primarily to visual, hearing, or motor handicaps, to mental retardation, emotional disturbance or to environmental deprivation.

National Advisory Committee on Handicapped Children to the Bureau of Education for the Handicapped, Office of Education, Department of Health, Education, and Welfare, First Annual Report on Handicapped Children, 1968.

Public Law 94-142: Specific learning disability means a disorder in one or more of the basic psychological processes involved in understanding or in using language, spoken or written, which may manifest itself in an imperfect ability to listen, think, speak, read, write, spell, or to do mathematical calculations. The term includes such conditions as percep-

BOX 1.2

History of the Definitions of Learning Disabilities

tual handicaps, brain injury, minimal brain dysfunction, dyslexia, and developmental aphasia. The term does not include children who have learning problems which are primarily the result of visual, hearing, or motor handicaps, or mental retardation, or emotional disturbance or of environmental, cultural, or economic disadvantage.

National Joint Committee on Learning Disabilities (NJCLD; 1981): Learning disabilities is a generic term that refers to a heterogenous group of disorders manifested by significant difficulties in the acquisition and use of listening, speaking, reading, writing, reasoning or mathematical abilities. These disorders are intrinsic to the individual and presumed to be due to central nervous system dysfunction. Even though a learning disability may occur concomitantly with other handicapping conditions (e.g., sensory impairment, mental retardation, social and emotional disturbance), or environmental influences (e.g., cultural differences, insufficient/inappropriate instruction, psychogenic factors), it is not the direct result of those conditions or influences.

As reported in Hammill, D. D., Leigh, J. E., McNutt, G., & Larsen, S. C. (1981). A new definition of learning disabilities. *Learning Disability Quarterly, 4,* 336–342.

U.S. Interagency Committee on Learning Disabilities (1987): Learning disabilities is a generic term that refers to a heterogenous group of disorders manifested by significant difficulties in the acquisition and use of listening, speaking, reading, writing, reasoning, or mathematical abilities, *or of social skills.* These disorders are intrinsic to the individual and presumed to be due to central nervous *system* dys-

function. Even though a learning disability may occur concomitantly with other handicapping conditions (e.g., sensory impairment, mental retardation, social and emotional disturbance), *with socio*environmental influences (e.g., cultural differences, insufficient or inappropriate instruction, psychogenic factors), *and especially with attention deficit disorder, all of which may cause learning problems, a learning disability* is not the direct result of those conditions or influences.

Note: The Interagency Committee used underlining (reproduced here as italics) to indicate differences with the definition of the NJCLD.

National Joint Committee on Learning Disabilities (NJCLD; 1989): Learning disabilities is a generic term that refers to a heterogenous group of disorders manifested by significant difficulties in the acquisition and use of listening, speaking, reading, writing, reasoning, or mathematical abilities. These disorders are intrinsic to the individual, presumed to be due to central nervous system dysfunction, and may occur across the life span. Problems in self-regulatory behaviors, social perception, and social interaction may exist with learning disabilities but do not by themselves constitute a learning disability. Although a learning disability may occur concomitantly with other handicapping conditions (for example, sensory impairment, mental retardation, serious emotional disturbance) or with extrinsic factors (such as cultural differences, insufficient or inappropriate instruction), they are not the result of those conditions or influences.

As quoted in Myers, P. I., & Hammill, D. D. (1990). Learning disabilities: Basic concepts,

(continued)

BOX 1.2

History of the Definitions of Learning Disabilities *(continued)*

assessment practices, and instructional strategies. Austin, TX: Pro-Ed, p. 8.

Individuals with Disabilities Education Improvement Act of 2004:

IN GENERAL—The term "specific learning disability" means a disorder in 1 or more of the basic psychological processes involved in understanding or in using language, spoken or written, which disorder may manifest itself in the imperfect ability to listen, think, speak, read, write, spell, or do mathematical calculations.

DISORDERS INCLUDED—Such term includes such conditions as perceptual disabilities, brain injury, minimal brain dysfunction, dyslexia, and developmental aphasia.

DISORDERS NOT INCLUDED—Such term does not include a learning problem that is primarily the result of visual, hearing, or motor disabilities, of mental retardation, of emotional disturbance, or of environmental, cultural, or economic disadvantage.

There are numerous criticisms of using discrepancy formulas. Here are some from Smith (2004).

- IQ tests are not reliable and are unfair to many groups of children.
- Results have little utility in planning a student's educational program.
- The process is not helpful in determining which interventions might be successful.
- The outcomes are not related to performance in the classroom, in the general education curriculum, or on district- or statewide assessments.
- Children must fail before they qualify for needed services. (p. 114)

The Exclusionary Clause

The definition of learning disability under IDEA also has what is referred to as an "exclusionary clause." The exclusionary clause states that a learning disability "does not include a learning problem that is primarily the result of visual, hearing or motor disabilities, of mental retardation, of emotional disturbance, or of environmental, cultural, or economic disadvantage." The purpose of this exclusionary clause is to help prevent the improper labeling of children, especially those from distinct cultures who have acquired learning styles, language, or behaviors that are not compatible with academic requirements of schools in the dominant culture. However, the exclusionary clause has generated tremendous debate and controversy by experts in the field.

The wording of the exclusion clause in the federal definition of learning disabilities lends itself to the misinterpretation that individuals with LD cannot also have other disabilities or be from different cultural and linguistic backgrounds. It is essential to understand and recognize the LD as they might occur within the varying disability categories as well as different cultural and linguistic groups. Individuals within these groups frequently have received inappropriate educational assessment, planning, and instruction because they could not be identified as learning disabled.

The NJCLD supports the idea that learning disabilities are not the primary and direct result of other disabilities and should not be so confused. However, the NJCLD notes specifically that learning disabilities may occur concomitantly with other disabilities. Although these individuals may be served educationally through different service modes, a denial of the existence of significant learning disabilities will result in inappropriate assessment and educational instruction and can result in the denial of direct or indirect professional services. According to Mercer (1997; cited in Gargiulio, 2004), the word "primarily" suggests that a learning disability can exist with other exceptionalities.

Classification Criteria

Consistent with the IDEA and NJCLD definitions, most states and local school districts require that students meet three criteria for classification as having a learning disability (Mercer, Jordan, Allsopp, & Mercer, 1996; cited in Turnbull, Turnbull, Shank, & Smith, 2004, p. 105):

1. **Inclusionary criterion**—The student must demonstrate a severe discrepancy (a statistically significant difference) between perceived potential and actual achievement as measured by formal and informal assessments.
2. **Exclusionary criterion**—The student's learning disability may not result primarily from visual or hearing impairment, mental retardation, serious emotional disturbance, or cultural differences.
3. **Need criterion**—The student manifests a demonstrated need for special education services. Without specialized support, the student's disability will prevent him or her from learning.

Prevalence of Learning Disabilities

Your chances of knowing someone with learning disabilities are very good. Currently, almost 2.9 million school-aged children in the United States are classified as having specific learning disabilities and receive some kind of special education support. In fact, over half of all children who receive special education have a learning disability (24th Annual Report to Congress . . . , 2002). They are approximately 5% of all school-aged children in public schools. (These numbers do not include children in private and religious schools or home-schooled children.) Learning disabilities is by far the largest category of special education.

It should be noted that prevalence figures can vary widely between states and within a state, depending on the stringency of the method used to determine eligibility. For example,

> Kentucky reports the lowest prevalence figure (2.9%) and Massachusetts the highest (7.35%). A study completed in Michigan compared the learning disabilities eligibility criteria and procedures for identification across the 57 regional education service agencies in the state (RESA). The results indicated that 21% of the RESAs had no written eligibility criteria or policies, the length of the written policies varied from one sentence to 112 pages, and the severe discrepancy formula score varied from 15 to 30 standard score points! It is possible for a student to move a few miles to the next school district and no longer be considered to have a learning disability. (Smith, Pollaway, Patton, & Dowdy, 2004, p. 164)

Studies show that learning disabilities do not fall evenly across racial and ethnic groups. For instance, in 2001, 1% of white children and 2.6% of non-Hispanic black children were receiving LD-related special education services. The same studies suggest that this has to do with economic status and not ethnic background. Learning disabilities are not caused by economic disadvantage, but in low-income communities there is increased risk of exposure to harmful toxins (lead, tobacco, alcohol, etc.) at early stages of development.

Boys outnumber girls by about three to one in the LD category. Some researchers have suggested that the prevalence of learning disabilities among males is due to their biological vulnerability. However, others have suggested that "the higher prevalence of learning disabilities among males may be due to referral bias." They suggest that "academic difficulties are no more prevalent among boys than girls, but that boys are more likely to be referred for special education when they do have academic problems because of other behaviors, such as hyperactivity. Research on this issue is mixed" (Hallahan & Kauffman, 2003, p. 155).

The prevalence of LD also varies by age. Not surprisingly, the number of students receiving special education services increases steadily between the ages of 6 and 9. The bulk of students served (42%), however, are between the ages of 10 and 13, with a sharp decrease observed for individuals between 16 and 21 years of age (U.S. Department of Education, 2000; cited in Gargiulo, 2004, p. 210).

The true prevalence of learning disabilities is subject to much dispute because of the lack of a standard definition of LD and the absence of objective diagnostic criteria. Some researchers have argued that the currently recognized 5% prevalence rate is excessive and is based on vague definitions, leading to inaccurate identification. On the other hand, research efforts to identify objective early indicators of LD in basic reading skills have concluded that virtually all children scoring below the 25th percentile on standardized reading tests can meet the criteria for having a reading disorder. While less is known about LD in written expression, researchers estimate its true prevalence at between 8% and 15% of the school population. Research also indicates that approximately 6% of the school population has difficulties in mathematics which cannot be attributed to low intelligence, sensory deficits, or economic deprivation.

Finally, the dramatic increase in the number of students identified with LD is getting mixed reviews from learning professionals. For some, the increase is alarming, raising concerns that students are being overidentified. By contrast, other experts believe that the increased prevalence is reasonable, considering the newness of the field (Fuchs et al., 2001; cited in Turnbull et al., 2004).

Growth in the Identification of Students with Learning Disabilities

 Since 1975, when the category of LD was first included in public law, the number of students identified as having a learning disability has grown by almost 250%, from approximately 800,000 students to almost 3,000,000 students (U.S. Department of Education, 2002).

A number of reasons have been suggested for the enormous growth in the identification of students with learning disabilities. According to Hunt and Marshall (2002, p. 119), these reasons include:

1. Children who are underachieving are incorrectly identified as individuals with learning disabilities. The evaluation and identification criteria are too subjective and unreliable, and there are few, if any, alternative programs for these students.
2. The diagnosis of LD is more socially acceptable than many other special education classifications, particularly mild mental retardation and behavior disorders. Consequently, teachers and parents prefer this classification and "push" for it.
3. Greater general awareness of learning disabilities has resulted in more appropriate referrals and diagnoses. Teachers and parents are more aware of the types of services that are available.
4. The number of students identified with learning disabilities parallels the increased social and cultural risks that have arisen during the past two decades. Biological and psychosocial stressors may place more children at risk for acquiring learning disabilities, and therefore more children are identified.

Warning Signs of a Learning Disability

There is no single sign that shows a person has a learning disability. Experts look for a noticeable difference between how well a child does in school and how well he or she could do, given his or her intelligence or ability. There are also certain clues that may mean a child has a learning disability. We've listed a few below. Most relate to elementary school tasks, because learning disabilities tend to be identified in elementary school. A child probably won't show all of these signs, or even most of them. However, if a child shows a number of these problems, then parents and the teacher should consider the possibility that the child has a learning disability.

When a child has a learning disability, he or she may exhibit the following characteristics.

- Have trouble learning the alphabet, rhyming words, or matching letters to their sounds
- Make many mistakes when reading aloud, and repeat and pause often
- Not understand what he or she reads
- Have real trouble with spelling
- Have very messy handwriting or hold a pencil awkwardly
- Struggle to express ideas in writing
- Learn language late and have a limited vocabulary
- Have trouble remembering the sounds that letters make, or in hearing slight differences between words
- Have trouble understanding jokes, comic strips, and sarcasm
- Have trouble following directions
- Mispronounce words or use a wrong word that sounds similar
- Have trouble organizing what he or she wants to say or not be able to think of the word needed for writing or conversation
- Not follow the social rules of conversation, such as taking turns, and may stand too close to the listener
- Confuse math symbols and misread numbers
- Not be able to retell a story in order (what happened first, second, third)
- Not know where to begin a task or how to go on from there

Specific details about the warning signs and characteristics of individuals with learning disabilities are discussed in greater detail in Chapter 3.

Conclusion

As should be evident, the debate surrounding what constitutes a learning disability continues on as strong as ever. Remember, this is a multidisciplinary field that embraces sometimes competing viewpoints as the very nature of the construct and its causes. It is perhaps best to envision LD as "a family or syndrome of disabilities affecting a wide range of academic and/or behavioral performance (Gargiulio, 2004, p. 206). In particular, regardless of the definition used, children with learning disabilities have intellectual functioning within the normal range, there is a discrepancy between potential and achievement, the learning disability is not due to other causes, there is difficulty in learning, and there is a presumption of central nervous system dysfunction.

The field of special education is subject to the dynamic forces found in political and scientific arenas, as well as to the capacity of the special education workforce to be responsive to current and future changes. To the extent that the identification of individuals with learning disabilities serves those purposes, changes in definition and criteria are and should be part of the constant evolution in this field. To the consumer of information, a careful examination of the definition and criteria used to identify populations will allow the application of research to practice.

2

Theoretical Perspectives on the Causes of Learning Disabilities

Understandably, one of the first questions parents ask when they learn their child has a learning disability is *Why? What went wrong?* Mental health professionals stress that since no one knows what causes learning disabilities, it doesn't help parents to look backward to search for possible reasons. There are too many possibilities to pin down the cause of the disability with certainty. It is far more important for the family to move forward in finding ways to get the right help.

Scientists, however, do need to study causes in an effort to identify ways to prevent learning disabilities. Once, scientists thought that all learning disabilities were caused by a single neurological problem. But research has helped us see that the causes are more diverse and complex. New evidence seems to show that most learning disabilities do not stem from a single, specific area of the brain, but from difficulties in bringing together information from various brain regions. Therefore, causes of learning disabilities may be as diverse as the types of learning disabilities.

Clearly, the causes of learning disabilities are a nebulous area of research. There is lack of explicit cause and effect relationships, and studies have not been able to indicate any single factor directly responsible for causing learning disabilities. The condition is better understood by considering associated factors rather than cause and effect relationships. Research and practice in the field of learning disabilities have primarily focused on diagnosis and remedial education. To this end, it is necessary to explore the root cause of learning disabilities to be able to prevent them.

The field of learning disabilities has been plagued, almost since its inception, by fads and unproven theories. Little is actually known about the causes of learning disabilities, but we can presume that the students who exhibit them are as diverse as the indicators of the condition (Deutsch-Smith, 2004).

What is known about the etiology (cause) of learning disabilities is that abnormal brain structure and function play a significant role. Different abnormalities cause different types of learning disabilities. These neurological abnormalities can result from a variety of sources. The focus of this chapter will be to discuss the different theories regarding the etiology of learning disabilities.

Genetic Links

The genetic basis for learning disabilities has been researched through twin studies, sibling analysis, and family pedigree analysis (Raskind, 2001). Twin studies in the field of LD have indicated that if one twin has a reading disability, the probability of the other twin also having a reading disability is 68 percent for identical twins (monozygotic) and 40 percent for fraternal twins (dizygotic). The research evidence generally supports the hypothesis that certain types of learning problems, including reading disabilities, are more common among identical twins than fraternal twins (DeFries, Gills, & Wadsworth, 1993). Similar findings are also observed in twins with speech and language disorders (Lewis & Thompson, 1992).

Familial transmission of learning disabilities has shown that if there is a family history (parents, siblings, and extended family) of reading disabilities, the probability of having a reading disability is significantly increased (Culbertson, 1998). Several modes of transmission have been investigated. Although there are, as yet, no definitive conclusions, a possible linkage to chromosomes 6 and 15 has been identified.

The fact that learning disabilities tend to run in families indicates that there may be a genetic link (Alarçon-Cazares, 1998). Researchers have found that about 35 to 45 percent of the first-degree relatives (parents and siblings) of persons with reading disabilities also have reading disabilities (Pennington, 1990; cited in Hallahan & Kauffman, 2003). Children who lack some of the skills needed for reading, such as hearing the separate sounds of words, are likely to have a parent with a related problem. However, a parent's learning disability may take a slightly different form in the child. A parent who has a writing disorder may have a child with an expressive language disorder. For this reason, it seems unlikely that specific LD are inherited directly. Possibly, what is inherited is a subtle brain dysfunction that can in turn lead to a learning disability. Similar evidence has been found in the area of speech and language disorders (Castles, Datta, Gayan, & Olson, 1999) and spelling disabilities (Schulte-Korne, Deimel, Muller, Gutenbrunner, & Remschmidt, 1996).

Note that there may be an alternative explanation for why learning disabilities might seem to run in families. Familiality does not clearly prove hereditability. Some learning difficulties may actually stem from the family environment. For example, parents who have expressive language disorders might talk less to their children, or the language they use may be distorted. In such cases, the child lacks a good model for acquiring language and, therefore, may seem to have learning disabilities.

Abnormalities in Fetal Brain Development

Throughout pregnancy, the fetal brain develops from a few all-purpose cells into a complex organ made of billions of specialized, interconnected nerve cells called neurons. During this amazing evolution, things can go wrong that may alter how the neurons form or interconnect.

In the early stages of pregnancy, the brain stem forms. It controls basic life functions such as breathing and digestion. Later, a deep ridge divides the cerebrum—the thinking part of the brain—into two halves, a right and left hemisphere. Finally, the areas involved with processing sight, sound, and other senses develop, as well as the areas associated with attention, thinking, and emotion.

As new cells form, they move into place to create various brain structures. Nerve cells rapidly grow to form networks with other parts of the brain. The networks enable information to be shared among various regions of the brain. Throughout pregnancy, brain development is vulnerable to disruptions. If the disruption occurs early, the fetus may die, or the infant may be born with widespread disabilities and possibly mental retardation. If the disruption occurs later, when the cells are becoming specialized and moving into place, the result may be errors in the cell makeup, location, or connections. Some scientists believe that these errors may later show up as learning disabilities.

Maturational Delay

Another theory to explain learning disabilities suggests that they occur because there is maturational delay (rather than a permanent dysfunction) within the neurological system (Samango-Sprouse, 1999). Some children develop and mature at a slower rate than others in the same age group. As a result, they may not be able to do the expected school work. This kind of learning disability is called *maturational lag.* Here are some typical symptoms of maturational delay.

- Slow maturation of language skills, especially those of reading
- Delayed development of motor skills
- Uneven performance patterns on measures of intellectual development
- Visual–motor problems
- Incomplete or mixed dominance
- Right–left confusion
- Social immaturity
- Tendency for members within a family to show similar symptoms.

Brain Structure and Learning Disabilities

In comparing people with and without learning disabilities, scientists have observed certain differences in the structure and functioning of the brain (Richards, 2001). For example, new research indicates that there may be variations in the brain structure called the planum temporale, a language-related area found in both sides of the brain. In people with dyslexia, the two structures were found to be equal in size. In people without dyslexia, however, the left planum temporale was noticeably larger. Some scientists believe reading problems may be related to such differences (Leonard, 2001; Raskind, 2001).

It is now widely accepted that the brain structure or function of a person with LD is different from that of a person who does not have learning disabilities. There is a view that the language area in the brain of an individual is well developed in the left hemisphere and is tiny, and hence, dysfunctional in the right hemisphere. So, in the normal course of information processing, the nerve impulses set up in the visual cortices travel for interpretation to the left hemisphere of the brain. In the brains of individuals with LD, the language areas are well developed in both the hemispheres. In this case, the nerve impulses travel to both hemispheres simultaneously. Thus, the corpus callosum becomes "jammed" with nerve impulses as the two language areas refer the messages they receive from the visual cortices back and forth for comparison and analysis. This confusion caused by crisscrossing of the nerve impulses may be why a child with learning disabilities often reads *b* as a *d* and vice versa. With more research, scientists hope to learn precisely how differences in the structures and processes of the brain contribute to learning disabilities, and how these differences might be treated or prevented.

Measuring the Brain and Brain Function

A variety of methods are now available to measure the physical structure as well as the function of the brain. Neuroanatomical techniques include autopsy studies; neuro-imaging techniques include CT scan, MRI, PET, rCBF, and SPECT; electrophysiological measures include EEG, ERP, and AEP; and neuropsychological assessments evaluate brain/behavior relationships.

A number of studies of brain structure and function have been carried out on individuals with learning disabilities (Silver, 1999). One method of looking at structural differences in the brain is through postmortem or autopsy studies. Postmortem findings have indicated that the normal brain has asymmetries: one side of the brain is not a perfect mirror image of the other. These asymmetries are expected and considered normal (just as it is quite ordinary or typical for one foot to be longer than the other).

Important research efforts have focused on reading disabilities, since they represent the most common and frequently identified type of learning disability. Studies have shown that people with reading disabilities have symmetry in brain structures where there should be asymmetry. For example, in people without LD, the temporal lobe (planum temporale area) in the left hemisphere is often larger than the same area in the right hemisphere. However, in subjects with LD, this area in the left hemisphere has been found to be the same size as in the right hemisphere.

Another technique for studying the brain is the CT scan (computed tomography (roentgen-ray)). With this technique, a beam of X rays is aimed through the brain, identifying bone, grey matter, and fluid. A computer then reconstructs an image of each slice or brain section, allowing abnormalities in structure to be detected. CT scans of the occipital lobe for example, have shown asymmetry of the occipital pole in subjects without LD and symmetry in subjects with LD.

Magnetic resonance imaging (MRI) is a technique that involves detecting the electromagnetic energy of brain protons and constructing an image by superimposing magnetic fields. Recent advances in MRI technology have enabled researchers to discover that specific regions of the brains of some individuals with reading and language disabilities show activation patterns during phonological processing tasks that are different from the patterns found in the brains of persons without disabilities (Simos et al., 2000). MRI research has shown that individuals without LD showed leftward asymmetry in the angular gyrus of the parietal lobe, whereas people with LD did not show the expected asymmetry.

It has been demonstrated through autopsy, CT scan, and MRI studies that there are structural differences in the brains of subjects with LD in comparison to subjects without LD. It has also been demonstrated that in the subjects with LD, there are differences in brain function—that is, how the brain works. Functional neuroimaging techniques, including PET (positron emission tomography), rCBF (regional cerebral blood flow), fMRI (functional magnetic resonance imaging), and SPECT (single photon emission computed tomography), are used to measure brain activity while subjects are engaged in a task such as reading. An fMRI is a noninvasive method that measures blood flow, while PET and SPECT methods involve the injection of radioactive materials. SPECT scan results have indicated that subjects with LD show under-functioning in the occipital lobe while reading, in comparison to subjects without LD.

Electroencephalograms (EEGs), event-related potentials (ERPs), and averaged evoked potentials (AEPs) record electrical activity of the brain through electrodes. Research has shown that subjects with dyslexia showed less electrical activity in the parietal lobe, in comparison to subjects without dyslexia.

Neuropsychological assessments include a variety of tests of cognitive/intellectual, language, visual-perceptual, academic, motor, sensory, and emotional/behavioral abilities and functions. A profile of strengths and weaknesses is then correlated with known brain functions. The neuropsychological research has indicated significant findings as well. Deficiencies in language/verbal learning, reading, written language, verbal reasoning, verbal memory, arithmetic computation, and processing speed have been associated with left hemispheric dysfunction. Deficiencies in spatial function, nonverbal reasoning, nonverbal cues, social skills, and social/emotional information have been associated with right hemispheric dysfunction. Phonological processing deficits have been identified as a primary difficulty in persons with language and reading disabilities, and structural and functional abnormalities in the medial geniculate nuclei have been associated with these findings.

It is important to emphasize that individuals with LD can learn, but the process may be inefficient as a result of the specific differences in brain structure and function. Inefficiency refers to either low accuracy or low speed in learning or performing a task and is quite distinct from inability or incapacity. Information can be processed, but at a slower rate and/or by different methods as compared to individuals without learning disabilities. The educational process, learning strategies, compensatory techniques, and remedial intervention can significantly affect the learning process. Therefore, effective and efficient learning and teaching methods are needed to specifically meet the needs of individuals with learning disabilities.

Biological Basis for Reading Disabilities

Recent research has found convincing evidence that dyslexia is caused by a functional disruption in the brain (Gilger, 2001). The research, led by Dr. Sally Shaywitz, a Professor of Pediatrics at the Yale University School of Medicine, was published in the March 3, 1998 Proceedings of the National Academy of Sciences (NAS). These findings represent a critical new piece of evidence that builds on the already solid research in the area of reading disability.

The researchers used functional magnetic resonance imaging (fMRI), which enables researchers to look into the brain as it is working. The research used fMRI to image the brains of 32 adults with dyslexia and 29 adults without dyslexia while they attempted to perform a progressively complex series of reading tasks. The tasks included letter recognition, rhyming letters and words, and finally, categorizing words. The findings showed that brain activation patterns of readers with dyslexia were significantly different from those of readers without dyslexia.

Reading requires an ability to recognize that spoken words can be segmented into smaller units of sound (phonological awareness) and that the letters in the printed word represent these sounds. Individuals with dyslexia do not recognize these smaller sound units and have difficulty mapping alphabetic characters onto the spoken word.

The results of the study indicated that readers without dyslexia systematically increased their brain activation as the difficulty of mapping print into phonological structures increased. The readers with dyslexia did not systematically increase their brain activity. The demonstrated disruption in brain function among readers with dyslexia occurred in a part of the brain involving traditional visual and language regions. During reading, people with dyslexia showed a pattern of underactivation in a large posterior brain region, an area which connects the visual areas with the language areas.

These findings reconcile seemingly contradictory evidence from previous imaging studies which were not able to map out the full extent of the disruption. Of particular importance was the finding that the angular gyrus, a brain region considered pivotal in carrying out cross-modal (e.g., vision and language) associations necessary for reading, is involved. The current findings of underactivation in the angular gyrus of readers with dyslexia coincide with earlier studies of people who lost the ability to read due to brain damage centered in that same area of the brain. According to the authors,

> it is no coincidence that both the acquired and developmental disorders affecting reading have in common a disruption within the neural systems serving to link the visual representation of the letters to the phonological structures they represent.
>
> These findings have important implications for the large numbers of intelligent men, women and children with dyslexia. . . . If you have a broken arm, you can hold up an x-ray as evidence. Up to now, individuals with dyslexia were often doubted and there was little concrete evidence they could show to support the neurobiologic nature of their reading difficulty. These brain activation patterns,

by revealing a functional disruption in those neural systems responsible for reading, now provide neurobiologic evidence for what, up to now, has been a hidden disability. (Gilger, 2001, pp. 490–491)

Biochemical Abnormalities

Chemicals play an important role in brain activity, controlling and releasing electrical impulses between neurons. The absence or excessive presence of biochemical substances can cause abnormal electrical activity in the brain.

Endocrine Problems

The endocrine glands, located in the various parts of the body, secrete hormones or strong chemical substances directly into the blood stream. Hormones influence the functions of tissues and organs and thus help to determine behavior. There seems to be some relationship between these chemicals and hyperactivity and learning disorders.

Thyroxine Imbalance. Thyroxine, the hormone secreted by the thyroid gland, controls the basal metabolic rate of the body, that is, the rate of consumption of oxygen and energy output. A low level of thyroxine can result in poor memory, low I.Q. and a lack of energy. Excessive thyroxine can result in nervous hyperactivity, irritability, and difficulty in concentration. A minimal lowering of blood sugar levels can also result in word-finding problems and increased spelling errors.

Thyroid Dysfunction. Children born without a functioning thyroid system may be at risk for learning disabilities. Babies who are screened at birth for congenital hypothyroid syndrome receive a prompt and lifelong program of thyroid hormone therapy, which prevents serious developmental delays. However, longitudinal followup reveals that, though IQs may be in the normal range, there are usually profiles of deficits similar to learning disabilities. Research is underway on relationships between optimal levels of maternal thyroid during the entire period of gestation and optimal fetal development.

Nutritional Problems

Poor Nutrition. There seems to be a link between nutritional deprivation (either the child's or the mother's when she was pregnant) and poor biochemical functioning in the brain. A poor diet and severe malnutrition can reduce the child's ability to learn by damaging intersensory abilities and delaying development.

Recent studies and clinical trials conducted at Purdue University in the United States and Surrey and Oxford in the United Kingdom indicate that some learning disabilities, such as dyslexia and dyspraxia, may have a nutritional basis. And, as previously stated, researchers such as Feingold believe that some learning disabilities might be caused by allergies to certain foods, food additives, and dyes, or by environmental allergies.

Dietary Sensitivities.   In the early 1970s, Feingold (1975) proposed that much of the hyperactivity involved with LD could be attributed to food additives. This untested idea, based on testimonials, gained wide public acceptance. He believed that removing synthetic colors and flavors, as well as certain fruits and vegetables containing "salicylates" (natural pesticides), from the diet could treat behavioral disturbances. Feingold believed that as many as 10 to 25% of all children may be sensitive to salicylates. The success of the diet may depend on the degree of a person's sensitivity to salicylates and food additives, and the amount of additives present in foods. Feingold also speculated that certain foods, such as sugar, caused behavior changes.

Over the years, dozens of scientists put Dr. Feingold's theories to the test, but the evidence they gathered failed to support the theory that additives, sugar, or other substances in food cause or contribute to hyperactivity. Most professionals in learning disabilities and the scientific community give little credence to biochemical imbalance as a significant cause of children's learning problems (Heward, 2003; Kavale & Forness, 1983).

Vitamin Deficiency.   Another popular approach of the 1970s was megavitamin therapy. The chief advocate was Alan Cott, who theorized (1972) that learning disabilities can be caused by the inability of a person's blood to synthesize a normal amount of vitamins. In an effort to treat LD, large daily doses of certain vitamins were recommended to counteract the suspected vitamin deficiency. Again, scientific research (Arnold, Christopher, Huestis, & Smeltzer, 1978) has failed to substantiate the benefit of this treatment (Gargiulo, 2004).

Complications of Pregnancy and Birth

Other possible causes of learning disabilities involve complications during pregnancy. Damage may be inflicted on the neurological system at birth by conditions such as abnormal fetal positioning during delivery, anoxia (a lack of oxygen), or chemicals in the blood. When a baby's brain is given certain kinds of chemicals or does not get enough blood or oxygen, permanent brain damage can occur. Many students with learning disabilities have had some sort of trauma either before or during their birth.

In some cases, the mother's immune system reacts to the fetus and attacks it as if it were an infection. This type of disruption seems to cause newly formed brain cells to settle in the wrong part of the brain. Or during delivery, the umbilical cord may become twisted and temporarily cut off oxygen to the fetus. This, too, can impair brain functions and lead to learning disabilities.

Infants born prematurely and with low birthweights have increased in numbers over the last 20 years; however, in that same period, infant and neonatal mortality rates have dramatically improved. Being born too small or too soon entails high risk of serious morbidity contributing to long-term neurologic impairment. Premature infants have an increased risk for cerebral palsy, mental retardation, sensory impairment, developmental delays, and learning and school problems. Nutrition plays a key role in the prevention of prematurity and in neonatal care during hospitalization and in the followup period.

Low birthweight babies are at risk for learning disabilities. According to some studies, children whose birthweight was less than five pounds lagged behind their peers academically and displayed other subtle behavioral characteristics that undermined their efforts at school. During their preschool years, many of these children exhibited poor motor skills and neurological immaturity.

Prenatal Exposure to Harmful Substances

Drugs, prescribed or otherwise, taken by the mother, pass directly to the fetus. Research shows that use of cigarettes, alcohol, or other drugs during pregnancy may have damaging effects on the unborn child (Codina, Yin, Katims, & Zapata, 1998). Scientists have found that mothers who smoke during pregnancy may be more likely to bear smaller babies. This is a concern because small newborns, usually those weighing less than five pounds, tend to be at a risk for a variety of problems, including learning disabilities.

Cocaine.   Cocaine—especially in its smokable form, known as crack—seems to affect the normal development of brain receptors that help transmit incoming signals from our skin, eyes, and ears, and help regulate our physical response to the environment. Because children with certain learning disabilities have difficulty understanding speech sounds or letters, some researchers believe that LD may be related to faulty receptors (Murphy-Brennan & Oei, 1999).

Marijuana.   The main psychoactive ingredient in marijuana, THC, crosses the placenta and has the potential for harming pregnancy outcome. Some recent epidemiological studies suggest that maternal marijuana use during pregnancy may result in perinatal hypoxia (low oxygen to the baby), premature labor, low birthweight, and physical and behavior anomalies in the offspring. However, marijuana use has been difficult to measure in these reports, since it is an illegal drug, and therefore prone to under-reporting, and many of the women studied also used other drugs, raising the possibility of drug interactions with marijuana.

Six-year-old children are more likely to show signs of Attention-Deficit Hyperactivity Disorder if their mothers smoked six or more marijuana cigarettes (joints) per week. This was the conclusion after testing 126 children at the Department of Psychology, Carleton University, Canada. Fourteen of the children had mothers who admitted smoking between one and six joints per week and 19 had mothers who admitted smoking at least six marijuana joints per week during pregnancy.

The data pertaining to maternal use of marijuana, are suggestive of an association between that drug and particular aspects of attentional behavior—possibly sustained attention. Cognitive psychologists have frequently divided the attentional process into three sub-systems that perform different but interrelated functions. These include orienting toward sensory events, detecting signals to be focused on—including information stored in memory, and maintaining a vigilant state. The present findings suggest that prenatal exposure to cigarettes and marijuana may be associated differentially with subsystems within the attentional process. . . . In addition, Discriminant Function Analysis revealed a dose–response relationship between prenatal marijuana use and a higher rating by the mothers on an impulsive/hyperactive scale. (Fried & Watkinson, 1992, p. 1)

Prescription Heart Medication.   Recent research suggests that warnings should be given to pregnant women taking the heart arrhythmia drug Amiodarone (AMD). Researchers at the Department of Medicine, Mount Sinai Hospital (1999), Toronto, Canada have found that when women took this drug during pregnancy there was an observed increase in language disorders for their children who were exposed to the drug during pregnancy. In the research project, the offspring of twelve mothers were followed after giving birth while taking the drug.

Early speech delay and difficulties with written language and arithmetic are part of the Nonverbal Learning Disability Syndrome. An association between AMD exposure and such a syndrome is plausible. Firstly, language skills may be more sensitive to neurotoxic damage than measure of global cognitive function. Secondly, another antenatal exposure, congenital hypothyroidism, has also been associated with this syndrome. Thirdly, AMD may have a direct neurotoxic effect on the developing fetal brain. (p. 5)

Alcohol.   Alcohol also may be dangerous to the fetus' developing brain. It appears that alcohol may distort the developing neurons. Heavy alcohol use during pregnancy has been linked to fetal alcohol syndrome, a condition that can lead to low birthweight, intellectual impairment, hyperactivity, and certain physical defects. Any alcohol use during pregnancy, however, may influence the child's development and lead to problems with learning, attention, memory, or problem solving. Because scientists have not yet identified safe levels, alcohol should be used cautiously or avoided entirely by women who are pregnant or who may soon become pregnant. Research has also indicated:

- "Third trimester exposure may affect the developing hippocampus or allied structures, leading to deficits in the ability to encode visual or auditory information." (Coles, 1991)
- "Alcohol-exposed children are likely to experience academic difficulties, and it is possible that some of these children will develop specific learning disabilities." (Coles, 1991)

- "Lower verbal comprehension and spoken language scores were found among 84 children at 13 months of age whose mothers drank an average of .24 ounces of absolute alcohol per day—about one-half drink per day." (Gusella & Fried, 1984)

Nicotine.   According to Pressinger (1999),

> although the percentage of smoking in the general population is declining, the rate of this [decline] is slowest among women of childbearing age. The recent National Household Survey on Drug Abuse reported that among women of reproductive age, approximately one-third smoke cigarettes on a regular basis. These figures for the United States are within one or two percentages of those noted in Canada and Sweden. In five surveys throughout the U.S., the extent of cigarette use by women during pregnancy in non-ghetto, urban regions has been reported to be between 22% and 30%. An additional recent statistic that bears upon the issue of smoking habits and pregnancy is that the proportion of heavy smokers has increased in the past decade, particularly among women. In Sweden, the proportion of heavy smokers has almost doubled, while in Canada, the increase of heavy smokers was 57% among females versus 31% among males. This has important implications because the relationship between the consequences of maternal smoking and effects on the offspring appears to be dose related. Also of concern is that it is estimated by the Office of Smoking and Health that one-third to one-half of nonsmoking pregnant women are exposed to significant levels of involuntary or second-hand smoke. Demonstrating the increased toxic insults today's developing child has from cigarette smoke, figures show smoking has increased 3 to 4-fold from 1940 to the beginning of the 1980s, although it has since then decreased somewhat. (p. 1)

Smoking cigarettes has been found to have a possible causal effect on learning disabilities in children. Research suggests the following.

- "In pregnant women who smoke, accumulation of carbon monoxide in the fetal blood stream could lead to serious reductions in oxygen to the developing infant. Carboxyhemoglobin levels (hemoglobin that is carrying carbon monoxide instead of oxygen) can concentrate in the developing fetus reaching twice the levels of that in the mother." (Denson, Nanson, & McWatters, 1994)
- "Children of mothers who smoked 10 or more cigarettes a day are between three and five months behind in reading, mathematics, and general ability when compared to the offspring of non-smokers, after allowing for associated social and biological factors." (Makin & Fried, 1991)
- McCartney (1994) found overall poorer performance on central auditory processing tasks (SCAN) among 110, six- to eleven-year-old children exposed to prenatal cigarette smoke. Maternal smoking during pregnancy was linearly associated with the poorer performance on listening skills in a noisy background

and attending to simultaneous information in both ears. Children exposed to passive cigarette smoke performed more poorly than children of non-smokers and equal to that found in children exposed to "light" prenatal smoking.

- "Human reports as well as animal studies have recorded accelerated motor activity, learning and memory deficits in offsprings of mothers exposed to nicotine during pregnancy." (Roy, 1994)
- "Research has links increased hyperactivity, attention deficits, lower IQ, and learning disabilities in children with parents who smoked during pregnancy." (Roy, 1994)
- According to the Finland Department of Public Health (1994), "the more cigarettes a mother smoked during pregnancy, the greater the likelihood her child would demonstrate severe behavior problems as the child became older. Women who smoked at least a pack a day had children with twice the rate of extreme behavior problems—such as anxiety, conflict with others, or disobedience, when compared with children of non-smokers. School performance of the smokers' children was poorer than that of their controls when measured in terms of their mean ability on theoretical subjects. The children of the smokers were more prone to respiratory diseases than the others. They were also shorter in length by nearly 1 centimeter (a little less than a half an inch) and their mean ability at school was poorer than among the controls for mothers who smoked 10 cigarettes and 20 cigarettes per day."

Pesticide Exposure during Pregnancy.   Exposure among pregnant women to pesticides generates considerable concern, as these chemicals are intentionally designed to damage the nervous system. This concern increases when we realize the total extent to which all of us are exposed to pesticides. In fact, evidence now shows that everyone is exposed to some level of pesticides every second of the day. In June, 1993, the National Academy of Sciences released its long-awaited report on the health hazards posed to infants and young children from exposure to pesticides in the food supply. The NAS stated that any pesticides are harmful to the environment and are known or suspected to be toxic to humans. Pesticides can produce a wide range of adverse effects on human health that include acute neurologic toxicity, cancer, reproductive dysfunction, and possible dysfunction of the immune and endocrine systems. Among the NAS's critical findings were that existing pesticide policies do not protect the young adequately, instead treating kids as "little adults." Unique dietary patterns common among children (such as eating only a few favorite foods almost exclusively) are ignored in existing calculations, although such habits result in children's far greater exposure to multiple pesticides in food, by body weight, than occur in the adult population. The NAS expressed particular concern over children's dietary exposure to neurotoxic pesticides, stating that children tend to retain a greater portion of a given dose of certain toxins than adults and are not as capable of detoxifying them in their bodies because their livers are still developing. Children also are at greater risk from neurotoxins because the nervous system in an infant or young child has not yet developed fully.

Toxins in the Child's Environment

Toxic Metals

Researchers are looking into environmental toxins that may lead to learning disabilities, possibly by disrupting childhood brain development or brain processes. According to studies reviewed, more than 20% of the children in the United States have had their health or learning significantly adversely affected by toxic metals such as mercury, lead, and cadmium; and more than 50% of children in some urban areas have been adversely affected. Significant behavioral effects were also documented. Adults can be similarly affected. Many epidemiologists believe the evidence demonstrates that over 50% of all U.S. children have had their learning ability or mental state significantly adversely affected by prenatal or postnatal exposure to toxic substances. Toxic metals have been documented to be reproductive and developmental toxins, causing birth defects and damaging fetal development, as well as creating or contributing to neurological effects, developmental delays, learning disabilities, depression, and behavioral abnormalities in many children.

Lead Poisoning. Approximately 434,000 U.S. children aged 1 to 5 years have blood lead levels greater than the Center for Disease Control's (2004) recommended level of 10 micrograms of lead per deciliter of blood. Lead poisoning can affect nearly every system in the body. Because lead poisoning often occurs with no obvious symptoms, it frequently goes unrecognized. Lead poisoning can cause learning disabilities, behavioral problems, and, at very high levels, seizures, coma, and even death.

Lead is a metal that does not belong in the human body. Today, lead-based paint is the most common source of lead poisoning in children. Over many years, painted surfaces crumble and become common household dust. This dust coats the objects that curious children put in their mouths. Adults can also ingest lead in this way. It is the most common way for the lead in paint to get into a person. Children will also chew on windowsills or other painted surfaces. Sometimes they eat old paint chips.

The major source of lead exposure among U.S. children is lead-based paint and lead-contaminated dust found in deteriorating buildings. Lead-based paints were banned for use in housing in 1978. However, approximately 24 million housing units in the United States have deteriorated leaded paint and elevated levels of lead-contaminated house dust. More than 4 million of these dwellings are homes to one or more young children.

Other sources of lead poisoning are related to hobbies (making stained-glass windows), work (recycling or making automobile batteries), drinking water (lead pipes, solder, brass fixtures, valves can all leach lead), and home health remedies.

Certain children are at greater risk for lead poisoning. These children include the following.

- Children under the age of 6 years because they are growing so rapidly and because they tend to put their hands or other objects into their mouths.

- Children from all social and economic levels can be affected by lead poisoning, although children living at or below the poverty line (who generally live in older housing) are at greatest risk.
- Children of some racial and ethnic groups living in older housing are disproportionately affected by lead. For example, 22% of black children and 13% of Mexican-American children living in housing built before 1946 have elevated blood lead levels, compared with 6% of white children living in comparable types of housing.

Exposure to lead can have a wide range of effects on a child's development and behavior. Even when exposed to small amounts of lead levels, children may appear inattentive, hyperactive, and irritable. Children with greater lead levels may also have problems with learning and reading, delayed growth, and hearing loss. At high levels, lead can cause permanent brain damage and even death (American Academy of Pediatrics, 2000).

Cadmium.   There are some researchers that suggest that cadmium exposure is related to learning disabilities in children. Cadmium is a natural element in the earth's crust. It is usually found as a mineral combined with other elements such as oxygen (cadmium oxide), chlorine (cadmium chloride), or sulfur (cadmium sulfate, cadmium sulfide) (U.S. Department of Labor, 2004).

All soils and rocks, including coal and mineral fertilizers, contain some cadmium. Most cadmium used in the United States is extracted during the production of other metals such as zinc, lead, and copper. Cadmium does not corrode easily and has many uses, including batteries, pigments, metal coatings, and plastics. The health effects in children are expected to be similar to those in adults (kidney, lung, and intestinal damage). It is not known if cadmium causes birth defects in people. Cadmium does not readily pass from a pregnant woman's body into the developing child, but some portion can cross the placenta. Cadmium can also be found in breast milk. The offspring of animals exposed to high levels of cadmium during pregnancy had changes in behavior and learning ability. Cadmium may also affect birthweight and the skeleton in developing animals.

Animal studies also indicate that more cadmium is absorbed into the body if the diet is low in calcium, protein, or iron, or is high in fat. A few studies show that younger animals absorb more cadmium and are more likely to lose bone and bone strength than adults.

Severe Head Injuries

The signs of severe head injuries can be very different, depending on where the brain is injured and how severely. Spivak (1986) estimated that as many as 20% of children identified with a learning disability have had a prior brain injury. Children with brain injuries will often have LD, as well as other difficulties, such as those listed below.

Physical disabilities. Individuals with severe head injuries may have problems speaking, seeing, hearing, and using their other senses. They may have headaches and often feel tired. They may also have trouble with skills such as writing or drawing. Their muscles may suddenly contract or tighten (called spasticity). They may have seizures. Their balance and walking may also be affected. They may be partly or completely paralyzed on one side of the body, or both sides.

Difficulties with thinking. Because the brain has been injured, it is common that the person's ability to use the brain changes. For example, children with head injuries may have trouble with short-term memory (being able to re-member something from one minute to the next, such as what the teacher just said). They may also have trouble with their long-term memory (being able to remember information from a while ago, such as facts learned last month). People with severe head injuries may have trouble concentrating and only be able to focus their attention for a short time. They may think slowly. They may have trouble talking and listening to others. They may also have difficulty with reading and writing, planning, understanding the order in which events happen (called sequencing), and judgment.

Social, behavioral, or emotional problems. These difficulties may include sudden changes in mood, anxiety, and depression. Children with head injuries may have trouble relating to others. They may be restless and may laugh or cry a lot. They may not have much motivation or much control over their emotions.

Most individuals with severe head injuries display attention or concentration deficits. *Attention* or *concentration* refers to the amount of time an individual stays on task. It might mean the short amount of time it takes to hear information, or the length of time it takes to process that information.

An individual's ability to perceive and understand information seen, heard, or touched is considered *comprehension*. An individual with a brain injury will dis-play difficulties with comprehension, which is evidenced in the following ways: difficulty understanding written and pictorial directions, difficulty following con-versations (due to vocabulary problems), misinterpretation of auditory and visual information, literal interpretations of jokes and proverbs, and decreased under-standing of questions.

Social–Environmental Causes

Low Socio-Economic Status and Learning Disabilities

According to Blair and Scott (2002; cited in Deutsch-Smith, 2004, p. 119), "a strong relationship exists between learning disabilities and low socio-economic status (SES) .... Whether factors associated with poverty (such as limited access to health care) or the lack of supportive environment puts these children at great risk for learning disabilities is not known, but the relationship is clear." Although the IDEA definition and others specifically exclude SES conditions as etiological possibilities, many educators believe that this risk factor indirectly contributes to the learning and behavioral difficulties of some pupils.

The Relationship between Poor Instruction and Learning Disabilities

Another environmental variable that is likely to contribute to children's learning problems is the quality of instruction that they receive. As noted by Heward (2003), many special educators believe that Engelmann (1977) was correct when he claimed more than 25 years ago that the vast majority of "children who are labeled 'learning disabled' exhibit a disability not because of anything wrong with their perception, synapses, or memory, but because they have been seriously mistaught. Learning disabilities are made, not born." Lovitt (1978) also contends that learning disabilities may result from poor teachers and inadequate instruction. While implying that the poor quality of some learning environments contributes to learning disabilities, researchers also note that learning problems can be remediated by direct, systematic instruction (Gersten, Carnine, & Woodward, 1987; cited in Gargiulo, 2004).

Conclusion

Since no one knows for sure what causes learning disabilities, mental health professionals stress that it does not help to look backward to search for possible reasons. Despite substantial work related to this field, determining precise causation has been difficult, and the effort to do so still continues (Hardman, Drew, & Egan, 2003). As should be evident after reading this chapter, there are likely many causes of learning disabilities, and in some cases, a specific type of learning disability may have multiple causes. Teachers need to recognize that it is not certain what causes learning disabilities and to not make assumptions about the students they teach (Deutsch-Smith, 2004). Consequently, parents and teachers must adopt an eclectic, multidisciplinary approach and seek advice from professionals in the field. It is far more important to move forward in finding ways to cope effectively and overcome the difficulties.

3 Characteristics of Children with Learning Disabilities

Children with learning disabilities are a heterogeneous group. These children are a diverse group of individuals, exhibiting potential difficulties in many different areas. For example, one child with a learning disability may experience significant reading problems, while another may experience no reading problems whatsoever, but has significant difficulties with written expression.

Learning disabilities may also be mild, moderate, or severe. Students differ too, in their coping skills. According to Bowe (2005), "some learn to adjust to LD so well that they 'pass' as not having a disability, while others struggle throughout their lives to even do 'simple' things. Despite these differences, LD always begins in childhood and always is a life-long condition" (p. 71).

Over the years, parents, educators, and other professionals have identified a wide variety of characteristics associated with learning disabilities (Gargiulo, 2004). One of the earliest profiles, developed by Clements (1966), includes the following ten frequently cited attributes.

Hyperactivity	Impulsivity
Perceptual-motor impairments	Disorders of memory and thinking
Emotional lability	Academic difficulties
Coordination problems	Language deficits
Disorders of attention	Equivocal neurological signs

Almost 35 years later, Lerner (2000) identified nine learning and behavioral characteristics of individuals with learning disabilities.

Disorders of attention	Reading difficulties
Poor motor abilities	Written language difficulties
Oral language difficulties	Social skills deficits
Psychological process deficits and information processing problems	Quantitative disorders

33

According to Gargiulo (2004), not all students with learning disabilities will exhibit these characteristics, and many pupils who demonstrate these same behaviors are quite successful in the classroom. As Smith (1979) observes, it is the quantity, intensity, and duration of the behaviors that lead to the problems in school and elsewhere.

The focus of this chapter will be to discuss the most commonly seen characteristics of children with learning disabilities. In almost all cases, a single student will not have deficits in all areas. Understanding the characteristics of children with learning disabilities is absolutely essential as a future educator in developing pre-referral interventions, in making appropriate referrals, and in identifying effective adaptations and intervention strategies (Smith et al., 2004).

Academic Achievement Deficits

Children with learning disabilities often struggle with various areas of academic performance. During the elementary school years, a discrepancy between ability and achievement begins to emerge in students with learning disabilities. Often puzzling to teachers, these students seem to have strengths similar to their peers in several areas, but their rate of learning is unexpectedly slower (Smith et al., 2004). These problems usually persist from the primary grades through the end of formal schooling, including college (Bradshaw, 2001).

Academic deficits for children with learning disabilities normally fall into the following areas: reading, mathematics, and written expression. Some children have problems in only one select academic area, while others may experience difficulties in all three.

Reading Deficits

Reading provides a fundamental way for individuals to exchange information. It is also a means by which much of the information presented in school is learned. As a result, reading is the academic area most often associated with academic failure. Reading is a complex process that requires numerous skills for its mastery. Consequently, identifying the skills that lead to success in reading is extremely important.

Reading difficulties are observed among students with learning disabilities more than any other problem area of academic performance. It is the most prevalent type of academic difficulty for students with learning disabilities. It is estimated that as many as 90% of students with learning disabilities have reading difficulties, and even the low estimates are approximately 60% (Bender, 2001). Most authorities believe that this problem is related to deficient language skills, especially phonological awareness—the ability to understand that speech flow can be broken into smaller sound units such as words, syllables, and phonemes.

According to Hallahan and Kauffman (2003), it is easy to see why problems with phonology would be at the heart of many reading difficulties. A person who has problems breaking words into their component sounds will have trouble learning to read. And there is suggestive evidence that readers of English are more susceptible than readers of some other languages to problems with phonological awareness. Some have speculated that this is why reading disabilities are more prevalent in English-speaking countries than in some other countries (p. 162).

Becoming a skilled reader is so important in our culture that an unskilled reader is at a great disadvantage in school and in the workplace. The following problems may prevent a child with learning disabilities from learning to read (Kirk, Gallagher, & Anastaiow, 2003, p. 224).

- Faulty auditory perception without hearing impairment
- Slow auditory or visual processing
- Inability to distinguish or separate the sounds of spoken words
- Lack of knowledge of the purpose of reading
- Failure to attend to critical aspects of the word, sentence, or paragraph
- Failure to understand that letters represent units of speech

Recent research has begun to reveal a great deal about the fundamental nature of children's reading disabilities and the type of instruction most likely to remediate reading problems (Jenkins & O'Connor, 2001). In summarizing the research, Torgeson and Wagner (1998) state that (1) the most severe reading problems of children with learning disabilities lie at the word, rather than the text, level of processing (i.e., inability to accurately and fluently decode single words), and (2) the most common cognitive limitation of these children involves a dysfunction in the awareness of the phonological structure of words in oral language (p. 226).

Clearly, problems with the reading process are very prevalent among students identified as having learning disabilities. However, the specific problems that they have in reading vary as much as the many components of the reading process (Hardman et al., 2005). These difficulties include, but are not limited to oral reading, reading comprehension, word recognition skills, and reading habits.

Oral Reading Difficulties

Many students with learning disabilities have difficulties with reading fluency (Mercer, Campbell, Miller, Mercer, & Lane, 2000). Reading fluency, most frequently defined as the rate of accurate reading (correct words per minute), is more than a status symbol for children; it is an important indicator of reading ability (Hunt & Marshall, 2005). Students with fluency problems may read aloud in a word-by-word manner without appropriate inflection or rhythm, unable to relate the patterns of spoken language to the printed word. Students with weakness in this area often dread being asked to read in class (Friend, 2005).

According to Salvia and Ysseldyke (1998), common oral reading problems include the following.

Omissions. The student skips individual words or groups of words.

Insertion. The student inserts one or more words into the sentence being orally read.

Substitution. The student replaces one or more words in the passage by one or more meaningful words.

Gross mispronunciation of a word. The student's pronunciation of a word bears little resemblance to the proper pronunciation.

Hesitation. The student hesitates for two or more seconds before pronouncing a word.

Inversion. The student changes the order of words appearing in a sentence.

Disregard of punctuation. The student fails to observe punctuation; for example, may not pause for a comma, stop for a period, or indicate a vocal inflection, a question mark, or an exclamation point.

Analyzing Oral Reading Miscues.   An oral reading error is often referred to as a miscue. A miscue is the difference between what a reader states is on a page and what is actually on the page. According to Vacca, Vacca, and Grove (1986), differences between what the reader says and what is printed on the page are not the result of random errors. Instead, these differences are "cued" by the thought and language of the reader, who is attempting to construct what the author is saying. Analysis of miscues can be of two types. With quantitative miscues analysis, the number of reading errors made by the student is counted. With qualitative miscues analysis, the focus is on the quality of the error rather than the number of different mistakes. This type of analysis is not based on the problems related to word identification, but rather on the differences between the miscues and the words on the pages. Consequently, in qualitative miscue analysis some miscues are more significant than others (Vacca et al., 1986).

According to John (1985), a *miscue is significant* if it affects meaning. Miscues are generally significant when the following statements apply.

- The meaning of the sentence or passages is significantly changed or altered, and the student does not correct the miscue.
- A nonword is used in place of the word in the passage.
- Only a partial word is substituted for the word or phrase in the passage.
- A word is pronounced for the student.

Miscues are generally *not* significant in the following cases.

- The meaning of the sentence or passage undergoes no change or only minimal change.
- Miscues are self-corrected by the student.
- They are acceptable in the student's dialect.
- They are later read correctly in the same passage.

Through miscue analysis, teachers can determine the extent to which the reader uses and coordinates graphic, sound, syntactic, and semantic information from the text. According to Goodman and Burke (1972), to analyze miscues you should ask at least four crucial questions.

Does the miscue change meaning? If it does not, then it is semantically acceptable within the context of the sentence or passage.

Does the miscue sound like language? If it does, then it is grammatically acceptable within the context. Miscues are grammatically acceptable if they sound like language and serve as the same parts of speech as the text words.

Do the miscue and the text word look and sound alike? Substitution and mispronunciation miscues should be analyzed to determine how similar they are in approximating the graphic and pronunciation features of the text words.

Was an attempt made to self-correct the miscue? Self-corrections are revealing because they demonstrate that the reader is attending to meaning and is aware that the initial miscuing did not make sense.

Oral reading problems often cause tremendous embarrassment for children. Children with oral reading problems may read in a strained voice with poor phrasing, ignore punctuation, and grope for words like a much younger child would do when reading. Pollaway, Patton, and Serna (2001) confirm that a student's self-image and feelings of confidence are greatly affected by unhappy reading experiences. Deficits in reading skills can also lead to acting-out behavior and poor motivation.

Reading Comprehension Deficits

Students with learning disabilities often have difficulties with reading comprehension (Gersten, Williams, Fuchs, & Baker, 1998). These children often lack the skills required for understanding text and have poor word-analysis skills (Hunt & Marshall, 2005). Reading comprehension refers to a student's ability to understand what he or she is reading. Some students with reading comprehension difficulties are able to read a passage so fluently that you might assume they were highly proficient readers. However, when they are asked questions about what they have read, they have little or no understanding of the words. Students with this problem sometimes are referred to as word callers (Friend, 2005).

It is always necessary to assess not only decoding but also the ability to understand what is being decoded. According to Salvia and Ysseldyke (1998), there are six different types of reading comprehension skills:

Literal comprehension. The student reads the paragraph or story and is then asked questions based on it.

Inferential comprehension. The student reads a paragraph or story and must interpret what has been read.

Listening comprehension. The student is read a paragraph or story by the examiner and is then asked questions about what the examiner has read.

Critical comprehension. The student reads a paragraph or story and then analyzes, evaluates, or makes judgments about what he or she has read.

Affective comprehension. The student reads a paragraph or story, and the examiner evaluates his or her emotional responses to the text.

Lexical comprehension. The student reads a paragraph or story, and the examiner assesses his or her knowledge of vocabulary words.

Here are some common reading comprehension problems of children with LD.

- Difficulties recalling basic facts (unable to answer specific questions about a passage, such as *What was the dog's name in the story?*)
- Difficulties recalling sequence (unable to tell the sequence of the story that was read)
- Difficulties recalling the main theme (unable to recall the main topic of the story)

When evaluating a child for reading comprehension, it is important to ask the following questions.

- Does the student guess at answers to the questions presented?
- Does the student show unwillingness to read or make attempts at reading?
- Does the student skip unknown words?
- Does the student disregard punctuation?
- Does the student exhibit inattention to the story line?
- Does the student drop the tone of his or her voice at the end of sentences?
- Does the student display problems with sounding out word parts and blends?
- Does the student exhibit a negative attitude toward reading?
- Does the student express difficulty attacking unknown words?

Problems with Word Recognition

Students with learning disabilities often have difficulties with **word recognition,** which relates to the student's ability with respect to sight vocabulary. According to Salvia and Ysseldyke (1998),

> A student learns the correct pronunciation of letters and words through a variety of experiences. The more exposure a student has to specific words and the more familiar those words become, the more readily he or she recognizes those words and is able to pronounce them correctly. (p. 464)

In order to identify written words, we use a number of different skills. Here are some of the most important word analysis skills.

- The ability to associate sounds with the various letters and letter combinations used to write them (phonic analysis)

- Immediately recognizing and remembering words (sight-word reading)
- Using the surrounding text to help figure out a specific word (using context)

The skills listed above rely heavy on perception, selective attention, memory, and metacognitive skills. Thus, word recognition depends almost entirely on the cognitive skills that are most problematic for individuals with disabilities (Hunt & Marshall, 2005).

According to Gargiulo (2004), here are common word recognition errors.

Omissions. Omitting a word (*Tom saw [a] cat.*)
Insertions. Inserting words (*The dog ran [fast] after the cat.*)
Substitutions. Reversing letters in a word (*no* for *on, was* for *saw*)
Mispronunciations. (*Mister* for *miser*)
Transpositions. Reading words in the wrong order (*She away ran* instead of *she ran away.*)
Unknown words. Hesitating for 5 seconds at words they cannot pronounce
Slow choppy reading. Not recognizing words quickly enough (20 to 30 words per minute)

Poor Reading Habits

Children with reading difficulties often have poor reading habits. As a teacher, it is critical that you be aware of these actions when watching your students read on a daily basis. Gargiulo (2004) lists some behaviors that are exhibited by children with poor reading habits.

Tension movements. Frowning, fidgeting, using a high-pitched tone of voice
Insecurity. Refusing to read, crying, attempting to distract the teacher
Loses place. Losing place frequently
Lateral head movements. Jerking head
Holds material close. Deviating extremely from 15 to 18 inches

Dyslexia

Dyslexia is one of several distinct learning disabilities. It is a specific language-based disorder characterized by difficulties in single word decoding, usually reflecting insufficient phonological processing abilities. The difficulties in single word decoding are often unexpected in relation to age and other cognitive and academic abilities; they are not the result of generalized developmental disability or sensory impairment. Dyslexia is manifested by variable difficulty with different forms of language, often including, in addition to problems reading, a conspicuous problem with acquiring proficiency in writing and spelling.

Simply stated, dyslexia is a type of reading disorder in which the student fails to recognize and comprehend written words. Dyslexia is a severe impairment in the ability to read, despite normal intelligence, normal opportunities to read, and an adequate home environment. Although the precise organic cause of dyslexia is unknown, it is generally thought that this problem results from difficulties with phonological awareness—a lack of understanding of the rules that govern the correspondence between specific sounds and certain letters that make up words (Lyon & Moats, 1997; cited in Gargiulo, 2004, p. 216). In other words, letter-sound recognition is impaired.

Various types of reading disorders have been recently cited by the American Academy of Special Education Professionals' *Educator's Diagnostic Manual of Disabilities and Disorders* (in press). Listed below are the reading disorders most frequently seen in children with dyslexia.

Direct Dyslexia. Direct dyslexia refers to the ability of the individual to read words aloud correctly, yet not comprehend what he or she has just read.

Dyseidesia Dyslexia. Such an affected individuals will have poor sight-word vocabularies and will rely on using time consuming word attack skills (a phonetic approach) to decode many words. As a result, students with this condition will read laboriously. Decoding becomes inaccurate for many phonetically irregular words, *log* for *laugh*. Characteristic spelling errors include phonetic equivalents for irregular words, such as *rede* for *ready*.

Dyseidetic Dyslexia. Children with the dyseidetic type of dyslexia are able to sound out individual letters phonetically but have trouble identifying patterns of letters in groups. Their spelling tends to be phonetic even when incorrect (*laf* for *laugh*). Children in this group have deficits in vision and memory of letters and word shapes, making it difficult for them to develop a sight vocabulary. However, they have the ability to acquire adequate phonetic skills.

Dyslexia with Dysgraphia ("Deep Dyslexia"). With this condition, a person has a problem in writing letters and words, grasping word-meanings, integrating the sounds of letters, and in pronouncing unfamiliar and, sometimes, even familiar words. People in this category face the biggest challenge and need our closest attention for educational and career planning.

Dyslexia without Dysgraphia ("Pure Dyslexia"). This disorder occurs when a person has problems reading but not writing. Some students with pure dyslexia have trouble doing written arithmetic because they have to read the text and the numbers, but may not have any problem doing spoken arithmetic. Dyslexia without dysgraphia may never be identified, because, to confuse matters, a person may have nearly normal oral language and his or her writing and oral spelling may be virtually unimpaired.

Dysnemkinesia Dyslexia. Dysnemkinesia involves minimal dysfunction of the area of the motor cortex involved in letter formation. Individuals with this disorder can be characteristically distinguished by their frequent letter reversals, such as *d* for *b*, as in *doy* for *boy*.

Dysnomia. A type of dyslexia specifically associated with difficulties in naming and naming speed.

Dysphonetic Dyslexia. Dysphonic readers have difficulty relating letters to sounds, so their spelling is totally chaotic. They are able to recognize words they have memorized but cannot sound out new ones to figure out what they are. They may be able to read near the appropriate grade level but are poor spellers. Dysphonetic dyslexia is viewed as a disability in associating symbols with sounds. The misspellings typical of this disorder are phonetically inaccurate. The misreadings are substitutions based on small clues, and are also semantic.

Literal Dyslexia (Letter Blindness). With this condition, a person has difficulty identifying letters, matching upper case letters with lowercase, naming letters, or matching sounds with the corresponding letters. Here, a person may read individual letters of the word but not the word itself, or read a word, but not understand the meaning of the word. Some people with literal dyslexia may read words partially. For example, a person may read the word *lice* as *ice,* or *like.* The person may realize that these words are incorrect, but cannot read the words correctly. Some people with literal dyslexia do better by moving their finger along the outline of a word, or by tracing the letters in the air.

Mixed Reading Disability Dyslexia (Alexic Reading Disability). Children with mixed reading disabilities have both the dyseidetic and dysphonic types of reading disorder. This subtype combines the deficit of the first two groups. This person may have disability in both sight vocabulary and phonetic skills. People with this form of dyslexia are usually unable to read or spell.

Neglect Dyslexia. This condition occurs when a person neglects the left or the right side of words, a problem particularly highlighted in reading long words. For example, if asked to read *strowt,* he or she may read it as *owt.* Given a word such as *alphabetically,* persons with this particular form of dyslexia will miss some of the first few letters. For example, they may read it simply as *betically.* There may be a problem with compound words. For example, a compound word such as *cowboy* may be read partially, as *cow* or *boy.*

Phonological Dyslexia. This disorder occurs when an individual has difficulty in converting letters to their sounds. They can read words that are already familiar to them, but have trouble reading unfamiliar or novel words. They also have difficulty in reading a nonword such as *tord.* They may misread this nonword as a real word that looks similar. They sometime also misread actual words as other ones that look similar. The word *shut* may pose this particular problem, much to a listener's dismay.

Primary Dyslexia. This is a dysfunction of, rather than damage to, the left side of the brain (cerebral cortex) and does not change with maturity. Individuals with this type are rarely able to read above a fourth-grade level and may struggle with reading, spelling, and writing as adults. Primary dyslexia is hereditary and is found more often in boys than in girls.

Semantic Dyslexia. This occurs when a person distorts the meaning of a word or incorrectly reads a word because of the confusion in the meaning of the given word. People with semantic dyslexia may say an antonym, a synonym, or a subordinate of a word instead of the word proper. For example, they may misread *dog* as *cat* or *fox*. They may misread *twist* as *twisted,* or *buy* as *bought.* Some have trouble reading function words such as *of, an, not,* and *and.*

Spelling Dyslexia. This occurs when a person has problems reading all types of words and sometimes has trouble identifying individual letters. Their reading is extremely slow and hesitant, particularly on long words. While a normal reader takes about 30 milliseconds for reading each additional letter, a spelling dyslexic may take about a second to do the same. Some dyslexics tend to read words one letter at a time, even if the words are short and familiar.

Surface Dyslexia. This condition occurs when a person can read words phonetically but has problems with whole word recognition (i.e., *yacht = yachet*).

Trauma Dyslexia. This condition usually occurs after brain trauma or injury to the area of the brain that controls reading and writing. This type of dyslexia is rarely diagnosed in today's school-age population because they will often receive a classification in special education of Traumatic Brain Injury (TBI) rather than LD.

Visual Dyslexia. People with this condition usually cannot learn words as a whole component. There are problems with visual discrimination, memory synthesis, and sequencing of words. Reversal of words or letters when reading, writing, and spelling is common.

It is important to identify students with dyslexia or other severe reading disabilities early, before they fall far behind their peers in word-recognition skills. Students who appear to be learning letter-names, sounds, and sight words at a significantly slower rate than their classmates are at a risk for developing later reading problems. And yet, despite the enormous problems children with dyslexia face, the general consensus among researchers is that they can improve. When the diagnosis of dyslexia is made in the first two grades, more than 80% of the children are brought up to grade level. However, if the diagnosis is not made until the fifth grade, only 10 to 15% are helped (Kirk et al., 2003).

Finally, it is critical to remember that not all children with learning disabilities suffer from dyslexia. The term *dyslexia* is overused in the popular press, which often gives an inaccurate impression that everyone with a reading or literacy problem suffers from dyslexia. For more details on teaching students with learning disabilities in reading, see Chapter 10.

Math Deficits

Although disorders of reading have traditionally received more emphasis than problems with mathematics, the latter are gaining a great deal of attention (Hunt & Marshall, 2005). Authorities now recognize that math difficulties are second only to reading disabilities as an academic problem area for students with LD (Hallahan &

Kauffman, 2003). Researchers estimate that about one out of every four pupils with LD receives assistance because of difficulties with mathematics (Rivera, 1997). According to Lerner (2003), each student with mathematical difficulties is unique; not all children exhibit the same deficiency or impairment.

Students with learning disabilities may have problems in both math calculations and math reasoning (USOE, 1977). These students often have a number of problems in mathematical thinking (Hunt & Marshall, 2005). Mathematical thinking is a process that begins early in most children. Even before formal education begins, children are exposed to various situations that involve the application of mathematical concepts. As they enter formal schooling, they take the knowledge of what they had previously learned and begin to apply it in a more formal manner.

It is necessary to understand that mathematics and arithmetic are actually two different terms. Although most people use them interchangeably, they each have distinct meanings. According to Merriam-Webster (m-w.com), arithmetic is

> a branch of mathematics that deals usually with the nonnegative real numbers including sometimes the transfinite cardinals and with the application of the operations of addition, subtraction, multiplication, and division to them

while mathematics is

> the science of numbers and their operations, interrelations, combinations, generalizations, and abstractions and of space, configurations and their structure, measurement, transformations, and generalizations.
>
> Mathematics involves many different abilities, as suggested by the list below.

Estimating	Doing computational skills
Solving problems	Understanding measurement
Using mathematics for prediction	Creating and reading graphs and charts
Recognizing how to interpret results	Applying mathematics in practical situations

Schools begin the process of learning math skills in kindergarten and proceed throughout the child's formal education. Even at the college level, mathematics is often a core requirement in many liberal arts schools. In general, next to reading, mathematics is probably the area most frequently assessed in school systems.

Analysis and Interpretation of Math Skills

According to McLoughlin and Lewis (1990), mathematics is one of the school subjects best suited for error analysis because students respond in writing on most tasks, thereby producing a permanent record of their work. Also, there is usually only one correct answer to mathematics questions and problems, making scoring unambiguous.

Today, the most common use of error analysis in mathematics is assessment of computation skills. Cox (1975) differentiates between systematic computation errors and errors that are random or careless mistakes. With systematic errors, students are consistent in their use of an incorrect number fact, operation, or algorithm (p. 354). McLoughlin and Lewis (1990) identified four error types in computational analysis:

Incorrect operation. The student selects the incorrect operation. For example, the problem requires subtraction, and the student adds.

Incorrect number fact. The number fact recalled by the student is inaccurate. For example, the student recalls the product of 9×6 as 52.

Incorrect algorithm. The procedures used by the student to solve the problem are inappropriate. The student may skip a step, apply the correct steps in the wrong sequence, or use an inaccurate method.

Random error. The student's response is incorrect and apparently random. For example, the student writes 100 as the answer to 42×6. (p. 354)

Different types of errors can occur in the mathematics process other than these four mentioned. For example, a student may make a mistake or error in applying the appropriate arithmetical operations. Such an example would be $50 - 12 = 62$. Here, the student used the operation of addition rather than subtraction. The student may understand how to do both operations, but consistently gets these types of questions wrong on tests due to the improper use of the sign involved.

Another problem the student may encounter is a **slip.** When a slip occurs, it is more likely due to a simple mistake rather than a pattern of problems. For example, if a child correctly subtracts $20 - 5$ in eight problems but for some reason not in the ninth problem, his or her error is probably due to a simple slip rather than a serious operational or processing problem. One error on one problem is not an error pattern. Error patterns can be assessed by analyzing all correct and incorrect answers. When designing a program plan for a particular child in mathematics, it is critical to establish not only the nature of the problems but also the patterns of problems that occur in the child's responses.

Also, handwriting can play an important role in mathematics. Scoring a math test often involves reading numbers written down on an answer sheet by the student. If a student's handwriting is difficult to interpret or impossible to read, this can create serious problems for the evaluator with respect to obtaining valid scores. When a student's handwriting is not clear on a math test, it is important that the evaluator ask the student for help in reading the answers. By doing so, the evaluator is analyzing the math skills that need to be assessed rather than spending time trying to decode the student's responses.

Robinson, Manchetti, and Torgeson propose that for some children, math difficulties may be due to either deficits in phonological processing of the features of spoken numbers or failure to grasp meaningful concepts. They note that 43% of the students with a math disability also have reading problems (2002; cited in Smith et al., 2004).

Dyscalculia

Arithmetic involves recognizing numbers and symbols, memorizing facts, aligning numbers, and understanding abstract concepts such as place value and fractions. Any of these may be difficult for children with developmental arithmetic disorders, also called *dyscalculia*, which refers to selective impairment in mathematical thinking or in calculation skills (Fletcher & Forman, 1994). Problems with number or basic concepts are likely to show up early. Disabilities that appear in the later grades are more often tied to problems in reasoning.

Various types of mathematical disorders have been cited by the American Academy of Special Education Professionals' *Educator's Diagnostic Manual of Disabilities and Disorders* (in press). Below are mathematical disorders frequently seen in children with dyscalculia:

> **Basic Number Fact Disorder.** Individuals with a Basic Number Fact Disorder have problems memorizing and retaining basic arithmetic facts, such as the answers to 8 − 2, 7 + 1, or 12 × 2. It is not that individuals with Basic Number Fact Disorder do not remember any arithmetic facts, but rather they have problems memorizing as many facts as other children do. Furthermore, they appear to forget facts rather easily. These children may struggle for years, will count their fingers to add and subtract, and seem unable to develop efficient memory strategies on their own.
>
> **Calculation Disorder.** By definition, calculation is problem solving that involves numbers or quantities. The calculation of numbers often gives students with learning disabilities great difficulties. Inconsistent calculation can lead to numerous errors when doing math work. Students with calculation difficulties often perform the incorrect mathematical operations. For example, when calculating 8 + 2, they may respond 6, because they subtracted rather than added the two numbers.
>
> **Mathematical Abstraction Limitation Disorder.** Individuals with this disorder do not possess the ability to function at a high level of mathematical abstraction and as a result can only function on a concrete level of understanding. Individuals with this disorder tend to reach a ceiling in their ability to comprehend abstract math concepts.
>
> **Mathematical Estimation Disorder.** Children with dyscalculia seem to have an impaired sense of number size. This may affect tasks involving estimating numbers in a collection and comparing numbers.
>
> **Mathematical Language Disorder.** According to Garnett (1998), some students with LD are particularly hampered by the language aspects of math, resulting in confusion about terminology, difficulty following verbal explanations, and weak verbal skills for monitoring the steps of complex calculations. Teachers can help by slowing the pace of their delivery, maintaining normal timing of phrases, and giving information in discrete segments. Such slowed-down chunking of verbal information is important when asking questions, giving directions, presenting concepts, and offering explanations.

Mathematical Measurement Disorder. Individuals with this disorder may have difficulty with concepts involving measurements, such as speed (miles per hour), temperature (energy per unit of mass), averages, and proportional measures.

Mathematical Navigation Disorder. Children with this disorder can usually learn the sequence of counting words, but may have difficulty navigating back and forth, especially in twos, threes, or more.

Mathematical Organization Disorder. Individuals with this disorder may have an inability to organize objects in a logical way. They may be unable to comprehend or mentally picture mechanical processes. They may lack "big picture/whole picture" thinking. They may have a poor ability to visualize the location of the numbers on the face of a clock, the geographical locations of states, countries, oceans, streets, and so on.

Mathematical Sequencing Disorder. People with this disorder have trouble with sequence, including left/right orientation. They will read numbers out of sequence and sometimes do operations backwards. They also become confused on the sequence of past or future events.

Symbolic Mathematical Operations Disorder. Individuals with this disorder may find it especially difficult to translate between number words, where powers of ten are expressed by new names (ten, hundred, and thousand) and numerals (where powers of ten are expressed by the same numerals but in terms of place value).

Temporal/Monetary Math Disorder. People with this disorder tend to have difficulties in topics relating to time, telling time, keeping track of time, estimating time, monetary concepts, and counting money. Older children may exhibit difficulties with money and credit and cannot do financial planning or budgeting (e.g., balancing a checkbook). Individuals may have fear of money and cash transactions and may be unable to mentally figure change due back, the amounts to pay for tips, taxes, and so forth.

Visual–Spatial Math Disorder. Students with this disorder have disturbances in visual–spatial–motor organization, which may result in weak or missing understanding of concepts, very poor number sense, specific difficulty with pictorial representations, poorly controlled handwriting, and confused arrangements of numerals and signs on the page. Students with this disorder might have spatial problems and difficulty aligning numbers into proper columns.

Written Symbol System Disorder. According to Garnett (2000), many younger children who have difficulty with elementary math actually bring to school a strong foundation of informal math understanding. They encounter trouble in connecting this knowledge base to the more formal procedures, language, and symbolic notation system of school math (Allardice & Ginsburg, 1983). The collision of their informal skills with school math is like a tuneful, rhythmic child experiencing written music as something different from what she already can do. In fact, it is quite a complex feat to map the new world of written math symbols onto the known world of quantities, actions and, at the same time, to learn the peculiar language we use to talk about arithmetic.

Whether because of the reading requirement or the ability to understand the mathematical concepts captured in a problem, students with learning disabilities may be unable to sort critical extraneous information, to recognize the correct computational procedure, or to determine whether the answer they obtain is reasonable (Jordan & Hanich, 2003). Mathematical difficulties are often major obstacles in the academic paths of students with LD and frequently continue to cause problems throughout high school. Mastery of fundamental quantitative concepts is vital to learning more abstract and complex mathematics, a requirement for youth with learning disabilities who are seeking to complete high school and attend colleges or universities (Cirino, Morris, & Morris, 2002; cited in Hardman et al., 2005). Further research on difficulties with mathematics and on effective instruction for students encountering such problems grows more important as such young people seek to achieve more challenging educational goals (p. 178).

Given these difficulties, it is not surprising that 50% of students with learning disabilities have IEP goals in math. As with reading and writing, explicit, systematic instruction that provides guided meaningful practice with feedback usually improves the math performance of students with learning disabilities (Fuchs & Fuchs, 2001; cited in Heward, 2003). For details on teaching students with learning disabilities in math, see Chapter 11.

Written Expression Deficits

Many individuals with LD exhibit deficits in written language (Hallahan, Kauffman, & Lloyd, 1999). Learning disabilities in the area of written expression are beginning to receive more recognition as a serious problem (Smith et al., 2004). Writing is a highly complex method of expression involving the integration of eye–hand, linguistic, and conceptual abilities. As a result, it is usually the last skill children master. Whereas reading is usually considered the receptive form of a graphic symbol system, writing is considered the expressive form of that system. The primary concern in the assessment of composition skills is the content of the student's writing, not its form.

The term *written language* refers to a variety of interrelated graphic skills.

Composition. The ability to generate ideas and to express them in an acceptable grammar, while adhering to certain stylistic conventions

Spelling. The ability to use letters to construct words in accordance with accepted usage

Handwriting. The ability to execute physically the graphic marks necessary to produce legible compositions or messages (Hallahan et al., 1999)

The impact of written language problems increases with a student's age because so many school assignments require a written product. Students with written language problems often exhibit the following characteristics.

- Feel overwhelmed by the idea of getting started
- Struggle to organize and use the mechanics of writing
- Struggle to develop their fluency
- Have difficulties spelling and constructing written products in a legible fashion
- Submit written work that is too brief

Many students with difficulties with written language use a "retrieve-and-write" approach, in which they retrieve from immediate memory whatever seems appropriate and write it down. They seldom use the self-regulation and self-assessment strategies of competent writers: setting a goal or plan to guide their writing, organizing their ideas, drafting, self-assessing, and rewriting. As a result, they produce poorly organized compositions containing a few poorly developed ideas (Sexton, Harris, & Graham, 1998; cited in Heward, 2003).

Handwriting Difficulties

Handwriting refers to the actual motor activity that is involved in writing. Most students are taught manuscript (printing) initially and then move to cursive writing (script) in later grades. Some educators advocate that only manuscript or only cursive should be taught. In truth, problems may appear among students using either system. Children's writing changes as they mature. The focus of a youngster's writing shifts from the process of writing (handwriting and spelling), to the written product (having written something), to communication with readers (getting across one's message) (Hallahan et al., 1999, p. 396).

Gargiulo (2004) notes that early on, pupils focus on becoming competent in mastering the mechanical aspects of composition—spelling and handwriting; in the later grades, they learn to organize and present their ideas in a lucid and logical fashion. Children with learning disabilities, however, lag behind their nondisabled peers. Investigators have observed that individuals with LD use less complex sentence structure, incorporate fewer ideas, produce poorly organized paragraphs, and write less complex stories (p. 219).

Dysgraphia.   Dysgraphia, the learning disability associated with written expression, entails writing skills that fall substantially below those expected given the individual's age, IQ, and education, such that academic achievement or activities of daily living are significantly impaired. Dysgraphia is the inability to perform motor movement, in other words, extremely poor handwriting. It is associated with a neurological dysfunction. Agraphia is an acquired disorder in which the ability to write and make patterns is impaired (Birsch, 1999; cited in Kirk et al., 2003). Students' handwriting problems can rise from any of the following conditions.

- A lack of fine motor coordination
- Failure to attend to task
- Inability to perceive and/or remember visual images accurately
- Inadequate handwriting instruction in the classroom

In general, students with dysgraphia often learn less from an assignment because they must focus on the mechanics of writing instead of on the content of their assignment (Turnbull et al., 2004).

Three different types of writing disorders have been recently cited by the American Academy of Special Education Professionals' *Educator's Diagnostic Manual of Disabilities and Disorders* (in press). Below are the writing disorders most frequently seen in children with dysgraphia.

Dyslexic Dysgraphia. With this disorder, spontaneously written text is illegible, especially when the text is complex. Oral spelling is poor, but drawing and copying of written text are relatively normal. Finger-tapping speed (a measure of fine-motor speed) is normal.

Motor Dysgraphia. With this disorder, both spontaneously written and copied text may be illegible, oral spelling is normal, and drawing is usually problematic. Finger-tapping speed is abnormal.

Spatial Dysgraphia. Individuals with this disorder display illegible writing, whether spontaneously produced or copied. Oral spelling is normal. Finger-tapping speed is normal, but drawing is very problematic.

Spelling Problems

Spelling is the ability to use letters to construct words in accordance with accepted usage. Spelling ability is viewed by some teachers and school administrators equally with other academic skills. Being a poor speller does not necessarily mean that a child has a learning disorder. However, when poor spelling occurs with poor reading and/or arithmetic, then there is reason for concern. It appears that many of the learning skills required for good spelling are the same ones that enable students to become good readers.

Learning to spell is a developmental process, and young children go through a number of stages as they begin to acquire written language skills. Writing begins in the preschool years as young children observe and begin to imitate the act of writing.

Dysorthographia is the learning disability associated with spelling. Individuals with this disorder have difficulties utilizing clues from several sources that aid in deciding on the correct spelling of a word. Marshall and Hunt (2005) note that many students with learning disabilities spell a word as if it were being approached for the first time, without reference to an image of the word held in memory. The difficulties students with LD have in learning and applying the rules of phonics, visualizing the word correctly, and evaluating spellings result in frequent misspellings, even as they become more adept at reading. It is not uncommon to find the same word spelled five or six different ways on the same paper, regardless of whether the student is in the fifth grade or college (e.g., *ther, there, thare,* and *they're* for *their*).

Analysis of Spelling Skills.   Several questions should be addressed before one begins to analyze a child's spelling abilities (Pierangelo & Giuliani, 2005).

> **Does the child have sufficient mental ability to learn to spell?** This information can be obtained from the school psychologist if an intellectual evaluation was administered. However, if no such test was administered, you may be able to find the results of a group school abilities index, which may be present in the child's permanent folder.
>
> **Are the child's hearing, speech, and vision adequate?** This information can be obtained through the permanent record folder, information in the nurse's office, or informal screening procedures.
>
> **What is the child's general level of spelling ability according to teacher comments, past evaluations, or standardized tests?** Teacher comments and observations about the child's spelling history are very important to show patterns of disability. Also, look at standardized tests to see if patterns exist through the years on such tests.

It is also important to look at these attributes.

- The child's attitude toward spelling in the classroom
- The extent to which the child relies on a dictionary in the classroom
- The extent of spelling errors in classroom written work
- Any patterns of procrastination or avoidance of written work
- The student's study habits and methods of work in the classroom
- The history of scores on classroom spelling tests
- Any observable handwriting difficulties
- Any evidence of fatigue as a factor in the child's spelling performance

Spelling Errors Primarily Due to Auditory or Visual Channel Deficits.   Certain spelling errors may be evident in students with auditory channel deficits (Pierangelo & Giuliani, 2005).

> **Auditory discrimination problems.** The child substitutes *t* for *d* or *sh* for *ch* and/or confuses vowels; for example, spells *bit* as *bet*.
>
> **Auditory acuity or discrimination problems.** The child does not hear subtle differences in, nor discriminate between, sounds and often leaves vowels out of two-syllable words.
>
> **Auditory–visual association.** The child uses a synonym such as *house* for *home* in spelling.
>
> **Auditory–visual associative memory.** The child takes wild guesses with little or no relationship between the letters or words used and the spelling words dictated, such as spelling *dog* for *home* or writing *phe* for *home*.

These spelling errors may be evident in students with certain visual channel deficits.

Visual memory problems. The child visualizes the beginning or the ending of words but omits the middle of the words; for example, spells *hppy* for *happy*.

Visual memory sequence. The child gives the correct letters but in the wrong sequence, for example, writes the word *the* as *teh* or *hte*.

Visual discrimination problems. The child inverts letters, writing *u* for *n*, *m* for *w*.

Visual memory. The child spells words phonetically that are nonphonetic in configuration, for example, *tuff* for *tough*.

In general, common spelling errors to look for in students with dysorthographia include the addition of unneeded letters, reversal of vowels, reversal of syllables, and the phonemic spelling of nonphonemic words. Fortunately, the writing and spelling skills of most students with LD can be improved through strategy instruction, frequent opportunities to practice writing, and systematic feedback (Heward, 2003). For details on teaching students with writing disorders, see Chapter 12.

Language Deficits

Students with learning disabilities often have difficulties with the mechanical and social uses of language (Hallahan & Kauffman, 2003). Specific mechanical deficits difficulties are often present in the three different areas (Gargiulo, 2004).

Syntax. Rule systems that determine how words are organized into sentences
Semantics. Word meanings
Phonology. The study of how individual sounds make up words

Language deficits are found in the areas of oral expression and listening comprehension. These two areas control our ability to communicate with others, and therefore a deficit in either or both can have a major impact on the quality of life of a child with a learning disability, as well as his or her life in education (Smith et al., 2004). Studies have found that more than 60% of students with LD have some type of language disorder (Bryan, Bay, Lopez-Reyna, & Donahue, 1991).

Oral Language Problems

Students with LD frequently experience difficulties with oral expression—a problem that can affect both academic and social interactions. Common problems associated with oral language include the following.

- **Choosing the appropriate word.** Children with LD will often use a less appropriate word because the right word will not come to them.

- **Understanding complex sentence structures**
- **Responding to questions**
- **Difficulties in retrieving words.** The response rate of children with learning disabilities may be slower than that of their nondisabled peers, and they may speak more slowly.

Listening Comprehension Problems

Listening problems can also be misinterpreted. A child with a disability in listening demonstrates that disability in a negative way, for example, by failing to follow directions or by appearing oppositional or unmotivated. A teacher's careful observation and assessment of a student's language ability is important for ensuring the student's success (Smith et al., 2004).

Problems with Pragmatics

One aspect of oral expression that is receiving increased attention is pragmatics, the functional use of language in social situations. Researchers note that children with learning disabilities sometimes experience communication problems in social settings (Bryan, 1998). Research in the field of children with language–learning disabilities has begun to focus more and more on the area of pragmatics. Simply stated, pragmatics is the use of language in social situations. Children with learning disabilities often have problems with social conversations. These students may exhibit the following characteristics.

- Need extra time to process incoming information
- Not understand the meaning of the words or sequences
- Miss nonverbal language cues
- Not understand jokes
- Laugh inappropriately or at the wrong times
- Have difficulty doing group work
- Have difficulties giving or following directions
- Have conversations marked by long silences
- Not be skilled in responding to statements
- Not be skilled at responding to questions
- Have a tendency to answer their questions
- Make those with whom they talk feel uncomfortable (Hallahan & Kauffman, 2003)

Participating in conversations with friends can be especially troublesome for someone with a learning disability. The ebb and flow that is characteristic of conversations may elude them, and nonverbal language clues may also be overlooked. In short, many individuals with learning disabilities are not good conversationalists (Gargiulo, 2004). They have great difficulties trying to engage in the mutual give and take that conversation between two people requires.

Disorders of Attention

Attention is a critical skill in learning. Conte (1991) suggests that to be effective learners, children must be able to initiate attention, direct their attention appropriately, sustain their attention according to the task demands, and shift attention when appropriate. Deficits in these areas can have an impact on all areas of school. When children are not paying attention, they cannot respond appropriately to questions, follow directions, or take notes during a lecture. Social problems occur when the student interrupts others and does not listen to peers. Estimates of the number of students with LD that have attention problems range from 41% to 80% (Smith et al., 2004).

Attention problems for children with learning disabilities are often characterized as short attention span. A short attention span is defined as an inability to focus one's attention on a task for more than a few seconds or minutes. Parents and teachers note that many children with LD share the following characteristics.

- Cannot sustain attention for more than a short period of time
- Exhibit excessive daydreaming
- Are highly distractible

Individuals with learning disabilities often have attention problems (Kotkin, Forness, & Kavale, 2001). Their attention difficulties are often severe enough for them to be diagnosed as also having Attention-Deficit Hyperactivity Disorder (ADHD). ADHD is a diagnosis normally made by either a psychiatrist or psychologist, using the criteria as established by the American Psychiatric Association (1994). Although estimates vary, researchers have consistently found an overlap of 10 to 25% between ADHD and learning disabilities (Forness & Kavale, 2002).

Several characteristics of ADHD have long been recognized in many children with learning disabilities, and there is a significant level of comorbidity (a situation in which multiple conditions occur together) between the two conditions (some experts estimate as high as 25%).

Overview of ADHD

Attention-Deficit Hyperactivity Disorder is a condition that can make it hard for a person to sit still, control behavior, and pay attention. These difficulties usually begin before the person is 7 years old. However, these behaviors may not be noticed until the child is older. Doctors do not know just what causes ADHD. However, researchers who study the brain are coming closer to understanding what may cause it. They believe that some people with ADHD do not have enough of certain chemicals (called neurotransmitters) in their brain. These chemicals help the brain control behavior. Parents and teachers do not cause ADHD. Still, there are many things that both parents and teachers can do to help a child with ADHD. As many as 5 out of every 100 children in school may have ADHD. Boys are three times more likely than girls to have ADHD. There are three main signs, or symptoms, of ADHD.

These are (1) Problems with paying attention, (2) Being very active (called hyperactivity), and (3) Acting before thinking (called impulsivity).

More information about these symptoms is listed in the *Diagnostic and Statistical Manual of Mental Disorders* (4th ed. rev.) *(DSM IV-TR)*, published by the American Psychiatric Association (2000). Based on these symptoms, three types of ADHD have been defined.

- *Inattentive ADHD.* The person can't seem to get focused or stay focused on a task or activity
- *Hyperactive-impulsive ADHD.* The person is very active and often acts without thinking
- *Combined ADHD.* The person is inattentive, impulsive, and too active

Inattentive ADHD. Many children with ADHD have problems paying attention. Children with the inattentive type of ADHD often exhibit the following characteristics.

- Do not pay close attention to details
- Can't stay focused on play or school work
- Don't follow through on instructions or finish school work or chores
- Can't seem to organize tasks and activities
- Get distracted easily
- Lose things such as toys, school work, and books (APA, 2000, pp. 85–86)

Hyperactive-Impulsive ADHD. Being too active is probably the most visible sign of ADHD. The hyperactive child is "always on the go," although as he or she gets older, the level of activity may go down. These children also act before thinking. For example, they may run across the road without looking or climb to the top of very tall trees. They may be surprised to find themselves in a dangerous situation. They may have no idea of how to get out of the situation. Hyperactivity and impulsivity tend to go together. Children with the hyperactive-impulsive type of ADHD often may:

- Fidget and squirm
- Get out of their chairs when they're not supposed to
- Run around or climb constantly
- Have trouble playing quietly
- Talk too much
- Blurt out answers before questions have been completed
- Have trouble waiting their turn
- Interrupt others when they're talking
- Butt in on the games others are playing (APA, 2000, p. 86)

Combined ADHD. Children with the combined type of ADHD have symptoms of both of the types described above. They have problems with paying attention, with hyperactivity, and with controlling their impulses. Of course, from time to time, all children are inattentive, impulsive, and too active. With children who have ADHD, these behaviors are the rule, not the exception. Such behavior can cause a child to have real problems at home, at school, and with friends. As a result, many children with ADHD feel anxious, unsure of themselves, and depressed. These feelings are not symptoms of ADHD. They come from having problems again and again at home and in school. There is no quick treatment for ADHD. However, the symptoms of ADHD can be managed. It's important that the child's family and teachers find out more about ADHD, learn how to help the child manage his or her behavior, create an educational program that fits the child's individual needs, and provide medication, if parents and the doctor feel this would help the child.

For details on teaching students with ADHD, see Chapter 13.

Achievement Discrepancy

Although students who receive special education services under the learning disabilities category are an extremely heterogeneous group, it is important to remember that the fundamental defining characteristic of students with learning disabilities is specific and significant achievement deficits in the presence of adequate overall intelligence (Heward, 2003). Students with LD perform below expectations based on their measured potential, in addition to scoring below their peers in overall achievement. Attempts to quantify the discrepancy between academic achievement and academic potential for students with LD have appeared in the literature for some time, but the field still lacks a broadly accepted explanation of the phenomenon (Roderiques, 2002; cited in Hardman et al., 2005).

Early in the school years, youngsters with LD may find themselves two to four years behind their peers in level of academic achievement, and many fall even further behind as they continue in the educational system. This discouraging pattern often results in students dropping out of high school or graduating without proficiency in basic reading, writing, or math skills (U.S. Department of Education, 2002; cited in Hardman et al., 2005, p. 178).

The difficulties experienced by children with learning disabilities—especially for those who cannot read at grade level—are substantial and pervasive and usually last across the lifespan (Mercer, 1997). The tendency to think of learning disabilities as a mild disability erroneously supports "the notion that a learning disability is little more than a minor inconvenience rather than the serious, life-long condition it is [and] often detracts from the real needs of these students" (Hallahan, 1998, p. 4; cited in Heward, 2003).

Memory Deficits

It is well documented that children and adolescents with LD have significant difficulties remembering academic information and nonacademic information, such as doctors' appointments, homework assignments, multiplication facts, directions, and telephone numbers. Teachers frequently comment that, with these students, it seems to be "in one ear and out the other," which can be highly aggravating for teachers as well as parents (Gargiulo, 2004). Teachers and parents also report that memory skills are inconsistent. For example, a student may know the multiplication facts on Thursday and then fail the test on Friday (Hardman et al., 2005).

Parents often state that they cannot understand how their children can be so intelligent and forget such simple things. Early research in learning disabilities has documented that students with LD have a real deficit in memory (Hallahan & Kauffman, 2003). Teachers have long complained that children with LD have poor memory.

Several studies have suggested that students with LD have more deficits in memory than students without LD except in the area of long-term memory (Swanson, 1994). Students with memory deficits have difficulty retaining learned information, repeating information read or heard, following multiple directions, and performing tasks in the right sequence (Smith et al., 2004).

The memory difficulties faced by students are normally either in short-term memory (STM) or working memory (WM). STM involves the ability to recall information after a short period of time. Short-term memory tasks involve the recall, in correct order, of either aurally or visually presented information (such as a list of digits, letters, or pictures) shortly after hearing or seeing the items several times (Hallahan, 1999). Working memory requires that the individual retain information while simultaneously engaging in another cognitive activity. According to Silver (2001), people with LD are more likely to have concerns with short-term rather than long-term memory. He explained that children and youth with these limitations need to concentrate on new information, and to repeat it continually, in order to keep it in short-term memory. If their attention is disrupted, the information may be lost (Bowe, 2005). Working memory is involved, for example, when we try to remember a person's address while also listening to directions on how to arrive there (Swanson, 1994). Deficits in memory, particularly working memory, often translate into difficulties in the classroom. Success with reading and math seems to depend more on working memory than short-term memory. Working memory also appears to be crucial for word recognition and reading comprehension (Ashbaker & Swanson, 1996).

Although there are various theories as to why students with learning disabilities have difficulties with memory tasks, it appears that they do not use "strategies for remembering" the way their nondisabled peers do. For example, when presented with a list of words to memorize, most children will rehearse the names to themselves. They will make use of categories by rehearsing the words and grouping them together. Students with learning disabilities are not likely to use these names spontaneously (Hallahan & Kauffman, 2003).

O'Shaughenessy and Swanson (1998) suggest that the problem is mainly with an inability to code new information for memory storage and a decreased motivation for difficult mental effort. On a positive note, when children with learning disabilities are taught a memory strategy, they perform memory tasks as well as non learning-disabled students (Smith et al., 2004).

Cognition Deficits

Students with learning disabilities will often demonstrate problems in cognition. Cognition is a broad term covering many different aspects of thinking and problem solving. Students with learning disabilities often exhibit disorganized thinking that results in problems with planning and organizing their lives at home (Hallahan & Kauffman, 2003). Research suggests that children with LD have differing, rather than uniformly deficient, cognitive abilities (Henry, 2001). This finding has led to the development of specific, highly focused instruction for individuals with learning disabilities to replace generic curricula, reflecting the assumption that their cognitive skills are generally poor (Hardman et al., 2005). According to Smith and colleagues (2004), students with problems in cognition may share the following characteristics.

Make poor decisions
Make frequent errors
Have delayed verbal responses
Require more supervision
Have trouble getting started
on a task

Have trouble adjusting to change
Require concrete demonstrations
Have difficulties understanding social
expectations
Have trouble using previously learned
information in a new situation

Metacognition Deficits

Students with learning disabilities often have problems with metacognition. Metacognition is defined as one's understanding of the strategies available for learning a task and the regulatory mechanisms needed to complete the task. Metacognition has at least three components.

Recognize task requirements. Students with LD frequently have problems judging how difficult tasks can be. For example, they may approach the reading of highly technical information with the same level of intensity as reading for pleasure.

Select and implement appropriate strategies. Students with LD often do not come up with strategies to help themselves in and outside of school. For example, if asked to name ways in which they can help themselves remember to bring their homework into school the next day, they may not have any ideas, whereas the nondisabled peers will suggest writing a note to themselves, putting the homework by the front door, and so on.

Monitor and adjust performance. Students with LD often have problems with comprehension monitoring. Comprehension monitoring is the ability to keep track of one's own comprehension of reading material and to make adjustments to comprehend better while reading. For example, a student with LD may not have a good sense he does not understand what he is reading. Good readers are often able to make the necessary adjustments, such as slowing down or rereading difficult passages. Students with reading problems are also likely to have problems picking out the main ideas of paragraphs.

Hallahan and colleagues (1999) refer to metacognition as "thinking about thinking." Students with problems in this area might have difficulty focusing on listening, purposefully remembering important information, connecting that information to prior knowledge, making sense out of the new information, and using what they know to solve a problem. They often lack strategies for planning and organizing, setting priorities, and predicting and solving problems. An important component of metacognition is the ability to evaluate one's own behavior and behave differently when identifying inappropriate behavior or mistakes (Smith et al., 2004). Competency as a learner requires that students exhibit these metacognitive skills (Kluwe, 1987).

Social–Emotional Problems

The literature suggests that to be socially accepted, students should be cooperative, share, offer pleasant greetings, have positive interactions with peers, ask for and give information, and make conversation (Gresham, 1982). Some children with LD have a real strength in the area of social skills. However, several characteristics of learning disabilities, such as those noted concerning language, can create difficulties in social and emotional life (Smith et al., 2004).

Although not all children with LD have social–emotional problems, they do run a greater risk than their nondisabled peers of having these types of problems. In the early years they are often rejected by their peers and have poor self-concepts (Sridhar & Vaughn, 2001). As adults, the scars from years of rejection can be painful and not easily forgotten (McGrady, Lerner, & Boscardin, 2001). A possible reason for these social–emotional problems is that students with LD often have deficits in social cognition. They may have the following characteristics.

- Misread social cues
- Misinterpret the feelings of others
- Not know when they are bothering others
- Be unaware of the effect of their behavior on someone else
- Be unable to take the perspective of others or put themselves in someone else's shoes

Research has consistently found a higher-than-normal rate of behavioral problems in the classroom among students with learning disabilities (Cullinan, 2002). In a study of 790 students enrolled in K–12 LD programs in Indiana, the percentage of students with behavioral problems (19%) remained consistent across grade levels.

However, it should be noted that the relationships between students' behavioral problems and academic difficulties are not known. In other words, we do not know whether the academic deficits or the behavioral problems cause the other difficulty. Furthermore, many children with LD exhibit no behavioral problems at all (Heward, 2003). Research further suggests that social interaction problems for students with LD seem to be more evident in those who have problems in math, visual-spatial tasks, tactual tasks, self-regulation, and organization (Worling, Humphries, & Tannock, 1999).

After reviewing 152 different studies, Kavale and Forness (1996) concluded that 75% of students with LD exhibit deficits in social skills. Studies of teacher ratings also suggested that students with learning disabilities have lower social status than other students. Social skills deficits include the following.

- Acceptance by peers
- Difficulty making friends
- Being seen by peers as overly dependent
- Being less likely to become leaders
- Resolving conflict
- Managing frustrations
- Initiating or joining a conversation or play activities
- Listening
- Demonstrating empathy
- Maintaining a friendship
- Working in groups

Some students with LD, however, experience no problems getting along with peers and teachers. For example, Sabornie and Kauffman (1986) reported no significant difference in sociometric standing of 46 high school students with LD and 46 peers without disabilities. Moreover, they discovered that some of the students with LD enjoyed socially rewarding experiences in inclusive classrooms. One interpretation of these contradictory findings is that social competence and peer acceptance are not characteristics of LD but are outcomes of the different social climates created by teachers, peers, parents, and others with whom students with LD interact (Vaughn, McIntosh, Schumm, Haager, & Callwood, 1993; cited in Heward, 2003).

In some cases, the social dimensions of life pose greater problems for students with LD than their specific academic deficits, and yet this dimension is essentially ignored in the definitions and labels that relate to learning disabilities. Many professionals would not support broadening the definition of learning disabilities to incorporate social and emotional dimensions, although it is clear that these are substantial (Hutchinson, Freeman, & Bell, 2002; cited in Hardman et al., 2005).

Years of failure can create other concerns. Wright-Strawderman and Watson (1992) found that 36% of a sample of students with learning disabilities indicated depression. Other researchers have reported psychological problems including feelings of inadequacy, anxiety, frustration, and anger (Bender, 2002).

Many students with LD are inept at understanding and interpreting social cues and social situations, which can easily lead to strained interpersonal relationships. Bryan (1977) suggests that the social–emotional difficulties of persons with learning disabilities may be the result of social imperceptiveness—a lack of skill in detecting subtle affective cues.

Nonverbal Learning Disorders (NLD)

Nonverbal learning disorders (NLD) is a neurological syndrome consisting of specific assets and deficits. The assets include early speech and vocabulary development, remarkable rote memory skills, attention to detail, early reading skills development, and excellent spelling skills. In addition, these individuals have the verbal ability to express themselves eloquently. Moreover, persons with NLD have strong auditory retention. Four major categories of deficits and dysfunction also present themselves.

> **Motoric dysfunction.** Lack of coordination, severe balance problems, and difficulties with graphomotor skills
>
> **Visual–spatial–organizational dysfunction.** Lack of image, poor visual recall, faulty spatial perceptions, difficulties with executive functioning (the brain's ability to absorb information, interpret this information, and make decisions based on this information), and problems with spatial relations
>
> **Social dysfunction.** Lack of ability to comprehend nonverbal communication, difficulties adjusting to transitions and novel situations, and deficits in social judgment and social interaction
>
> **Sensory dysfunction.** Sensitivity in any of the sensory modes: visual, auditory, tactile, taste, or olfactory

Foss (2004) reports that statements like the following are often true of individuals with a nonverbal learning disability.

- They talk a lot but really say very little.
- They see the trees, not the forest.
- They focus on details, but do not apprehend the main idea.
- They do not see the whole picture.
- They do not "read" facial expressions, gestures, nor other nonverbal aspects of communication; they miss the subtleties, nuances.
- They may be inappropriate in their social interactions.
- They have few friends; friendships tend to be with older or younger persons rather than peers.
- They tend to process information in a linear, sequential fashion, not seeing multiple dimensions.
- In spite of relative strength in sequencing or recalling sequences, they may confuse abstract temporal concepts; they have significant difficulty recognizing cause–effect relationships. (NLD Online, 2004)

Motivational and Attribution Problems

Students with LD will often lose the motivation to succeed in school. As failure starts to become more prominent, they begin to take on an external locus of control. External locus of control is a motivational term whereby an individual believes that he no longer has control over his fate in life. People with external locus of control believe that they will have a good day or a bad day depending on how outside influences affect them. They feel powerless and no longer believe that they control their own destiny. This differs from people with an internal locus of control, who believe that they are "the captain of their ship," that they control their successes and failures. Students with LD and external locus of control believe that their lives are dictated by luck or fate, rather than by their own internal factors such as determination, hard work, or ability.

Chronic difficulties with academic assignments often lead children with learning disabilities to anticipate failure; success is seen as an unattainable goal no matter how hard they try. Seligman (1992) identifies this outlook as learned helplessness. Youngsters who maintain this attitude frequently give up and will not even attempt to complete the task. As a result, even when success is possible, the individual no longer tries because she has the mindset that failure is inevitable anyway. What individuals believe about the source of their own success or failure on a task is known as *attribution*. Many students with LD attribute success not to their own efforts but to situations or events beyond their control.

Because of their propensity for academic failure, individuals with learning disabilities tend to become passive or inactive learners. They are not actively involved or engaged in their own learning (Torgeson, 1977) and often fail to demonstrate initiative in the learning process. Swanson (1998) calls these pupils "actively inefficient learners." Motivation is the desire to engage in an activity. Many special education and general education teachers, especially those in middle and high schools, comment that students with learning disabilities are not motivated to learn, and research suggests that this is a common characteristic (Fulk, Brigham, & Lohman, 1998).

Perceptual Deficits

Many students with LD exhibit perceptual problems (Lerner, 2003). Perception does not pertain to whether a student sees or hears but rather to how that student's brain interprets what is seen or heard. Perceptual disorders affect the ability to recognize stimuli received through sight, hearing, and touch, and to discriminate between and interpret the sensations appropriately. A child with a learning disability might not have any problems in these areas, or he might have deficits in any or all of them (Smith et al., 2004). For example, a student with a visual perception problem may see perfectly well the letters *b-a-t* written on the page. What the brain interprets them to be is *t-a-b*. Problems in auditory perception often include difficulties with perceiving sounds that are not attributable to a hearing loss (Kruger, Kruger, Hugo, & Campbell, 2001). For example, some students may have trouble understanding whether the word spoken was *king* or *kin, hot* or *hut, fire* or *file*. The result can be misunderstood directions, poor communication, and awkwardness in social situations (Friend, 2005).

Conclusion

In conclusion, it should be evident that children with LD are truly a heterogeneous group. The characteristics exhibited by one child with a learning disability may be quite different than another one with a learning disability. As a future educator, it is essential that you understand all of the possible characteristics that may be seen in these children. By knowing what to look for and being able to identify the common characteristics, you may be able to help in the identification, diagnosis, and assessment of a child with a suspected learning disability. Ultimately, depending on where a student's problems lie, understanding these characteristics or learning styles can lead to significant improvement in the academic performance, social awareness, and overall self-esteem of a child with a learning disability in your classroom.

II Identifying a Student with a Learning Disability

The Special Education Process

The process of identifying a student with a suspected disability is referred to as the special education process. This process involves a variety of steps that must follow federal, state, and district guidelines. These guidelines have been created to protect the rights of students, parents, and school districts. Working together within these guidelines allows for a thorough and comprehensive assessment of a student and the proper special education services and modifications, if required. When a student is having difficulty in school, the professional staff makes many attempts to resolve the problem. When these interventions do not work, a more extensive look at the student is required.

The chapters in Part II outline in detail the step-by-step process that is normally followed in special education. A brief explanation of this assessment continuum follows. Each step is covered in depth in the chapters noted.

Step 1. Prereferral. A concerned classroom teacher attempts simple classroom interventions such as meeting with the child, giving extra help, simplifying assignments, scheduling parent conferences, and arranging for peer tutoring (discussed in Chapter 4). If these measures are unsuccessful, then . . .

Step 2. Child Study Team and prereferral strategies. Referral to a school-based Child Study Team (sometimes called the Prereferral Team or Pupil Personnel Team) for a prereferral intervention plan is usually made by the classroom teacher (although anyone can make a request for a meeting). More involved prereferral strategies are considered, such as direct classroom intervention strategies, which include the following: classroom management, classroom modifications, observation by professional staff, observation and analysis of teaching methods, in-school counseling, assessment of environment, extra help, classroom modifications, change of program, consolidation of program, disciplinary actions, further parent conferences, medical referral, and so forth (discussed in Chapter 4). If such strategies prove unsuccessful, then . . .

Step 3. Screening. The child is screened for a suspected disability by members of the school staff, such as the school psychologist, educational evaluator, or speech and language clinician. If screening reveals a possible disability, then a referral is made for a more comprehensive assessment (discussed in Chapter 4) to the . . .

Step 4. Multidisciplinary team (MDT). This team is made up of members of the school staff, parents, and other professionals. When required, they decide which evaluations and professionals will be involved in this specific assessment. The team then provides a thorough and comprehensive assessment for possible special education services. Assessments may include such measures as standardized tests, portfolio assessments, curriculum-based assessment, criterion-referenced assessments, and the like (discussed in Chapter 5). If the findings of this team indicate the existence of a disability, then . . .

Step 5. Putting it all together. Members of the MDT determine the student's strengths and weaknesses, a possible diagnostic category, level of severity of the problem, recommendations to the school, teachers, and parents, and other information that later will be used to determine any appropriate special education recommendations (discussed in Chapter 6), then . . .

Step 6. Prepare for presentation to the IEP Committee. The MDT puts together the information packet for the presentation to the IEP Committee. This packet contains all the necessary forms, reports, and results of assessment that will be used to determine possible classification and special education services (discussed in Chapter 7). Once the packet is complete . . .

Step 7. IEP meetings. A meeting of the IEP Committee (also known as the Committee on Special Education or Eligibility Committee) is scheduled. This committee determines whether the student meets the criteria for a disability, a special education program, and services (discussed in **Chapter 7**). If the student is classified, then . . .

Step 8. IEP development and alternate planning. Final IEP development occurs and placement is instituted. If eligibility is not accepted by the local school, alternate planning is formulated and suggested by the IEP Committee (discussed in Chapter 7).

Step 9. Transition services. Chapter 8 focuses on transition services for classified students as they move from high school into adult life.

Roles and Responsibilities of the Child Study Team and Multidisciplinary Team

The Child Study Team (CST)

When teachers in general education are having difficulty with a student in their class, they may attempt several strategies to see if the problem can be resolved within the classroom. These strategies may include meeting with the child, providing extra help, simplifying assignments, scheduling parent conferences, arranging for peer tutoring, and so on. If there is no progress within a realistic amount of time, the teacher may decide to refer the student to a school-based team, often known as the Child Study Team (CST), School Building Level Committee (SBLC), Pupil Personnel Team (PPT), or Prereferral Team (PRT), depending on the state in which the student resides. Depending on the type of referral, this team may be drawn from the following staff members.

CHILD STUDY TEAM

Classroom teacher	School nurse
Principal	Social worker
School psychologist	Speech/language clinician
Special education teacher	Guidance counselor (secondary level)
Reading teacher	

Many school districts recommend or require that, before a formal assessment of a student for a suspected disability occurs, the teacher meet with the prereferral team to discuss the nature of the problem and what possible modifications to instruction or the classroom might be made. These procedures are known as prereferral strategies. Historically, prereferral strategies have arisen out of a number of research studies documenting faulty referral practices. Included among other practices is the overreferral of students who come from backgrounds that are culturally or linguistically different from the majority culture, those who are hard to teach, or those who are felt to have behavioral problems. According to Overton (1992), "the more frequent use of better pre-referral intervention strategies is a step forward in the prevention of unnecessary evaluation and the possibility of misdiagnosis and over-identification of special education students" (p. 6).

This process recognizes that many variables affect learning; rather than first assuming that the difficulty lies within the student, the prereferral team and the teacher look specifically at what variables (e.g., classroom, teacher, student, or an interaction of these) might be affecting this particular student. Examining student records and work samples and conducting interviews and observations are part of the team's efforts. These approaches to gathering data are intended to specify the problem more precisely and to document its severity. Modifications to the teacher's approach, to the classroom or to student activities may then be suggested, attempted, and documented. It is important for teachers to keep track of the specific modifications they attempt with a student who is having trouble learning or behaving, because such information can provide valuable information to the school-based team if the student is referred for a comprehensive assessment.

Prior to doing an evaluation for possible classification and services in special education, it is important to make sure that the school has made every effort to remediate the problems through other means. The assessment process is a very significant and important piece in addressing such concerns, but it should never be the first step. Before a full battery of tests is administered, many preventative measures are attempted to try to forestall further difficulties. The rest of this chapter is devoted to discussing the most common prereferral procedures in school systems.

Members of the CST (the prereferral team) usually meet on a regular basis, once or twice a week, depending on the caseload. Normally, there is a chairperson of the CST, to whom the entire faculty and staff can make a request during the week to be put onto the agenda for the next meeting. For example, if the CST meets on Friday, a teacher can go to the chairperson on Tuesday and say:

> I have been trying to work with Kristen by making some changes in my class. However, she does not seem to be responding, and I am becoming increasingly concerned about her deterioration. I think I need help and would like to discuss her at the next team meeting.

This type of statement would allow the teacher to come to the team meeting for help in developing more formal and comprehensive prereferral strategies that can then be attempted in the classroom. The next statement typifies a different need:

> We have been working with James for a while on prereferral strategies but they do not seem to be working. Therefore, I would like to meet with the CST again to discuss James because he is still doing very poorly in my class and nothing we developed is working.

This type of statement would probably require the team to consider screening James for a suspected disability, since prereferral strategies have been attempted over a period of time and under a variety of conditions and have made no impact.

The chairperson then puts Kristen and James on the list of students to discuss at the next CST meeting. He or she informs the members of the CST in writing that both students are on the CST agenda. It is each team member's responsibility to bring any important and relevant documentation on Kristen and James to the next CST meeting. When the CST meets, team members discuss whatever agenda is put forth for that particular day. Some days, there may be very little to discuss, whereas on other days, the CST meeting may run for a few hours based on the number of students that need to be discussed.

The CST Meeting

Once a referral is made to the CST, team members will gather all available information before the meeting to better understand the child and his or her educational patterns. This information may come from a variety of sources, and the presentation of this information at the meeting is crucial for determining the most appropriate direction to proceed. Schools usually have a wealth of information about all of the students, distributed among a number of people and a number of records. Gathering and reviewing this information after a referral, and prior to screening, could reduce the need for more formal testing and provide a very thorough picture of the child's abilities and patterns (Pierangleo & Giuliani, 2005).

Sources of Student Information.

School Records. School records can be a rich source of information about the student and his or her background. For instance, the number of times the student has changed schools may be of interest. Frequent school changes can be disruptive emotionally, as well as academically, and may be a factor in the problems that have resulted in the student's being referred to the CST.

Prior Academic Achievement. The student's past history of grades is usually of interest to the CST. Is the student's current performance in a particular subject typical of the student, or is the problem that is being observed something new? Are patterns noticeable in the student's grades? For example, many students begin the year with poor grades, then show gradual improvement as they get back into the swing of school. For others, the reverse may be true: During the early part of the year, when prior school material is being reviewed, they may do well, with declines in their grades coming as new material is introduced. Also, transition points such as beginning the fourth grade or middle school may cause some students problems; the nature and purpose of reading, for example, tends to change when students enter the fourth grade, because reading to learn content becomes more central. Similarly, middle school requires students to assume more responsibility for long-term projects (Hoy & Gregg, 1994). These shifts may bring about a noticeable decline in grades.

Prior Test Scores. Test scores are also important to review. Comparing these scores to a student's current classroom performance can indicate that the student's difficulties are new ones, perhaps resulting from some environmental change that needs to be more fully investigated. Further, the comparison may show that the student has always found a particular skill area to be problematic. "In this situation, the current problems the student is experiencing indicate that the classroom demands have reached a point [where] the student requires more support to be successful" (Hoy & Gregg, 1994, p. 37).

Group Standardized Achievement Test Results. Much information can be obtained from group achievement test results. Whereas individual tests should be administered when evaluating a child's suspected disability, group achievement results may reflect certain very important patterns. Most schools administer group achievement tests annually or every few years. If these results are available on a student, you may want to explore the various existing patterns. It is helpful to have several years of results to analyze. Over time, this type of pattern can be more reliable for interpretation.

Attendance Records. Attendance records can provide the CST with a great deal of important information, especially if team members know what they are looking for. Many patterns are symptomatic of more serious concerns, and being able to recognize these patterns early can only facilitate the recognition of a potential high-risk student. When we look at a student's attendance profile over the years, several things may stand out. For instance, a child's pattern of absences might include consistent absences during a specific part of the year, as is the case with some students who have respiratory problems or allergies. In other cases, there may be a noticeable pattern of declining attendance that may be linked to a decline in motivation, an undiagnosed health problem, or a change within the family. Specific points to keep in mind when reviewing attendance records include the following:

- *The number of days absent in the student's profile.* Ordinarily, more than 10 days a year may need to be investigated for patterns. If a child is out more than 15 to 20 days, this could be indicative of a serious issue if a medical or some other logical reason did not substantiate the absences.
- *The patterns of days absent.* Single days of absence may indicate the presence of possible school avoidance, phobia, or a dysfunctional or chaotic home environment.
- *Prior teacher reports.* Comments written on report cards or in permanent record folders can provide the CST with a different perspective on the child under a different style of teaching. Successful years and positive comments may be clues to the child's learning style and the conditions under which he or she responds best. Also, write-ups about conferences between previous teachers and parents can provide information important to understanding the child's patterns and history.
- *Group IQ test information.* This information is usually found in the permanent record folder. Many schools administer a group IQ type of test (e.g., Otis Lennon—7) in grades three, six, and nine. Be aware that the

term *School Abilities Index* has replaced the term *IQ* or *intelligence quotient* on many group IQ tests.

- *Prior teacher referrals.* The CST should investigate school records for prior referrals from teachers. There could have been a time when a teacher referred but no action was taken due to time of year, parent resistance, delay in procedures, and so on. These referrals may still be on file and may reveal useful information.

- *Medical history in the school nurse's office.* The CST should also investigate school medical records for indications of visual or hearing difficulties, prescribed medication that may have an effect on the child's behavior (e.g., antihistamines), or medical conditions in need of attention or that could be contributing to the child's current difficulties.

- *Student work.* Often, an initial part of the assessment process includes examining a student's work, either by selecting work samples that can be analyzed to identify academic skills and deficits or by conducting a portfolio assessment, whereby folders of the student's work are examined (see Chapter 1). When collecting work samples, the teacher selects work from the areas in which the student is experiencing difficulty and systematically examines them. The teacher might identify such elements as how the student was directed to do the activity (e.g., orally, in writing), how long it took the student to complete the activity, the pattern of errors (e.g., reversals when writing), and the pattern of correct answers. Analyzing the student's work in this way can yield valuable insight into the nature of his or her difficulties and suggest possible solutions.

CST Recommendations—Prereferral Strategies

After analyzing all of the information presented at the meeting, the CST has to make a decision: What does it recommend at this point? If this is the first time a student is being reviewed by the team, then the CST is very likely to recommend prereferral strategies to the teacher. These are techniques and suggestions to attempt to resolve the child's issues without the need for a more comprehensive assessment (Pierangelo & Giuliani, 2005). What are the benefits of prereferral intervention?

- Alternatives are reviewed and referrals made to other programs. Instructional assistance can be provided if needed.
- Students who do not have a disability, but who need instructional support, will receive it in the regular program.
- Problem solving as a team facilitates professional growth in needed areas; staff development is formative and directly in response to teacher needs. Teachers in the regular program develop a network of peer support.
- Later referrals to special education, if they happen, are more valid; that is, students are more likely to truly have a disability.

Examples of Prereferral Intervention Strategies

Team Meeting with Teachers. A team meeting with teachers is a prereferral procedure whereby teachers who have previously worked with, or have ideas about, this student come together to determine what strategies can be implemented to help this child. In this prereferral procedure, teachers share information about a student to identify patterns of behavior reflective of some particular condition or disability. Sometimes, a group meeting with all of the child's teachers can preclude the need for further involvement. One or several teachers may be using techniques that could benefit others also working with the child. By sharing information or observations, it is possible to identify patterns of behavior reflective of some particular condition or disability. Once this pattern is identified, the student may be handled in a variety of ways without the need for more serious intervention.

Parent Interviews. A parent interview as a prereferral procedure involves meeting with the parent(s) to discuss what motivates this child, along with finding out any family information that may be contributing to the child's behavior in the classroom (e.g., recent separation, death of a loved one). Meeting the parent(s) is always recommended when a child is having difficulty in school. The initial meeting can be informal, with the purpose of clarifying certain issues and gathering pertinent information that may help the child as well as the teacher in the classroom. If testing or serious intervention is required, then a more formal and in-depth parent meeting must take place.

Medical Exam. The CST should try to rule out any possibility of a medical condition causing or contributing to the existing problems. If the teacher or any other professional who works with the child feels that there is any possibility of such a condition, and the need for a complete medical workup is evident, then a recommendation for a medical exam should be made. Available records should be reviewed, and if they are inadequate in light of the presenting problems and symptoms, outside recommendations to the parents such as a neurological examination or opthamological examination should be considered.

Hearing Test. A hearing test should be one of the first prereferral procedures recommended if one has not been administered to the student within the last six months to one year. Be aware of inconsistencies in test patterns from year to year that might indicate a chronic pattern. Some symptoms that might indicate the need for an updated audiological examination are when the child

- Turns head when listening
- Asks you to repeat frequently
- Consistently misinterprets what he or she hears
- Does not respond to auditory stimuli
- Slurs speech, speaks in a monotone voice, or articulates poorly

Vision Test. As with the hearing exam, this evaluation should be one of the first prereferral procedures recommended. Again, if a vision test has not been done within six months to a year, then request this immediately. Possible symptoms that may necessitate such an evaluation are when the child

- Turns head when looking at board or objects
- Squints excessively
- Rubs eyes frequently
- Holds books and materials close to the face or at unusual angles
- Suffers frequent headaches
- Avoids close work of any type
- Covers an eye when reading
- Consistently loses place when reading

Classroom Management Techniques. There are times when the real issue may not be the child but rather in the teaching style of the classroom teacher, that is, having unrealistic expectations, being critical, or being overly demanding. In such instances, help for the teacher can come in the form of classroom management techniques. Classroom management techniques are strategies developed to help handle various problems and conflicts within a classroom. An administrator, psychologist, or any realistic and diplomatic team member who feels comfortable with this type of situation may offer these practical suggestions to the teacher. There are many classroom techniques and modifications that should be tried before taking more serious steps. These include the following:

Display daily class schedule with times so that the student has a structured idea of the day ahead
Change seating
Seat the student with good role models
Use peer tutors when appropriate
Limit number of directions
Simplify complex directions
Give verbal as well as written directions
Provide extra work time
Shorten assignments
Modify curriculum but change content only as a last resort
Identify and address preferred learning styles
Provide manipulative materials
Provide examples of what is expected
Use color coding of materials to foster organizational skills
Develop a homework plan with parental support
Develop a behavior modification plan, if necessary
Uses lots of positive reinforcement
Use technology as an aid

Help Classes. Certain children may require only a temporary support system to get them through a difficult academic period. Some schools provide additional non special education services, such as help classes, that may be held during lunch or before or after school. These classes can clarify academic confusion that could lead to more serious problems if not addressed.

Remedial Reading or Math Services. Remedial reading or math services are academic programs within a school designed to help the student with reading or math by going slower in the curriculum or placing him or her with a smaller number of students in the classroom for extra attention. These services can be recommended when reading or math is the specific area of concern. Remedial reading and math classes are not special education services and can be instituted as a means of alleviating a child's academic problems.

In-School Counseling. In-school counseling is normally done by the school psychologist, social worker, or guidance counselor, and is designed to help the child deal with the issues that are currently problematic for him or her. Sometimes, a child may experience a situational or adjustment disorder (a temporary emotional pattern that may occur at any time in a person's life without a prior history of problems) resulting from separation, divorce, health issues, newness to school district, and so on. When this pattern occurs, it may temporarily interfere with the child's ability to concentrate, remember, or attend to tasks. Consequently, a drop in academic performance can occur. If such patterns occur, the school psychologist may want to institute in-school counseling, with the parent's involvement and permission. This recommendation should be instituted only to address issues that can be resolved in a relatively short period of time. More serious issues may have to be referred to outside agencies or professionals for longer treatment.

Progress Reports. A progress report is a synopsis of the child's work and behavior in the classroom sent home to the parents in order to keep them updated on the child's strengths and weaknesses over a period of time (e.g., every day, each week, biweekly, or once a month). Sometimes, a child who has fallen behind academically will "hide" from the real issues by avoiding reality. Daily progress reports for a week or two at first and then weekly reports may provide the child with the kinds of immediate gratification and positive feedback necessary to get back on track. They offer the child a greater sense of hope and control in getting back to a more normal academic pattern.

Disciplinary Action. This recommendation is usually made when the child in question needs a structured boundary set involving inappropriate behavior. If a child demonstrates a pattern of inappropriate behavior, disciplinary action is usually used in conjunction with other recommendations because such patterned behavior may be symptomatic of a more serious problem. The appropriate disciplinary actions necessary should be discussed with the school psychologist, and how it should be implemented must be carefully considered before it begins.

Change of Program. A change of program involves examining the child's program and making adjustments to his or her schedule based on the presenting problem. This recommendation usually occurs when a student has been placed in a course that is not suited to his or her ability or needs. If a student is failing in an advanced class, then the student's program should be changed to include more modified classes.

Consolidation of Program. There are times when reducing a student's course load is necessary. Consolidation of a program involves taking the student's program and modifying it so that the workload is decreased. If a child is "drowning in school," then that child's available energy level may be extremely limited. In such cases, you may find that he or she is failing many courses. Temporarily consolidating or condensing the program allows for the possibility of salvaging some courses, because the student's available energy will not have to be spread so thin.

Referral to Child Protective Services. Child Protective Services is a state agency designed to investigate cases of possible neglect and abuse of children. A referral to Child Protective Services (CPS; name can vary by state) is mandated for all educators if there is a suspicion of abuse or neglect. The school official or staff does not have a choice as to referral if such a suspicion is present. Referrals to this service may result from physical, sexual, or emotional abuse and/or educational, environmental, or medical neglect.

Screening. If the CST feels the prereferral strategies are not working after a realistic period of time, team members may recommend a screening for a suspected disability. The source of this suspicion may emanate from the team, a staff member, or the parent. Keep in mind that the team does not have to diagnose a specific disability, but only suspect one in order to begin the referral for a more comprehensive assessment to a multidisciplinary team. This team will administer a comprehensive evaluation conducted by a multitude of professionals to decrease the possibility of subjective and discriminatory assessment.

Screening measures may include a variety of tests and procedures that can be sensitive enough to allow team members the opportunity to determine the presence of a suspected disability. Other than the very obvious cases involving attempted suicide, neglect, abuse and so on, which must be dealt with immediately, a child with a suspected disability is defined as a child who exhibits one or more of the following symptoms for more than six months:

- Serious inconsistencies in intellectual, emotional, academic, or social performance
- Inconsistency between ability and achievement and/or ability and classroom performance
- Impairment in one or more life functions, that is, socialization, academic performance, or adaptive behavior

In order to accomplish this screening, team members utilize

- Abbreviated intelligence tests
- Selected subtests or screening versions of individual achievement tests
- Informal reading inventories
- Checklists
- Observation scales
- Rating scales
- Prereferral data already discussed

If the screening determines the possibility of a suspected disability, then the CST must make a more formal referral to the district's multidisciplinary team for a comprehensive assessment.

The Multidisciplinary Team (MDT)

Purpose of the Multidisciplinary Team

As a result of the Individuals with Disabilities Education Act (IDEA 2004) regulations, schools are moving toward a more global approach to the identification of students with suspected disabilities, through the development of a district-based team. This team may be referred to as the Multidisciplinary Team (MDT), Multifactor Team (MFT), or School-Based Support Team (SBST), depending on the state in which the student resides. Throughout this text, we refer to this team as the multidisciplinary team. This team usually comes into operation when the local school-based team (Child Study Team) has conducted a screening and suspects a disability. Once that is determined, then the MDT takes over. This team is mandated by IDEA 2004 so the child and his or her parents are guaranteed that any comprehensive evaluation will be conducted by different professionals to decrease the possibility of subjective and discriminatory assessment.

The role of the MDT is to work as a single unit in determining the possible cause, contributing behavioral factors, educational status, prognosis (outcome), and recommendations for a student with a suspected disability. The MDT's major objective is to bring together many disciplines and professional perspectives to help work on a case, so that a single person is not required to determine and assimilate all of the factors that affect a particular child. The MDT is responsible for gathering all the necessary information on a child in order to determine the most effective and practical direction for his or her education. In many states, the MDT's findings are then reviewed by another committee (sometimes referred to as the IEP Committee, Eligibility Committee, or Committee on Special Education). Its role is to determine whether the findings of the MDT fall within the guidelines for classification as having an exceptionality and requiring special education services. In accomplishing this task, the team members employ several types of assessment and collect data from many sources.

To further comply with IDEA, the following guidelines must be followed by the MDT (IDEA: 20 U.S.C. sec. 1400 et seq.):

a) Testing and assessment materials and procedures used for the purposes of assessment and placement of individuals with exceptional needs are selected and administered so as not to be racially, culturally, or sexually discriminatory.

b) Tests and other assessment materials are provided and administered in the pupil's primary language or other mode of communication, unless the assessment plan indicates reasons why this provision and administration are not clearly feasible.

c) Tests and other assessment materials have been validated for the specific purpose for which they are used.

d) Tests and other assessment materials are administered by trained personnel in conformance with the instructions provided by the producer of the tests and other assessment materials, except that individually administered tests of intellectual or emotional functioning shall be administered by a credentialed school psychologist.

e) Tests and other assessment materials are selected and administered to best ensure that when a test administered to a pupil with impaired sensory, manual, or speaking skills produces test results that accurately reflect the pupil's aptitude, achievement level, or any other factors the test purports to measure and not the pupil's impaired sensory, manual, or speaking skills unless those skills are the factors the test purports to measure.

f) No single procedure is used as the sole criterion for determining an appropriate educational program for an individual with exceptional needs.

g) The pupil is assessed in all areas related to the suspected disability including, where appropriate, health and development, vision, including low vision, hearing, motor abilities, language function, general ability, academic performance, self-help, orientation and mobility skills, career and vocational abilities and interests, and social and emotional status. A developmental history is obtained, when appropriate. For pupils with residual vision, a low vision assessment shall be provided.

h) Persons knowledgeable of that disability shall conduct the assessment of a pupil, including the assessment of a pupil with a suspected low incidence disability. For instance, if the screening reveals a suspected learning disability then a learning disabilities specialist becomes part of the team. If the child is suspected of having a hearing impairment then an audiologist becomes a member of the team. Special attention shall be given to the unique educational needs, including, but not limited to, skills and the need for specialized services, materials, and equipment.

Members of the Multidisciplinary Team

Although specific state regulations may differ on the membership of the MDT, the members are usually drawn from individuals and professionals within the school and community. Depending on the school in which you work, your roles and responsibilities as an educational evaluator may be different than those of another professional with the same title in a different school. Listed here are the general roles and responsibilities of members of a multidisciplinary team.

School psychologist. The role of the school psychologist on the MDT usually involves administering individual intelligence tests, projective tests, personality inventories, and observing the student in a variety of settings.

School nurse. The role of the school nurse is to review all medical records, screen for vision and hearing, consult with outside physicians, and make referrals to outside physicians, if necessary.

Classroom teacher. The classroom teacher's role is to work with the local school-based Child Study Team to implement prereferral strategies, and plan and implement, along with the special education team, classroom strategies that create an appropriate working environment for the student.

School social worker. The social worker's role on the MDT is to gather and provide information concerning the family system. This may be accomplished through interviews, observations, conferences, and so forth.

Special education teacher. The roles of the special education teacher include consulting with parents and classroom teachers about prereferral recommendations, administering educational and perceptual tests, observing the student in a variety of settings, screening students with suspected disabilities, writing IEPs (including goals and objectives) with the team (based on assessed needs), and recommending intervention strategies to teachers and parents.

Educational diagnostician. This professional administers a series of evaluations including norm-referenced and criterion-referenced tests, observes the student in a variety of settings, and makes educational recommendations that get applied to the IEP as goals and objectives.

Physical therapist. The physical therapist is called upon to evaluate a child who may be experiencing problems in gross-motor functioning, living and self-help skills, and vocational skills necessary for the student to be able to function in certain settings. This professional may be used to screen, evaluate, provide direct services, or consult with the teacher, parent, or school.

Behavioral consultant. A behavioral consultant works closely with the team in providing direct services or consultation on issues involving behavioral and classroom management techniques and programs.

Speech/language clinician. This professional is involved in screening for speech and language developmental problems, provides a full evaluation on a suspected language disability, provides direct services, and consults with staff and parents.

Audiologist. This professional is called on to evaluate a student's hearing for possible impairments and, as a result of the findings, may refer the student for medical consultation or treatment. The audiologist may also help students and parents obtain equipment (i.e., hearing aids) that may improve the child's ability to function in school.

Occupational therapist. The occupational therapist is called on to evaluate a child who may be experiencing problems in fine-motor skills and living and self-help skills. This professional may be used to screen, evaluate, provide direct services, consult with the teacher, parent, or school, and assist in obtaining the appropriate assistive technology or equipment for the student.

Guidance counselor. This individual may be involved in providing aptitude test information; providing counseling services; working with the team on consolidating, changing, or developing a student's class schedule; and assisting the Child Study Team in developing prereferral strategies.

Parents. The parent plays an extremely important role on the MDT by providing input for the IEP; working closely with members of the team; and carrying out, assisting, or initiating academic or management programs within the child's home (parents' roles will be discussed in more detail later in this chapter).

Formal Referral to the Multidisciplinary Team

Once the CST determines that a suspected disability may exist, a formal referral is made to the multidisciplinary team. A formal referral is nothing more than a form starting the special education process. A referral for evaluation and possible special education services is initiated by a written request. However, you should understand that people other than the CST have the right under due process to initiate a formal referral for a child with a suspected disability. Depending on state regulations, these could include:

- The child's parent, advocate, person in parental relationship, or legal guardian
- A classroom teacher
- Any professional staff member of the public or private school district
- A judicial officer—a representative of the court
- A student on his or her own behalf if he or she is 18 years of age or older or an emancipated minor (a person under the age of 18 who has been given certain adult rights by the court)
- The Chief School Officer of the State or his or her designee responsible for welfare, education, or health of children

Contents of a Referral to the Multidisciplinary Team.   The signed formal referral is usually sent to the MDT so the team can begin the process of formal assessment. At the same time, the referral is sent to the chairperson of the IEP Committee (see Chapter 7) indicating that a child with a suspected disability will be reviewed by the committee in the near future. This referral should be in written form and should be dated. This makes it official and gives a start date, because time lines are involved. A referral from the CST should include a great deal of information to assist the MDT in its assessment. Further documentation as to why a possible disability exists, descriptions of attempts to remediate the child's behaviors (prereferral strategies), or performance prior to the referral should all be included. All of these are important, especially the attempts that have been made prior to the referral. Remember, the district should try to keep the child in the mainstream, and the documentation it provides at this step in the process should ensure that it has done everything possible to preclude the referral process.

Referrals from the CST for a formal assessment are forwarded to the MDT. If the referral is not from the parents, the district must inform the parents in writing immediately that their child has been referred for assessment as a result of a suspected disability. The referral states that the child may have a disability that adversely affects educational performance. An important point to remember is that a referral to the MDT does not necessarily mean that the child has a disability. It signals that the child is having learning and/or behavioral difficulties, and that there is a concern that the problem may be due to a disability.

Initial Referral to the MDT from the School Staff. As previously stated, once the CST has determined that a suspected disability may exist, the team must alert the chairperson of the MDT that a child with a suspected disability is being referred for review. This, in all actuality, begins the special education process.

Initial Referral to the MDT from a Parent/Guardian. An Initial Referral to the MDT from the School Staff alerts the chairperson of the MDT that the local school has made every attempt to resolve the student's difficulties prior to the formal referral. The form also informs the chairperson that the parent's rights have been followed. In other cases, a student's parent or guardian may initiate a referral to the MDT for suspicion of a disability under special education laws or Section 504 of the Rehabilitation Act. A fully completed referral form and any relevant information is sent to the appropriate special education administrator. Usually, upon the receipt of the parent's referral, the chairperson of the MDT will send to the parent/guardian an assessment plan (discussed next) and the parent's due process rights statement.

Note: If a release for testing (assessment plan) is not secured at a separate meeting, the chairperson of the MDT will mail one to the parent with the letter indicating that a referral has been made. However, no formal evaluations may begin until the district has received signed permission from the parent or guardian.

Consent for Evaluation

Prior to any assessment, the MDT must secure an agreement by the parent to allow the members of the team to evaluate the child. This release is part of the assessment plan and the following characteristics should be included.

- It is in a language easily understood by the general public.
- It is provided in the primary language of the parent or other mode of communication used by the parent, unless to do so is clearly not feasible.
- It explains the types of assessments to be conducted.

- It states that no individualized educational program (IEP) will result from the assessment without the consent of the parent.
- It states that no assessment shall be conducted unless the written consent of the parent is obtained prior to the assessment. The parent shall have at least 15 days (may vary from state to state) from the receipt of the proposed assessment plan to arrive at a decision. Assessment may begin immediately upon receipt of the consent.
- The copy of the notice of parent rights shall include the right to record electronically the proceedings of the IEP Committee meetings.
- The assessment shall be conducted by persons competent to perform the assessment, as determined by the school district, county office, or special education local plan area.
- Any psychological assessment of pupils must be conducted by a qualified school psychologist.
- Any health assessment of pupils shall be conducted only by a credentialed school nurse or physician who is trained and prepared to assess cultural and ethnic factors appropriate to the pupil being assessed.

Assessment Options of the Multidisciplinary Team

Only when the parents have been informed of their rights, a release has been obtained, and the assessment plan has been signed, can assessment begin. The MDT has several evaluation options from which to choose. The areas most often considered by the MDT to assess a child with a suspected disability include the following evaluations.

Academic Achievement Evaluation. An academic achievement evaluation is frequently recommended when a child's academic skill levels (reading, writing, math, and spelling) are unknown or inconsistent. The evaluation will determine strengths and weaknesses in the child's academic performance. The primary objectives of an academic achievement evaluation are listed below.

- Help determine the child's stronger and weaker academic skill areas. The evaluation may give the team useful information when making practical recommendations to teachers about academic expectations, areas that need remediation, and how to best provide information to improve the child's ability to learn.
- Help the teacher gear the materials to the learning capacity of the individual child. A child reading two years below grade level may require modified textbooks or greater explanations prior to a lesson.
- Develop a learning profile that can help the classroom teacher understand the best way to present information to the child and therefore increase his or her chances of success.
- Help determine whether the child's academic skills are suitable for a regular class or so severe that he or she may require a more restrictive educational setting (an educational setting or situation best suited to the

current needs of the student other than a full-time regular class placement; e.g., resource room, self-contained class, special school, etc.).
- Whatever achievement battery the special educator chooses, it should be one that covers enough skill areas to make an adequate diagnosis of academic strengths and weaknesses.

Some symptoms that might suggest the need for an academic achievement evaluation are as follows.

- Consistently low test scores on group achievement tests
- Indications of delayed processing when faced with academic skills
- Labored handwriting after grade three
- Poor word recall
- Poor decoding (word attack) skills
- Discrepancy between achievement and ability
- Consistently low achievement despite remediation

In most cases of a suspected disability, the academic achievement evaluation is always a part of the formal evaluation.

Intellectual and Psychological Evaluation. This recommendation is appropriate when the child's intellectual ability is unknown or when there is a question about his or her inability to learn. It is useful when the CST suspects a potential learning, emotional, or intellectual problem. The psychological evaluation can rule out or rule in emotionality as a primary cause of a child's problem. Ruling this factor out is necessary before a diagnosis of LD can be made. Listed below are the objectives of a psychological evaluation.

- Determine the child's present overall levels of intellectual ability
- Determine the child's present verbal intellectual ability
- Determine the child's nonlanguage intellectual ability
- Explore indications of greater potential
- Find possible patterns involving learning style—that is, verbal comprehension, concentration, and the like
- Ascertain possible influences of tension and anxiety on testing results
- Determine the child's intellectual ability to deal with present grade-level academic demands
- Explore the influence of intellectual ability as a contributing factor to a child's past and present school difficulties—for example, limited intellectual ability, as is found in retardation

Here are some symptoms that might signal the need for such an evaluation.

- High levels of tension and anxiety exhibited in behavior
- Aggressive behavior
- Lack of motivation or indications of low energy levels

- Patterns of denial
- Oppositional behavior
- Despondency
- Inconsistent academic performance, ranging from very low to very high
- History of inappropriate judgment
- Lack of impulse control
- Extreme and consistent attention-seeking behavior
- Pattern of provocative behavior

As with the academic assessment, the psychological evaluation is a normal part of a referral for a suspected disability.

Perceptual Evaluation.   A perceptual evaluation is suggested when the team suspects discrepancies in the child's ability to receive and process information. This assessment may focus on the following perceptual areas.

- **Auditory modality.** The delivery of information through sound
- **Visual modality.** The delivery of information through sight
- **Tactile modality.** The delivery of information through touching
- **Kinesthetic modality.** The delivery of information through movement
- **Reception.** The initial receiving of information
- **Perception.** The initial organization of information
- **Association or organization.** Relating new information to other information and giving meaning to the information received
- **Memory.** The storage or retrieval process that facilitates the associational process to give meaning to information or help in relating new concepts to other information that might have already been learned
- **Expression.** The output of information through vocal, motoric, or written responses

The primary objectives of the perceptual assessment are to:

- Help determine the child's stronger and weaker modality for learning. Some children are visual learners, some are auditory, and some learn best through any form of input. However, if a child is a strong visual learner in a class in which the teacher relies on auditory lectures, then it is possible that his or her ability to process information may be hampered. The evaluation may give the team useful information when making practical recommendations to teachers about how to best provide information to assist the child's ability to learn.
- Help determine a child's stronger and weaker process areas. A child having problems in memory and expression will very quickly fall behind the rest of his or her class. The longer these processing difficulties continue, the greater the chance for secondary emotional problems (emotional problems resulting from continued frustration with the ability to learn) to develop.

- Develop a learning profile that can help the classroom teacher understand the best way to present information to the child, thereby increasing the child's chances of success.
- Help determine whether the child's learning process deficits are suitable for a regular class or so severe that he or she may require a more restrictive educational setting (an educational setting or situation best suited to the current needs of the student other than a full-time regular class placement; e.g., resource room, self-contained class, special school).

Oral Language Evaluation. This recommendation usually occurs when the child is experiencing significant delays in speech or language development, problems in articulation, or problems in receptive or expressive language. Some symptoms that might warrant such an evaluation are:

- Difficulty pronouncing words through grade three
- Immature or delayed speech patterns
- Difficulty labeling thoughts or objects
- Difficulty putting thoughts into words

Occupational Therapy Evaluation. This evaluation may be considered by the team when the child is exhibiting problems involving fine-motor–upper-body functions. Examples of these would include abnormal movement patterns, sensory problems (sensitive to sound, visual changes etc.), hardship with daily living activities, organizational problems, attention span difficulties, equipment analysis, and interpersonal problems.

Physical Therapy Evaluation. This evaluation may be considered by the team when the child is exhibiting problems with lower body and gross motor areas. Examples of these problems might be range of motion difficulties; architectural barrier difficulties; problems in posture, gait, and endurance; joint abnormalities; and lack of manual dexterity. Possible remediations include training on special equipment and checking prosthetic and orthotic equipment.

Parental Participation in the Assessment Process

Once the CST has made a formal referral for assessment to the MDT for a child with a suspected disability, the parents need to be asked to provide pertinent background information that will assist in the assessment process. The participation of the parents is crucial to this process.

Whereas designing, conducting, interpreting, and paying for the assessment are the school system's responsibilities, parents have an important part to play before, during, and after the evaluation. There is a range of ways in which parents may involve themselves in the assessment of their child. The extent of their involvement, however, is a personal decision and will vary from family to family.

Waterman (1994) lists parental options, responsibilities, and expectations prior to an assessment for a suspected disability:

- Parents may initiate the assessment process by requesting that the school system evaluate their child for the presence of a disability and the need for special education.
- Parents must be notified by the school, and give their consent, before any initial evaluation of the child may be conducted.
- Parents may wish to talk with the professional responsible for conducting the evaluation to find out what the evaluation will involve.
- Parents may find it very useful to become informed about assessment issues in general and any specific issues relevant to their child (e.g., assessment of minority children, use of specific tests or assessment techniques with a specific disability).
- Parents should advocate for a comprehensive evaluation of their child—one that investigates all skill areas apparently affected by the suspected disability and that uses multiple means of collecting information (e.g., observations, interviews, alternative approaches).
- Parents may suggest specific questions to the MDT they would like to see addressed through the assessment.
- Parents should inform the MDT of any accommodations the child will need (e.g., removing time limits from tests, conducting interviews/testing in the child's native language, adapting testing environment to child's specific physical and other needs).
- Parents should inform the MDT if they themselves need an interpreter or other accommodations during any of their discussions with the school.
- Parents may prepare their child for the assessment process, explaining what will happen and, where necessary, reducing the child's anxiety. It may help the child to know that he or she will not be receiving a "grade" on the tests.
- Parents need to share with the MDT their insights into the child's background (developmental, medical, and academic) and past and present school performance.
- Parents may wish to share with the MDT any prior school records, reports, tests, or evaluation information available on their child.
- Parents may need to share information about cultural differences that can illuminate the MDT's understanding of the student.
- Parents need to make every effort to attend interviews the MDT may set up with them and provide information about their child.

Confidentiality

Information about the child collected through assessment automatically becomes a part of a child's school records. The school district should establish policies regarding confidentiality of information contained in the school record, such as informing the parent and the child (above age 18) of their right to privacy, of who has access to the information, and their right to challenge those records should they be inaccurate, misleading, or otherwise inappropriate. To communicate this information to the parent, handouts describing the district's policy on confidentiality of school records are usually given out on the day of the parent intake.

Because professionals conducting the evaluation are involved in collecting confidential information about a child's health status and educational development, it is very important that verbal as well as written accounts of the child's performance be held in the strictest confidence. Personnel involved in the evaluation should treat their own impressions and concerns about the children they see in a confidential manner and should refrain from talking about children and their performance with people not directly involved with conducting the evaluation. If parents ask how their child is doing during the evaluation, explain that the screening results are meaningful only after all the testing has been completed and their child's performance in all areas is recorded. You should also inform them at this time that they are entitled to receive a complete typed report from the evaluation personnel. The person in charge of evaluation may choose to designate certain persons responsible for answering specific questions about the evaluation instruments, children's responses, and reports.

Conclusion

Once written consent of the parent or legal guardian is given for assessment, the MDT will move to the evaluation phase of the assessment process. The next several chapters address the various evaluation instruments available to the MDT in the formal evaluation of a child with a suspected disability.

The MDT plays a critical role in the assessment of a child with a suspected disability. An effective MDT works as an interdisciplinary team to make many of the most important decisions for a child and his or her possible future in special education. By working as a professional team, the members of the MDT have the opportunity to help numerous children. An efficient MDT gathers much data and takes significant time to analyze each child's potential problems. In the end, its recommendations may be the most important ones for children who are in need of services.

It is very important to remember that referring a child for a suspected disability could have tremendous impact on his or her life. Because this is a formal referral for special education, it has legal implications, and, therefore, it is extremely important that the MDT follow all procedures, complete all necessary forms, and make sure that it complies with the specific time limits required by the state in which the child resides.

Parents have many rights during the assessment process. Regardless of race, creed, color, socioeconomic status, and so on, all parents are afforded the same legal rights and protections under federal law. The differences arise in the parents' exercising of their rights. Some parents will be heavily involved in their child's assessment for a suspected disability, whereas others will show little, if any, interest—only signing the release form and never participating nor attending any optional sessions for them. Parents need to be aware of their rights. As a special educator, there are many ways to make parents comfortable when you meet with them. Remember, most parents are scared and confused about the entire process. Normally, all they want is for their child to be evaluated so that success, both in and out of school, becomes a future possibility.

5

Overview of Assessment in the Special Education Process

To understand the assessment and diagnosis of a learning disability, you need to know about the various assessment techniques used in the special education process. Assessment in special education involves collecting information about a student for the purpose of making decisions. According to Gearheart and Gearheart (1990), assessment is "a process that involves the systematic collection and interpretation of a wide variety of information on which to base instructional/intervention decisions and, when appropriate, classification and placement decisions. Assessment is primarily a problem-solving process" (p. 3). Clearly, gathering information about a student using a variety of techniques and information sources should shed considerable light on the student's strengths and needs, the nature of a suspected disability and its probable effect on educational performance, and realistic and appropriate instructional goals and objectives.

Components of a Comprehensive Assessment

An evaluation for special education should always be conducted on an individual basis. When completed, it is a comprehensive assessment of the child's abilities. Under the Individuals with Disabilities Education Improvement Act of 2004, no single procedure is used as the sole criterion for determining an appropriate educational program for a child. Further, the child must be assessed in all areas related to the suspected disability. These areas include, where appropriate, health, vision, hearing, social and emotional status, general intelligence, academic performance, communicative status, and motor abilities. In light of these mandates, a comprehensive assessment should normally include many of the following:

- An individual psychological evaluation, including general intelligence, instructional needs, learning strengths and needs, and social–emotional dynamics
- A thorough social history based on interviews with parents and student

- A thorough academic history with interviews or reports from past teachers
- A physical examination, including specific assessments that relate to vision, hearing, and health
- A classroom observation of the student in his or her current educational setting
- An appropriate educational evaluation specifically pinpointing the areas of deficit or suspected disability including, but not limited to, educational achievement, academic needs, learning strengths and needs, and vocational assessments
- A functional behavioral assessment to describe the relationship between a skill or performance problem and variables that contribute to its occurrence. The purpose of a functional behavioral assessment is to gather broad and specific information in order to better understand the specific reasons for the student's problem behavior
- A bilingual assessment for students with limited English proficiency
- Auditory and visual discrimination tests
- Assessment of classroom performance
- Speech and language evaluations, when appropriate
- Physical and/or occupational evaluations, when indicated
- Interviewing the student and significant others in his or her life
- Examining school records and past evaluation results
- Using information from checklists completed by parents, teachers, or the student
- Evaluating curriculum requirements and options
- Evaluating the student's type and rate of learning during trial teaching periods
- Evaluating which skills have been and not been mastered, and in what order unmastered skills need to be taught
- Collecting ratings on teacher attitude toward students with disabilities, peer acceptance, and classroom climate

This information can be gathered in a variety of ways, including norm-referenced tests, informal assessment, criterion-referenced tests, ecological assessment, curriculum-based assessment, curriculum-based measurement, dynamic assessment, portfolio assessment, authentic/naturalistic/performance–based assessment, task analysis, outcome-based assessment, and learning styles assessment (Pierangelo & Giuliani, 2005).

Norm-Referenced Tests

Scores on norm-referenced tests are not interpreted according to an absolute standard or criterion (e.g., eight out of ten correct) but rather, according to how the student's performance compares with that of a particular group of individuals. For this comparison to be meaningful, a valid comparison group—called a norm group—must be defined. A norm group is a large number of children who are representative of all the children in that age group. Such a group can be obtained by selecting a group of children that have the characteristics of children across the United States—that is, a certain percentage must be from each gender, from various ethnic backgrounds (e.g., Caucasian, African American, American Indian, Asian, Hispanic), from each geographic area (e.g., Southeast, Midwest), and from each socioeconomic class. By having all types of children take the test, the test publisher can provide information about how various types of children perform on the test. (This information—what type of students comprised the norm group and how each type performed on the test—is generally given in the manuals that accompany the test.) The school will compare the scores of the child being evaluated to the scores obtained by the norm group. This helps evaluators determine whether the child is performing at a level typical for, below, or above that expected for children of a given ethnicity, socioeconomic status, age, or grade.

Thus, before making assumptions about a child's abilities based upon test results, it is important to know something about the group to which the child is being compared—particularly whether the student is being compared to children who are similar in ethnicity, socioeconomic status, and so on. The more unlike the child the norm group is, the less valuable the results of testing will generally be. This is one of the areas in which standardized testing has fallen under considerable criticism. Often, test administrators do not use the norm group information appropriately, or there may not be children in the norm group who are similar to the child being tested. Furthermore, many tests were originally developed some time ago, and the norm groups reported in the test manual are not similar at all to the children being tested today.

Norm-referenced tests include basal and ceiling levels. These are used to prevent the examiner from having to administer all of the items with each test. A basal is the "starting point." It represents the level of mastery of a task below which the student would correctly answer all items on a test. All of the items prior to the basal are not given to the student. These items are considered already correct. For example, on an IQ test, the examiner may start with question 14 because of the age of the child. That is the basal. Here, the student starts with credit given for the first 13 questions. Once the basal is determined, the examiner will administer all items until the student reaches a ceiling. The ceiling is the point at which the student has made a predetermined number of errors, and, therefore, all other items stop being administered because it is assumed that the student will continue to get the answers wrong. The ceiling is the "ending point." It represents the level of mastery of a task above which the student would incorrectly answer all future items on a test. For example, if on a spelling test a child got numbers 15 to 24 wrong, and the ceiling is 10 incorrect in a row, this means that the examiner would stop administering spelling words to the child because the ceiling has been obtained.

Norm-referenced tests compare a person's score against the scores of a group of people who have already taken the same exam, called the norming group. When you see scores in the paper that report a school's scores as a percentage—"the Lincoln school ranked at the 49th percentile"—or when you see your child's score reported that way—"Jamal scored at the 63rd percentile"—the test is usually a norm-referenced test. Norm-referenced tests are designed to "rank order" test takers— that is, to compare students' scores. A commercial norm-referenced test does not compare all the students who take the test in a given year. Instead, test makers select a sample from the target student population (say, ninth graders). The test is "normed" on this sample, which is supposed to fairly represent the entire target population (all ninth graders in the nation). Students' scores are then reported in relation to the scores of this "norming" group. To make comparing easier, test makers create exams in which the results end up looking at least somewhat like a bell-shaped curve. Test makers make the test so that most students will score near the middle, and only a few will score low (the left side of the curve) or high (the right side of the curve).

Standardized Testing

All norm-referenced tests include standardized procedures. Standardization refers to structuring test materials, administration procedures, scoring methods, and techniques for interpreting results (Venn, 2000). Standardized tests have detailed procedures for administration, timing, scoring, and interpretation procedures that must be followed precisely to obtain valid and reliable results. Standardized tests are very much a part of the education scene. Most of us have taken many such tests in our lifetime. A wide variety of standardized tests is available to assess different skill areas. In the field of special education, these include intelligence tests; math, reading, spelling, and writing tests; perceptual tests; and many others. The fact is, standardized tests are a tremendous source of information when assessing a child.

Concerns with Standardized Testing.

Criticisms of standardized tests seem to have grown in proportion to the frequency with which, and the purposes for which, they are used (Haney & Madaus, 1989). Pikulski (1990) suggests that the greatest misuse of standardized tests may be their overuse. Many districts now administer such tests at every grade level, define success or failure of programs in terms of test scores, and even link teacher and administrator salaries and job security to student performance on standardized test performance. Three areas often criticized in regard to standardized tests are content, item format, and item bias. Standardized tests are designed to provide the best match possible to what is perceived to be the "typical" curriculum at a specific grade level. Because a bilingual education program is built on objectives unique to the needs of its students, many of the items on a standardized test may not measure the objectives or content of that program. Thus a standardized test may have low content validity for specific bilingual education programs. In such a situation, the test might not be sensitive to actual student progress. Consequently, the program, as measured by this test, would appear to be ineffective.

Standardized achievement tests generally rely heavily on multiple-choice items. This item format allows for greater content coverage as well as objective and efficient scoring. However, the response required by the format is recognition of the correct answer. This type of response does not necessarily match the type of responses students regularly make in the classroom, for example, the production or synthesis of information. If students are not used to responding within the structure imposed by the item format, their test performance may suffer. On the other hand, students may recognize the correct form when it is presented as a discrete item in a test format, but fail to use that form correctly in communication contexts. In this case, a standardized test may make the student appear more proficient than performance would suggest.

Further, some tests have been criticized for including items that are biased against certain kinds of students (e.g., ethnic minorities, limited English proficiency, rural, inner-city). The basis for this criticism is that the items reflect the language, culture, and/or learning style of the middle-class majority culture (Neill & Medina, 1989). Although test companies have attempted to write culture-free items, the removal of questions from a meaningful context has proved problematic for minority students.

Thus, there are strong arguments in favor of educators considering the use of alternative forms of assessment to supplement standardized test information. These alternate assessments should be timely, not time-consuming, truly representative of the curriculum, and tangibly meaningful to the teacher and student. Techniques of informal assessment have the potential to meet these criteria as well as programmatic requirements for formative and summative evaluations. Validity and reliability are not exclusive properties of formal, norm-referenced tests. Informal techniques are valid if they measure the skills and knowledge imparted by the project; they are reliable if they measure consistently and accurately. According to Hart (1994, p. 7, cited in Taylor, 1997), important criticisms of standardized testing include the following:

- It puts too much value on recall and rote learning at the expense of understanding and reflection.
- It promotes the misleading impression that a single right answer exists for almost every problem or question.
- It turns students into passive learners who need only recognize, not construct, answers and solutions.
- It forces teachers to focus more on what can be easily tested than on what is important for students to learn.
- It trivializes content and skill development by reducing whatever is taught to a fill-in-the-bubble format.

Informal Assessment

Formal and *informal* are not technical psychometric terms; therefore, there are no uniformly accepted definitions. As the term is used here, informal tests include techniques that can easily be incorporated into classroom routines and learning activities. Informal assessment techniques can be used at any time without interfering with instructional time. Their results are indicative of the student's performance on the skill or subject of interest. Unlike standardized tests, they are not intended to provide a comparison to a broader group beyond the students in the local project.

This is not to say that informal assessment is casual or lacking in rigor. Formal tests assume a single set of expectations for all students and come with prescribed criteria for scoring and interpretation. Informal assessment, on the other hand, requires a clear understanding of the levels of ability the students bring with them. Only then may assessment activities be selected that students can attempt reasonably. Informal assessment seeks to identify the strengths and needs of individual students without regard to grade or age norms.

Criterion-Referenced Tests

Criterion-referenced tests (CRTs) are scored according to a standard, or criterion, that the teacher, school, or test publisher decides represents an acceptable level of mastery. An example of a criterion-referenced test might be a teacher-made spelling test in which there are twenty words to be spelled. The teacher has defined an "acceptable level of mastery" as sixteen correct (or 80%). These tests, sometimes called content-referenced tests, are concerned with the mastery of specific, defined skills; the student's performance on the test indicates whether he or she has mastered those skills. Examples of criterion-referenced questions would be

- Does John correctly read the word *happy*?
- Does Jane do eighth-grade math computation problems with 85% accuracy?
- Did Joe get 90% of the questions correct on the social studies exam?

As you can see, in criterion-referenced assessment, the emphasis is on passing one or a series of questions. The test giver is interested in what the student can and cannot do, rather than how his or her performance compares with those of other people (Salvia & Ysseldyke, 1998, p. 35). Informal reading inventories (IRIs) are examples of criterion-referenced tests. IRIs generally consist of two main sections: word recognition and passage reading. According to Bigge and Stump (1999),

> the interpretation of an IRI is based on criteria or levels of performance, and identifies three reading levels; independent, instructional, and frustration. The independent reading level is the level at which a student reads fluently and for pleasure (word recognition of 96% to 99% correct paired with correct comprehension of 75% to 90%). The instructional reading level is the level at which the student can experience success with assistance (word recognition of 92% to 95% correct paired with correct comprehension of 60% to 75%). The frustration level is the level at which the reading process breaks down for the student (word recognition of 90% to 92% or less paired with correct comprehension of 60% to 75% or less), as demonstrated by depressed comprehension and difficulties with word recognition (p. 197).

Ecological Assessment

Ecological assessment involves directly observing and assessing a child in the many environments in which he or she routinely operates. The purpose of conducting such an assessment is to probe how the different environments influence the student and his or her school performance. Critical questions to ask in an ecological assessment include:

- In what environments does the student manifest difficulties?
- Are there instances in which he or she appears to function appropriately?
- What is expected of the student academically and behaviorally in each type of environment?
- What differences exist in the environments in which the student manifests the greatest and the least difficulty?
- What implications do these differences have for instructional planning?

As Wallace, Larsen, and Elksnin (1992) remark: "An evaluation that fails to consider a student's ecology as a potential causative factor in reported academic or behavioral disorders may be ignoring the very elements that require modification before we can realistically expect changes in that student's behavior" (p. 19).

According to Overton (1996), an ecological assessment analyzes a "student's total learning environment" (p. 276). A thorough ecological assessment should include the following:

- Interaction between students, teachers, and others in the classroom and in other school environments
- Presentation of materials and ideas
- Selection and use of materials for instruction
- Physical arrangement and environment of the classroom or target setting
- Students' interactions in other environments

Ecological assessment can also draw on the culture and beliefs of the child; the teacher's teaching style; the way time is used in the classroom; academic, behavioral, and social expectations within the learning environment; and the overall tone of the class (Bigge & Stump, 1999). The components of an ecological assessment clearly reveal that it involves numerous aspects of the student's life to get a detailed picture of his or her situation.

Common Observational Techniques Used in Ecological Assessment.

Anecdotal Records. The observer describes incidents or behaviors observed in a particular setting in concrete, narrative terms (as opposed to drawing inferences about feelings or motives). This type of record allows insight into cause and effect by detailing what occurred before a behavior took place, the behavior itself, and consequences or events that occurred after the behavior.

Event Recording. The observer is interested in recording specific behavioral events (such as how many times the student hits or gets out of his or her seat). A tally sheet listing the behaviors to be observed and counted is useful; when the observer sees the behavior of interest, he or she can simply make a tick mark on the sheet.

Duration Recording. This method usually requires a watch or clock, so that a precise measurement of how much time a student spends doing something of concern to the teacher or assessment team (e.g., talking to others, tapping, rocking) can be recorded.

Time-Sampling Recording. With this technique, observers count the number of times a behavior occurs during a specific time interval. Rather than observe for long periods of time and tally all incidences of the behavior causing concern, the observer divides the observation period into equal time units and observes and tallies behavior only during short periods of time. Based on the time sampling, predictions can then be made about the student's total behavior.

Checklists and Rating Scales. A checklist usually requires the observer to note whether a particular characteristic is present or absent, while a rating scale typically asks the observer to note the degree to which a characteristic is present or how often a behavior occurs. There are many commercially available checklists and rating scales, but they may be developed locally as well.

Interviews

Interviewing the student in question, his or her parents, teachers, and other adults or peers can provide a great deal of useful information about the student. Ultimately, "an interview should be a conversation with a purpose" (Wallace, Larsen, & Elksnin, 1992, p. 16), with questions designed to collect information that "relates to the observed or suspected disability of the child" (p. 260). Preparing for the interview may involve a careful review of the student's school records or work samples, for these may help the assessment team identify patterns or areas of specific concern that can help determine who should be interviewed and some of the questions to be asked. Parents, for example, may be able to provide detailed information about the child's academic or medical background. It is especially important that they contribute their unique, "insider" perspective on their child's functioning, interests, motivation, difficulties, and behavior in the home or community. They may have valuable information to share about possible solutions to the problems being noted. Teachers can provide insight into the types of situations or tasks that the child finds demanding or easy, what factors appear to contribute to the child's difficulties, and what has produced positive results (e.g., specific activities, types of rewards) (Wodrich & Joy, 1986). The student, too, may have much to say to illuminate the problem. "All persons interviewed should be asked if they know of information important to the solution of the academic or behavior problem that was not covered during the interview" (Hoy & Gregg, 1994, p. 44).

Organizing interview results is essential. Hoy and Gregg (1994) suggest that the interviewer might summarize the "perceptions of each person interviewed in a way that conveys similarities and differences in viewpoints" (p. 46), including perceptions of the primary problem and its cause, what attempts have been made to solve or address the problem, any recent changes in the problem's severity, and student strengths and needs.

Curriculum-Based Assessment and Curriculum-Based Measurement

Direct assessment of academic skills is one alternative that has recently gained in popularity. Although a number of direct assessment models exist (Shapiro, 1989), they are similar in that they all suggest that assessment needs to be tied directly to instructional curriculum.

Curriculum-based assessment (CBA) is one type of direct evaluation. CBA is defined as a data collection procedure that is a direct measure of a student's progress within a curriculum, with the data serving as a basis for confirmation of adequate and expected progress as well as determination that effective teaching and learning is occurring (King-Sears, 1994, p. 9). "Tests" of performance in this case come directly from the curriculum. For example, a child may be asked to read from his or her reading book for one minute. Information about the accuracy and the speed of reading can then be obtained and compared with other students in the class, building, or district. CBA is quick and offers specific information about how a student may differ from his or her peers.

Because the assessment is tied to curriculum content, it allows the teacher to match instruction to a student's current abilities and pinpoints areas in which curriculum adaptations or modifications are needed. Unlike many other types of educational assessment, such as intelligence tests, CBA provides information that is immediately relevant to instructional programming (Berdine & Meyer, 1987, p. 33).

CBA also offers information about the accuracy and efficiency (speed) of performance. The latter is often overlooked when assessing a child's performance but is an important piece of information when designing intervention strategies. CBA is also useful in evaluating short-term academic progress.

Curriculum-based measurement (CBM) is an assessment method that involves timing tasks and then charting performance. CBM is most concerned with fluency. This means that we are looking at the rate at which a student is able to perform a given task. After assessing the speed at which the student performs the task, we then chart performance over time so that we can clearly see on a graph the student's progress (or decline) from the initial performance to the goal point. An example of curriculum-based measurement would be to examine the number of words correctly read from a book in five minutes and then continually charting the student's progress over the course of the school year with the goal being set at a predetermined number of 150 words.

Portfolio Assessment

Perhaps the most important type of assessment for the classroom teacher is the portfolio assessment. According to Paulson, Paulson, and Meyer (1991), a portfolio is "a purposeful collection of student works that exhibits the student's efforts, progress, and achievement in one or more areas" (p. 60). The student must participate in the selection of items for a portfolio. It must include the criteria for selection, the criteria for judging merit, and evidence of student self-reflection. A portfolio collection contains work samples, permanent products, and test results from a variety of instruments and measures. For example, a portfolio of reading might include a student's test scores on teacher-made tests including curriculum-based assessments, work samples from daily work and homework assignments, error analyses on work and test samples, and the results of an informal reading inventory with miscues noted and analyzed (Overton, 1996, p. 250).

Batzle (1992; cited in Bigge & Stump, 1999) identifies three general types of portfolios:

1. Working portfolio: Teacher, student, and parents all contribute to the portfolio. Both works in progress and final product pieces are included.
2. Showcase portfolio: The portfolio houses only the student's best work and generally does not include works in progress. The student manages the portfolio and decides what to place in it.
3. Teacher portfolio or record keeping: The portfolio houses student test papers and work samples maintained by the teacher. It contains work not selected by the student for inclusion in the showcase portfolio.

When portfolios are used in the classroom, they allow teachers to assess student progress more closely over time, aid teachers and parents in communicating about student's performance, assist in program evaluation efforts, and provide a means through which students can actively participate with their teachers in the assessment process (Hart, 1994).

Authentic/Naturalistic/Performance-Based Assessment

Another technique that is becoming increasingly popular with classroom teachers to assess classroom performance is authentic assessment. This performance-based assessment technique involves the application of knowledge to real-life activities, real-world settings, or simulations of such settings using real life, real-world activities (Taylor, 1997). For example, when an individual is being assessed in the area of artistic ability, typically she presents examples of her own artwork and is evaluated according to various criteria; it is not simply the person's knowledge of art, the materials, artists, or art history.

Authentic assessment is sometimes referred to as naturalistic-based assessment or performance-based assessment. The terms can be used interchangeably. These assessment methods share common characteristics, which include the following (Herman et al., 1992, p. 6; cited in Bigge & Stump, 1999, p. 183).

- Ask students to perform, create, produce, or do something
- Tap higher-level thinking and problem-solving skills
- Use tasks that represent meaningful instructional activities
- Invoke real-world applications

- Let people, not machines, do the scoring, using human judgment
- Require new instructional and assessment roles for teachers

Performance assessment has several advantages. Students are assessed in real and complex situations, considering both process and product (Maker, 1993). In addition, the gap between testing and instruction is reduced (Frechtling, 1991). There is a concern, however, that performance-based assessment relies on the teacher's observations or judgments, increasing the role of subjectivity over that of other measurement strategies (Frechtling, 1991). In performance assessment, judgments are made about student knowledge and skills based on observation of student behavior or examination of student products (Lam, 1995). Although the instructional advantages of performance assessment are obvious when teachers focus on higher-order thinking skills, there is no evidence that assessment bias vanishes with performance assessment (Linn, Baker, & Dunbar, 1991). Performance assessment may generate its own potential sources of bias, including the students' limitations or ability to use higher-order thinking skills and metacognitive skills; cultural problem-solving patterns; shyness; inadequate communication skills in presenting, discussing, arguing, or debating; inadequate or undue help; lack of resources inside and outside of school; incompatibility in language and culture between assessors and students; and subjectivity in rating (Lam, 1995).

Task Analysis

Task analysis is very detailed; it involves breaking down a particular task into the basic sequential steps, component parts, or skills necessary to accomplish the task. The degree to which a task is broken down into steps depends upon the student in question; "it is only necessary to break the task down finely enough so that the student can succeed at each step" (Wallace et al., 1992, p. 14).

Applying this approach to assessment offers the teacher several advantages. For one, the process identifies what is necessary for accomplishing a particular task. It also tells the teacher whether the student can do the task, which part or skill causes the student to falter, and the order in which skills must be taught to help the student learn to perform the task. According to Bigge (1990), task analysis is a process that can be used to guide decision making in the following situations.

- Question: What to teach next?
- Problems students encounter when they are attempting to complete a task but are not able to
- The steps necessary to complete an entire task
- Adaptations that can be made to help the student accomplish a task
- Options for students when learning a task is not a possible goal

Task analysis is an approach to assessment that goes far beyond the need to make an eligibility or program placement decision regarding a student. It can become an integral part of classroom planning and instructional decision making.

Primary Areas of Assessment

Now that you have an understanding of the different types of assessment, we can examine in detail the primary areas in which students are assessed. In this section, we will look at what skills are involved in these traditional areas of assessment (e.g., intelligence, language, and so on) and how schools may collect information about how a student performs in each area. When the disability is related to a medically related condition (e.g., sensory deficit, orthopedic impairment, and arthritis), assessment information from physicians or other medical practitioners needs to be included as well. While standardized testing is often the default means of gathering information about a student, it is highly recommended that other methods be used as well, including interviews, observations, and methodologies such as ecological or dynamic assessment.

Intelligence

While a person's intelligence is typically measured by an intelligence test, there is considerable controversy over what, precisely, is meant by the term "intelligence." Binet, who was largely responsible for the development of the first intelligence test, viewed intelligence as a collection of faculties, including judgment, practical sense, initiative, and the ability to adapt to circumstances (Wallace, Larsen, & Elksnin, 1992). Thurman, in contrast, developed a multifactor theory of intelligence, which included such mental abilities as verbal, number, perceptual speed, reasoning, memory, word fluency, and spatial visualization. Wechsler, on the other hand, believed that intelligence was the ability of the person "to act purposefully, to think rationally, and to deal effectively with his environment" (Wechsler, 1958, p. 7, as cited in Wallace, Larsen, & Elksnin, 1992, p. 105).

It is important to know that different intelligence tests are based on different definitions of what constitutes intelligence. As a result, different tests may measure different skills and abilities. It is critical, therefore, that administrators of such tests "be completely aware of an author's definition of intelligence when selecting and interpreting an intelligence test" and "to view the scores as highly tentative estimates of learning ability that must be verified by other evidence" (Wallace, Larsen, & Elksnin, 1992, p. 106).

The theory underlying intelligence tests (e.g., how does one define intelligence or develop tests of intelligence?) is not the only controversy surrounding their use. How fairly they assess certain populations (e.g., minority children, persons with limited experience, children with severe language deficits), and whether or not such tests are reliable and valid (Elliott, 1987) are also areas of hot debate. In the past, intelligence measures have been misused, particularly with African American children, Native Americans, and non English-speaking children, who, based on their scores, were placed in classes for those with mental retardation or with learning disabilities. However, given the many court cases involving standardized intelligence testing as a means of assessing minority children (e.g., *Diana v. State Board of Education*, 1970; *Covarrubias v. San Diego Unified School District*, 1971; *Larry*

P. v. Riles, 1979; *Guadalupe v. Tempe Elementary District,* 1972), and given the strength and volume of advocates' protests, evaluators are now becoming more sensitive to issues of test bias, the importance of testing in a child's native language, the need for specialized training when administering and interpreting standardized tests, and the importance of combining any test scores with information gathered in other ways.

Issues related to the definition of intelligence and the fairness of using measures of intelligence also become less concerning if one knows the purpose for which the test is being used. Intelligence tests are most helpful (and probably most appropriate) when they are used to determine specific skills, abilities, and knowledge that the child either has or does not have and when such information is combined with other evaluation data and then directly applied to school programming.

There are a number of skills that an intelligence test appears to measure—social judgment, level of thinking, language skill, perceptual organization, processing speed, and spatial abilities. Questions that attempt to measure social judgment and common sense, numerical reasoning, concrete and abstract thinking, the ability to recognize similarities and differences between objects or concepts, and vocabulary and language skill (e.g., the ease with which a person can find words in memory) appear very dependent on experience, training, and intact verbal abilities. Perceptual organization, processing speed, and spatial abilities seem less dependent on experience and verbal skill.

Intelligence tests can also yield valuable information about a student's ability to process information. In order to learn, every person must take in, make sense of, store, and retrieve information from memory in an efficient and accurate way. Each of us can process certain kinds of information more easily than other kinds. The artist sees and reproduces accurate depictions of the world, while others struggle to produce stick figures. The musician creates beautiful sounds from a mixture of separate tones. The writer crafts words to create a mood. Others of us do none of these things well. In school, children need certain skills to function effectively. They must be able to listen attentively so that other movements, sounds, or sights do not distract them. They must be able to understand the words spoken to them. This often requires children to hold multiple pieces of information in memory (e.g., page number, questions to answer) and to act upon them. They must be able to find the words they need to express themselves and, ultimately, commit these words to paper. This involves another series of processing skills—holding a writing implement, coordinating visual and motor actions, keeping information in memory until it can be transferred to paper, transforming sounds into written symbols, and understanding syntax, punctuation, and capitalization rules. Students also must be able to interpret the nonverbal messages of others, such as a frown, a smile, a shake of the head. Equally important, they must do all of these things quickly and accurately and often in a setting with many distractions.

A thorough interpretation of an intelligence test can yield information about how effectively a child processes and retrieves information. Most individually administered intelligence tests can determine, at least to some degree, a child's ability to attend, process information quickly, distinguish relevant from less relevant details, put events in sequence, and retrieve words from memory. Kamphaus (1993, p. 65) summarizes a number of research findings related to the use of intelligence tests:

1. Intelligence test scores are more stable for school-aged children than for preschoolers and more stable among individuals with disabilities than those without disabilities;
2. Intelligence test scores can change from childhood to adulthood;
3. It is likely that environmental factors, socioeconomic status, values, family structure, and genetic factors all play a role in determining intelligence test scores;
4. Factors such as low birth weight, malnutrition, anoxia (lack of oxygen), and fetal alcohol exposure have a negative impact on intelligence test scores; and
5. Intelligence and academic achievement appear to be highly related.

This last finding supports the notion that intelligence and achievement tests may not be so different from each other and that "intelligence tests may be interpreted as specialized types of achievement measures" (Kamphaus, 1993, p. 65). This is consistent with the suggestion that intelligence tests may be best used to determine specific skills, abilities, and knowledge.

Language

Language provides the foundation upon which communication, problem solving, and expanding, integrating, analyzing, and synthesizing knowledge take place. Deficits in language, therefore, can have a profound impact on the ability of an individual to learn and function competently and confidently as he or she interacts in the world.

Language is complex and involves multiple domains—nonverbal language, oral language (i.e., listening and speaking), written language (i.e., reading and writing), pragmatic language (e.g., using language for a specific purpose such as asking for help), phonology, and audiology. How quickly a person can access words or ideas in memory further influences his or her use of language. A child who must struggle to find an appropriate term is at a great disadvantage in a learning and social environment. As he or she struggles to retrieve a word or information, others have moved on. The student may miss critical pieces of knowledge, connect incorrect bits of information in memory, and have an ineffective means of showing others all that he or she knows. Such problems can result in lowered levels of achievement and in feelings of confusion, helplessness, and frustration.

It is clear how important language processing can be to a child's successful adaptation to the school environment and, therefore, it is an important area to be considered in the assessment process. Speech and language pathologists are specially trained professionals who, working with school psychologists and classroom teachers, are frequently the primary individuals gathering data related to a child's language functioning.

Bloom and Lahey (1978) divide language processes into three general categories: form, content, and use. Phonology, morphology, and syntax are all considered to be components of *form.* The first of these processes, *phonology,* refers to the knowledge a person has of the sounds in the language. While the number of sounds that exist are limited, a nearly endless number of words can be constructed from these sounds. Awareness of the basic sound units of language appears important to a child's ability to quickly and accurately locate words in memory when speaking, comprehend oral sentences, and learn to read (Liberman & Shankweiler, 1994). It is important to note that the ability to blend or separate sounds (i.e., phonological processing ability) is often overlooked in the assessment process. This may be an unfortunate oversight, given its apparent importance to the reading process.

Morphology, the second form element, refers to the smallest meaningful unit of language. Morphology involves the stringing together of sounds (phonemes) and includes such structures as prefixes, suffixes, word endings that describe number (e.g., dog vs. dogs), and tense (e.g., walk vs. walked). *Syntax* refers to the rules used in combining words to make a sentence. As with the sounds of language (phonology), the rules of language are finite. The acquisition of syntax is also developmental.

While syntax determines the rules that guide how sentences are put together, such knowledge alone is not sufficient for constructing sentences. The meaning of words constrains what words may or may not be used together. For example, the sentence *I saw the house flying over the orchard* would make little sense, although it is syntactically correct. It is this aspect of language, the importance of meaning, that Bloom and Lahey (1978) refer to as *content.* Content involves knowledge of vocabulary, the relationships between words, and "time-and-event" relationships (Swanson & Watson, 1989). The child must also be able to associate words with the correct environmental experience. It is generally expected that a child understands the meaning of more words than he or she can express at any point in time. As Swanson and Watson (1989) point out, when an individual appears able to express more information than he or she is able to receive and comprehend, it may suggest that he or she has difficulty in auditory input and processing.

Use, the final component in the Bloom and Lahey model, refers to "the pragmatic functions of language in varying contexts" (Swanson & Watson, 1989, p. 151). It views the child as an active communicator whose words and sentences are intentionally selected in relation to the effect the speaker wishes to have on a listener. The speaker needs to be able to (1) change what is said in some way when it is apparent that he or she is not being understood, (2) vary language use when talking with different groups (e.g., peers or adults), and (3) use language in a variety of functional ways (e.g., to begin or end a conversation). Thus, use (or *pragmatics,* as it is sometimes called) is a vital area to assess in language; to ignore how a student uses language is to ignore a basic element of language—that we communicate in a context, for a particular purpose or reason (Heward & Orlansky, 1992).

Assessing a Child's Language Abilities.   IDEA regulations provide a definition of speech–language impairment as "a communication disorder such as stuttering, impaired articulation, a language impairment, or a voice impairment that adversely affects" a child's educational performance [34 CFR Section 300.7(b)(11)]. In more specific terms, a child with a speech disorder may have difficulty in *producing* sounds properly, speaking in a normal flow or rhythm, or using his or her voice in an effective way. A child with a *language* disorder would have problems using or understanding the rules, sounds, or symbols that we use to communicate with each other. This relates to language form, content, and/or use, as discussed above (Heward & Orlansky, 1992). A child with a speech impairment, a language impairment, or both, would be eligible for services under IDEA.

There are many standardized measures of speech and language ability. Some "provide a *comprehensive* view of all language functioning," while others "measure *specific* components of linguistic performance (for example, phonology, linguistic structure, or semantics)" (Wallace, Larsen, & Elksnin, 1992, p. 252). The range of tests and what they measure may be identified through consulting resource books on speech/language assessment or more general test references such as *Tests* (Sweetland & Keyser, 1991), or by contacting organizations such as the American Speech-Language-Hearing Association (ASHA).

It is important to realize, however, that "standardized diagnostic tests are generally insensitive to the subtleties of ongoing functional communication" (Swanson & Watson, 1989, p. 155). Therefore, in addition to or in place of standardized tests, a typical speech/language evaluation should include obtaining a language sample that seeks to capture how the student performs in an actual communication situation. Language samples can be obtained through checklists or observational recording systems, or through informally conversing with the student. Great care must be taken to ensure that assessment of students is culture-free and dialect-sensitive, as many children will speak nonstandard English or another language entirely. [The issue of cultural bias in language assessment is considered in *Topics in Language Disorders* (Terrell, 1983)]. Obtaining such a language sample from the student is often the responsibility of the speech-language pathologist.

Through interviews, observations, and teaching, teachers can also gather valuable information about a student's language use. By engaging in what is known as diagnostic teaching, the teacher can become an invaluable participant in the ongoing assessment and remediation of a child's language deficiencies. It is important, however, for teachers to be thoroughly familiar with the developmental milestones of normal language functioning.

Obtaining a case history of the child (in most cases, from the parents) can also be valuable in the initial stages of assessment. Knowing in detail how the child's language has developed can yield information relevant to the problem and includes gaining an understanding of the early stages of the disorder, any physical or emotional condition that may have been or be involved, whether the disorder occurs in other settings and, if so, how it manifests itself, and any insights the parents may have into how best to assess and work with their child (Wallace, Larsen, & Elksnin, 1992, p. 260).

It is also important to realize that the ability to receive and understand language, and to use language verbally, in part depends on how well the body performs physically. Before embarking on an extensive (and expensive) battery of tests, examiners should ensure that any apparent speech or language impairment is not actually the result of a hearing impairment which, in effect, prevents the child from hearing words clearly and learning to use or understand them. Similarly, many children with physical disabilities may not be able to speak clearly enough to be understood but, when provided with assistive technology (e.g., speech synthesizers, computers), may show themselves to be competent users of language.

Perceptual Abilities

Perceptual abilities determine how individuals perceive information and how they respond. These abilities can be subdivided into at least four general areas: visual-perceptual, auditory-perceptual, perceptual-motor skills, and attention. Assessing a student in these areas is intended to determine strengths and needs in information and sensory processing and can help the assessment team gain an understanding of how the child learns best.

The idea of "perceptual deficits" has long been linked to learning disabilities. It is important to realize that research results in this area have been mixed and controversial, and offer only small support for including evaluation of perceptual abilities in any assessment battery or approach (Overton, 1992). Linguistic issues, rather than perceptual abilities, may more often explain learning deficits. Nevertheless, since assessing perceptual abilities continues to be part of the evaluation process at present, we will briefly discuss them below.

Visual-Perceptual Ability. Visual perception includes the ability to discriminate between two or more visual stimuli, locate a particular figure within a larger scene, and understand position in space. Perceptual skills include detecting specific colors, shapes, and sizes. In reading, it requires the ability to detect the visual features of a letter or word so that the 26 letters of the alphabet can be distinguished from each other. The student must also discriminate between ten written digits.

Auditory-Perceptual Ability. Auditory perception includes the ability to detect certain auditory features such as changes in volume, discrimination of vowel or consonant sounds, and nonphonemic sound discrimination (e.g., the sound of a bell from the sound of a buzzer). In a school setting, then, the student would need the ability to discriminate between different sounds, identify spoken words that are the same or different, and hear sounds in order.

Perceptual-Motor Ability. Most assessments include one or more measures of perceptual-motor ability. It has been an assumption of many educators that perceptual-motor or visual-motor problems are often associated with learning problems and, therefore, should be included in most assessment batteries (Salvia & Ysseldyke, 1991). Historically, tests of perceptual-motor skill have been second only to intelligence tests in terms of use in the assessment of school-aged children. Tests of perceptual-motor skill or perceptual-motor integration most often ask students to copy geometric designs that are placed in front of them. This requires the child to see the design, attend to and remember the relevant features, and then carry out the motor actions necessary to reproduce the design on paper.

Attention. The ability to focus on a given activity for extended periods is important if a student is to take in information or complete the day-to-day tasks in school. Keogh and Margolis (1976) have suggested three phases of attention: the ability to (1) come to attention; (2) focus attention; and (3) maintain attention. The issue of "selective" attention must also be considered here. Students must be able to attend, *and* they must be able to sustain attention on the most relevant stimuli. For example, a student must be able to attend to the teacher's words rather than to his or her clothing. Difficulties in any of the three phases of attention can interfere with a student's ability to learn or share what he or she knows in a consistent fashion. While the ability to attend effectively is seldom assessed through a formalized instrument, information related to attention can be gathered through classroom observations, observations of test behaviors, and rating scales (e.g., Connor's Scales).

Assessing Perceptual Ability. As was mentioned above, assessing perceptual abilities is not without its controversies. There are certainly a number of issues that need to be considered when addressing this area.

- The first issue relates to the importance of ensuring that a student's apparent perceptual difficulties are not actually the result of a lack of visual or auditory acuity (as opposed to a difficulty with processing stimuli). Before beginning an assessment of perceptual ability, then, the student's eyesight and hearing should be tested (Overton, 1992; Swanson & Watson, 1989). This can be part of the assessment process, with the school referring the student to the appropriate facilities for such screenings.
- The second issue is related to the relevance of such measures to the goals of assessment. There has been little to suggest that direct training in perceptual skills improves academic performance (Salvia & Ysseldyke, 1991; Vellutino, 1979). If there is little applicability, then it seems reasonable to question whether formal tests of perceptual skill are necessary as part of the assessment battery.
- The third issue is related to the validity and reliability of the perceptual test measures. There is some suggestion that tests purported to measure perceptual abilities may actually measure other factors such as language or verbal memory skill (Vellutino, 1979). Information gained from tests thought to measure perceptual processing may actually result in incorrect explanations for learning problems. This may lead those working with the child towards strategies that are not useful (perceptual training such as copying designs) and away from ones that may be helpful, such as training in phonological processing. There are also concerns that many of the instruments currently available do not meet acceptable standards of reliability and validity (Swanson & Watson, 1989, p. 217), making their use of questionable value.

Academic Achievement

Academic achievement refers to how well the child is performing in core skill areas such as reading, mathematics, and writing. Assessment batteries typically include an individual measure of academic achievement, although it is important to realize that standardized achievement tests may be inappropriate for use with immigrant or minority group children. Information about the child's placement (i.e., below, at, or above) in his or her peer group and knowledge about the specific skills the child possesses are important both for the planning and evaluation of instruction.

Reading. Reading is an extension of the language process. It provides a way for individuals to exchange information. Reading also represents the means by which much of the information presented in school is learned and is the academic area most often implicated in school failure. Reading, like language, is an extremely complex process, a process that is, for many, so natural or fluent that many of the subskills are not recognized or identified as a part of the process. Identifying these subskills is important, however, if an adequate assessment in this area is to occur. Prereading involves the following skills.

- General language competence
- Understanding that reading is a means of exchanging ideas (e.g., the ability to "read" pictures)
- The ability to complete rhymes and identify words that do not rhyme
- The ability to distinguish between verbal and nonverbal sounds, recognize when words are the same or different, and segment and blend language sounds
- The ability to store and retrieve sounds one has heard

Having opportunities for abundant language experiences, while not a skill, is also important to the development of prereading and later reading ability.

Reading skills can be divided into two general categories: word recognition and comprehension. A number of skills are used when attempting to identify, pronounce, or retrieve a word. Four types of analyses can be used by the child: visual analysis (i.e., the use of visual features), contextual analysis (i.e., using the surrounding words for clues about a given word), phonological analysis (i.e., using information about the sounds in the word), and structural analysis (i.e., recognizing and giving meaning to specific word parts such as prefixes, suffixes, or syllables). Phonological analysis appears particularly important as children attempt to gain reading skill. It allows the child to decode (i.e., read) a word he or she has never seen before, either in isolation or in context. This is not possible with visual, contextual, or structural analysis alone. The ability, then, to engage in phonemic analysis is important to becoming a proficient reader and, therefore, is an area that should be considered in any assessment of any child who is struggling with reading.

Gaining meaning from text (comprehension) is the most common goal of reading. The general approach of the reader (active or passive), use of prior knowledge, and contextual analysis are all skills that appear related to comprehension. The ability to grasp literal information and to predict, interpret, critically analyze, or create new ideas in response to a paragraph are examples of the use of context at the comprehension level. Listening comprehension also appears to be related to reading comprehension, particularly at the higher reading skill levels (Stanovich, 1982).

The assessment of reading, then, needs to address the ability of the child to recognize individual words and to comprehend text. Assessment instruments should be selected that assure that test content and test tasks are as similar as possible to school reading tasks. Both formal and informal assessment may be useful here. Informal measures may include asking the student to do one or more of the following activities.

- Read aloud, which permits the teacher to identify errors in decoding and to determine the student's fluency and accuracy when reading
- Answer questions after reading, to determine the student's ability to understand the main idea of the story, capture its details, or place events in sequence
- Paraphrase or re-tell the story in his or her own words
- Fill in missing words in a passage he or she has not read
- Identify which sentence out of several means the same thing as a sentence supplied by the teacher
- Provide synonyms of selected words

Mathematics.   Another critical area of school achievement is that of mathematics. The terms "mathematics" and "arithmetic" are often used interchangeably but actually mean different things. *Mathematics* refers to the study of numbers and their relationships to time, space, volume, and geometry, whereas *arithmetic* refers to the operations or computations performed. Subskills related to mathematics include the following.

- Problem-solving
- The ability to perform mathematics in practical situations
- Performance of appropriate computational skills
- Use of mathematics to predict
- Understanding and use of concepts related to measurement
- Interpretation and construction of charts or graphs
- Ability to estimate
- Understanding and application of geometric concepts
- Ability to recognize the reasonableness of results
- Computer knowledge

For more information, see Lerner (1988), Reid and Hresko (1981), and Roth-Smith (1991).

For a student to learn and act on knowledge of mathematics, he or she must understand terms regarding amount or direction (i.e., language-based knowledge), understand that numbers stand for a quantity, hold multiple pieces of mathematical information in memory and perform mathematical operations (e.g., add, multiply) on them, and know that numbers can be manipulated in meaningful ways.

The assessment of mathematics should measure a student's ability in both calculation and reasoning (application). Like reading, an evaluation of mathematical understanding and performance should also be structured so that it closely matches the demands made on the child in the actual classroom situation. Assessment might begin by analyzing actual samples of the student's work and identifying specific errors and any apparent pattern to those errors. Curriculum-based assessment techniques are also useful, and can be combined with task analysis and error analysis to identify where, specifically, the student is having problems. Interviewing can be useful as well, and may include "asking the student to solve a problem and explain the steps used in the process" (Overton, 1992, p. 257). Such an approach can be invaluable in providing insight into a student's mathematical reasoning. Conducting several such interviews is important, however, to avoid drawing hasty conclusions about the nature of a student's difficulties. Observations can also provide productive information to the assessment team and should focus on student behavior during—and his or her approach to—written assignments, working at the chalkboard, and classroom discussions.

Written Language. Written language is a complex form of communicating that consists of three general areas: spelling, handwriting, and written expression or composition. Like reading, writing tasks are an important part of the school curriculum and are often utilized in evaluating a student's understanding of a given concept. Written language is directly tied to reading, listening, and speaking, and skills in all of these areas overlap.

Spelling. Spelling has often been considered a difficult task (Henderson, 1985). In English, the difficulty arises because there is no one-to-one correspondence between letters and their representative sounds. This can cause problems for the reader and may cause even greater problems for the speller. In spelling there are even fewer cues to aid in recreating a spoken word in print. As Lerner (1988) explains:

> Several clues aid the reader in recognizing a word in print: context, phonics, structural analysis, and configuration. There is no opportunity, however, to draw on peripheral clues in reproducing a word. (p. 105)

Both language and reading experience appear to be important to the development of connections between letters and their sounds. Thus, knowledge of spelling patterns, analysis of word parts, and knowledge of syllable rules all need to be measured.

It is important to consider that any approach that does not require a child to independently reconstruct a word (e.g., one that simply asks a child to select a misspelled word from among a group of words) does little to give information about the child's ability to recreate accurate spelling in a sentence he or she is writing. Assessment of spelling is particularly well-suited to informal approaches such as curriculum-based measurement or interviews. A number of standardized, commercially available spelling tests are available, as well.

Handwriting.   This refers to the actual motor activity that is involved in writing. Most students are taught manuscript (printing) initially and then move to cursive writing. Some educators advocate that only manuscript or only cursive should be taught (Reid & Hresko, 1981). In truth, problems may appear among students in either system. Wiederhold and colleagues (1978) have suggested a number of areas that may be assessed related to both manuscript and cursive writing. The assessment of manuscript includes evaluating the position of the hand and paper, size of letters and the proportion of letters to each other, quality of the actual pencil lines, the amount and regularity of the slant of the letters, letter formation and alignment, letter or word spacing, and speed of production. Cursive writing can be considered according to many of the same qualities but should also include an evaluation of the way in which letters are connected.

Composition.   This term refers to the more creative parts of written expression. Alley and Deshler (1979) suggest three general areas that need to be addressed in any assessment of written expression.

- The student's attitude toward writing
- Ability of the individual to express content (e.g., skill in describing or reporting events, or in expressing views or feelings)
- The student's ability to "craft" a paragraph (e.g., the student's ability to organize, sequence, choose effective words, use punctuation and capitalization, or take notes)

Both formal and informal measures of assessment of written expression are available and should be considered in a thorough evaluation. Analyzing work samples produced by the student can be particularly useful, as can interviewing the student regarding his or her perceptions of the writing process.

Behavior and Emotional–Social Development

Behavior—how a student conducts himself or herself in school—is often a key factor in educational performance. Certainly, behavior that is off-target academically or socially—inattention, being out of seat, talking too much, hitting or biting, skipping school—can detract from learning. When a student's behavior appears to be interfering with school performance and relationships with others, or when that behavior is maladaptive, bizarre, or dangerous, it becomes important to assess the student's behavior (when the behavior occurs, how often, and for what reasons) as well as his or her emotional and social development. Wallace, Larsen, and Elksnin (1992) "stress the need to take an *ecological* perspective when assessing a student's nonacademic behaviors in order to obtain a complete picture and examine the relationship between the behavior and the environment" (pp. 164–165).

Negative or inappropriate behaviors may occur for different reasons. One child may be disruptive in class because of attention-deficit disorder. A second child may exhibit similar behaviors due to a mental illness, while another's inappropriate behavior may be linked to environmental factors such as his or her parents' recent divorce. Still another child may be disruptive only in one or two classes, for reasons associated with the way instruction is organized (e.g., a predominance of small-group, large-group, or self-paced activities) or something in that environment which the student finds disturbing. Thus, identifying *why* a child is exhibiting certain behaviors is an important part of the assessment process. The reasons why, if they can be determined, will influence whether the child is determined eligible for special education services and, if so, will certainly affect the nature of decisions made regarding educational and other interventions.

Assessing Problem Behavior.   For children exhibiting signs of emotional, social, or behavioral problems, the assessment team will generally conduct a *behavioral assessment*. The goal of behavioral assessment is to gain an increased understanding of how environmental factors may be influencing the child's behavior. This includes identifying (1) what expectations and rules are established by significant others in the settings where the problem behavior occurs, and (2) what "specific variables in a particular situation . . . may be maintaining problem behaviors" (Berdine & Meyer, 1987, p. 151). This knowledge will then be used directly in designing intervention strategies. "Behavioral assessment depends on keen observation and precise measurement" (Swanson & Watson, 1989, p. 246). Assessment is tied to observing a specific situation (e.g., how the child responds during lunch or reading) at a particular point in time. It is important that a behavioral assessment involve multiple measures and take place in various settings (e.g., the classroom, school playground, chorus, home) and at different times during the day (e.g., morning, afternoon, and night). The ability to observe and record behavior, select the most appropriate places to observe the child, and find efficient and clear means of interpreting results are all critical in behavioral assessment. Collectively, the observations should provide information that

- Pinpoints and quantifies the nature of the behavior problem (including what variables in the environment are contributing to or maintaining the behavior),
- Allows eligibility and placement decisions to be made,
- Illuminates what type of instruction or intervention is needed, and
- Provides baseline information against which progress can be measured once intervention begins.

Interviews are also a useful means of gathering information about a child's behavior. Parents and significant others may be able to offer insight into the nature and history of the child's difficulties. The child may also be an excellent source of information. Of primary interest here is determining the child's "awareness of the problem behaviors and their controlling variables, degree of motivation to change, and skill at behavioral self-control" (Berdine & Meyer, 1987, p. 174).

Assessing Adaptive Behavior.   Other aspects of behavior may be important to assess as well. *Adaptive behavior* is a frequent focus of assessment, and is a required area of assessment when a classification of mental retardation is being considered for a student. Adaptive behavior refers to "the effectiveness or degree with which individuals meet the standards of personal independence and social responsibility expected for age and cultural groups" (Grossman, 1983, p. 1). When assessing a person's adaptive behavior, examiners may investigate his or her strengths and needs in a variety of different skill areas, such as communication, self-care, home living, social skills, community use, self-direction, health and safety, functional academics, leisure, and work. According to the American Association on Mental Retardation (1992), these are the skills with which individuals most often require assistance or some specialized support.

IDEA specifies "deficits in adaptive behavior" as one of the two characteristics necessary for a student to be classified as having mental retardation (the other characteristic being "significantly subaverage general intellectual functioning" [34 CFR Section 300.7(b)(5)]. Measuring a student's adaptive behavior, however, should not be limited to only those students suspected of having mental retardation; this type of assessment has much to offer in the decision-making associated with students with other disabilities as well, particularly in regards to IEP development and instructional and transition planning.

Many commercially developed adaptive behavior instruments exist to help educators evaluate a student's adaptive skills. Using these instruments typically does not require the student to be involved directly; rather, examiners record information collected from a third person who is familiar with the student (e.g., parent, teacher, direct service provider) and who can report what types of adaptive skills the student has mastered and which he or she has not. Unfortunately, there is some concern that many of the available adaptive behavior scales do not meet the technical requirements of good instrumentation [for example, reliability and validity may not reported by the publisher (Berdine & Meyer, 1987; AAMR, 1992)] and that there may be bias inherent in assessing the behavior of children who are culturally or linguistically different from the majority culture. Therefore, care must be taken with the selection of the adaptive behavior scale to be used. It is also a good idea to use other methods to collect information about the student's skills, such as direct observation and interviewing the student. For minority students, it is imperative to develop an understanding of what types of behavior are considered adaptive (and, thus, appropriate) in the minority culture, before making judgments about the particular functioning of a student.

Assessing Emotional and Social Development.   No child lives in a vacuum. His or her relative freedom from internal and external stressors, ability to interact with others comfortably, and ability to respond consistently and positively in the learning environment all are important for the child to benefit maximally from school experiences. In assessing a child's emotional and social adjustment, questions need to be answered related to the child's intrapersonal and interpersonal experience. Assessment of the child's *intrapersonal* world involves knowledge about how the child views him or herself, how the child responds emotionally, how much conflict or anxiety he or she is currently experiencing, the degree to which the individual believes that personal behaviors can actually make a difference in his or her own life, his or her tolerance for frustration, and general activity level. *Interpersonal* characteristics are related to how the individual views the world and other people. Such characteristics are developed in response to the child's experiences within the environment. If the child sees the world as a hostile place and views people as untrustworthy, negative interactive patterns and behaviors may emerge.

The development of the child's intrapersonal experience and interpersonal behaviors is, at least in part, related to the way basic physiological and psychological needs (e.g., to be fed, feel safe, belong, be productive, unique, empowered) are being met. If a child is abused, ignored, or neglected, there are often negative behavioral, cognitive, and emotional outcomes. Problem behaviors such as tantrums, aggression toward others, or withdrawal may result from the child's emotional and social turmoil. However, as was mentioned above, it is important to remember that negative behaviors may arise from vastly different reasons than experiences of abuse or neglect (e.g., biochemical or physiological factors).

There are many instruments available to assess a child's emotional and social functioning. Salvia and Ysseldyke (1991) suggest several ways in which personality variables may be measured. The use of rating scales was discussed above under Behavioral Assessment and is applicable here as well. A second approach, using *projective techniques,* asks students to respond to vague or ambiguous stimuli such as inkblots or pictures, draw pictures, or express themselves through the use of puppets or dolls. The responses are then interpreted by a person trained in such procedures. A third approach is to administer personality inventories or questionnaires that vary in their focus. Some may measure self-concept or learning style, while others are intended to indicate the possible presence of mental illness. These latter instruments are generally lengthy and present the individual taking them with a substantial reading load, both in terms of how much there is to read and in terms of how complex and abstract many of the ideas are. Thus, many such inventories are not suitable for individuals with low literacy. Furthermore, as Berdine and Meyer (1987) remark, "Many of these measures suffer from technical inadequacies and yield esoteric results that are difficult to translate into treatment goals" (p. 144). For this reason, while information gathered through these instruments may help the assessment team understand the student more fully, information collected through approaches such as direct observation and interviews may be more useful and reliable.

Diagnosing a Learning Disability

One of the most crucial parts in the assessment of a learning disability is the ability to take all the information on a child—including test results, observations, background history, school performance, and so forth—and piece it all together into a practical, informative, accurate diagnosis. Determining the proper diagnosis and possible classification category requires the integration of many variables. In reality, learning disabilities will most likely be diagnosed by the local school-based team, since symptoms of LD would first show up in a classroom environment. With other disabilities, some will likely be diagnosed by medical professionals (e.g., visual impairment), while others (e.g., autism) will be diagnosed by a combination of agencies. The categories most likely to appear in the public schools for initial diagnosis, if not previously identified by parents and medical professionals prior to school enrollment, are referred to as higher incidence disabilities (disabilities that affect the largest percentage of children). The list of higher incidence disabilities includes the following.

- Learning disabilities
- Emotional disabilities
- Mental retardation—higher-level functioning other than Down syndrome
- Speech and language disabilities
- Other health impairment—ADHD prediagnosis

These diagnostic categories may first show up when the child enters formal schooling and is presented with educational and social demands that may prove to be too difficult (Pierangelo & Giuliani, 2001). In these cases, the Child Study Team will be directly involved in indentifying, evaluating, diagnosing, and recommending a classification, program, and services. It is not likely, in most of these cases, that outside agencies or medical personnel would need to be involved in this process unless the CST needed further substantiation of the diagnosis. An example might be an audiological exam to rule out hearing impairment, in the case of a child with a suspected language disorder.

The classification categories most likely diagnosed by medical professionals or early medical screening prior to formal schooling are referred to as lower incidence disabilities (disability categories affecting the least number of children). These lower incidence disabilities include the following.

- Autism
- Orthopedic impairment
- Visual impairment
- Hearing impairment
- Other health impairment
- Traumatic brain injury
- Deaf-Blind
- Deafness
- Mental retardation—lower levels of functioning

These categories would most likely be diagnosed by doctors, early screening programs, or outside agencies involved in early education (birth to age 5). A child with one or more of these conditions would most likely come to school at age 5 with a classification from the district's IEP Committee or preschool special education. These conditions, if present prior to formal schooling, would not require the diagnosis by the CST. However, there may be times when some of these conditions might occur after entrance into school at age 5; for example, traumatic brain injury, deafness, and the like. These conditions would be diagnosed by medical professionals, but school professionals would follow the child's progress, determining educational levels, providing the triennial review, and so forth.

The classification categories most likely diagnosed by a combination of professionals and agencies during school could be as follows.

- Visual impairments
- Hearing impairments
- Other health impairments, such as Attention-Deficit Hyperactivity Disorder (ADHD)

There may be times when school professionals are the first to notice a suspected medical problem. In these cases, the school would initially be involved in recommending outside evaluations for diagnosis and recommendations.

To diagnose a suspected learning disability properly, you need to understand the necessary information gathered from the assessment process. This material will be quite comprehensive. The key question becomes, "Now what do I do with all this information?"

You need to know about the many different types of learning disabilities so that you become aware of the direction the assessment results may be heading, just as (for example) medical doctors should know about different types of viruses while they are interpreting test results so they can rule out a specific condition.

The diagnosis of a learning disability can be difficult, especially in the early grades. However, if some practical guidelines are followed, the diagnosis can be more easily substantiated. To accurately diagnose a child with a suspected learning disability, consider the following procedures and criteria.

Exclusion Factors

To properly diagnose a true learning disability, several other possible problems or causes must be ruled out. Among these exclusion factors are the following.

Mental retardation. This can usually be ruled out if the child's IQ is 70 or higher on the Wechsler Scales or any other standardized measure of intelligence.

Primary emotional issues. Sometimes serious emotional issues, which lead to increasing levels of tension, can mirror learning disability symptoms. However, these are learning problems, not learning disabilities, if the primary causes are determined to be emotionally based. In such a case, the patterns of academic difficulties may be inconsistent, indicating the effects of ongoing anxiety and stress.

Problems in acuity. Any mechanical difficulties with the eye and ear must be ruled out, and should be done first, prior to any other evaluation. Screening can be done in school and, if need be, substantiated by a doctor's exam. If acuity is causing the distorted perception, then the child cannot be considered truly learning disabled. A child with LD has intact acuity, and the perceptual distortion occurs in the internal psychological processes involved in the learning process.

Poor teaching. Poor teaching or inadequate schooling may cause severe learning problems that can be misinterpreted as a learning disability.

Cultural confusion. A student from a foreign country may experience learning problems as a result of cultural confusion. If this is found to be the case, it is not a true learning disability. If this student were to be taught and tested in his native language, he would exhibit no learning problems. However, be careful here to determine whether cultural confusion is the only factor. Some students would (or did) have difficulty in their native land as well, which suggests there may be a learning difficulty at play.

Motivational factors. If a child does not possess a serious emotional disturbance, but is simply unmotivated for school, this is not a true learning disability. However, note that lack of motivation can actually be a symptom of a true learning disability.

Observing and Assessing Performance

Ecological Assessment

Ecological assessment involves observing the child in a variety of settings such as the classroom, playground, and other structured and nonstructured settings to determine where the student manifests the greatest difficulties. In the case of a child with a suspected learning disability, you may observe these symptoms.

- Social withdrawal
- Alienation from peers
- Inability to focus in unstructured settings
- "Class clown" type behaviors as a means of being removed from academically stressful settings

You should review all the symptoms that were addressed in Chapter 3 before doing this observation.

Dynamic Assessment

Dynamic assessment is concerned with learning what a student is able to do when provided support in the form of prompts, cues, or physical supports, some of which naturally exist in the environment. For instance, in the case of a child with a suspected learning disability you may observe some of the following behaviors: gaps in thinking, difficulty grasping concepts and directions, difficulty with generalizations despite repeated modeling of a task, difficulty manipulating objects, and significant strengths in one modality over another (e.g., auditory over visual).

Curriculum-Based Assessment (CBA) and Curriculum-Based Measurement (CBM)

In the case of a child with a suspected learning disability, the teacher may use curriculum-based assessment or curriculum-based measurement, as previously discussed in Chapter 5, to find that the child is unable to fully comprehend information read from a textbook within the curriculum or unable to decode or comprehend information from class texts as fast as other children in the classroom. This difficulty may result from poor memory, slow processing, or inadequate reading skills.

Task Analysis

Task analysis, from an educational standpoint, involves breaking down a learning task into the skills required so a student can better understand the assigned task. Task analysis is especially useful when you are teaching students with LD and special needs. However, task analysis also is useful in determining a possible learning disability in children who have impaired learning styles. A task analysis should be done with any child with a suspected disability, to see what specific area may be impaired. A task analysis will assist you in locating and possibly pinpointing the area in the child's learning style that may need attention or that reflects a problem.

Learning Style Assessment

In a learning style assessment you will be looking for any indications in the child's academic, social, perceptual, intellectual, or behavioral styles that might offer some clues to how the child learns best, despite a possible learning disability. Some of the common elements included here would be the way in which material is typically presented (visual, auditory, tactile) in the classroom, the environmental conditions of the classroom (temperature, noise level, brightness), the child's personality characteristics, the expectations for success that the child and others hold, the response the child receives while engaging in the learning process (e.g., praise or criticism), and the type of thinking the child generally utilizes in solving problems (e.g., trial and error, analyzing). Identifying the factors that positively impact the child's learning may help you develop effective intervention strategies.

Other Diagnostic Symptoms

Other diagnostic symptoms may be the first indication of a possible learning disability and, if exhibited, should be investigated as soon as possible. These symptoms include, but are not limited to, delays, disorders, or discrepancies in listening and speaking; difficulties with reading, writing, and spelling; difficulty in performing arithmetic functions or in comprehending basic concepts; difficulty organizing and integrating thoughts, difficulty in organizing all facets of learning, a short attention span, poor letter or word memory, an inability to distinguish between letters or between sounds; erratic performance that fluctuates from day to day; poor gross- or fine-motor development; difficulty telling time; trouble with spatial relationships; difficulty developing right or left dominance; difficulty making friends; difficulty adjusting to change; and inappropriate responses to questions or situations.

Interviews

Clinical Interview

The clinical interview involves a series of discussions with the child to assess where the ultimate problems may lie. When interviewing the child with a suspected disability, you may want to look and listen for confusion over questions, poor use of vocabulary, problems expressing ideas and thoughts, awkward gait, poor memory, short attention span, lack of focus, poor fine-motor skills, and a history of academic difficulties.

Parent Interview

A parent interview requires a personal meeting with the parents to determine essential background history that may be essential for appropriate diagnosis. In the case of a child with a suspected learning disability, you may want to listen during this type of interview for behaviors such as has difficulties dressing, avoids homework, is disorganized, has a short attention span, forgets easily, forgets to bring home books, gets stomachaches in the morning before school, gets frequent headaches, has few friends, is unwilling to try new things, and gives up easily.

Teacher Interview

Teacher interviews should be held with past and current teachers of the child. This may require several meetings in order to ascertain the child's basic intellectual, social, and academic performance over time. In the case of a child with a potential learning disability, the interviewer should be aware of certain LD symptom clusters that may appear in the classroom. Some examples include poor memory, gross-motor coordination difficulties, lack of focus, short attention span, procrastination, failure to hand in written work or homework, lack of confidence, self-derogatory statements such as *I'm so stupid,* consistently low academic performance in certain subjects over time, social difficulties, lack of motivation for schoolwork, poor handwriting, and poor fine-motor skills.

Testing

Intelligence Testing

In the case of a child with a suspected learning disability, the psychologist will administer an individual intelligence test to look for an average to above-average potential intellectual level. Many children are commonly misdiagnosed as having a learning disability when they may actually be slow learners, children with emotional issues, or underachievers not performing for reasons other than a learning disability.

Achievement Testing

Children with learning disabilities usually exhibit a severe discrepancy between potential ability (as measured on an individual IQ test) and academic achievement. This is a debatable criterion because it is possible that a child functioning on grade level, according to standardized achievement tests, may actually have a severe discrepancy if one takes into account ability levels. For instance, consider these 5th grade students.

- Susan—Grade 5—IQ 125: With this IQ score, one would expect Susan's potential achievement levels to be above grade level, perhaps by one to two years. Therefore, scores within the seventh-grade range (80th to 90th percentiles) would be more in line with her ability levels, which, based on her IQ score, are at around the 95th percentile. If Susan were to score on the second-grade level in achievement areas (around the 10th percentile), then this would represent an 85th percentile difference between ability and achievement potential, a definite criterion for a possible learning disability.

- Devin—Grade 5—IQ 100: With this IQ score (50th percentile, one should expect Devin to be functioning right on grade level, according to his ability potential. This means that, because he is in the fifth grade, scores in that area would be right where we expect. If one uses percentile comparisons, then achievement scores around the 50th percentile would indicate no significant discrepancy between ability and achievement.

- Shamika—Grade 5—IQ 130: With this IQ score, one would expect Shamica's potential achievement levels to be above grade level, perhaps by one to two years. Therefore, scores within the seventh-grade range (80th to 90th percentiles) would be more in line with her ability levels, which, based on her IQ score, are at the 98th percentile. If Shamika were to score on the fifth-grade level in achievement areas (around the 50th percentile), then this would represent a 40% difference between ability and achievement potential, a definite criterion for a possible learning disability. However, this pattern indicating a discrepancy may not be identified in the early grades because the child is "keeping up with the class." The discrepancy between ability and performance is more likely to begin to show in later grades, as work becomes more difficult.

The Wechsler Individual Achievement Test–2 and the Peabody Individual Achievement Test–R are examples of tests that are used to measure overall academic achievement.

Criterion-Referenced Tests and Authentic Assessment

Performance assessments can take many forms. Ascher (1990), for example, described station activities as one way to employ performance assessment. In station activities, students proceed through a series of discrete tasks, either individually or in teams, in a given amount of time. Ascher gave the example of a science laboratory in which a variety of tasks, such as inferring the characteristics of objects sealed in boxes, measuring electrical currents, and sorting seeds are set in various places around the lab. Students may participate in individual or group projects, which serve as comprehensive demonstrations of skills or knowledge. Interviews or oral presentations allow students to verbalize their knowledge (Rudner, 1991). In the case of a child with a suspected learning disability, you may see an inability to focus on task, or that the child is not able to multitask, appears confused, becomes easily frustrated, cannot keep up with peers, is unable to complete the task, and so on.

More traditional formats can also serve as performance assessments. For example, Rudner (1991) required students to produce their own answers rather than select from an array of possible answers. Assessment questions can vary from filling in a blank or writing a short answer, to drawing a graph or diagram, or writing all the steps of a geometry proof. Essays have long been used by teachers so that students employ critical thinking, analysis, and synthesis. Experiments test how well a student understands scientific concepts and can carry out scientific processes. In these types of assessment, you may notice the child with a suspected learning disability is unable to complete the written assignment, is sloppy or makes frequent misspellings in the assignment, avoids completion of the task, is unable to use a pencil and ruler simultaneously (indicating poor hand–eye coordination), and is unable to write a coherent response.

Perceptual Testing

One of the underlying assumptions with a true learning disability is that it is the result of a subtle neurological impairment. This impairment, if present, affects the child's ability to process information in a timely manner, thereby interfering with performance. Perceptual testing needs to be administered to determine if, and where, such processing difficulties occur.

In the case of a learning disability, the examiner may look for deficits in memory, perception, expression, organization, or reception of information. Further, such deficits may also affect the child's ability to process information if it is received through certain weak channels, such as auditory or visual. These factors, when present, might explain the lack of performance in certain academic areas.

Psychological Tests/Scales

Many children with learning disabilities have some form of anxiety or low self-esteem because of their difficulties in the classroom. By using psychological tests, the psychologist can determine if a child shows signs of emotional issues such as depression, anxiety, school phobia, and other types of disorders that are being caused by the effects of a learning disability. However, it will also be the job of the psychologist to determine that emotional factors are not the primary cause of the child's difficulties in learning. To diagnose a learning disability, emotional factors as a primary cause must be ruled out.

Reviewing Documents

Review of Cumulative Reports and Records

Very important clues to the diagnosis of a learning disability can be found in the child's permanent record folder. Therefore, a complete review of report cards, attendance records, standardized tests, and so forth will be necessary to determine possible patterns of behavior and performance. In the case of the child with a potential learning disability, a review of cumulative records may reveal consistently low group achievement scores in certain subjects over a period of years. Past teacher comments may show a pattern similar to what the child's current teacher reports. The report cards may reveal a historical pattern of academic difficulties, frequent absences (which may occur when the child feels frustrated and overwhelmed by the work), and a discrepancy between ability and class performance.

Portfolio Review

In the case of a child with a suspected learning disability, a portfolio assessment may reveal that the child is missing homework, shows incomplete work, and has consistent academic problems in one or more areas. There may be work that has been crumpled in frustration or embarrassment, and evidence of failure to complete group assignments. Select work samples from the areas where the student is experiencing difficulty and systematically examine them. Try to identify such elements as how the student was directed to do the activity (i.e., orally or in writing), how long it took the student to complete the activity, the pattern of errors (e.g., reversals when writing, etc.), and the pattern of correct answers. Analyzing the student's work in this way can yield valuable insight into the nature of her difficulties and suggest possible solutions.

Look for Historical Patterns

A learning disability does not usually just appear out of nowhere for the first time in the later grades, unless it has been undiagnosed due to inadequate screening. If the child has performed up to ability without any historical pattern of achievement deficit areas, and then has problems in learning or performance, check out other possibilities as the cause. In the case of a child with a learning disability, there is greater likelihood that consistent patterns of deficits in specific areas would have been present over time.

Behavioral Manifestations

Students who have LD may exhibit a wide range of behavioral manifestations, including inattention, uneven and unpredictable test performance, perceptual impairments, motor disorders, and behaviors such as impulsiveness, low tolerance for frustration, and problems in handling daily social interactions and situations. Evidence for these problems should be in the paperwork comprising the cumulative reports and records.

Conclusion

Assessment is a complex process that needs to be conducted by a multidisciplinary team of trained professionals. It involves both formal and informal methods of collecting information about the student. Although the team may choose to administer a series of tests to the student, by law assessment must involve much more than standardized tests. Interviews of all key participants in the student's education, and observations of student behaviors in the classroom or in other sites, should be included as well. To develop a comprehensive picture of the student and to develop practical intervention strategies to address that student's special needs, the team must ask questions and use assessment techniques that will help them determine the factors that are facilitating—and interfering with—the child's learning. Ecological assessment, dynamic assessment, curriculum-based assessment, learning styles inventories, and other less traditional approaches may be particularly helpful in answering such questions.

It is also important that assessment be an ongoing process. The process begins even before the student is referred for formal evaluation; a teacher or parent may have noticed that some aspect of the student's performance or behavior is below expectations and, so, requests an official assessment. After eligibility has been established and the IEP has been developed for the student, assessment should continue, through teacher-made tests, through ongoing behavioral assessment, or through incorporating curriculum-based assessment or task analysis into the classroom. This allows teachers and parents to monitor the student's progress toward the goals and objectives stated in his or her IEP. Thus, assessment should not end when the eligibility decision is made or the IEP is developed; it has great value to contribute to the daily, weekly, and monthly instructional decision making that accompanies the provision of special education and related services.

A thorough and comprehensive assessment of a child can greatly enhance his or her educational experience. The assessment process has many steps and needs to be appropriately done. Furthermore, no one individual makes all of the decisions for a child's classification; it is done by a multidisciplinary team. As a future special educator, it is your professional responsibility to understand the laws, steps, and various assessment measures and procedures used in the special education process so that you can have a significant and positive impact on all the students whose lives you touch.

7 Eligibility Procedures and IEP Development

The IEP Committee

Once the evaluation process is completed by the MDT, the IEP Committee will arrange to meet to discuss the results of the evaluations and the school's recommendations. Normally, the individuals who have completed each evaluation discuss the results of the evaluations with the parents prior to the IEP Committee meeting. However, this is an informal process, and recommendations for classification and placement usually are not discussed because that is the responsibility of the IEP Committee. Formally, parents will receive a notice indicating the time and date of an IEP Committee meeting.

According to IDEA 2004, every public school district is required to have an IEP Committee, which, as previously mentioned, may be referred to as the Eligibility Committee, Committee on Special Education, and so forth. If the population of students with special needs reaches a certain level, then more than one IEP Committee may be formed. IEP Committees are responsible for the identification of children with disabilities within the district and recommending appropriate education at public expense for students identified as having disabilities.

Members of the IEP Committee

The IEP Committee is usually made up of members mandated by IDEA 2004 and assigned members whom the board of education deems necessary. Most states require that certain professionals and individuals be core members. Consistent with IDEA 2004, these members must include the following persons.

- The parents of a child with a disability;
- Not less than one regular education teacher (if the child is, or may be, participating in the regular education environment);
- Not less than one special education teacher, or when appropriate, not less than one special education provider;

- A representative of the local educational agency (LEA) who is qualified to provide, or supervise the provision of, specially designed instruction to meet the unique needs of children with disabilities; is knowledgeable about the general education curriculum; and is knowledgeable about the availability of resources of the LEA;
- An individual who can interpret the instructional implications of evaluation results, who may be a member of the team described above;
- Other individuals, at the discretion of the parent or the agency, who have knowledge or special expertise regarding the child, including related services personnel as appropriate; and
- Whenever appropriate, the child with a disability.

Responsibilities of the IEP Committee

The IEP Committee is charged with many important responsibilities both before and after a child is classified in special education.

During the Initial Eligibility Meeting.   Some of the responsibilities of IEP Committee are as follows:

- Following appropriate procedures and taking appropriate action for a child referred as having a suspected disability
- Determining the suitable classification for a child with a suspected disability
- Reviewing and evaluating all relevant information that may appear on each student with a disability
- Determining the least restrictive environment for any child having been classified as having a disability
- Finalizing the child's IEP

After the Child Receives a Classification in Special Education

- Reviewing, at least annually, the status of the child. This annual review will be discussed later in this chapter.
- Evaluating the adequacy of programs, services, and facilities for the child.
- Maintaining ongoing communication in writing to parents in regard to planning, modifying, changing, reviewing, placing, or evaluating the program, classification, or educational plan of the child.
- Advising the board of education as to the status and recommendations of the child.
- Making sure that every three years, the child is retested with a full educational and psychological battery. This triennial review will be discussed later in this chapter.

Most IEP Committees try to remain as informal as possible to reduce the anxiety of the situation. This is a crucial issue, because a parent may enter a room with numerous professionals and feel overwhelmed or intimidated.

The parent member usually serves as a liaison and advocate for the parent(s), establishing contact before the meeting to reduce anxiety and alleviate any concerns that the parent(s) may have. School personnel should also be in contact with the parent(s) prior to the meeting to go over the process, their rights, and what may take place at the meeting. At no time should anyone in contact with the parent(s) prior to the meeting give them false hope, make promises, or second-guess the IEP Committee.

What needs to be communicated are procedural issues and options, and the awareness that it is the IEP Committee that will make the recommendation, not one individual. Further, the parent(s) must be made aware of their rights, and you should make sure they understand their right to due process if they do not agree with the IEP Committee's recommendations. Making sure parents understand their rights before the meeting may reduce the possibility of conflict.

IDEA 2004 and IEP Committee Meetings—What to Know

The Reauthorized IDEA 2004 made clear that parents have a right to participate in IEP Committee meetings with respect to the identification, evaluation, educational placement, and the provision of FAPE (Free and Appropriate Public Education) for their child. IDEA 2004 regulations provide that a meeting does not include informal or unscheduled conversations involving school district personnel and conversations on issues such as teaching methodology, lesson plans, or coordination of service provision if those issues are not addressed in the child's IEP. IDEA 2004 regulations also provide that if neither parent can participate in a meeting in which a decision is to be made relating to the educational placement of their child, the school district must use other methods to ensure their participation, including individual conference calls or video conferencing.

The IEP Committee may make a placement decision without the parent's participation in the decision, but in such an instance the school district must have a record of its attempt to ensure the parent's involvement. This includes the following items.

- Detailed records of telephone calls made or attempted and the results of those calls
- Copies of correspondence sent to the parents and any responses received
- Detailed records of visits made to the parents' home or place of employment and the results of those visits.

IDEA 2004 regulations require that school districts inform parents of the purpose of an IEP meeting, and explain who will be in attendance, in addition to the time and location of the meeting.

IDEA 2004 regulations indicate that it may be appropriate for a school district to encourage parents to bring supportive individuals to the IEP meeting. The school district may request advance notification of any such persons who will attend.

Developing the Information Packet for the IEP Committee

Once the MDT has considered all the information and completed the evaluations, intakes, assessments, and so on, team members need to prepare the information packet that the district's IEP Committee will use when reviewing the case for possible classification and special education programs and services. This information will be viewed by all the members of the IEP Committee, along with the parents and other designated individuals, such as an advocate or lawyer. The IEP Committee packet is a crucial part of the special education process because most of the committee members will not be familiar with the child. The information gathered and forwarded will be used to determine the child's educational future. Therefore, it is imperative that the MDT present the most thorough and practical information to the committee.

To facilitate the process of preparing the required documentation for presentation, the team usually designates a case manager, the specific individual whose responsibility it will be to gather, organize, and forward the packet to the IEP Committee. The case manager can be anyone, but in many cases it will be either the special education teacher or the psychologist. All districts have their own specific forms and guidelines for presentation to the committee. However, in most of these cases the information presented, regardless of the forms, will be somewhat the same.

This section of the chapter presents an example of what the case manager may need to forward to the IEP Committee. It is a typical list of materials included in the eligibility packet that might be required by the committee when reviewing a student for classification. These materials may vary from district to district and from state to state.

Required Forms

Initial referral to the MDT from school staff. The Child Study Team fills out this form when the team suspects that the child being reviewed may have an educational disability. This type of referral occurs when a child is being assessed for special education by the MDT for the very first time and usually involves children previously in general education who have had no prior services.

Initial referral to MDT from parent/guardian. This form is filled out if the parent makes the initial referral for assessment to the MDT for a suspected disability, which is part of the parent's due process rights.

Assessment plan and parent consent. This plan and form must be signed and dated by a parent prior to evaluation and is part of the parent's due process rights.

Social history form. This form is the result of a recent parent intake and provides the most recent pertinent background information on the child.

Medical report form. This is usually filled out by the teacher or school nurse and includes the latest medical information on the child (within the last year) that may be related to the child's learning problems.

Classroom observation form. This form is the result of an on-site visit observation by some member of the Child Study Team.

Evaluations (Initial Referral)

Psychological. A full psychological evaluation includes all identifying data, reason for referral, background and developmental history, prior testing results, observations, tests administered, test results (including a breakdown of scaled scores), conclusions, and recommendations. This required evaluation must be conducted within one year of the IEP Committee meeting. It may also be helpful to include any prior evaluations done over the years.

Educational. An educational evaluation includes identifying data, reason for referral, academic history, prior testing results, observations, tests administered, test results, conclusions, and recommendations. This required report should identify achievement strengths and weaknesses.

Speech/language. A speech/language evaluation including identifying data, reason for referral, observations, tests administered, test results, conclusions, and recommendations should be included if applicable. A description of the severity of the language deficit should also be included and, if possible, the prognosis.

Vocational (secondary level only). A copy of the child's Differential Aptitude Test results or other measures of vocational aptitude should be included, if applicable.

Other (e.g., occupational therapist, physical therapist, ESL, reading). From time to time, parents or the school will have a variety of reports from outside agencies, such as medical, neurological, psychiatric, occupational therapy screening, physical therapy screening, psychological, audiological, visual training, and so forth. These reports should be included only when they are relevant to the possible disability. If outside reports are to be used in place of the district's own evaluations, they should be fairly recent, within the past six months to one year.

Guidance and School Materials (Initial Referral)

Child's schedule. This would be a copy of the student's daily school schedule.

Transcript of past grades. All the child's report card grades should be attached as far back as possible, or a report indicating the patterns of grades throughout the child's school career should be included.

Latest report card. The most current report card should be included.

Teachers' reports. Teacher reports in behavioral terms should be included from all the child's teachers.

Standardized achievement test scores. Many schools require standardized achievement testing in certain grades. Any and all scores should be provided, to document historical patterns or levels of ability.

Discipline information. Any referrals to the principal, dean, and so on should be included, as well as descriptions of incidents and disposition.

CST-related documents (i.e., minutes). This provides the IEP Committee with pertinent information regarding prior intervention strategies and procedures the Child Study Team followed prior to the referral.

Attendance records. Attendance patterns and records should be provided, especially if poor attendance is a recurring issue and a serious symptom.

Other Materials

Some schools also may include the following materials in a draft form. This draft becomes a working model at the IEP Committee meeting between the Committee and the parent, and the final version is mailed to the parent after the meeting. These may include the following.

SPAM (Social, Physical, Academic, Management Needs). In some states and school districts, a working draft copy of the child's needs should be included in the eligibility packet. These needs will provide the IEP Committee with an idea of the environmental, educational, social, and physical requirements under which the child may learn best.

Draft IEP, Including Goals and Objectives. In some states and school districts, a working draft copy of the IEP is prepared prior to the Eligibility meeting. This is a basic working draft of the IEP, not the final draft, because no IEP can be finalized without parental involvement.

Testing Modifications Worksheet. This worksheet outlines the suggested test and classroom modifications being suggested and the supporting data for such recommendations. As will be discussed, testing modifications are a component of the child's IEP. The modifications must be consistent with the criteria established. The worksheet may be completed by a member of the MDT or school staff to be processed as a draft recommendation for discussion at the IEP Committee meeting. Depending on the state, there are usually four circumstances in which students with disabilities may be eligible to receive test modifications.

1. Students with disabilities whose individualized education program includes test modifications
2. Students who are "declassified" by the IEP Committee as special education recipients but are determined to still need test modifications
3. Students with disabilities whose Section 504 Accommodation Plan includes test modifications
4. Students who acquire disabilities shortly before test administration

In making its decision regarding the need for test modifications, the IEP Committee reviews all available information regarding the student's individual needs. Such information might include recent evaluations, previous school records and IEPs, classroom observations, and the student's experience on previous tests. Information and suggestions from the student's teachers, related service providers, and parents should also be sought. Testing modifications must be limited to specific needs of the student.

If such a determination is made by the IEP Committee and documented in the recommendation for declassification, the test modification(s) must continue to be consistently provided to the student for the balance of his or her public school education. The continuation of test modifications upon declassification, however, is not automatic. During subsequent school years, if it is felt that test modifications are no longer appropriate, the school staff is to meet with the student's parent to review and document their revision or discontinuation.

The school principal may modify testing procedures for general education students who experience temporary (e.g., broken arm) or long-term (e.g., paraplegic) disabilities shortly before the administration of state exams. In such cases when sufficient time is not available for the development of an IEP or 504 plan, principals may authorize testing modifications. However, if the student is expected to continue to need test modifications, the principal should make the appropriate referral for the development of an IEP or 504 plan.

Extended School Year Worksheet.   This worksheet provides the IEP Committee with the information and criteria necessary to make a recommendation for extended school services during the summer months. At annual review meetings, parents of students with disabilities may ask for special education services during the summer (extended school year).

Extended School Year Criteria.   Depending on the state, the law may indicate that extended school year service be considered by the IEP Committee when a student experiences substantial regression. Substantial regression means a student's inability to maintain developmental levels due to a loss of skill or knowledge during the months of July and August of such severity as to require an inordinate period of review at the beginning of the school year to reestablish and maintain IEP goals and objectives mastered at the end of the previous school year. For example, a teacher would project November 1 of the upcoming school year as the target date for the student to reacquire skills demonstrated at the end of the previous school year (a typical period of review or reteaching is up to 40 school days). Classroom teachers and/or service providers are expected to provide documentation (qualitative and/or quantitative) as to the evidence of regression in the discussion at the IEP Committee meeting.

An analysis of students' substantial regression, if any, may be monitored during school vacation periods (winter, spring, summer). Note the above definition includes not only regression but also an inordinate period of time to reestablish and maintain IEP goals/objectives. Extended school year services are not provided in order for students to improve their skills. Such instruction is a parent responsibility. Extended year services may differ from services provided during the school year. The IEP Committee will determine the type, amount, and duration of services to be provided. Extended school year services may be provided at a different location than provided during the school year.

Adaptive Physical Education Worksheet.   If a child's disability prevents him or her from participating in the general education physical education program, then the district must provide adaptive alternatives that capitalize on the student's abilities. This worksheet outlines the criteria exhibited by the child for possible adaptive physical education. The behaviors, supporting reports, and data are included for the IEP Committee in order to make a recommendation. The physical education teacher in consultation with other IEP Committee staff members usually completes this. This worksheet then becomes a draft recommendation for discussion at the IEP Committee.

Other Information.   This includes any other information not noted in the categories discussed above.

In conclusion, the above forms and information will represent a picture of the child with a disability including strengths, weaknesses, recommendations, and any other information that will assist the IEP Committee in making the most educationally sound decision.

How Recommendations for Classification Are Made by the IEP Committee

In developing recommendations, all the members of the IEP Committee who are present will discuss the evaluations presented and any other pertinent information on the child. The first issue decided will be whether the child has an educational disability that adversely affects his or her educational performance. The EC will review the IEP Committee packet prepared by the school and ask any sitting member pertinent questions necessary to clarify the information. If in fact it is found that this is the case, the child will be classified according to the categories outlined in IDEA 2004.

The concept of least restrictive education (LRE) applies to the placement of students with disabilities in the most advantageous educational placement suitable for their needs. Contrary to the belief of many teachers and parents, LRE does not mean every student with a disability be placed in a regular classroom.

Specific Placement (LRE) Considerations According to IDEA 2004

A placement is the location where the special educational program will be provided. According to IDEA 2004, the requirements involving least restrictive environment are as follows.

- In selecting the LRE for a student with a disability, school districts must consider any potential harmful effect on the child or on the quality of services that the child needs.

- School districts may not remove a student with a disability from education in age-appropriate regular classrooms solely because of needed modifications in the general curriculum.
- LRE requirements apply to both nonacademic and extracurricular activities, including meals and recess periods, athletics, transportation, health services, recreational activities, special interest groups or school-sponsored clubs, and referral to agencies that provide assistance to individuals with disabilities and employment of students, including both employment by the public agency and assistance in making outside employment available.

IDEA 2004 regulations also indicate the two following points.

- The determination of an appropriate placement for a child whose behavior is interfering with the education of others requires careful consideration of whether the child can appropriately function in the regular classroom if provided appropriate behavioral supports, strategies, and interventions.
- If a student's behavior in the regular classroom, even with the provision of appropriate behavioral supports, strategies, and interventions, would significantly impair the learning of others, that placement would not meet her needs and would not be appropriate for that child.

The placement of students with disabilities is the responsibility of the IEP Committee with the input of staff and parents and final consent by the parents. This committee must analyze all the available information and determine the best starting placement for the child that will ensure success and provide the child with the highest level of stimulation and experience for his or her specific disability and profile of strengths and weaknesses.

To accomplish this task, the IEP Committee has a variety of placements from which to choose, which range in levels of restriction, including class size, student–teacher ratio, length of program, and the degree to which the child will be included in the general education population. In the normal course of events, it is hoped that children should be placed in a more restrictive environment only if it is to their educational advantage. However, they should be moved to a less restrictive setting as soon as they are capable of being educated in that environment. The following placements follow a path from least restrictive to most restrictive (Gargiulio, 2004; Pierangelo & Giuliani, 2002; see also Box 7.1).

General Education Classroom.   General education class placement is the least restrictive placement for all children. This placement alone, without some type of special education supportive services, is not suitable for a child with a disability and is usually considered unsuitable by the IEP Committee.

Inclusion Classroom.   There are various models of inclusion classrooms that are available as options in special education. Use of these models can vary from state to state, and even district to district. In many instances, inclusion classroom place-

BOX 7.1

Continuum of Services

REGULAR CLASSES FULL-TIME

The IEP is implemented in the regular educational environment with consultation and monitoring services by a special education teacher. This may include some resource room instruction or related service outside the classroom for less than 21% of a child's full school day.

SPECIAL CLASSES PART-TIME

The IEP is implemented in an environment other than the regular classroom for 21 to 60% of the school day. It must also address supplementary aids and services, modifications, supports and related services delivered in the regular classroom.

SPECIAL CLASSES FULL-TIME

The IEP is implemented in a special class environment full-time for more than 60% of a child's full school day. The team must consider the child's opportunities for *inclusion* in nonacademic and extracurricular services offered to nondisabled children.

SPECIAL SCHOOLS

Implementation of the IEP requires placement in a special day school program at a location other than the regular school setting.

HOME INSTRUCTION

The IEP specifies that the needs of the child require that instruction be provided in the home environment. The special education and related services are supervised and delivered by appropriately qualified personnel. Frequency and duration of services are determined by the IEP team on an individual basis.

INSTRUCTION IN HOSPITALS

Implementation of the IEP requires instruction in a hospital setting. The frequency and duration of services are determined by the team based on the individual needs of the child, and are delivered by appropriately qualified personnel.

INSTRUCTION IN OTHER SETTINGS

The IEP requires implementation in nontraditional and alternative settings such as an alternative education program.

INSTRUCTION IN INSTITUTIONS OR RESIDENTIAL FACILITY

The IEP requires implementation in a residential institution or other residential care facility.

ment involves including the child in a general education classroom assisted by the presence of a second teacher who is certified in special education.

General Education Class Placement with Consulting Teacher Assistance.   A consultant teacher model is used when supportive special education services are required but the IEP Committee feels that the child will be better served while remaining in the classroom rather than being pulled out for services. Because the child remains within the class, even though he or she is receiving services, this placement is considered the next LRE setting.

General Education Class Placement with Some Supportive Services.   Regular class placement with supportive services may be used for students with mild disabilities who require supportive services but can remain in the regular class for the majority of the day. The services that may be applied to this level include adaptive physical education, speech and language therapy, in-school individual or group counseling, physical therapy, and occupational therapy.

General Education Class Placement with Itinerant Specialist Assistance.   Itinerant services are services subcontracted by the district and provided by outside agencies. These services are usually provided for students when the disability is such that the district wishes to maintain the child in the district, but there is not a sufficient number of students with that disability to warrant hiring a teacher. An example of this may be a hard-of-hearing child who can maintain a regular class placement as long as supportive itinerant services by a teacher specializing in hearing impairments are provided.

General Education Class Placement with Resource Room Assistance.   A resource room program is usually provided for students who need supportive services but can successfully remain within the regular classroom for the majority of the day. This type of program is a "pullout" program, and the services are usually provided in a separate room. The student–teacher ratio with this type of service is usually 5:1, and the amount of time spent within the resource room cannot exceed 50% of the child's day.

General Education Class Placement with Part Time in Regular Class.   Part-time placement is for students who need a more restrictive setting for learning, behavioral, or intellectual reasons; cannot be successful in a full-time regular class or with a pullout supportive service; but can be successfully included in general education classroom (part-time participation in a general education classroom setting) for a part of the school day.

General Education Full-Time Special Class in a General Education School.   A full-time special class in a regular school placement is viewed as the LRE setting for students whose disability does not permit successful participation in any type of regular class setting, even for part of the day. The students in a special class usually require a very structured, closely monitored program on a daily basis but not so restrictive as to warrant an out-of-district placement. These students can handle the rules and structure of a regular school building but not the freedom or style of a less restrictive setting within the school.

Special Day School Outside the School District.   A special day school is a type of restrictive educational setting that is a desirable placement for students whose disability is so severe that they may require a more therapeutic environment and closer monitoring by specially trained special education teachers or staff members. The child is transported by district expense to the placement, and many state policies try to limit travel time on the bus to no more than one hour.

These types of programs may have student–teacher–aide ratios of 6:1:1, 6:1:2, 9:1:1, 9:1:2, 12:1:1, or 15:1:1, depending upon the severity of the child's disability. The more severe the disability, the lower the number of student–teacher ratio. These programs can run 10 or 12 months, again depending upon the severity of the disability and the individual needs of the child.

Residential School.   Residential school placements are considered the next most restrictive placement. Not only does the student with a disability receive his education within this setting but also usually resides there for the school term. The nature and length of home visits depend on several factors that are usually determined by the residential school staff after evaluation and observation. For some students, home visits may not take place at all, whereas others may go home every weekend. Some students are placed in residential placements by the court. In this case, the child's local school district is only responsible to provide the costs of the educational portion, including related services if needed.

Homebound Instruction.   Homebound instruction provides a very restrictive setting that is usually for students who are in the process of transition between programs and have yet to be placed. It should never be used as a long-term placement because of the social restriction and limitations. This option is also used when a child is restricted to his or her house because of an illness, injury, and so on, and this option remains the only realistic educational service until the child recovers. Homebound instruction requires an adult at home when the teacher arrives or can be held at a community center, library, or some other site deemed appropriate by the IEP Committee.

Hospital or Institution.   The most restrictive setting used is a hospital or institution. Although this is the most restrictive setting, it may be the LRE setting for certain students, such as situations of attempted suicide by an adolescent, pervasive clinical depression, or severe or profound retardation. In conclusion, the least restrictive environment is not something that is etched in concrete. It is normally reviewed every year at the annual review, and changes are made in either direction should the situation warrant it.

LRE Placements the IEP Committee May Consider

Once the IEP Committee determines the most suitable LRE, committee members need to determine the facility or program that best fits their decision. The following examples are types of placements that the IEP Committee may consider for the LRE and are listed in order of educational restriction.

Local School District.   The child's home school of the local school district, depending on the severity of the disability, will generally provide the types of services he or she requires. This is preferential for the many reasons previously discussed. Maintaining the child in his or her home school should be the parents' and the district's goal. This, of course, is not always possible. If not, the next step is another school in the district.

Neighboring School District.   Due to the nature of special education programs, not all special education services are offered within every district. The child's local school may arrange for participation in necessary programs and services in a neighboring school district if they cannot be provided within the child's home district.

Cooperative Educational Services.   Cooperative educational service agencies are usually set up by your state to assist local districts with the student population or specific services one or more districts could not provide themselves.

Home/Hospital Settings.   There may be times when a child needs temporary instruction at home or in a hospital setting due to severe illness or special circumstances indicated on the IEP. The key term here is *temporary*. The instruction should approximate what is offered in school within reasonable limits. Home and hospital instruction is highly restrictive; the continuing need for such services should be assessed frequently, and this service should be seen as temporary. State laws may vary on the minimum amount of educational time allotted to children involved in these services. A general guide should be two hours per day of individual instruction for a secondary student and one hour per day for an elementary-grade student.

Private Approved Schools.   School districts may place students in private schools, special act schools (schools set up by the state to provide services for a child with a disability), or residential placements approved by the State Education Department. These private approved schools may be located in or out of state. Students placed in such facilities have such diverse needs that the home school district may not be able to serve them due to the severity of their medical, physical, mental, or emotional needs.

State Operated Schools for the Deaf, Blind, and Severely Emotionally Disturbed.
These state operated schools are examples of educational programs that are available for students with educational needs who require a school with a special focus.

It is the responsibility of the IEP Committee to provide programs based on the least restrictive environment concept. Remember, it is important to provide programs that are near the child's home (some states limit this to one hour on the bus). The child should have involvement with his or her peers without disabilities. Finally, the program must be based on the student's needs.

When considering any of the above placements, everyone works toward providing the best possible placement for the child in the least restrictive environment. However, the school district, on the other hand, needs to provide only an appropriate placement, not the best placement in a program that is appropriate to the child's needs, as close to home as possible.

Appealing the Decision of the IEP Committee

The process of identifying and finding an appropriate educational placement for a child with a disability should be a joint process between the district and the family. Assuming that the parents agree with the IEP Committee's decisions, the parents will sign off on the IEP, and the child's program will begin as of the start date mandated in the IEP. When both the parents and the IEP Committee work in the best interests of the child, the process can be very positive and rewarding. However, there can be times when the family and the district disagree. When this occurs, the parents or the school has the right to due process. This procedure protects the rights of both the school and the family and allows for another avenue for resolution.

An impartial hearing officer may be requested to intervene when there is a difference of opinion. This is an independent individual assigned by the district's board of education or commissioner of education to hear an appeal and render a decision. Impartial hearing officers can in no way be connected to the school district, may have to be certified (depending upon state regulations), are trained, and usually must update their skills.

Although due process rights of parents to continue this appeal to the State Department of Education exist, if they disagree with the impartial hearing officer's decision, it is hoped that through a thorough understanding of the needs of the parent and the child, conflict resolution, and a positive working relationship, a solution that is acceptable to both sides can be established at the local level.

Other Roles of the IEP Committee

Special Meetings.   Sometimes, the parents or IEP Committee will call a special meeting. This type of review can occur for several reasons and is always held for a child who has been previously classified. Some of the reasons for such a meeting are listed below.

- Change in a child's IEP
- Change in a child's program
- Addition or deletion of a modification
- Parental request for an IEP Committee meeting
- Disciplinary concerns
- New student to district previously identified as disabled
- Referral from the building administrator

The Annual Review.   Each year the IEP Committee is required to review the existing program of a child with a disability. Annual review meetings are required for all students receiving special instruction or related services. The required IEP Committee participants of an annual review meeting may include the IEP Committee chairperson, psychologist, special education teacher, general education teacher (if the student is in general education or will receive general education services), parent of child, parent member, and student (if over 16 years of age). During this process, the IEP Committee will make recommendations, based on a review of the records, that will continue, change, revise, or end the child's special education program. Based on these findings, the IEP Committee will make adjustments to the IEP and recommendations to the board of education.

The annual review occurs within a year of initial placement and yearly thereafter. The date of the annual review should be part of the child's IEP. A parent, the child's teacher, or a school administrator may request an IEP Committee review at any time to determine if a change in placement is needed. If this occurs, the next review must be conducted within one year.

The parents are notified of the date, time, location, and individuals expected to attend their child's meeting. They will also be given a statement about their right to bring other people to the meeting. Parents have the same rights as at the initial IEP Committee meeting. They will also be notified that if they cannot attend the meeting, they will have the opportunity to participate in other ways such as through telephone calls or written reports of the annual review meeting. If necessary, they will be able to have an interpreter provided at no cost. The parents' notice of their child's annual review will include their right to have information about the planned review. They may at any time inspect their child's school files, records, and reports and make copies at a reasonable cost. If medication or a physical condition is part of the child's disability, the parent may request that a physician attend the meeting. The parent may request an independent evaluation, an impartial hearing, or appeal the decision from the impartial hearing to the State Review Office of the State Education Department.

In some cases, the parent may be entitled to receive free or low-cost legal services and a list of where those services can be obtained. Parents also are entitled to have the child stay in the current educational placement during formal due process proceedings, unless both parties agree otherwise.

After the annual review, the parents will receive another notice regarding the recommendation that has been made to the board of education. A copy of their child's IEP will be sent to them indicating that their child has been recommended to continue to receive special education. The notice will also explain all factors used to make the recommendation. Again, the notice will describe the parents' due process rights.

Suggestions for the Special Educator's Participation in the Annual Review.
When you attend an annual review meeting as a special educator, there are some key points that you should follow. These include the following.

- Suggest ways to meet the child's proposed goals and objectives as specified in the IEP.
- Discuss changes or additions for the child's upcoming program and services. Talk about what worked and what needs adjustment, from your point of view.
- Present the areas in which the child showed success and significant progress.
- Discuss high school diploma and credential options, if applicable.

- Discuss need for a referral to an adult service provider—that is, state vocational rehabilitation coordinator—for services the child may need as an adult, if applicable.
- Review problems that the child has experienced or encountered throughout the year with the IEP Committee and parent.
- When the child is 13, you should begin to consider plans for occupational education and transition services and become very familiar with the transitional process and all the factors involved.

The Triennial Review.   A child in special education will have a triennial review (evaluation) that occurs every three years to provide current assessment information to help determine his or her continued placement in special education. At this triennial evaluation, updated information is provided through reexamining many of the areas previously tested in the initial evaluation. The results of this evaluation, which is usually conducted by school officials, must be discussed at an IEP Committee meeting.

Declassification Procedures of a Child in Special Education.   It is the responsibility of the IEP Committee to declassify students previously classified with a disability who no longer meet the requirements for special education. The rationale for declassification is as follows.

- The child demonstrates effective compensatory skills.
- The student no longer exhibits difficulty in the classroom (there is no classroom impact on performance) despite a process deficit and discrepancy.
- The student no longer exhibits difficulty in the classroom (performance) or a discrepancy between ability and achievement (there is no classroom impact) despite a process deficit.
- The student no longer exhibits difficulty in the classroom (performance) or a process deficit (there is no classroom impact) despite a discrepancy between ability and achievement.
- Depending on the state regulations, the child who is declassified may be entitled to transition services that offer up to one year of support following the declassification. However, testing modifications can continue after the student is declassified when the student graduates from high school or receives an IEP Diploma (a diploma offered to children with disabilities who meet the criteria of their IEP but do not meet district or state standards for graduation).

IEP Development

All students in special education are expected to leave school prepared to do the following.

- Live independently
- Enjoy self-determination

- Make choices
- Contribute to society
- Pursue meaningful careers
- Enjoy integration in the economic, political, social, cultural, and educational mainstream of U.S. society

As previously discussed, the school district's committee on eligibility for special education services (IEP Committee) is charged with ensuring that each student with a disability is educated to the maximum extent appropriate in classes and programs with peers who do not have disabilities. For school-age students with disabilities, this committee must consider the supports, services, and program modifications necessary for a student to participate in general education classes and extracurricular and nonacademic activities. To better ensure that this occurs, the Individuals with Disabilities Education Act (IDEA 2004) requires that all students in special education have an Individualized Education Program, or IEP.

The IEP is the key document developed by the parent and his or her child's teachers and related services personnel that lays out how the child receives a free appropriate public education in the least restrictive environment. Among other components, the IEP lays out the child's academic achievement and functional performance, describes how the child will be included in the general education curriculum, establishes annual goals for the child and describes how those goals will be measured, states what special education and related services are needed by the child, describes how the child will be appropriately assessed including through the use of alternate assessments, and determines what accommodations may be appropriate for the child's instruction and assessments.

Components Included in the IEP

According to IDEA 2004, the components of an IEP must include a statement of the child's present levels of academic achievement and functional performance, including how the child's disability affects the child's involvement and progress in the general education curriculum. For preschool children, as appropriate, the IEP must describe how the disability affects the child's participation in appropriate activities.

For children with disabilities who take alternate assessments aligned to alternate achievement standards, a description of benchmarks or short-term objectives is included in the IEP. The IEP also includes a statement of measurable annual goals, including academic and functional goals, designed to meet the child's needs that result from the child's disability, to enable the child to be involved in and make progress in the general education curriculum. The measurable annual goals must meet each of the child's other educational needs that result from the child's disability. The IEP includes a description of how the child's progress toward meeting the annual goals is measured, and when (how often) periodic reports on the child's progress will be provided. The IEP also contains a statement of the special education and related services and supplementary aids and services, based on peer-reviewed research to the extent practicable, that will be provided to the child, or on behalf of the child, and a statement of the program modifications or supports for school personnel that will be provided for the child. See Appendix A for more information about IEPs under IDEA 2004.

Conclusion

The IEP Committee packet is a crucial piece of the special education process because it represents the culmination of gathering information, evaluations, observations, intakes, professional opinions, and recommendations necessary for the proper educational direction of a child with a suspected disability. This information will be viewed by all the members of the IEP Committee, along with the parents and other individuals so designated, such as an advocate or lawyer. This packet is also crucial because most of the IEP Committee members will not be familiar with the child, and they will use the information gathered and forwarded to determine the child's educational future. Therefore, it is imperative that the MDT present the most thorough and practical information to the IEP Committee.

Unless the student's IEP requires some other arrangement, the student with a disability must be educated in the school he or she would have attended if the disability were not present. The determination of the recommended placement is the final step in developing an IEP. The placement decision must address the full range of the student's cognitive, social, physical, linguistic, and communication needs. According to the least restrictive environment (LRE) requirements of federal and state law and regulations, a student may be removed from the general education environment only when the nature or severity of the disability is such that the student's education cannot be satisfactorily achieved even with the use of supplementary supports and services in the general education setting.

If a child is classified with a disability, several other procedures will occur in the special education process. Some of these may occur during the year, at the end of the year, or every three years. These procedures are also part of due process rights for students with disabilities and their parents. The IEP Committee handles many types of issues, but the three more common ones are special meetings, annual reviews, and triennial reviews. All of these meetings are for the sole purpose of protecting the rights of both the children and the parents. In the end, the IEP Committee plays a very significant role within the school district. An effective IEP Committee, working as an interdisciplinary team, can make a tremendous difference in the lives of children with disabilities. It is truly the link between the child and his or her educational future.

Transition Services for Students with Learning Disabilities

The Transitional Process

The last two decades have witnessed significant changes for people with disabilities, in large part due to the disability rights movement that, in many ways, paralleled the civil rights movement. People with disabilities used to be thought of as the invisible minority. Individuals with disabilities are now a presence in all the media, commercial advertising, and many forms of public life. Changes in the laws, and progress and technology, have helped make these advances possible. Despite these gains, the barriers to acceptance remain society's myths, fears, and stereotypes about people with disabilities. Consequently, the efforts for change need to be viewed as an ongoing process. The implementation of transition services is a significant component of this pathway to acceptance (Pierangelo & Giuliani, 2004).

Since the number of students with learning disabilities composes the largest number of individuals in the disability community (50.5%; Gargiulio, 2004), the need for special education governing the transition to adult life is a major concern for this population. The need for such services becomes more apparent as students with learning disabilities prepare for the adult world. Feelings of anxiety may arise because students with LD are uncertain about their future, which may include postsecondary education, employment, and independent community living (Pierangelo & Giuliani, 2004). The legislation governing transition services was passed to prevent all children with disabilities from being ill-prepared for postsecondary life. Since many aspects of learning disabilities continue through adulthood, it is imperative that students with LD be provided with a suitable transition plan to increase their chances of being productive members of society.

As many adults know from their own experience, adolescence is often the most difficult and unsettling period of adjustment in one's development. It is a time filled with physical, emotional, and social upheavals. Until a child leaves secondary school, parents and teachers may experience a sense of protective control over the child's life. This protective guidance normally involves educational, medical, financial, and social input to assist the child's growth. When the child leaves this setting, there is normally a personal struggle on the part of parents in letting go. There is always a normal amount of apprehension associated with the child's entrance into the adult world. Today, greater responsibility for adjustment falls on educators.

However, for the child with a learning disability, this developmental period can be fraught with even greater apprehension, for a variety of reasons. Depending on the nature and severity of the learning disability, parents may play more of an ongoing role in their child's life even after he or she leaves secondary education. Historically, parents and their children have spent years actively involved in IEP development and meetings, transitional IEP development, and Eligibility Committee meetings concerning educational and developmental welfare. Depending on the severity of the learning disability and its interference in making reasoned decisions, some parents may have to continue to make vital decisions affecting all aspects of their child's life.

Because planning for the future of a student with LD can arouse fear of the unknown, there may be a tendency for parents to delay addressing these issues and instead focus only on the present. However, working through these fears and thinking about the child's best future interest has a greater chance of ensuring a meaningful outcome. Regardless of the nature and severity of the learning disability, educators and parents will be exposed to a transitional process during the child's school years that will provide a foundation for the adult world. This transitional process will include many facets of planning for the future and should be fully understood by everyone concerned, each step of the way. Planning for the future is an investment in a child's well-being.

The Intent of Transition Services

For many years, educators have been concerned about the lack of success in adult life for students with disabilities. Many did not go for further training, and often did not receive postschool support and services. As these children "aged out" (students were no longer eligible for a free and appropriate education, including services and support of the educational system), the families felt that they were being dropped into a void. Although there were many services out in the community, parents were left to their own devices and would find out about such services and supports by chance, luck, or fate. Parents and students were confronted with a complex array of service options and resources, each with unique roles, services, funding sources, forms, and eligibility requirements. A need for a collaborative, readily accessible system was obvious.

What seemed to be missing was the bridge between a student's school system and services for postsecondary-school life. As a result, the concept of transitional services was developed to bridge this gap and hopefully provide students who have special needs with a more structured path to adulthood.

The Importance of Transition Services for Individuals with Learning Disabilities

Even though transition planning has been mandated for all students with disabilities for more than 10 years, transition planning for individuals with LD has lagged behind that of other groups. A major reason for this lack of attention has been an assumption that individuals with LD have a mild disability that primarily affects academic achievement; therefore, they have the ability to move from secondary to postsecondary environments without a lot of difficulty. Unfortunately, this is not the case for many students with learning disabilities. The results of a number of recent studies have suggested that many adolescents with LD do encounter difficulties in making the transition to adult life, including problems related to unemployment, underemployment, job changes, participation in community and leisure activities, pay, dependency on parents and others, satisfaction with employment, postsecondary academics, and functional skills (Council for Learning Disabilities, 2004).

The Introduction of Transition Services

In 1990, the laws governing the education of children with disabilities took a major step forward with the introduction of transition services. The rules and regulations for IDEA 1990 define transition services as:

> A—a coordinated set of activities for a student, designed within an outcome oriented process that promotes movement from school to postschool activities, including postsecondary education, vocational training, integrated employment (including supported employment), continuing and adult education, adult services, independent living, or community participation.

> B—the coordinated set of activities must be based on the individual student's needs, taking into account the student's preferences and interests; include instruction, community experience, the development of employment and other postschool adult living objectives and if appropriate, acquisition of daily living skills and functional evaluation. (IDEA, P.L. 101–476, 34 C.F.R. 300.18)

Simply put, transition services help students and family think about life after high school, identify long-range goals, and design the high school experience to ensure that students gain the skills and connections they need to achieve these goals (see Box 8.1). Transition services also provide funding and services to local school districts to assist families and students in the transition process.

In May 1994, President Clinton signed the School to Work Opportunities Act. This act contains the blueprint to empower all individuals, including those with disabilities, to acquire the skills and experiences they need to compete. This landmark bill demonstrated that transition was clearly a national priority, important to ensure our economic viability as well as to offer every young person a chance at a productive life.

Every state receives federal special education moneys through Part B of IDEA, and in turn, most of these funds flow through to local school districts and other state-supported programs providing special education services. As a requirement for receiving these funds, state education agencies monitor the programs for which the funds are made available (Pierangelo & Giuliani, 2004).

BOX 8.1

From the National Center on Secondary Education and Transition

This document identifies the major changes between IDEA 1997 and IDEA 2004 concerning transition services (**bold** text indicates language changes from IDEA 1997).

Individuals with Disabilities Education Act of 1997	H.R. 1350: Individuals with Disabilities Education Improvement Act of 2004

PART A: GENERAL PROVISIONS

Section 601: SHORT TITLE; TABLE OF CONTENTS; FINDINGS; PURPOSES	*Section 601: SHORT TITLE; TABLE OF CONTENTS; FINDINGS; PURPOSES*
(d) PURPOSES. The purposes of this title are—	(d) PURPOSES. The purposes of this title are—
(1)(A) to ensure that all children with disabilities have available to them a free appropriate public education that emphasizes special education and related services designed to meet their unique needs and prepare them for employment and independent living	(1)(A) to ensure that all children with disabilities have available to them a free appropriate public education that emphasizes special education and related services designed to meet their unique needs and prepare them **for further education,** employment, and independent living
Section 602: DEFINITIONS	*Section 602: DEFINITIONS*
(30) TRANSITION SERVICES.	(34) TRANSITION SERVICES:
The term "transition services" means a coordinated set of activities for a student with disability that—	The term "transition services" means a coordinated set of activities for a **child** with a disability that—
(A) is designed within an outcome-oriented process, which promotes movement from school to post-school activities, including postsecondary education, vocational training, integrated employment (including supported employment), continuing and adult education, adult services, independent living, or community participation;	(A) is designed to be **within a results-**oriented process, **that is focused on improving the academic and functional achievement of the child with a disability to facilitate the child's** movement from school to postschool activities, including postsecondary education, vocational **education,** integrated employment (including supported employment), continuing and adult education, adult services, independent living, or community participation;
(B) is based upon the individual student's needs, taking into account the student's preferences and interests; and	(B) is based on the individual child's needs, taking into account the **child's strengths,** preferences, and interests; and
(C) includes instruction, related services, community experiences, the development of employment and other post-school adult living objectives, and when appropriate, acquisition of daily living skills and functional vocational evaluation.	(C) includes instruction, related services, community experiences, the development of employment and other post-school adult living objectives, and when appropriate, acquisition of daily living skills and functional vocational evaluation.

(continued)

B O X 8 . 1

From the National Center on Secondary Education and Transition *(continued)*

PART B: ASSISTANCE FOR EDUCATION OF ALL CHILDREN WITH DISABILITIES

Section 614: INDIVIDUALIZED EDUCATION PROGRAMS

(c) ADDITIONAL REQUIREMENTS FOR EVALUATION AND REEVALUATIONS

(5) EVALUATIONS BEFORE CHANGE IN ELIGIBILITY—

A local educational agency shall evaluate a child with a disability in accordance with this section before determining that the child is no longer a child with a disability.

Section 614: INDIVIDUALIZED EDUCATION PROGRAMS

(c) ADDITIONAL REQUIREMENTS FOR EVALUATION AND REEVALUATIONS

(5) EVALUATIONS BEFORE CHANGE IN ELIGIBILITY—

(A) IN GENERAL—**Except as provided in subparagraph (B),** a local educational agency shall evaluate a child with a disability in accordance with this section before determining that the child is no longer a child with a disability.

(B) EXCEPTION—

(i) IN GENERAL—The evaluation described in subparagraph (A) shall not be required before the termination of a child's eligibility under this part due to graduation from secondary school with a regular diploma, or due to exceeding the age eligibility for a free appropriate public education under State law.

(ii) SUMMARY OF PERFORMANCE—For a child whose eligibility under this part terminates under circumstances described in clause (i), a local education agency shall provide the child with a summary of the child's academic achievement and functional performance, which shall include recommendations on how to assist the child in meeting the child's postsecondary goals.

Section 614, INDIVIDUALIZED EDUCATION PROGRAMS

(d) INDIVIDUALIZED EDUCATION PROGRAMS

(1) DEFINITIONS

(A) INDIVIDUALIZED EDUCATION PROGRAM

(vii)(I) beginning at age 14, and updated annually, a statement of the transition service needs of the child under the applicable components of the child's IEP that focuses on the child's courses of study (such as participation in advanced-placement courses or a vocational education program);

(II) beginning at age 16 (or younger, if determined appropriate by the IEP Team), a state-

Section 614, INDIVIDUALIZED EDUCATION PROGRAMS

(d) INDIVIDUALIZED EDUCATION PROGRAMS

(1) DEFINITIONS

(A) INDIVIDUALIZED EDUCATION PROGRAM

(VIII) beginning not later than the first IEP to be in effect when the child is 16, and updated annually thereafter—

(aa) appropriate measurable postsecondary goals based upon age appropriate transition assessments related to training, education, employment, and, where appropriate, independent living skills;

BOX 8.1

From the National Center on Secondary Education and Transition

ment of needed transition services for the child, including, when appropriate, a statement of the interagency responsibilities or any needed linkages; and

(III) beginning at least one year before the child reaches the age of majority under State law, a statement that the child has been informed of his or her rights under this title, if any, that will transfer to the child on reaching the age of majority under section 615(m); and

(viii) a statement of—

(I) how the child's progress toward the annual goals described in clause (ii) will be measured; and

(II) how the child's parents will be regularly informed (by such means as periodic report cards), at least as often as parents are informed of their nondisabled children's progress of—

(aa) their child's progress toward the annual goals described in clause (ii); and

(bb) the extent to which that progress is sufficient to enable the child to achieve the goals by the end of the year.

(bb) the transition services (including courses of study) needed to assist the child in reaching those goals; and

(cc) beginning **not later than** 1 year before the child reaches the age of majority under State law, a statement that the child has been informed of the child's rights under this title, if any, that will transfer to the child on reaching the age of majority under section 615(m).

(ii) RULE OF CONSTRUCTION—nothing in this section shall be construed to require—

(I) that additional information be included in a child's IEP beyond what is explicitly required in this section; and

(II) the IEP Team to include information under 1 component of a child's IEP that is already contained under another component of such IEP.

[Note: The following text appears in Part B, Section 614 (d)(1)(A)(i), as part of the definition of what an IEP includes.]

(II) a statement of measurable annual goals, including **academic and functional goals**, designed to—

(aa) meet the child's needs that result from the child's disability to enable the child to be involved in and **make** progress in the general education curriculum; and

(bb) meet each of the child's other educational needs that result from the child's disability;

(III) a description of how the child's progress toward meeting the annual goals described in subclause (II) will be measured and when periodic reports on the progress the child is making toward meeting the annual goals (such as through the use of quarterly or other periodic reports, concurrent with the issuance of report card) will be provided;

(3) DEVELOPMENT OF IEP—

(A) IN GENERAL—In developing each child's IEP, the IEP Team, subject to subparagraph (C), shall consider—

(i) the strengths of the child and the concerns of the parents for enhancing the education of their child; and

(3) DEVELOPMENT OF IEP—

(A) IN GENERAL—In developing each child's IEP, the IEP Team, subject to subparagraph (C), shall consider—

(i) the strengths of the child;

(ii) the concerns of the parents for enhancing the education of their child;

(continued)

BOX 8.1

From the National Center on Secondary Education and Transition (continued)

(ii) the results of the initial evaluation or most recent evaluation of the child.

(6) CHILDREN WITH DISABILITIES IN ADULT PRISONS—

(A) IN GENERAL—The following requirements do not apply to children with disabilities who are convicted as adults under State law and incarcerated in adult prisons:

(i) The requirements contained in section 612(a)(17) and paragraph (1)(A)(v) of this subsection (relating to participation of children with disabilities in general assessments.)

(ii) The requirements of subclauses (I) and (II) of paragraph (1)(A)(vii) of this subsection (relating to transition planning and transition services), do not apply with respect to such children whose eligibility under this part will end, because of their age, before they will be released from prison.

(iii) the results of the initial evaluation or most recent evaluation of the child; and

(iv) the academic, developmental, and functional needs of the child.

(7) CHILDREN WITH DISABILITIES IN ADULT PRISONS—

(A) IN GENERAL—The following requirements **shall** not apply to children with disabilities who are convicted as adults under State law and incarcerated in adult prisons:

(i) The requirements contained in section 612(a)**(16)** and paragraph (1)(A)**(i)(VI)** (relating to participation of children with disabilities in general assessments).

(ii) The requirements of items **(aa) and (bb)** of paragraph (1)(A)**(i)(VIII)** (relating to transition planning and transition services), do not apply with respect to such children whose eligibility under this part will end, because of **such children's age, before such children** will be released from prison.

The Individualized Transition Plan (ITP)

The IEP, as it has been defined over the years by legislation and court rulings, is not changed by the presence of the transition services section. The IEP is still a contract between the students, the parents, and the school. It is not a performance contract. The IEP spells out what the school will do (services and activities). If transition services are included in the IEP, the school is responsible for performing this service activity.

The IEP should carry the information about transition services that only the school district can provide, though perhaps indirectly (by arranging for another agency to provide services coordinated with the school services). As in previous interpretations of the IEP, parents cannot be listed as responsible for achieving an outcome or providing a service. These are the school district's responsibility.

The Individual Transitional Education Plan (ITP) is a part of the overall IEP but represents a very important piece in determining a child's future. The ITP should include long-term adult outcomes from which annual goals and objectives are defined. The ITP should address the following:

- The child's preferences, interests, and needs
- The beginning date for the service

- Annual goals and objectives, such as employment services and living arrangements
- Long-term adult outcomes, including statements regarding the student's participation in employment, postsecondary education, and community living
- A coordinated set of activities that demonstrate the use of various strategies, including daily living and functional vocational evaluation activities, community experiences, adult living objectives, and instruction (If one of these activities is not included in the IEP in a particular year, then the IEP must explain why that activity is not reflected in any part of the student's program.)
- A list of participants involved in planning and developing the ITP

Transition Services

Transition services are aimed at providing students and their families with the practical and experiential skills and knowledge that will assist in a successful transition to adult life. Although transition services are provided in each of the following areas, it is important to understand that not every student with disabilities will need to receive all of these services. The available services included in the transition process involve services and experiences for both students and parents, such as:

Employment services	Financial services
Living arrangements	Postsecondary education services
Leisure/recreational services	Assistive technology
Transportation services	Medical services

As an educator working with students with learning disabilities, it is crucial for you to become familiar with the aspects of transition that affect this specific population so you can help parents help their student in the progress toward adulthood. To accomplish this, you will need to become familiar with the different areas associated with transition that may be faced by students with learning disabilities. A brief explanation of the areas involved in the transition process follows.

Special Considerations for Students with Learning Disabilities

Several special factors need to be considered in the transition planning for students with LD. One of these factors is the drop-out rate. Students with LD are at great risk for dropping out of school. Recent drop-out estimates for this population range from 17% to 42% (Scanlon & Mellard, 2002). Dropping out engenders numerous consequences relating to job opportunities, income, and self-esteem. Within the student with LD population, those students most at risk for dropping out are boys from urban communities and low-income homes who are members of a racial minority. Such students should receive intensified support, and their progress should be monitored.

According to the Council for Learning Disabilities (2004), another critical factor in transition planning for students with LD is individualized planning that matches a student's postsecondary goals. Because the population of students with disabilities is so heterogeneous, a wide range of postsecondary goals and transition planning should be considered. For some students, the next step after high school will be employment, for other students it will be further career or technical training, and for still others it will be attending a 2- or 4-year college or university. To be successful in the postsecondary environment, these students must be provided with appropriate training and experiences. For example, for a student whose postsecondary goal is attending a university, the high school curriculum must include participation in college preparatory courses and the development of independent study skills. For a student whose postsecondary goal is employment, the high school curriculum must include participation in career/technical education courses and work experiences. For all students, the curriculum should include the development of self-determination skills, social and interpersonal skills, community integration and participation skills, and independent living skills, if appropriate.

A final critical aspect of transition planning for students with LD is self-determination, which has been defined as "one's ability to define and achieve goals based on a foundation of knowing and valuing oneself" (Field & Hoffman, 1994, p. 164). It is highly related to positive adult outcomes. For example, Wehmeyer and Schwartz (1997) found that students with high levels of self-determination were more likely to be employed for pay, have a savings or checking account, and have expressed an interest in living outside of the home. Skills related to self-determination include self-evaluation, self-awareness, self-knowledge, self-management, choice making, decision making, problem solving, goal setting and attainment, and social collaboration (Field, Hoffman, & Spezia, 1998).

Employment Services

Crossing the threshold from the world of school to the world of work brings a significant change in anyone's life. School is an entitlement—an environment that our system of government supplies for all citizens. The workplace is the opposite; no one is "entitled" to a job. The workplace is governed by the competitive market, and students with or without disabilities have to be able to function in that setting or they will not succeed.

One of the first and most important aspects of transition planning is the preparation for some students for the world of work. This is a very practical issue that can create many concerns. With the proper information and resources, this phase of the transition process can also be rewarding. Parents and teachers must fully understand the options in order to help the child make the best decision for his or her future. The first step in planning for employment may begin with vocational assessments to help determine the best direction based on the child's interests and skill levels (Pierangelo & Giuliani, 2004).

Vocational Assessments

One of the techniques used to determine a child's interests, aptitudes, and skills is a vocational assessment. A vocational assessment is the responsibility of the district's special education program. It begins by assessing referrals for special education services and continues throughout subsequent annual reviews. The planning of transitional services includes the IEP Committee's development of transitional employment goals and objectives based on the child's needs, preferences, and interests. These will be identified through the child-centered vocational assessment process.

A good vocational assessment should include the collection and analysis of information about a child's vocational aptitudes, skills, expressed interests, and occupational exploration history (volunteer experiences, part-time or summer employment, club activities). The collection of this information should also take into account the child's language, culture, and family.

Level I Vocational Assessment. A Level I vocational assessment is administered at the beginning of a child's transitional process, usually around age 13 or 14, and is based on the student's abilities, expressed interests, and needs. The Level I assessment may include a review of existing school information and the results of informal interviews. Level I takes a look at the student from a vocational perspective. A trained vocational evaluator or knowledgeable special education teacher should be designated to collect the Level I assessment data. The information gathered for analyses should include existing information from

Cumulative records	Achievements
Student interviews	Interests
Special education eligibility data	Behaviors
A review of the child's aptitudes	Occupational exploration activities
Parent/guardian and teacher interviews	

The informal student interview involved in a Level I assessment should consider the student's vocational interest, interpersonal relationship skills, and adaptive behavior.

Level II Vocational Assessment. A Level II vocational assessment usually includes the administration of one or more formal vocational evaluations. A Level II assessment follows and is based on the analyses obtained from the Level I assessment. This may be recommended by the IEP Committee at any time to determine the level of a student's vocational skills, aptitudes, and interests, but not before the age of 12. The same knowledgeable staff members involved in prior assessments should be used. Collected data should relate to

Writing
Learning styles
Interest inventory
Motor skills (dexterity, speed, tool use, strength, coordination)
Spatial discrimination
Verbal reading
Perception (visual/auditory/tactile)
Speaking
Numerical operations (measurement, money skills)
Comprehension (task learning, problem solving)
Attention (staying on task)

Level III Vocational Assessment.   A Level III vocational assessment is a comprehensive vocational evaluation that focuses on real or simulated work experiences (Pierangelo & Giuliani, 2004). This assessment is the basis for vocational counseling. Unlike Level I and Level II assessments, a trained vocational evaluator should administer or supervise this level of assessment. Level III assessment options include

Vocational evaluations. This includes aptitudes and interests that are compared to job performance to predict vocational success in specific areas. Work samples must be valid and reliable.

Situational vocational assessments that occur in real work settings. This on-the-job assessment considers what has been learned and how.

Work study assessments. These are progress reports from supervisors or mentors that provide information on the student's job performance. A standard observational checklist may be utilized.

Assessments Helpful for Postsecondary Education Planning

A student who plans a postsecondary educational program may benefit from two types of assessments

- General assessments of postsecondary education skills are necessary to determine academic skills, critical thinking skills, requirements for reasonable accommodations, social behaviors, interpersonal skills, self-advocacy and self-determination skills, learning strategies, and time management or organizational skills. This information is usually obtained through consultation with peers, teachers, or a self-evaluation.
- Assessments specific to a field of study or setting are necessary to assess needs in relation to daily living skills that may be experienced in a classroom setting or on the college campus, such as dormitory living versus commuting, lab work, or large lecture versus seminar courses.

- Parents should be encouraged to visit campuses that provide supportive services for children with disabilities. Sources of information regarding colleges that provide these services can be obtained in the local libraries, bookstores, or high school guidance offices.

Leisure/Recreational Experiences

Leisure activities are what we do by choice for relaxation rather than for money as part of our job. When a student with a learning disability is involved in the transition from school to adult life, a healthy part of this journey should include leisure activities. Teachers and parents may generally discover the student's leisure interests by having him or her sample a variety of activities to find which ones are the most interesting and exciting. Parents of very young children in today's society normally expose them to a wide variety of experiences, such as

Dance classes	Music lessons
Sports activities	Travel
Little League	Scouting
Cultural experiences	Art lessons

As students without disabilities grow older, this process of sampling leisure interests depends less on the parents and more on their peer group. For young people with LD, however, teachers, parents, and other family members may continue to guide or structure leisure experiences. This extended period of guidance and involvement should be considered a realistic part of a student with disabilities' transitional process to adulthood. Learning specific leisure skills can be an important component for successful integration into community recreation programs. Research has shown that leisure skill training contributes to a sense of competence, social interaction, and appropriate behavior.

Advantages of Special Leisure Programs.   One of the conflicts that teachers and parents have to address is whether the child should participate in activities designed specifically for people with disabilities or enter activities that are geared for a more mainstreamed population. The advantages of special programs designed for children with disabilities are:

- They may be the only opportunity for some children with severe disabilities to participate (e.g., Special Olympics).
- They engender for a sense of group identity.
- They provide a setting for social interaction.
- They create a more level playing field so that the individual's abilities become the focus rather than the disability.

On the other hand, concentrating on "disabled only" activities may unnecessarily exclude individuals from many leisure opportunities and prevent interaction with the nondisabled community.

Individuals' Concerns When Faced with Leisure Activities.   One of the greatest concerns of individuals with disabilities is the problem they may face assimilating into the social world. Many students receive special services while in school that expose them to other children with disabilities. This social interaction and connection provide a foundation for improving social skills. However, once the school experience ends and the child is confronted with the mainstream world, there are fewer social opportunities, and social isolation is often the result. Social isolation could be a painful aspect that individuals with learning disabilities face when they enter adulthood. Therefore, parents play a crucial role in assisting their child by providing exposure to leisure and recreational activities. Parents may often find themselves as the only agent for this particular aspect of life, especially once the child leaves the school setting.

Parents and professionals should be aware of the enormous benefit of recreational activities in the role of social and personal confidence. Having a learning disability should not preclude a person from activities that enhance enjoyment. It is always important in one's life to maintain a balance between work and play.

Recreation activities have been one of the most visible areas of change for people with learning disabilities. There is hardly a sport activity that cannot include the participation of people with learning disabilities. For those who accept the challenge, nothing is off limits. Not everyone needs or wants to be a superstar, but everyone can attain a level of confidence in an activity that is personally interesting. Parents and educators need to support and encourage children to develop a range of interests and skills because, for all people, it is through the mastery of tasks that we raise our self-esteem.

Postsecondary Education Options

Some students with disabilities may be capable of graduating high school with all the requirements and moving to a postsecondary education experience. A number of years ago, students with disabilities had limited choices when it came to choosing a college or university that could provide accommodations. With the advent of the Americans with Disabilities Act (ADA), and the disabilities rights movement, accommodations for students with disabilities are relatively common today. However, many colleges require documentation of the existence of a learning disability. According to Barr, Hartman, and Spillane (2004), documentation is defined in the following manner:

> A high school student with a learning disability is one who has been evaluated by professionals. Such professionals (a school psychologist or educational diagnostician), after reviewing the results of various tests and other evidence, provide for each student a written diagnosis that a learning disability exists. Recommendations for accommodative services and programs are also usually part of the written document. This document can serve as a vehicle for the student to understand his or her strengths and weaknesses, as well as a "ticket" to obtain the accommodative services necessary to participate in regular college programs. There are several points for a student planning to go to college to keep in mind concerning the documenta-

tion of a learning disability: IDEA requires reevaluations to be conducted at least every three years, therefore, students with learning disabilities may be wise to have a comprehensive reevaluation conducted close to high school graduation time. This will ensure, for students who are going directly into postsecondary education, that the documentation that they take with them will be timely. If the student is unable to be evaluated close to graduation from high school, it is possible that a college or university, after receiving documentation, may decide that the documentation is too old. This may occur if the college or university feels that the information does not adequately describe the student's current academic strengths and weaknesses, learning styles, etc. Such current information can be invaluable in determining the most appropriate accommodations for the student. While an agreed upon definition does not exist within the postsecondary/disability community of "how old is too old," evidence from the field suggests a range of two–five years. While it is ultimately the student's responsibility to obtain necessary documentation, some colleges and universities do provide testing services. Students should ask about campus-based possibilities before going to a private diagnostician. Students and parents should study and discuss the documentation in order to fully understand what it conveys about the student's strengths, weaknesses, and recommended accommodative services. If the report is not clear, discuss it with the school psychologist or whoever has prepared it. Many high schools routinely destroy copies of student records after a predetermined number of years. As students with learning disabilities will need copies of select items in their records to show to the college or university as documentation of their disability, students should make sure that they have complete copies of all of their records upon leaving high school.

When to Begin College Planning

IDEA requires that the IEP Committee consider postschool goals when the student is about to enter high school at about age 14. Beginning at age 16 (or younger, if appropriate) a statement of transition services needed by the student must be included in the IEP. High school experiences, both academic and social, greatly influence future options for all students. For adolescents with disabilities, these experiences are pivotal.

Transition plans should be grounded in the student's goals and vision for life as an adult, career interests, extracurricular and community activities, and the skills the student needs to progress toward his or her goals. Planning should include preparation for proficiency tests and other assessments needed for postsecondary academic work (e.g., SATs), as well as the development of self-determination and self-advocacy skills.

During the last two years of high school, diagnostic testing should be conducted to further define the LD or ADHD. Colleges require documentation of a disability (i.e., results of tests indicating the presence of a disability) in order to provide support services; having an IEP or Section 504 plan in high school is not enough documentation to obtain services from colleges. Students entering postsecondary programs will need to present current assessment data in order to receive accommodations at college.

Even for students who have struggled academically in high school, postsecondary education may very well be a possibility. Students who wonder whether college is a realistic option can explore summer pre-college courses for high school students who have completed their junior or senior year. Alternatively, students can take a college course the summer before they enroll to get to know the campus, learn how to use the library, and sharpen their study strategies and time management skills.

Colleges offer an opportunity for individuals with disabilities to continue their education and earn tangible evidence of education such as a certificate or degree. Junior and community colleges offer a variety of courses that, upon successful completion of the prescribed courses, lead to a Certificate or Associate's degree. Community colleges are publicly funded, have either no or low-cost tuition, and offer a wide range of programs, including vocational and occupational courses. They exist in or near many communities; generally the only admissions requirement is a high school diploma or its equivalent. Junior colleges are usually privately supported, and the majority provide programs in the liberal arts field. Four-year colleges and universities offer programs of study that lead to a Bachelor's degree after successful completion of four years of prescribed course work.

Understanding Legal Rights Pertaining to Postsecondary Education

Once students with disabilities graduate from high school, they are no longer eligible for services provided by the school system and will not have an IEP. If they have been receiving rehabilitation services as part of their transition plans, they can continue to receive them. They will have an Individual Written Rehabilitation Plan (IWRP) and may be eligible for services such as postsecondary education, counseling, and vocational evaluation and assessment.

ADA bars discrimination against students with disabilities in the college application process. Once admitted, students may request reasonable accommodations to allow them to participate in courses, exams, and other activities. Most colleges and universities have a disability support services office to assist in providing accommodations.

Identifying the Desirable Characteristics of a College

Once the student's strengths, learning needs, and level of support needed have been delineated, it is time to look at the characteristics of colleges that might be a good match for the student. Consider various types of colleges: two-year colleges, public community colleges, private junior colleges, four-year colleges and universities, as well as graduate and professional schools. Students with LD can succeed in all types of schools, including the most prestigious.

Students must determine the characteristics of colleges that will make them happy and support their success. For example, how big is their high school? Will they feel more comfortable in a larger or a smaller college? Will they be happier in an urban or a rural area? Can they meet the academic requirements? Should they find a college that doesn't impose rigid prerequisites? Should they consider enrolling part-time rather than taking a full course load? What are their academic and extracurricular interests?

In looking at colleges, students may also want to consider whether progressive attitudes toward instruction prevail. Colleges that are using instructional techniques and electronic technology in a flexible way can increase students' success. For example, if courses are web-based so lecture notes or videos of presentations are available online and can be viewed multiple times, then students have natural supports built into a course. Nevertheless, according to the Heath Resource Center (2004), a student can get a good idea about the nature of the college by asking questions such as:

- Does this college require standardized college admissions test scores? If so, what is the range of scores for those admitted?
- For how many students with learning disabilities does the campus currently provide services?
- What are their major fields of study?
- What types of academic accommodations are typically provided to students with learning disabilities on your campus?
- Will this college provide the specific accommodations that I need?
- What records or documentation of a learning disability is necessary to arrange academic accommodations for admitted students?
- How is the confidentiality of applicants' records, as well as those of enrolled students, protected? Where does the college publish Family Education Rights and Privacy Act guidelines which I can review?
- How is information related to the documentation of a learning disability used? By whom?
- Does the college or university have someone available who is trained and understands the needs of adults with learning disabilities?
- What academic and personal characteristics have been found important for students with learning disabilities to succeed at this college?
- How many students with learning disabilities have graduated in the past five years?
- What is the tuition? Are there additional fees for LD-related services? If so, what services beyond those required by Section 504 and the ADA does one get for those fees?

In addition to talking with college staff, try to arrange a meeting with several college students with LD and talk with them about the services they receive and their experiences on campus. Such a meeting can be requested when you schedule the interview with the college staff. While you will certainly be interested in the answers to the questions, the impressions that you get during the conversations will be equally important and may serve as a way to make final refinements to the short list. (HEATH's *How to Choose a College: Guide for the Student with a Disability* contains more detailed advice.)

Students with disabilities must also look at other factors. They should investigate the support services offered by candidate colleges, discuss them with college staff (e.g., personnel in the Office of Disability Support Services), and verify that the services advertised by the college will actually be available to the student. For example, is tutoring available? Will extended time be allowed for taking tests? Is someone available to help with taking notes or preparing written work? Will college policies allow extended time to complete a course of study so that fewer classes may be taken over a longer period of time? Furthermore, students with LD must decide whether and to whom to disclose the presence of the disability. To obtain support services, students must self-disclose their disabilities to the Office of Disability Support Services. That office will notify professors of the necessary accommodations. Students are not required to give faculty information about a disability, but to obtain the best course work accommodations, they must be able to explain their needs to instructors. Therefore, students will want to investigate specific classes before they register for them. Some strategies for becoming informed about classes are listed below.

Participate in orientation programs. These programs provide opportunities to become familiar with campus life and to ask questions of continuing students and advisors about classes, faculty, resources, and services.

Don't procrastinate. Do not wait until the last minute to begin gathering information about courses and professors. Most Offices for Disability Support Services will allow students with disabilities to register a few days before other students, but you must be prepared.

Talk to other students. Other students are an excellent source of information about classes and professors.

Audit classes. It is possible to observe a class for a limited period of time to determine whether this is the right class. Students who audit a course are not responsible for exams or assignments.

Check the Internet. Most colleges and universities offer an increasing amount of information, including the course syllabus (outline of the course), objectives, textbook, readings, and assignments.

Meet the professor. Professors schedule office hours to answer questions about the course. Getting the textbooks and reading list ahead of time also allows students an opportunity to get a head start on the course.

For many individuals with LD, the transition to adulthood will be a time of positive self-discovery, but it will take trial and error. Goals and successes can sometimes be elusive, and the hidden nature of LD can pose special challenges. Careful preparation for the transition to college can help.

Disability-Related Support Services

Many college campuses have an office of student services or special services for students with disabilities. Others have designated the dean of students or some other administrator to provide this information and to coordinate necessary services and accommodations. At vocational schools or other training programs, the person responsible for disability services can usually provide this information. There are also many publications that can tell more about the policies and programs that individual colleges and universities have established to address the needs of students with disabilities.

Assistive Technology. Technology has become ubiquitous as a tool for teachers and students. P.L. 100-407, The Technology-Related Assistance for Individuals with Disabilities Act of 1988 (Tech Act), was designed to enhance the availability and quality of assistive technology (AT) devices and services to all individuals and their families throughout the United States. Public Law 105-17, IDEA, uses the same definitions for assistive technology as the Tech Act and mandates that assistive technology be considered in developing IEPs for students with disabilities. IDEA also emphasizes access to the general education curriculum for all students with disabilities.

The Tech Act and IDEA define an AT device as any item, piece of equipment, or product system (whether acquired off the shelf, modified, or customized) that is used to increase, maintain, or improve the functional capabilities of a person with a disability. AT devices may be categorized as no technology, low technology, or high technology (LD Online, 2001).

No-technology or *no-tech* refers to any assistive device that is not electronic. No-tech items range from pieces of foam glued to the corners of book pages to make turning easier, to the provision of a study carrel to reduce distractions. Low-technology or low-tech devices are electronic but do not include highly sophisticated computer components; examples include an electronic voice-recording device or a talking watch (Behrmann & Schaff, 2001). High-technology or high-tech devices utilize complex, multifunction technology and usually include a computer and associated software.

Lahm and Morissette (1994) identified areas of instruction in which AT can assist students. Six of these are described here: (1) organization, (2) note taking, (3) writing, (4) academic productivity, (5) access to reference and general educational materials, and (6) cognitive assistance.

Organization. Low-tech solutions include teaching students to organize their thoughts or work using flow-charting, task analysis, webbing, and outlining. These strategies can also be accomplished using high-tech, graphic, software-based organizers to assist students in developing and structuring ideas. Graphic organizers, whether low or high tech, allow students to manipulate and reconfigure brainstormed ideas and color code and group those ideas in ways that visually represent their thoughts. Another high-tech solution might be the outline function of word processing software, which lets students set out major ideas or topics and then add subcategories of information. Using the Internet, local area networks, or LCD projection systems enables students and their teachers to collaborate, give feedback, and modify these applications either as a group or individually at different times.

Note Taking.   A simple, no-tech approach to note taking is for the teacher to provide copies of outlines of the lectures, which students fill in with detailed information as they listen. Low- and high-tech methods include:

- Videotaping class sessions for visual learners or those who are unable to attend class for extended periods of time
- Sending web-cam photography across the Internet to allow students to see and hear what is happening in class (for students who are unable to attend class)
- Sending class notes or presentations to students via e-mail
- Translating print-based notes to voice by using optical character recognition (OCR) software with a voice synthesizer
- Using notebook computers, personal digital assistants (PDAs), or portable word processing keyboards to help students with the mechanics of note taking

Writing.   Word processing may be the most important application of assistive technology for students with mild disabilities. Writing barriers for students with mild disabilities include the following.

Mechanics: spelling, grammar, and punctuation errors
Process: generating ideas, organizing, drafting, editing, revising, and producing a neat, clear final copy
Motivation: interest in writing

Grammar and spell-checkers, online dictionaries, and thesaurus programs assist in the mechanics of writing. Macros are available that will insert an entire phrase with the touch of a single key. Word prediction software helps students recall or spell frequently used words.

During the writing process, word processors allow teachers to make suggestions on the student's disk. If computers are networked, students can read each other's work and make recommendations for revision. Computer editing also reduces or eliminates problems such as multiple erasures, torn papers, and poor handwriting. The final copy is neat and legible.

Motivation is often increased through the desktop publishing and multimedia capabilities of computers. A variety of fonts and styles allow students to customize their writing and highlight important features. Graphic images, drawings, video, and audio can provide interest or highlight ideas. Multimedia gives the student the means and the motivation to generate new and more complex ideas. For early writers, there are programs that allow students to write with pictures or symbols as well as text. In some of these programs, the student selects a series of pictures to represent an idea, then the pictures are transformed to words that can be read by a synthesizer for the student to edit.

Academic Productivity.   Tools that assist productivity can be hardware-based, software-based, or both. Calculators, for example, can be separate, multifunction devices or part of a computer's software. Spreadsheets, databases, and graphics software enhance productivity in calculating, categorizing, grouping, and predicting events. The Internet, computers, and PDAs can also aid productivity in note taking, obtaining assignments, accessing reference material and help from experts, and communicating with peers. Instead of relying on the telephone, students are increasingly sharing documents, using instant messaging, and transferring documents to each other as email attachments.

Access to Reference and General Educational Materials.   Access to the general education curriculum is emphasized by IDEA and includes the ability to obtain materials as well as the ability to understand and use them. Many students with mild disabilities have difficulty gathering and synthesizing information for their academic work. In this arena, Internet communications, multimedia, and universal design are providing new learning tools.

Internet communications can transport students beyond their physical environments, allowing them to interact with people far away and engage in interactive learning experiences. This is particularly appropriate for individuals who are easily distracted when going to new and busy environments such as the library, who are poorly motivated, or who have difficulty with reading or writing. Students can establish "CompuPals" via email or instant messaging with other students, which often motivates them to generate more text and thus gain more experience in writing. Students can also access electronic multimedia encyclopedias, library references, and online publications. However, these experiences should be structured, because it is easy to get distracted or lost as opportunities are explored.

Multimedia tools are another way in which information can be made accessible to students. Multimedia use of text, speech, graphics, pictures, audio, and video in reference-based software is especially effective in meeting the heterogeneous learning needs of students with mild disabilities. While a picture can be worth a thousand words to one student, audio or text-based descriptive video or graphic supports may help another student focus on the most important features of the materials.

Used in conjunction with assistive technology, e-books can use the power of multimedia to motivate students to read. They include high-interest stories: the computer reads each page of the story aloud, highlighting the words as they are read. Fonts and colors can be changed to reduce distraction. Additional clicks of the mouse result in pronunciation of syllables and a definition of the word. When the student clicks on a picture, a label appears. A verbal pronunciation of the label is offered when the student clicks the mouse again. Word definitions can be added by electronic dictionaries and thesaurus. These books are available in multiple languages, including English and Spanish, so students can read in their native language while being exposed to a second language.

The Center for Applied Special Technology (CAST) promotes the concept of universal design (Rose & Meyer, 2000), which asserts that alternatives integrated in the general curriculum can provide access to all students, including a range of backgrounds, learning styles, or abilities. Providing material in digital form, which can easily be translated, modified, or presented in different ways, can often attain the goal of universal design.

Cognitive Assistance.   A vast array of application software is available for instructing students through tutorials, drill and practice, problem solving, and simulations. Many of the assistive technologies described previously can be combined with instructional programs to develop and improve cognitive, reading, and problem-solving skills. Prompting and scheduling through PDAs, pagers, and Internet software also can assist students in remembering assignments or important tasks. They can help students to follow directions or a sequence of events, establish to-do lists, take and retrieve notes, check spelling, or look up words in a dictionary.

Special educators are familiar with the need to create or customize instructional materials to meet the varied needs of students with disabilities. Today, assistive technology can be more specifically targeted to address an individual's needs through the emergent power and flexibility of electronic tools and the ways in which they are combined and used. These innovations affect teaching and learning as well as individual capabilities. For students with mild disabilities, assistive technology can help to balance weak areas of learning with strong areas.

Conclusion

It has only been through the personal struggles and efforts of parents, professionals, and individuals with disabilities that laws and attitudes have changed. Initially, the collaborative efforts of parents and professionals best meet the needs of young children with learning disabilities. However, as these children enter the adult world, they should become partners of this collaborative team in promoting issues that promote their own well-being.

III

Teaching Students with Learning Disabilities

Over the years, teaching methods and intervention strategies for students with learning disabilities have been controversial. Not long ago, instruction of students with learning disabilities emphasized the remediation of basic skill deficits, often at the expense of providing opportunities for students to express themselves, learn problem-solving skills, or contact the general education curriculum in a meaningful way.

In recent years, however, the field has begun to shift its instructional focus from a remediation-only mode to an approach designed to give students with learning disabilities meaningful access to and success with the core curriculum. Many approaches have gained acceptance as research-based methods for improving the skills and developing the abilities of students with learning disabilities. Teachers need to be well informed on these approaches so that they can provide objective information to parents who seek to understand and address their child's difficulties. Ultimately, teachers need to be able to design instruction to meet the specific needs of children with special needs.

Part III of the text focuses on learning strategies and instructional strategies and practices for students with learning disabilities. After explaining what learning strategies entail (Chapter 9), chapters focus specifically on instructional strategies and practice for reading (Chapter 10), mathematics (Chapter 11), and written expression (Chapter 12). The final chapter (Chapter 13) addresses instructional strategies and practice for students with attention-deficit hyperactivity disorder.

Overview of Learning Strategies

Learning is the process of acquiring—and retaining—knowledge so it may be applied in life situations. Learning is not a passive process. As any teacher can attest, students are not vessels into which new information is poured and then forever remembered. Rather, learning new information and being able to recall and apply it appropriately involves a complex interaction between the learner and the material being learned. Learning is fostered when the learner has opportunities to practice the new information, receive feedback from an expert, such as a teacher, and apply the knowledge or skill in familiar and unfamiliar situations, with less and less assistance from others.

To each new learning task, students bring their own ideas, beliefs, opinions, attitudes, motivation, skills, and prior knowledge; they also bring with them the strategies and techniques they have learned in order to make their learning more efficient. All these aspects will contribute directly to the students' ability to learn, and to remember and use what has been learned.

The focus of this chapter is on helping students with LD become more efficient and effective learners by teaching them *how* to learn. By equipping them with a repertoire of strategies for learning—ways to organize themselves and new material; techniques to use while reading, writing, and doing math or other subjects; and systematic steps to follow when working through a learning task or reflecting upon their own learning—teachers can provide students with learning disabilities with the tools for a lifetime of successful learning.

Learning Difficulties of Students with LD

It is no secret that many students with learning disabilities find learning a difficult and painful process. For them, learning may be made more difficult by any number of factors, including inadequate prior knowledge, poor study skills, problems with maintaining attention, and cultural or language differences. Students who have LD are often overwhelmed, disorganized, and frustrated in learning situations. Learning can become a nightmare when there are memory problems, difficulties in following directions, trouble with the visual or auditory perception of information, and an inability to perform paper-and-pencil tasks (i.e., writing compositions, notetaking, doing written homework, taking tests).

Another aspect of learning that presents difficulties for students with LD relates to their beliefs about why they succeed or fail at learning. Due to their history of academic problems, such students may believe that they cannot learn, that school tasks are just too difficult and not worth the effort, or that, if they succeed at a task, it must have been due to luck. They may not readily believe that there is a connection between what they do, the effort they make, and the likelihood of academic success. These negative beliefs about their ability to learn, and the nature of learning itself, can have far-reaching academic consequences.

The Need to Be Strategic Learners

Notwithstanding the learning difficulties that students with LD often experience, they have the same need as their peers without disabilities to acquire the knowledge, skills, and strategies—both academic and nonacademic—that are necessary for functioning independently on a daily basis in our society. Perhaps one of the most important skills they need to learn is *how* to learn. Knowing that certain techniques and strategies can be used to assist learning, knowing which techniques are useful in which kinds of learning situations, and knowing how to use the techniques are powerful tools that can enable students to become strategic, effective, and lifelong learners.

Surprisingly, most students with LD (and most students in general) know little about the learning process, their own strengths and weaknesses in a learning situation, and what strategies and techniques they naturally tend to use when learning something new. Yet, we all do use various methods and strategies to help us learn and remember new information or skills. For example, when encountering a new word while reading, some of us may try to guess its meaning from the context of the passage and be satisfied with an approximate idea of what it means, while others may look the word up in the dictionary or ask someone nearby what it means. Still others may go a step further and write the new word down or try to use the word in a sentence before the day is through. Some of these methods are more effective than others for learning and remembering new information, and some of us are more conscious of our own learning processes than others.

Because of the nature of their learning difficulties, students with LD need to become *strategic* learners, not just haphazardly using whatever learning strategies or techniques they have developed on their own, but becoming consciously aware of what strategies might be most useful in a given learning situation and working to become capable of using those strategies effectively. Teachers can be enormously helpful in this regard. They can introduce students to specific strategies and demonstrate when and how the strategies are used. Students can then see how a person thinks or what a person does when using the strategies. Teachers can provide opportunities for students to discuss, reflect upon, and practice the strategies with classroom materials and authentic tasks. By giving feedback, teachers help students refine their use of strategies and learn to monitor their own usage. Teachers may then gradually fade out these reminders and guidance so that students begin to assume responsibility for strategic learning.

Learning Strategies

Research Base for Learning Strategies

As our knowledge has grown regarding the learning strategies that help students with LD learn new information and perform various tasks, so has our knowledge regarding how to *teach* those strategies to these students. In the past twenty years, a sizeable research base has developed that demonstrates the usefulness of directly teaching students with LD how to use strategies to acquire skills and information and how to apply those strategies, skills, and information in other settings and with other materials (known as *generalization*). Unfortunately, a lengthy discussion of the research is beyond the scope of this chapter. Presented here is an overview of the conclusions that many researchers have drawn regarding learning strategy instruction.

Researchers at the University of Kansas have been deeply involved in researching learning strategies since the 1970s and have done much to define and articulate the benefits of strategy instruction in general and for individuals with LD, in particular. Chief among the benefits is the fact that instruction in learning strategies helps students with learning disabilities approach and complete tasks successfully and provides them with techniques that promote independence in acquiring and performing academic skills (Ellis, Deshler, Lenz, Schumaker, & Clark, 1991).

The work at the University of Kansas has also resulted in one of the most well-researched and well-articulated models for teaching students to use learning strategies. This model has been known for years as the Strategies Intervention Model, or SIM, and was recently renamed the Strategies Integration Model. The SIM is designed as a series of steps that a teacher can use to effectively teach students to use any number of strategies or strategic approaches. (The model is described more fully on the next pages.) The SIM is not the only model available to guide how teachers provide students with strategy instruction; not surprisingly, researchers around the country tend to advocate similar methods, drawing from what is known about effective teaching methodology and about learning.

In a nutshell, teaching methods need to provide students with the opportunity to observe, engage in, discuss and reflect upon, practice, and personalize strategies that can be used with classroom and authentic tasks now and in the future (Rosenshine & Stevens, 1986). In using these teaching methods, teachers promote student independence in use of the strategies. Research makes it clear, however, that if students are to use learning strategies and generalize their strategic knowledge to other academic and nonacademic situations, teachers must understand both the strategies that provide students with the necessary learning tools and the methods that can be used to effectively teach those learning strategies to students.

Types of Learning Strategies

Learning strategies are "techniques, principles, or rules that facilitate the acquisition, manipulation, integration, storage, and retrieval of information across situations and settings" (Alley & Deshler, 1979, p. 13). Strategies are efficient, effective, and organized steps or procedures used when learning, remembering, or performing.

More simply put, learning strategies are the tools and techniques we use to help ourselves understand and learn new material or skills; integrate this new information with what we already know in a way that makes sense; and recall the information or skill later, even in a different situation or place. When we are trying to learn or do a task, our strategies include what we *think* about (the cognitive aspect of the strategy) and what we *physically do* (the behavioral or overt action we take).

Strategies can be simple or complex, unconsciously applied or used with great awareness and deliberation. Simple learning strategies that many of us have used, particularly in school settings, include notetaking, making a chart, asking the teacher questions, asking ourselves questions, re-reading when something does not make sense, looking at the reading questions before beginning to read, checking our work, making an outline before beginning to write, asking a friend to look over our composition, rehearsing a presentation aloud, making up a goofy rhyme to remember someone's name, using resource books, drawing a picture that uses every new vocabulary word we have to learn, or mapping in sequence the events of a story. Complex strategies tend actually to be a set of several different strategies that are used in tandem (and recursively) to accomplish a complex learning task, such as writing a composition or reading a passage and answering questions.

For example, a complex set of strategies for writing a composition might involve three recursive stages: planning, writing, and revising. Each of these stages can involve using many different strategies. When planning, for instance, we might (1) think hard about the audience that will be reading what we've written (e.g., what do they need or want to know, or how can we best capture and hold their attention?), (2) write an outline, and (3) identify points where we need to gather more information in order to write effectively.

When actually writing, we might focus on stating our main ideas well, supporting them with appropriate details, and summarizing our main points in the conclusion. Revising may have several mini-stages: looking back while writing to make sure we're following our outline (or deciding to abandon parts of the outline), or laying aside the composition for a day, then re-reading it with a fresh eye. We might also check to make sure we've used correct punctuation and grammar, consult a dictionary or other resource guide when we're uncertain, and ask someone else to read what we've written and give us feedback. We also move back and forth between these three stages—thinking and planning, writing for a while, re-reading to see how we're doing, thinking of how to fix mistakes or add new information, writing again—until we're finished.

The research literature abounds with descriptions of these strategy sets, often called strategy interventions, which are intended to make learners highly aware of what they doing, thus making their approach to completing specific tasks more purposeful, systematic, and, according to the research findings, more effective. The writing intervention called DEFENDS is an example of such a strategy set (see Box 9.1). The name is actually an acronym; each letter stands for one of the steps in the strategy. Remembering the acronym helps students remember the steps they are to use when writing.

Strategies can also be categorized in many different ways. Distinctions have been made, for instance, between cognitive and metacognitive strategies.

> **Cognitive strategies** help a person process and manipulate information. Examples include taking notes, asking questions, or filling out a chart. Cognitive strategies tend to be very task-specific, meaning that certain cognitive strategies are useful when learning or performing certain tasks.
>
> **Metacognitive strategies** are more executive in nature. They are the strategies that a student uses when planning, monitoring, and evaluating learning or strategy performance. For this reason, they are often referred to as self-regulatory strategies.

The use of metacognitive strategies indicates that the student is aware of learning as a process and of what will facilitate learning. Taking the time to plan before writing, for example, shows that the student knows what is involved in writing a good composition. Similarly, he or she might monitor comprehension while reading and take action when something does not make sense—for example, look back in the text for clarification or consciously hold the question in mind while continuing to read. Evaluating one's work, learning, or even using a strategy is also

BOX 9.1

Example of a Strategy Intervention

DEFENDS is the acronym for a strategic approach that helps secondary students write a composition in which they must take a position and defend it (Ellis, 1994). Each letter stands for a strategic step, as follows:

Decide on audience, goals, and position
Estimate main ideas and details
Figure best order of main ideas and details
Express the position in the opening
Note each main idea and supporting points
Drive home the message in the last sentence
Search for errors and correct

highly metacognitive in nature, because a learner who does these things is aware of and thinking about how learning takes place.

Metacognitive strategies are at the core of self-regulated learning, which, in turn, is at the core of successful and lifelong learning. Self-regulation involves such strategies as goal-setting, self-instruction, self-monitoring, and self-reinforcement (Graham, Harris, & Reid, 1992). It's easy to see why self-regulated learners tend to achieve academically. They set goals for learning, talk to themselves in positive ways about learning, use self-instruction to guide themselves through a learning problem, keep track of (or monitor) their comprehension or progress, and reward themselves for success. Just as students can be helped to develop their use of cognitive, task-specific strategies, so can they be helped to use self-regulatory, metacognitive ones as well. In fact, the most effective strategy interventions combine the use of cognitive and metacognitive strategies.

Strategies have also been categorized by their purpose or function for the learner (Lenz, Ellis, & Scanlon, 1996). Is a strategy being used to help the student initially learn new information or skills? Such strategies are *acquisition strategies.*

Is a strategy being used to help the student manipulate or transform information so that it can be effectively placed in memory? These types of strategies are *storage strategies.*

Is a strategy being used to help the learner recall or show what he or she has learned? Such strategies are *demonstration* and *expression of knowledge strategies.*

The Importance of Teaching Children to Be Strategic

The Individuals with Disabilities Education Improvement Act of 2004 (IDEA 2004) and the No Child Left Behind (NCLB) Act of 2001 focus on improved achievement by all students. IDEA 2004 mandates that all students access and progress in the general education curriculum. This includes students with disabilities, English language learners, and gifted students. NCLB has established performance goals that drive the efforts of public schools, especially in requiring proficiency in reading/language arts and mathematics by all students by the year 2013–2014. The outcomes listed below help ensure student progress. Additionally, when students become strategic, independent learners, they also become literate and productive lifelong learners.

When children are taught to be strategic, the following outcomes can be expected:

- Students trust their minds.
- Students know there's more than one right way to do things.
- They acknowledge their mistakes and try to rectify them. They evaluate their products and behavior.
- Memories are enhanced.

- Learning increases.
- Self-esteem increases.
- Students feel a sense of power.
- Students become more responsible.
- Work completion and accuracy improve.
- Students develop and use a personal study process.
- They know how to "try."
- On-task time increases; students are more "engaged."

Essential Strategies to Teach

The most essential strategies to teach students with LD are determined, in large part, by assessing what successful, efficient learners do. It has been found that successful learners use numerous strategies across subjects and tasks, such as taking notes, asking questions, and filling out a chart. Efficient learners know when to use strategies and for what purposes.

Strategic Learning: Examples from the Reading Field

Decades of research into reading has resulted in a substantial knowledge base about how we learn to read, what effective readers do, what not-so-effective readers do and don't do, and how good reading skills might be fostered or poor reading skills remediated. Much of this knowledge base has been put to use in the form of strategy instruction—helping beginning readers, and those whose skills need remediating, develop the strategies the good reader uses. Good readers, for example, successfully construct understanding and meaning through interacting with the text using learning strategies, including thinking about what they already know on the topic, being aware when they are not understanding something in the text, and taking some sort of corrective action to clear up the difficulty (Pressley, Brown, El-Dinary, & Afflerbach, 1995). They also paraphrase or summarize as they go along, and they ask questions of themselves or others to maximize their comprehension. Studies have shown that children with LD and other low-achievers can master the learning strategies that improve reading comprehension skills (e.g., Deshler, Shumaker, Alley, Clark, & Warner, 1981; Idol, 1987; Palincsar & Brown, 1987; Schunk & Rice, 1989; Wong & Jones, 1982). Techniques that help students learn to ask questions and to paraphrase and summarize what they are reading have been shown to help them develop higher-level reading comprehension skills. For students with learning problems, learning to use questioning strategies is especially important, since these students do not often spontaneously self-question or monitor their own reading comprehension (Bos & Filip, 1984).

This section looks briefly at some of the strategies that researchers and teachers have focused their attention upon, with the purpose of illustrating concretely what strategies might be helpful to students, particularly those with learning disabilities.

Questioning and Paraphrasing.   Several strategic approaches have been designed to foster student interaction with the text being read. **Reciprocal Teaching** is one such approach (Brown & Palincsar, 1988). In Reciprocal Teaching, students interact deeply with the text through the strategies of questioning, summarizing, clarifying, and predicting. Organized in the form of a discussion, the approach involves one leader (students and teacher take turns being the leader) who, after a segment of the text is read, frames a *question* to which the group responds. Participants can then share their own questions. The leader then *summarizes* the gist of the text. Participants comment or elaborate upon that summary. At any point in the discussion, either the leader or participants may identify aspects of the text or discussion that need to be clarified, and the group joins together to *clarify* the confusion. Finally, the leader indicates it's time to move on when he or she makes or solicits *predictions* about what might come up next in the text.

Paraphrasing, self-questioning, and finding the main idea are the strategies used in an approach developed and researched by Deshler and colleagues (1981). Students divide reading passages into smaller parts such as sections, subsections, or paragraphs. After reading a segment, students are cued to use a self-questioning strategy to identify main ideas and details. The strategy requires students to maintain a high level of attention to reading tasks, because they must alternate their use of questioning and paraphrasing after reading each section, subsection, or paragraph.

Questioning to Find the Main Idea.   Wong and Jones (1982) developed a self-questioning strategy focused primarily on identifying and questioning the main idea or summary of a paragraph. They first taught junior high students with LD the concept of a main idea. A self-questioning strategy was then explained. Students practiced the self-questioning strategy, with cue card assistance, on individual paragraphs. Following the practice, students were provided with immediate feedback. Eventually, following successful comprehension of these short paragraphs, students were presented with lengthier passages and the cue card use was phased out. Continuing to give corrective feedback, Wong and Jones (1982) finished each lesson with a discussion of students' progress and of strategy usefulness. Their results indicated that students with LD who were trained in a self-questioning strategy demonstrated greater comprehension of what was read than untrained students.

Story-Mapping.   Idol (1987) used a story-mapping strategy to help students read a story, generate a map of its events and ideas, and then answer questions. To fill in the map, students had to identify the setting, characters, time and place of the story, the problem, the goal, the action that took place, and the outcome. Idol modeled for students how to fill in the map, then gave them extensive opportunities to practice the mapping technique for themselves and receive corrective feedback. She stated that if comprehension instruction provides a framework for understanding, conceptualizing, and remembering important story events, students will improve their comprehension of necessary information. Idol further recognized that comprehension improves only through direct teacher instruction on the use of the strategy, high expectation of strategy use, and a move toward students' independent use of the strategy.

This is just a sampling of the strategies that can be used by students to improve their reading comprehension technique. Many other strategies can be used in reading, and there are also many strategies designed for math, writing, and other academic and nonacademic areas.

Effective Teaching Methods

Just as there are effective approaches to learning, there are effective approaches to teaching. Much research has been conducted into the nature of effective teaching, and much has been learned. Educational researchers (e.g., Englert, 1984; Nowacek, McKinney & Hallahan, 1990; Rosenshine & Stevens, 1986; Sindelar, Espin, Smith, & Harriman, 1990) have concluded, for example, that a systematic approach to providing instruction greatly improves student achievement. These researchers also state that teachers can learn the specific components of an effective, systematic approach to providing instruction and can modify and thereby enhance their teaching behavior. Using such a systematic approach with whatever is being taught can only help to further improve educational opportunities for all students, especially those who have learning disabilities.

Rosenshine and Stevens (1986) have identified common teaching practices of successful teachers, such as teaching in small steps, practicing after each step, guiding students during initial practice, and providing all students with opportunities for success. Englert (1984) pointed out that successful teachers use lesson strategies to provide students with both direct instruction and the opportunity for practice. Lesson strategies include communicating the rules and expectations of the lesson, stating instructional objectives and linking them to previous lessons, providing numerous examples, prompting student responses, and providing drill and further practice immediately following incorrect responses. Sindelar and colleagues (1990) add that the more time an actively engaged educator spends in the instructional process, the more positive student behavior and achievement will be. Sindelar and colleagues (1990) suggest that effective teachers limit seatwork activities, provide ample opportunities for student overlearning through teacher questioning, and allow time to socially interact with students. They conclude that encouraging higher levels of student participation, providing effective classroom transitions (i.e., concluding one activity and moving on to another), and bringing lessons to a close by providing assignments for further practice are consistent with teacher-directed learning.

Nowacek and colleagues (1990) indicate that teacher-directed, rather than student-directed, activities provide for an effective educational experience that is more likely to improve student achievement. Higher levels of student achievement occur because teachers, using a systematic approach, are more organized, have clearer expectations, maintain student attention, and provide immediate, corrective, and constructive feedback. Because their instruction is highly structured, these teachers provide a positive environment in which to learn.

Using a systematic approach to teaching does not suggest that teacher and student creativity is not a vital part of the process. It merely lays out an organizational framework that provides a means for enhanced, successful, and efficient learning.

Teaching Students to Use Learning Strategies

As with the basic tenets of effective teaching, much has been learned through research regarding effective learning strategy instruction. As mentioned earlier, a well-articulated instructional approach known as the Strategies Integration Model (SIM) has emerged from the research conducted at the University of Kansas. Based on cognitive behavior modification, the SIM is one of the field's most comprehensive models for providing strategy instruction. It can be used to teach virtually any strategic intervention to students.

First, of course, the teacher must select a strategy—most likely, a set of strategies—to teach to students. The decision of what strategy to teach, however, should not be arbitrary. Rather, the strategy should be clearly linked to (i.e., useful in completing) the tasks that students need to perform and where they need to perform them. When the strategy instruction is matched to student need, students tend to be more motivated to learn and use the strategy.

Once the teacher has decided which strategy or approach to teach, he or she may find the steps of the SIM particularly useful for guiding how the actual instruction should proceed. A fairly detailed description of suggested steps is given below.

Step 1: Pretest Students and Get Them Interested in Learning the Strategy.
Although the teacher may not wish to call this step "testing," it is nonetheless important to know how much the students with LD already know about using the strategy, and to secure their commitment to learning the strategy from top to bottom.

Letting students with LD know that gains in learning can occur when the strategy is used effectively is one of the keys to motivating them. Studies have shown that it is important to tell students directly that they are going to learn a strategy that can help them in their reading, writing, or whatever skill is being addressed through the strategy. They also need to know that their effort and persistence in learning and in using the strategy can bring them many learning benefits. In a study by Schunk and Rice (1989), for example, students were put into three groups and taught the strategy of finding the main idea of a reading passage. The groups, however, were given different *goals* for their work. One group was told that the goal of the activity was to learn the strategy, which would help them answer several reading questions. Another group was told that the goal was to answer several reading questions; the third group was simply told to "do their best." Results indicated that students whose learning goal was to learn the strategy performed the best when posttested. Understanding, knowing, and applying a strategy that assisted comprehension, Schunk and Rice (1989) reported, gave students a sense of control over their learning outcomes and, therefore, encouraged students to use the strategy. Use of the strategy also fostered a sense of task involvement among students. These results indicate the importance of overtly teaching students both the strategy and the *power* of the strategy—in other words, making sure they understand that the strategy can help them learn, and *how* it can help.

The pretest can be instrumental in helping students with learning disabilities see the need to learn the strategy. To this end, it is critical that the teacher pretest students using materials and tasks that are similar to the materials and tasks that the students actually encounter in their classes. The strategy should also be useful when working with those materials and tasks—in other words, students will find it easier to work with those materials or perform those tasks if they apply the strategy.

The pretest should primarily focus on completing the task (e.g., reading a passage and answering questions). Following the pretest, the students should discuss results. How did students do? Were they able to perform the task successfully? What types of errors did they make? What did they do, or think about, to help themselves while taking the pretest? What difficulties did they have, and how did they address those difficulties? If students did not perform particularly well, the teacher then indicates that he or she knows of a strategy or technique that will help students perform that task more successfully in the future.

Obtaining a commitment from students with LD to learn the strategy, according to the SIM model, can involve any number of approaches, including discussing the value of the strategy, the likelihood that success will not be immediate upon learning the strategy but will come if the student is willing to persevere and practice the strategy, and the teacher's own commitment to helping the students learn the strategy (Lenz, Ellis, & Scanlon, 1996). With elementary school students, student-teacher collaboration in use of the strategy is especially important; teachers need to discuss and practice strategies with young students frequently. Commitments can be verbal or in writing, but the idea here is to get the students involved and to make them aware that their participation in learning and using the strategy is vital to their eventual success.

Step 2: Describe the Strategy. In this stage, teachers "present the strategy, give examples, and have students discuss various ways the strategy can be used" (Day & Elksnin, 1994, p. 265). A clear definition of the strategy must be given, as well as some of the benefits to learning the strategy. The teacher should also identify real assignments in specific classes where students can apply the strategy and ask students if they can think of other work where the strategy might be useful. Students should also be told the various stages involved in learning the strategy, so they know what to expect.

Once this type of overview is provided and the teacher feels that students are ready to delve more deeply into hearing about and using the strategy, instruction must become more specific. Each separate step of the strategy must be described in detail. It is important that the strategy be presented in such a way that students can easily remember its steps. Many strategies have been given an acronym to help students remember the various steps involved. Students may also benefit from having a poster or chart about the strategy and its steps displayed in plain view.

During the description stage, the students may also discuss how this new approach to a specific task differs from what students are currently using. The stage should conclude with a review of what has been said.

Step 3: Model the Strategy.   Modeling the strategy for students with LD is an essential component of strategy instruction. In this stage, teachers overtly use the strategy to help them perform a relevant classroom ("authentic") task, talking aloud as they work so that students can observe how a person thinks and what a person does while using the strategy, including deciding which strategy to use to perform the task at hand, working through the task using that strategy, monitoring performance (i.e., is the strategy being applied correctly, and is it helping the learner complete the work well?), revising one's strategic approach, and making positive self-statements.

The self-talk that the teacher provides as a model can become a powerful guide for students, as responsibility for using the strategy transfers to them. In fact, Lenz, Ellis, and Scanlon (1996) suggest that teachers model the strategy intervention more than once and involve students in these subsequent modelings by asking questions such as "What do I do in this step?" Teachers can prompt this type of student involvement by asking "Now what's next? How do we do that step? What questions should you be asking yourself?" (p. 109). Student responses will help the teacher determine how well the students understand when and where they might use the strategy intervention, as well as the steps involved in the intervention.

Step 4: Practice the Strategy.   Repeated opportunities to practice the strategy are important, as well. The more students and teachers collaborate to use the strategy, the more internalized the strategy will become in students' strategic repertoire. Initial practice may be largely teacher-directed, with teachers continuing to model appropriate ways of thinking about the task at hand and deciding (with increasing student direction) which strategy or action is needed to work through whatever problems arise in completing the task.

Students may also be called upon to think aloud as they work through the practice tasks, explaining the problems they are having, decisions they are making, or physical actions they are taking, and what types of thoughts are occurring to them as they attempt to solve the problems, make the decisions, or take the physical actions. These student think-alouds should increasingly show the strategy being used to help them complete the task successfully. While these think-alouds may initially be part of teacher-directed instruction, students may benefit greatly from practicing as well in small groups, where they listen to each other's think-alouds and help each other understand the task, why the strategy might be useful in completing the task, and how to apply the strategy to the task. Practice opportunities should eventually become self-mediated, where students work independently to complete tasks while using the strategy.

In the beginning, students should practice using the strategy with materials that are at or slightly below their comfort level, so they do not become frustrated by overly difficult content. Using materials that are well matched to the strategy is also important, because then students can readily see the strategy's usefulness. As time goes by and students become more proficient in using the strategy, materials that are more difficult should be used.

Step 5: Provide Feedback.   The feedback that teachers give students with learning disabilities on their strategy use is a critical component in helping students learn how to use a strategy effectively and how to change what they are doing when a particular approach is not working. Much of the feedback can be offered as students become involved in thinking aloud about the task and about strategy use, in the modeling and practice steps described above. It is also important to provide opportunities for students to reflect upon their approach to and completion of the task. What aspects of the task did they complete well? What aspects were hard? Did any problems arise, and what did they do to solve the problems? What might they do differently the next time they have to complete a similar task?

Step 6: Promote Generalization.   It is important for students with learning disabilities to be able to apply the strategy in novel situations and with novel tasks. Surprisingly, many students will not recognize that the strategy they have been learning and practicing may be ideal for helping them to complete a learning task in a different classroom or learning situation; this is particularly true of students with learning disabilities (Borkowski, Estrada, Milstead, & Hale, 1989). Thus, mere exposure to strategy training appears insufficient for both strategy learning and strategy utilization (Wood, Rosenburg, & Carran, 1993). Consistent, guided practice at generalizing strategies to various settings and tasks is, therefore, vital for students with learning disabilities (Pressley, Symons, Snyder, & Cariglia-Bull, 1989), as are repeated reminders that strategies can be used in new situations (Borkowski, Estrada, Milstead & Hale, 1989).

Therefore, teachers need to discuss with students what "generalization" is and how and when students might use the strategy in other settings. An important part of this discussion will be looking at the actual work that students have in other classes and discussing with students how the strategy might be useful in completing that work. Being specific—actually going through the steps of the strategy with that work—is highly beneficial. Students can also be called upon to generate their own lists of instances where they might apply the strategy in other classes. (An example of a student-generated list of opportunities to use the strategy COPS is given in Box 9.2.) Additionally, teachers may wish to coordinate with a colleague to promote student use of strategies across settings, so that the strategies being taught in one classroom are mentioned and supported by other teachers as well. All of these approaches will promote student generalization of the strategy.

The Importance of Positive Self-Statements

Teachers may find that it's important to address the negative feelings that many students with LD have about learning and about themselves. Often, students with learning disabilities believe that they cannot learn, that the work is simply

BOX 9.2

An Acronym to Help Students Remember Steps in Using a Strategy

COPS is the acronym for a strategic approach that helps students detect and correct common writing errors. Each letter stands for an aspect of writing that students need to check for accuracy.

Capitalization of appropriate letters
Overall appearance of paper
Punctuation used correctly
Spelling accuracy

Here is a list of opportunities for using COPS that students generated in a brain-storming session:

Love letters	Written math problems
Homework assignments	Health questions
Spelling practice	History exam questions
Job applications	Friendly letters
English papers	Written instructions

(Shannon & Polloway, 1993, p. 161)

too difficult, or that any success they might achieve is due to luck. They may not readily believe they can achieve success in learning through their own effort and strategic activities and thoughts, and so they may not persist in using strategies.

Just as teachers can help students develop strategic approaches to learning, teachers can help students learn to attribute success in learning to their own effort and use of strategies. Modeling positive self-statements, and encouraging students to use such self-talk, are essential. Examples of positive self-statements that attribute success to effort and not to luck include:

"I can probably do this problem because I've done similar ones successfully."

"I'm usually successful when I work carefully and use the learning strategy correctly."

"If I make a mistake, I can probably find it and correct it." (Corral & Antia, 1997, p. 43)

Changing students' perceptions about themselves and about the connection between effort and success can be a vital element in their willingness to keep trying in the face of challenge, using learning strategies as a valuable tool.

Other Approaches to Strategy Instruction

The steps given above have been drawn primarily from research conducted at the University of Kansas and represent one strong approach to teaching the wide range of strategies that learners can use to tackle challenging learning situations. Other approaches to strategy instruction exist as well, with most experts recommending many of the steps articulated in the SIM. Much effort has gone into defining, testing, and refining their components, and in validating their effectiveness in promoting student achievement.

While the SIM and other strategy instruction models present educators with an overall structure for *teaching* students about learning and about learning strategies and techniques, the research literature also abounds with descriptions of specific strategies that *students* can use to enhance their reading, writing, and math skills. There are also many descriptions of strategies designed for use in specific academic (e.g., science) and nonacademic (e.g., social skills) areas. Some strategy interventions are designed for use at the elementary level, while others are appropriate for secondary students. Although much is known about strategy instruction, new instruction and instructional methodologies continue to unfold, as do our understanding of both strategies and strategy instruction. Therefore, strategy techniques and instruction should not be looked upon as a cure-all when working with students who have learning disabilities, but as another possible approach to meeting learners' needs.

The Extent to Which Strategy Instruction Is Taking Place in Classrooms

Currently, there are little data available to determine how many teachers teach strategic learning skills to students with learning disabilities. It is not even known how many teachers are aware of their existence, or if they are aware, have the skills to teach them. Few teachers demonstrate to their students their own personal strategy use. In general, teachers are not aware of the importance of these skills. The fact that there is so little data leads to the assumption that strategy instruction is not a general classroom practice. Following are a few possible explanations for this:

- Early strategy instruction research was done specifically with students with learning disabilities. General education preservice and inservice programs have not generalized these research findings to all learners.
- How students learn takes a back seat to what is learned. Teachers assume students will "get it" on their own, or with more teacher-directed instruction or practice.
- The idea of focusing on the learner is still in its infancy.
- "Educator overload" is a factor. Teachers, experiencing the pressures of accountability for student progress, feel they don't have time to "learn one more

thing," especially something they are not convinced will improve student learning.

- Numerous researchers are assisting educators in turning strategies research into practice. An increasing number of strategies instruction curricula are available, especially in reading and writing.

Conclusion

Learning strategy instruction appears to hold great educational potential, especially for students who have learning disabilities. This is because strategy training emphasizes helping students learn how to *learn* and how to use strategies that are known to be effective in promoting successful performance of academic, social, or job-related tasks. Students need these skills not only to cope with immediate academic demands but also to address similar tasks in different settings under different conditions throughout life. Strategies are, thus, skills that empower. They are resources for an individual to use, especially when faced with new learning situations.

Good strategy instruction makes students with learning disabilities aware of the purposes of strategies, how they work, why they work, when they work, and where they can be used. To accomplish this, teachers need to talk about strategies explicitly, describe and name them, model how they are used by thinking aloud while performing tasks relevant to students, provide students with multiple opportunities to use the strategies with a variety of materials, and provide feedback and guidance to help students refine and internalize strategy use. Ultimately, responsibility for strategy use needs to shift from teacher to students, so that students can become independent learners with the cognitive flexibility necessary to address the many learning challenges they will encounter in their lives.

Of course, no single technique or intervention can be expected to address the complex nature of learning or the varied needs of all learners. When working with students with learning disabilities, teachers will find it highly beneficial to have a variety of interventions and techniques with which to foster student success. Strategies are one such technique—and a powerful one at that! When students are given extensive and ongoing practice in using learning strategies within the context of daily school instruction, they become better equipped to face current and future tasks. Learning how to learn provides them with the ability to be independent lifelong learners, which is one of the ultimate goals of education. Ultimately, we want to teach students "how to fish" rather than "giving them a fish." When students with learning disabilities learn, they grow and change intellectually. They acquire more than knowledge. They enhance their sense of competence and their ability to achieve.

10

Strategies and Instructional Practices for Students with Learning Disabilities in Reading

Teaching Reading to Students with Learning Disabilities: An Overview

No other skill taught in school and learned by school children is more important than reading. It is the gateway to all other knowledge. If children do not learn to read efficiently, the path is blocked to every subject they encounter in their school years.

The past twenty years have brought major breakthroughs in our knowledge of how children learn to read and why so many fail. These new insights have been translated into techniques for teaching reading to beginning readers, including the many students who would otherwise encounter difficulties in mastering this fundamental skill. Researchers have come to appreciate that early identification and treatment of such students can make all the difference. Researchers have also documented the problems—personal, social, and educational—that too often result when early attention and intervention do not occur (Torgeson & Wagner, 1998).

Chapter 3 of this textbook presents a detailed overview of learning disabilities associated with reading difficulties (dyslexia). In case you have not had a chance to read this chapter or have forgotten some of the key points, let's review.

Most children begin reading and writing by the first, second, or third grade. By the time they are adults, most can't recall or can't remember what it was like not to be able to read and write, or how difficult it was to figure out how to translate patterns on a page into words, thoughts, and ideas. These same adults usually cannot understand why some children have not yet begun to read and write by the third grade. They have even more difficulty understanding how adults can function in our society with only the most rudimentary literacy skills.

Dyslexia is perhaps the learning disability that is most widely known. Stories about children (and adults) trying to overcome their learning disabilities appear in the mass media with some regularity. Despite the relative familiarity of the word *dyslexia*, there is no clear-cut, widely accepted definition for it. In the broadest sense, dyslexia refers to the overwhelming difficulty in learning to read and write by normally intelligent children exposed to suitable educational opportunities in school and at home. These often very verbal children's reading levels fall far below what would have been predicted for their quick and alert intelligence. According to The International Dyslexia Association (2005), dyslexia is defined as

> a neurologically-based, often familial, disorder which interferes with the acquisition and processing of language. Varying in degrees of severity, it is manifested by difficulties in receptive and expressive language, including phonological processing, in reading, writing, spelling, handwriting, and sometimes in arithmetic.
>
> Dyslexia is not the result of lack of motivation, sensory impairment, inadequate instructional or environmental opportunities, or other limiting conditions, but may occur together with these conditions.
>
> Although dyslexia is lifelong, individuals with dyslexia frequently respond successfully to timely and appropriate intervention. (p. 1)

Just as educators and researchers cannot agree on a specific and precise definition of dyslexia, they do not agree on the cause or causes. In the late 1980s, research (Vellutino, 1987) challenged many commonly held beliefs about dyslexia: dyslexia results in reversal of letters; dyslexics show uncertain hand preference; children whose first language is alphabetic rather than ideographic are more likely to have dyslexia; and dyslexia is correctable by developing strategies to strengthen the child's visual-spatial system. Instead, dyslexia appears to be a complex linguistic deficiency marked by the inability to represent and access the sound of a word in order to help remember the word and the inability to break words into component sounds.

It is important to remember that not all individuals who have problems with reading are dyslexic. And the diagnosis of dyslexia should only be made by a qualified reading professional. Many slow readers who are not dyslexic, however, can be helped with a variety of reading experiences to improve fluency. For more details on dyslexia, refer back to Chapter 3.

Phonological Awareness

Phonological awareness is the understanding of different ways that oral language can be divided into smaller components and manipulated. Spoken language can be broken down in many different ways, including sentences into words and words into syllables (e.g., in the word simple, /sim/ and /ple/), onset and rime (e.g., in the word *broom*, /br/ and /oom/), and individual phonemes (e.g., in the word *hamper*, /h/, /a/, /m/, /p/, /er/). Manipulating sounds includes deleting, adding, or substituting syllables or sounds (e.g., *Say can*; *Say it without the /k/*; *Say can with /m/ instead of /k/*). Being phonologically aware means having a general understanding at all of these levels (Chard & Dickson, 1999).

Over the past two decades, researchers have focused primarily on the contribution of phonological awareness to reading acquisition. However, the relationship between phonological awareness and reading is not unidirectional but reciprocal in nature. Early reading is dependent on having some understanding of the internal structure of words, and explicit instruction in phonological awareness skills is very effective in promoting early reading. However, instruction in early reading—specifically, explicit instruction in letter-sound correspondence—appears to strengthen phonological awareness, and in particular the more sophisticated phonological awareness (Snow, Burns, & Griffin, 1998).

Research has shown that phonological awareness is a predictor of future reading success. The child who can discriminate sounds in words, whether these sounds are beginning or ending sounds, is likely to be a successful reader. This may be because this child is able to concentrate, pay attention to detail, and articulate her thoughts and ideas. She is aware of similarities and differences in the sounds contained within the English language.

Some children have the ability to isolate and detect relatively large units of sound, such as syllables. These children are able to hear the rhyme and alliteration in and between words. This learning has by and large been absorbed over time, perhaps because the child has been read to regularly and has been exposed to language activities such as rhyming, sorting, matching, and so on (Bradley, 2003).

Educators are always looking for valid and reliable predictors of educational achievement. One reason educators are so interested in phonological awareness is that research indicates it is the best predictor of the ease of early reading acquisition (Stanovich, 1993), better even than IQ, vocabulary, and listening comprehension.

Phonological awareness is not only correlated with learning to read, but research indicates a stronger statement is true: phonological awareness appears to play a causal role in reading acquisition. Phonological awareness is a foundational ability underlying the learning of spelling–sound correspondences (Stanovich & Siegel, 1994). Although phonological awareness appears to be a necessary condition for learning to read (children who do not develop phonological awareness do not go on to learn how to read), it is not a sufficient condition. Adams (1990) reviews the research that suggests that it is critical for children to be able to link phoneme awareness to knowledge of letters.

Children can show us that they have phonological awareness in several ways, including the following.

- Identifying and making oral rhymes
    "The pig has a (wig)."
    "Pat the (cat)."
    "The sun is (fun)."

- Identifying and working with syllables in spoken words
    "I can clap the parts in my name: An-drew."

- Identifying and working with onsets and rimes in spoken syllables or one-syllable words
    "The first part of sip is s-."
    "The last part of win is -in."

- Identifying and working with individual phonemes in spoken words
  "The first sound in sun is /s/."

Once beginning readers have some awareness of phonemes and their corresponding graphic representations, research has indicated that further reading instruction
heightens their awareness of language, assisting them in developing the later stages
of phonological awareness mentioned above. Phonological awareness is both a prerequisite for and a consequence of learning to read (Yopp, 1992).

Teaching Phonological Awareness to Students with Learning Disabilities

Research indicates that phonological awareness can be taught and that students
with learning disabilities who increased their awareness of phonemes (the smallest parts of sound in a spoken word that make a difference in the word's meaning)
facilitated their subsequent reading acquisition (Lundberg et al., 1988). Teachers
need to be aware of instructional activities that can help their students with LD to
become aware of phonemes before they receive formal reading instruction, and
they need to realize that phonological awareness will become more sophisticated
as students' reading skills develop. The following recommendations for instruction
in phonological awareness are derived from Spector (1995).

- At the preschool level, engage children in activities that direct their attention
  to the sounds in words, such as rhyming and alliteration games.
- Teach students to segment and blend.
- Combine training in segmentation and blending with instruction in letter-
  sound relationships.
- Teach segmentation and blending as complementary processes.
- Systematically sequence examples when teaching segmentation and blending.
- Teach for transfer to novel tasks and contexts.

Yopp (1992) offers the following general recommendations for phonological awareness activities.

- Keep a sense of playfulness and fun, avoid drill and rote memorization.
- Use group settings that encourage interaction among children.
- Encourage children's curiosity about language and their experimentation
  with it.
- Allow for and be prepared for individual differences.
- Make sure the tone of the activity is not evaluative but, rather, fun and informal.

Solutions in the Classroom

Teaching students with learning disabilities to read must be highly purposeful and
strategic. Effective techniques have been developed for helping students with

learning disabilities, to develop phonological awareness, word recognition, and other advanced skills required for reading. Phonological awareness activities build on and enhance children's experiences with written (e.g., print awareness) and spoken language (e.g., playing with words). A beginning reader with successful phonological awareness and knowledge of letters learns how words are represented in print.

Intervention for students with learning disabilities who have difficulty with phonological awareness must be early, strategic, systematic, and carefully designed. It must be based on a curriculum that recognizes and balances the importance of both phonics instruction and the appreciation of meaning.

For children with LD who have difficulty reading, effective reading instruction strategies should be used to build phonological awareness and alphabetic understanding. These strategies should be explicit, making phonemes prominent in children's attention and perception. For example, teachers can model specific sounds and in turn ask the children to produce the sounds. In addition, opportunities to engage in phonological awareness activities should be plentiful, frequent, and fun.

Instructional strategies should consider the characteristics that make a word easier or more difficult to read. These include the following.

- The number of phonemes in the word
- Phoneme position in words (initial sounds are easier)
- Phonological properties of words (e.g., continuants, such as /m/, are easier than stop sounds, such as /t/)
- Phonological awareness dimensions, including blending sounds, segmenting words, and rhyming

Many early readers require greater teacher assistance and support. Using a research-based strategy known as scaffolding, teachers should provide students with lots of instructional support in the beginning stages of reading instruction, and gradually reduce the support as students learn more reading skills. The ultimate goal is for students to read on their own without the help of a teacher.

We do not know precisely why acquisition of phonological awareness is delayed in some students with learning disabilities. We do know that certain kinds of language activities for the pre-academic child make a substantial difference. For example, rhyming games can have an important effect (Bradley & Bryant, 1985). Children who have difficulty with rhyming often seem to have difficulty learning to read. Therefore, utilizing rhyming games and songs with young children can assist in identifying those children who may have difficulty reading later, so that useful interventions can be made to strengthen their skills. Keith Stanovitch (1993) outlines several activities that enhance phonological awareness:

Phonemic deletion. What word would be left if the /k/ sound were taken away from cat?

Word-to-word matching. Do pen and pipe begin with the same sound?

> **Blending.** What word would we have if we put these sounds together: /s/, /a/, /t/?
>
> **Sound isolation.** What is the first sound in *rose*?
>
> **Phoneme segmentation.** What sounds do you hear in the word *hot*?
>
> **Phoneme counting.** How many sounds do you hear in the word *cake*?
>
> **Deleted phoneme.** What sound do you hear in *meet* that is missing in *eat*?
>
> **Odd word out.** What word starts with a different sound: *bag, nine, beach, bike*?
>
> **Sound-to-word matching.** Is there a /k/ in *bike*?

Activities of this kind can be fun and interesting to all children. To those for whom increased phonological awareness is essential, they are a godsend. Nevertheless, even if we were to achieve a perfect record of teaching phonological awareness, there will still be a significant number of students with learning disabilities who will have difficulty with reading and other language tasks. Researchers in the medical and educational fields are pursuing avenues for understanding the root causes of these problems. It is hoped that such understanding will bring about some additional ways of presenting reading, so that yet another subset of poor readers can be helped.

With phonological awareness, we have the opportunity to establish modes of teaching that are based on solid research. Annual data supplied by the U.S. Department of Education (2003) show that more than 50% of school-age youngsters being provided special education services have learning disabilities and that of these, more than 80% manifest their difficulties in reading and language. It is clear that a major effort in teaching phonological awareness at the earliest possible opportunity will have a significant impact on reducing the number of individuals who will require special services.

A major impediment to implementing a phonological approach is the poor level of phonological awareness among teachers who teach reading, and among teachers in general. This lack of awareness is reported in a major survey by Louisa Moats (1994), who found that teachers often were aware of their lack of knowledge and earnestly sought greater understanding, but they had received little training. Moats's findings suggest that shifting our approach to teaching reading means training teachers in phonological awareness. Teachers who do not understand the structural basis of language will have little success in teaching it or in perceiving the difficulties with language that some children have.

Anderson and colleagues (1985), in their seminal report *Becoming a Nation of Readers,* alerted the nation to the need for explicit phonic teaching. As early as 1985, they had observed a decline in reading scores among selected groups of children. The report, perhaps overshadowed by other more startling calls for school reform, never received the attention it merited. In the intervening years, little has changed, and test scores continue to decline. The nation has poured millions of tax dollars into research that supports phonological approaches, yet little has changed in the school systems. Emphasizing phonological awareness in teaching reading is an approach that appears to match the method to our body of knowledge. Phonological awareness has the potential to unravel the mysteries of reading to countless thousands of individuals, and to protect their well-being as well as that of the nation. The phonological approach to reading is an area where we actually have well-documented tools. We need to use them.

Phonemic Awareness

Over the past two decades, but particularly in the last ten years, there has been a burgeoning consensus about the critical importance of phonemic awareness to beginning reading success, and about its role in specific reading disability or dyslexia (Hempenstall, 2003). Phonemic awareness is the ability to notice, think about, and work with the individual sounds in spoken words. Before children learn to read print, they need to become aware of how the sounds in words work. They must understand that words are made up of speech sounds, or phonemes.

The issue of when to introduce phonemic awareness activities and instruction has also been investigated. Byrne, Fielding-Barnsley, and Ashley (2000) report that it is not only the attainment of phonemic awareness that is important in learning to read, but also its speed of acquisition.

Phonemes are the smallest parts of sound in a spoken word that make a difference in the word's meaning. For example, changing the first phoneme in the word *hat* from /h/ to /p/ changes the word from *hat* to *pat*, and so changes the meaning. (A letter between slash marks shows the phoneme, or sound, that the letter represents, and not the name of the letter. For example, the letter *h* represents the sound /h/.)

Children can show us that they have phonemic awareness in several ways, including the following.

- Recognizing which words in a set of words begin with the same sound (*"Bell, bike,* and *boy* all have /b/ at the beginning.")
- Isolating and saying the first or last sound in a word ("The beginning sound of *dog* is /d/." "The ending sound of *sit* is /t/.")
- Combining, or blending the separate sounds in a word to say the word ("/m/, /a/, /p/—*map.*")
- Breaking, or segmenting a word into its separate sounds ("up—/u/, /p/.").

Children who have phonemic awareness skills are likely to have an easier time learning to read and spell than children who have few or none of these skills.

Although phonemic awareness is a widely used term in reading, it is often misunderstood. One misunderstanding is that phonemic awareness and phonics are the same thing. Phonemic awareness is *not* phonics. Phonemic awareness is the understanding that the sounds of *spoken* language work together to make words. Phonics is the understanding that there is a predictable relationship between phonemes and graphemes, the letters that represent those sounds in *written* language. If children are to benefit from phonics instruction, they need phonemic awareness. The reason is obvious: children who cannot hear and work with the phonemes of spoken words will have a difficult time learning how to relate these phonemes to the graphemes when they see them in written words.

Another misunderstanding about phonemic awareness is that it means the same as phonological awareness. The two names are *not* interchangeable. Phonemic awareness is a subcategory of phonological awareness. The focus of phonemic awareness is narrow—identifying and manipulating the individual sounds in words. The focus of phonological awareness is much broader. It includes identifying and manipulating larger parts of spoken language, such as words, syllables, onsets and rimes, as well as phonemes (see Box 10.1). It also encompasses awareness of other aspects of sound, such as rhyming, alliteration, and intonation.

BOX 10.1

The Language of Literacy

Here are some definitions of terms used frequently in reading instruction.

PHONEME
A phoneme is the smallest part of spoken language that makes a difference in the meaning of words. English has about forty-one phonemes. A few words, such as "a" or "oh", have only one phoneme. Most words, however, have more than one phoneme: The word *if* has two phonemes (/i/ /f/); *check* has three phonemes (/ch/ /e/ /k/), and *stop* has four phonemes (/s/ /t/ /o/ /p/). Sometimes one phoneme is represented by more than one letter.

GRAPHEME
A grapheme is the smallest part of written language that represents a phoneme in the spelling of a word. A grapheme may be just one letter, such as b, d, f, p, s; or several letters, such as ch, sh, th, -ck, ea, -igh.

PHONICS
Phonics is the understanding that there is a predictable relationship between phonemes (the sounds of spoken language) and graphemes (the letters and spellings that represent those sounds in written language).

PHONEMIC AWARENESS
Phonemic awareness is the ability to hear, identify, and manipulate the individual sounds—phonemes—in spoken words.

PHONOLOGICAL AWARENESS
Phonological awareness is a broad term that includes phonemic awareness. In addition to phonemes, phonological awareness activities can involve work with rhymes, words, syllables, and onsets and rimes.

SYLLABLE
A syllable is a word part that contains a vowel or, in spoken language, a vowel sound (e-vent; news-pa-per; ver-y).

ONSET AND RIME
Onsets and rimes are parts of spoken language that are smaller than syllables but larger than phonemes. An onset is the initial consonant(s) sound of a syllable (the onset of bag is b-; of swim, sw-). A rime is the part of a syllable that contains the vowel and all that follows it (the rime of bag is -ag; of swim, -im).

What Does Scientifically Based Research Tell Us about Phonemic Awareness Instruction?

Key findings from the National Reading Panel's (2000) scientific research on phonemic awareness instruction provide the following conclusions of particular interest and value to classroom teachers.

Phonemic Awareness Can Be Taught and Learned. Effective phonemic awareness instruction teaches children to notice, think about, and work with (manipulate) sounds in spoken language. Teachers use many activities to build phonemic awareness, including the following.

- **Phoneme isolation:** Children recognize individual sounds in a word.
    Teacher: What is the first sound in *van*?
    Children: The first sound in *van* is /v/.

- **Phoneme identity:** Children recognize the same sounds in different words.
    Teacher: What sound is the same in *fix, fall,* and *fun*?
    Children: The first sound, /f/, is the same.

- **Phoneme categorization:** Children recognize the word in a set of three or four words that has the "odd" sound.
    Teacher: Which word doesn't belong? *Bus, bun, rug.*
    Children: *Rug* does not belong. It doesn't begin with /b/.

- **Phoneme blending:** Children listen to a sequence of separately spoken phonemes and combine the phonemes to form a word. Then they write and read the word.
    Teacher: What word is /b/ /i/ /g/?
    Children: /b/ /i/ /g/ is *big.*
    Teacher: Now let's write the sounds in *big*: /b/, write *b*; /i/, write *i*; /g/, write *g.*
    Teacher: (Writes *big* on the board.) Now we're going to read the word *big.*

- **Phoneme segmentation:** Children break a word into its separate sounds, saying each sound as they tap out or count it. Then they write and read the word.
    Teacher: How many sounds are in *grab*?
    Children: /g/ /r/ /a/ /b/. Four sounds.
    Teacher: Now let's write the sounds in *grab*: /g/, write *g*; /r/, write *r*; /a/, write *a*; /b/, write *b.*
    Teacher: (Writes *grab* on the board.) Now we're going to read the word *grab.*

- **Phoneme deletion:** Children recognize the word that remains when a phoneme is removed from another word.
    Teacher: What is *smile* without the /s/?
    Children: *Smile* without the /s/ is *mile.*

- **Phoneme addition:** Children make a new word by adding a phoneme to an existing word.
    Teacher: What word do you have if you add /s/ to the beginning of *park?*
    Children: *Spark.*

- **Phoneme substitution:** Children substitute one phoneme for another to make a new word.
    Teacher: The word is *bug.* Change /g/ to /n/. What's the new word?
    Children: *Bun.*

Phonemic Awareness Instruction Helps Children Learn to Read. Phonemic awareness instruction improves children's ability to read words. It also improves their reading comprehension. Phonemic awareness instruction aids reading comprehension primarily through its influence on word reading. For children to understand what they read, they must be able to read words rapidly and accurately. Rapid and accurate word reading frees children to focus their attention on the meaning of what they read. Of course, many other things, including the size of children's vocabulary and their world experiences, contribute to reading comprehension.

Phonemic Awareness Instruction Helps Children Learn to Spell. Teaching phonemic awareness, particularly how to segment words into phonemes, helps children learn to spell. The explanation for this may be that children who have phonemic awareness understand that sounds and letters are related in a predictable way (see Box 10.2). Thus, they are able to relate the sounds to letters as they spell words.

Phonemic Awareness Instruction Is Most Effective When Children Are Taught to Manipulate Phonemes by Using the Letters of the Alphabet. Phonemic awareness instruction makes a stronger contribution to the improvement of reading and spelling

B O X 1 0 . 2

Common Phonemic Awareness Terms:

PHONEME MANIPULATION
When children work with phonemes in words, they are manipulating the phonemes. Types of phoneme manipulation include blending phonemes to make words, segmenting words into phonemes, deleting phonemes from words, adding phonemes to words, or substituting one phoneme for another to make a new word.

BLENDING
When children combine individual phonemes to form words, they are blending the pho-

nemes. They also are blending when they combine onsets and rimes to make syllables and combine syllables to make words.

SEGMENTING (SEGMENTATION)
When children break words into their individual phonemes, they are segmenting the words. They are also segmenting when they break words into syllables and syllables into onsets and rimes.

when children are taught to use letters as they manipulate phonemes than when instruction is limited to phonemes alone. Teaching sounds along with the letters of the alphabet is important because it helps children to see how phonemic awareness relates to their reading and writing. Learning to blend phonemes with letters helps children read words. Learning to segment sounds with letters helps them spell words. If children do not know letter names and shapes, they need to be taught them along with phonemic awareness, as relating sounds to letters is the heart of phonics instruction.

Phonemic Awareness Instruction Is Most Effective When It Focuses on Only One or Two Types of Phoneme Manipulation, Rather Than Several Types. Children who receive instruction that focuses on one or two types of phoneme manipulation make greater gains in reading and spelling than do children who are taught three or more types of manipulation. One possible explanation for this is that children who are taught many different ways to manipulate phonemes may become confused about which type to apply. Another explanation is that teaching many types of manipulations does not leave enough time to teach any one type thoroughly. A third explanation is that instruction that includes several types of manipulations may result in teaching children more difficult manipulations before they acquire skill in the easier ones.

Questions about Teaching Phonemic Awareness to Students with Reading Disabilities

Which Activities Will Help My Students Acquire Phonemic Awareness? Your instruction to increase children's phonemic awareness can include various activities in blending and segmenting words. Clearly, however, you should provide your students with instruction that is appropriate for their level of literacy development. If you teach younger children or less able older readers, your instruction should begin with easier activities, such as having children identify and categorize the first phonemes in words. When the children can do these activities, move them on to more difficult ones.

Which Methods of Phonemic Awareness Instruction Will Have the Greatest Impact on My Students' Learning to Read? You can use a variety of teaching methods that contribute to children's success in learning to read. However, teaching one or two types of phoneme manipulation—specifically blending and segmenting phonemes in words—is likely to produce greater benefits to your students' reading than teaching several types of manipulation. Teaching your students to manipulate phonemes along with letters can also contribute to their reading success. Your instruction should also be explicit about the connection between phonemic awareness and reading. For example:

> Teacher: Listen: I'm going to say the sounds in the word *jam*—/j/ /a/ /m/. What is the word?
> Children: *Jam.*

> Teacher: You say the sounds in the word *jam.*
> Children: /j/ /a/ /m/.
> Teacher: Now let's write the sounds in *jam:* /j/, write *j*; /a/, write *a*; /m/, write *m*.
> Teacher: (Writes *jam* on the board.) Now we're going to read the word *jam.*

Which of My Students Will Benefit from Phonemic Awareness Instruction?
Phonemic awareness instruction can help essentially all of your students learn to read, including preschoolers, kindergartners, first graders who are just starting to read, and less able older readers. Phonemic awareness instruction can help most of your students learn to spell. Instruction can be effective with preschoolers, kindergartners, and first graders. It can help children from all economic levels.

How Much Time Should I Spend on Phonemic Awareness Instruction?   You do not need to devote a lot of class time to phonemic awareness instruction. Over the school year, your entire phonemic awareness program should take no more than 20 hours. Your students will differ in their levels of phonemic awareness. Some will need more instruction than others. The best approach is to assess students' phonemic awareness before you begin instruction. Assessment will let you know which students do and do not need the instruction, which students should be taught the easier types of phoneme manipulation (such as identifying initial sounds in words), and which should receive instruction in more advanced types (such as segmenting, blending, deletion/addition, and substitution).

Should I Teach Phonemic Awareness to Individual Students, to Small Groups, or to the Whole Class?   In general, small-group instruction is more effective in helping your students acquire phonemic awareness and learn to read. Small-group instruction may be more effective than individual or whole-group instruction because children often benefit from listening to their classmates respond and receive feedback from the teacher.

Do We Know Enough about the Effectiveness of Phonemic Awareness Instruction for Me to Implement It in My Classroom?   Yes. Bear in mind, however, that phonemic awareness instruction is not a complete reading program; it cannot guarantee the reading and writing success of your students. Adding well-thought-out phonemic awareness instruction to a beginning reading program or to a remedial reading program is very likely to help your students learn to read and spell. Whether these benefits are lasting, however, will depend on the comprehensiveness and effectiveness of the entire literacy curriculum.

Phonics Instruction

Phonics instruction teaches children the relationships between the letters (graphemes) of written language and the individual sounds (phonemes) of spoken language. It teaches children to use these relationships to read and write words.

Teachers of reading and publishers of programs of beginning reading instruction sometimes use different labels to describe these relationships, including the following.

- Graphophonemic relationships
- Letter-sound associations
- Letter-sound correspondences
- Sound-symbol correspondences
- Sound-spellings

Regardless of the label, the goal of phonics instruction is to help children learn and use the alphabetic principle: the understanding that there are systematic and predictable relationships between written letters and spoken sounds. Knowing these relationships will help children recognize familiar words accurately and automatically and "decode" new words. In short, knowledge of the alphabetic principle contributes greatly to children's ability to read words both in isolation and in connected text.

Critics of phonics instruction argue that English spellings are too irregular for phonics instruction to really help children learn to read words. The point is, however, that phonics instruction teaches children a system for remembering how to read words. Once children learn, for example, that *phone* is spelled this way rather than *foan*, their memory helps them to read, spell, and recognize the word instantly and more accurately than they could read *foan*. The same process is true for all irregularly spelled words. Most of these words contain some regular letter–sound relationships that can help children remember how to read them. In summary, the alphabetic system is a mnemonic device that supports our memory for specific words.

What Does Scientifically Based Research Tell Us about Phonics Instruction?

Key findings from the National Reading Panel's (2000) scientific research on phonics instruction include the following conclusions of particular interest and value to classroom teachers.

Systematic and Explicit Phonics Instruction Is More Effective Than Nonsystematic or No Phonics Instruction.
How do systematic programs of phonics instruction differ from nonsystematic programs? The hallmark of systematic phonics instruction programs is the direct teaching of a set of letter–sound relationships in a clearly defined sequence. The set includes the major sound–spelling relationships of both consonants and vowels.

The programs also provide materials that give children substantial practice in applying knowledge of these relationships as they read and write. These materials include books or stories that contain a large number of words that children can decode by using the letter–sound relationships they have learned and are learning. The programs also might provide children with opportunities to spell words and to write their own stories with the letter–sound relationships they are learning.

BOX 10.3

Phonics Instructional Approaches

Analytic phonics: Children learn to analyze letter–sound relationships in previously learned words. They do not pronounce sounds in isolation.

Analogy-based phonics: Children learn to use parts of word families they know to identify words they don't know that have similar parts.

Embedded phonics: Children are taught letter–sound relationships during the reading of connected text. (Because children encounter different letter–sound relationships as they read, this approach is not systematic or explicit.)

Onset–rime phonics instruction: Children learn to identify the sound of the letter or letters before the first vowel (the onset) in a one-syllable word and the sound of the remaining part of the word (the rime).

Phonics through spelling: Children learn to segment words into phonemes and to make words by writing letters for phonemes.

Synthetic phonics: Children learn how to convert letters or letter combinations into sounds, and then how to blend the sounds together to form recognizable words.

Most teachers are acquainted with several approaches to phonics instruction, including those listed in Box 10.3. The distinctions between approaches are not absolute, and some programs of instruction combine approaches.

Systematic and Explicit Phonics Instruction Significantly Improves Kindergarten and First-Grade Children's Word Recognition and Spelling.   Systematic phonics instruction produces the greatest impact on children's reading achievement when it begins in kindergarten or first grade. Both kindergarten and first-grade children who receive systematic phonics instruction are better at reading and spelling words than kindergarten and first-grade children who do not receive systematic instruction.

Systematic and Explicit Phonics Instruction Significantly Improves Children's Reading Comprehension.   Systematic phonics instruction results in better growth in children's ability to comprehend what they read than nonsystematic or no phonics instruction. This is not surprising because the ability to read the words in a text accurately and quickly is highly related to successful reading comprehension.

Systematic and Explicit Phonics Instruction Is Effective for Children from Various Social and Economic Levels.   Systematic phonics instruction is beneficial to children regardless of their socioeconomic status. It helps children from various backgrounds make greater gains in reading than nonsystematic instruction or no phonics instruction.

Systematic and Explicit Phonics Instruction Is Particularly Beneficial for Children Who Are Having Difficulty Learning to Read and Who Are at Risk for Developing Future Reading Problems.   Systematic phonics instruction is significantly more effective than nonsystematic or no phonics instruction in helping to prevent reading difficulties among at-risk students and in helping children overcome reading difficulties.

Systematic and Explicit Phonics Instruction Is Most Effective when Introduced Early. Phonics instruction is most effective when it begins in kindergarten or first grade. To be effective with young learners, systematic instruction must be designed appropriately and taught carefully. It should include teaching letter shapes and names, phonemic awareness, and all major letter–sound relationships. It should ensure that all children learn these skills. As instruction proceeds, children should be taught to use this knowledge to read and write words.

Phonics Instruction Is Not an Entire Reading Program for Beginning Readers. Along with phonics instruction, young children should be solidifying their knowledge of the alphabet, engaging in phonemic awareness activities, and listening to stories and informational texts read aloud to them. They also should be reading texts (both out loud and silently) and writing letters, words, messages, and stories.

Questions about Teaching Phonics to Students with Reading Disabilities

Do We Know Enough about the Effectiveness of Systematic and Explicit Phonics Instruction for Me to Implement It in My Classroom? Yes. Many teachers are teaching phonics systematically and explicitly and have been doing so for years. Their results, along with the findings of three decades of research, confirm the importance and effectiveness of systematic phonics instruction, particularly in kindergarten and first- and second-grade classrooms.

How Can I Tell if a Phonics Program Is Systematic and Explicit? A program of systematic phonics instruction clearly identifies a carefully selected and useful set of letter–sound relationships and then organizes the introduction of these relationships into a logical instructional sequence. The instructional sequence may include the relationships between the sounds associated with single letters (for example, the sound /m/ with the letter *m*), as well as with larger units of written language (for example, letter combinations such as *th* or *ing* or spelling patterns such as *ea* or *ie*). Furthermore, a systematic program of instruction provides children with ample opportunities to practice the relationships they are learning.

What Do Nonsystematic Programs of Phonics Instruction Look Like? Programs of phonics instruction that are not systematic do not teach consonant and vowel letter–sound relationships in a prescribed sequence. Rather, they encourage informal phonics instruction based on the teacher's perceptions of what students need to learn and when they need to learn it.

Nonsystematic instruction often neglects vowels, even though knowing vowel letter–sound relationships is a crucial part of knowing the alphabetic system. Nonsystematic programs of phonics instruction do not provide practice materials that offer children the opportunity to apply what they are learning about letter–sound relationships. The reading materials these programs do provide for children are selected according to other criteria, such as their interest to children or their literary value.

What Else Should I Look for in Programs of Phonics Instruction?   Programs should acknowledge that systematic phonics instruction is a means to an end. Some phonics programs focus primarily on teaching children a large number of letter–sound relationships. These programs often do not allot enough instructional time to help children learn how to put this knowledge to use in reading actual words, sentences, and texts. Although children need to be taught the major consonant and vowel letter–sound relationships, they also need ample reading and writing activities that allow them to practice using this knowledge.

What Kinds of Reading Practice Materials Should I Look For?   Usually, practice materials are in the form of short books or stories that contain words that provide children with practice in using the specific letter–sound relationships they are learning. Most programs of systematic phonics instruction also include materials for use in practicing writing. For example, children might have activity sheets on which they write the letters and letter combinations they are learning, and then combine these into words, sentences, messages, and their own stories.

Is Phonics Instruction More Effective When Students are Taught Individually, in Small Groups, or In Whole Classes?   You can teach phonics effectively to the whole class, to small groups, or to individual students. The needs of the students in your class and the number of adults working with them determine how you deliver instruction.

Doesn't Phonics Instruction Get in the Way of Reading Comprehension?   Quite the opposite is true. Because systematic phonics instruction helps children learn to identify words, it increases their ability to comprehend what they read. Reading words accurately and automatically enables children to focus on the meaning of text. The research is quite convincing in showing that phonics instruction contributes to comprehension skills rather than inhibiting them.

Does Phonics Instruction Slow Down the Progress of Some Children?   Again, the opposite is true. Phonics instruction contributes to growth in the reading of most children. It is important, however, to acknowledge that children vary greatly in the knowledge of reading that they bring to school. For phonics instruction to support the reading progress of all of your students, it is important to work in flexible instructional groups and to pace instruction to maximize student progress.

How Does Systematic and Explicit Phonics Instruction Affect Spelling?   Systematic programs of phonics instruction produce more growth in spelling among kindergarten and first-grade students than nonsystematic or no phonics programs.

However, systematic phonics instruction for normally developing and poor readers above first grade does not produce gains in spelling. The reason may be that as students move up in the grades, spelling is less a matter of applying letter–sound relationships and more a matter of combining word parts.

How Does Systematic and Explicit Phonics Instruction Affect the Reading and Spelling of Older Students?   Systematic phonics instruction by itself may not be enough to significantly improve the overall reading and spelling performance of readers beyond first grade. The effects of phonics instruction on students in second through sixth grades are limited to improving their word reading and oral text reading skills. The effects do not extend to spelling and reading comprehension. For these students, it is important to emphasize reading fluency and comprehension. In addition, these students also require explicit spelling instruction to improve their spelling.

How Long Should Phonics Be Taught?   Approximately two years of phonics instruction is sufficient for most students. If phonics instruction begins early in kindergarten, it should be completed by the end of first grade. If phonics instruction begins early in first grade, it should be completed by the end of second grade.

Fluency Instruction

Fluency is the ability to read a text accurately and quickly. When fluent readers read silently, they recognize words automatically. They group words quickly to help them gain meaning from what they read. Fluent readers read aloud effortlessly and with expression. Their reading sounds natural, as if they are speaking. Readers who have not yet developed fluency read slowly, word by word. Their oral reading is choppy and plodding. Fluency is important because it provides a bridge between word recognition and comprehension. Because fluent readers do not have to concentrate on decoding the words, they can focus their attention on what the text means. They can make connections among the ideas in the text and between the text and their background knowledge. In other words, fluent readers recognize words and comprehend at the same time. Less fluent readers, however, must focus their attention on figuring out the words, leaving them little attention for understanding the text.

Fluency develops gradually over considerable time and through substantial practice. At the earliest stage of reading development, students' oral reading is slow and labored because students are just learning to "break the code"—to attach sounds to letters and to blend letter sounds into recognizable words.

Even when students recognize many words automatically, their oral reading still may be expressionless, not fluent. To read with expression, readers must be able to divide the text into meaningful chunks. These chunks include phrases and clauses. Readers must know to pause appropriately within and at the ends of sentences and when to change emphasis and tone.

Fluency is not a stage of development at which readers can read all words quickly and easily. Fluency changes, depending on what readers are reading, their familiarity with the words, and the amount of their practice with reading text. Even very skilled readers may read in a slow, labored manner when reading texts with many unfamiliar words or topics. For example, readers who are usually fluent may not be able to read technical material fluently, such as a textbook about nuclear physics or an article in a medical journal.

A recent large-scale study by the National Assessment of Educational Progress (NAEP) found that 44% of a representative sample of the nation's fourth graders were low in fluency. The study also found a close relationship between fluency and reading comprehension. Students who scored lower on measures of fluency also scored lower on measures of comprehension, suggesting that fluency is a neglected reading skill in many U.S. classrooms, affecting many students' reading comprehension.

Although some readers may recognize words automatically in isolation or on a list, they may not read the same words fluently when the words appear in sentences in connected text. Instant or automatic word recognition is a necessary, but not sufficient, reading skill. Students who can read words in isolation quickly may not be able to automatically transfer this "speed and accuracy." It is important to provide students with instruction and practice in fluency as they read connected text.

What Does Scientifically Based Research Tell Us about Fluency Instruction?

Researchers have investigated two major instructional approaches related to fluency. In the first approach, repeated and monitored oral reading (commonly called "repeated reading"), students read passages aloud several times and receive guidance and feedback from the teacher. In the second approach, independent silent reading, students are encouraged to read extensively on their own.

Key findings from the National Reading Panel's (2000) scientific research on fluency instruction include the following conclusions about these two approaches that are of particular interest and value to classroom teachers.

Repeated and Monitored Oral Reading Improves Reading Fluency and Overall Reading Achievement.   Students who read and reread passages orally as they receive guidance and feedback become better readers. Repeated oral reading substantially improves word recognition, speed, and accuracy as well as fluency. To a lesser but still considerable extent, repeated oral reading also improves reading comprehension. Repeated oral reading improves the reading ability of all students throughout the elementary school years. It also helps struggling readers at higher grade levels.

Traditionally, many teachers have relied primarily on round-robin reading to develop oral fluency. In round-robin reading, students take turns reading parts of a text aloud (though usually not repeatedly). But round-robin reading in itself does not increase fluency. This may be because students only read small amounts of text, and they usually read this small portion only once.

Researchers have found several effective techniques related to repeated oral reading.

- Students read and reread a text a certain number of times or until a certain level of fluency is reached. Four re-readings are sufficient for most students.
- Oral reading practice is increased through the use of audiotapes, tutors, peer guidance, or other means.

In addition, some effective repeated oral reading techniques have carefully designed feedback to guide the reader's performance.

No Research Evidence Is Currently Available to Confirm That Instructional Time Spent on Silent, Independent Reading with Minimal Guidance and Feedback Improves Reading Fluency and Overall Reading Achievement. One of the major differences between good and poor readers is the amount of time they spend reading. Many studies have found a strong relationship between reading ability and how much a student reads. On the basis of this evidence, teachers have long been encouraged to promote voluntary reading in the classroom. Teacher-education and reading-education literature often recommends in-class procedures for encouraging students to read on their own, such as Silent Sustained Reading (SSR) or Drop Everything and Read (DEAR).

Research, however, has not yet confirmed whether independent silent reading with minimal guidance or feedback improves reading achievement and fluency. Neither has it proven that more silent reading in the classroom cannot work; its effectiveness without guidance or feedback is as yet unproven. The research suggests that there are more beneficial ways to spend reading instructional time than to have students read independently in the classroom without reading instruction.

Questions about Teaching Fluency to Students with Reading Disabilities

How Can I Help My Students Become More Fluent Readers? You can help your students become more fluent readers (1) by providing them with models of fluent reading and (2) by having students repeatedly read passages as you offer guidance. In addition, you can help students improve their fluency by combining reading instruction with opportunities for them to read books that are at their independent level of reading ability.

Model Fluent Reading, Then Have Students Reread the Text on Their Own. By listening to good models of fluent reading, students learn how a reader's voice can help written text make sense. Read aloud daily to your students. By reading effortlessly and with expression, you are modeling for your students how a fluent reader sounds during reading.

After you model how to read the text, you must have the students reread it. By doing this, the students are engaging in repeated reading. Usually, having students read a text four times is sufficient to improve fluency. Remember, however, that instructional time is limited, and it is the actual time that students are actively engaged in reading that produces reading gains.

Have other adults read aloud to students. Encourage parents or other family members to read aloud to their children at home. The more models of fluent reading the children hear, the better. Of course, hearing a model of fluent reading is not the only benefit of reading aloud to children. Reading to children also increases their knowledge of the world, their vocabulary, their familiarity with written language ("book language"), and their interest in reading.

Have Students Repeatedly Read Passages Aloud with Guidance.   The best strategy for developing reading fluency is to provide your students with many opportunities to read the same passage orally several times. To do this, you should first know what to have your students read. Second, you should know how to have your students read aloud repeatedly.

What Students Should Read.   Fluency develops as a result of many opportunities to practice reading with a high degree of success. Therefore, your students should practice orally rereading text that is reasonably easy for them—that is, text containing mostly words that they know or can decode easily. In other words, the texts should be at the students' independent reading level. A text is at students' independent reading level if they can read it with about 95% accuracy, or misread only about 1 of every 20 words. If the text is more difficult, students will focus so much on word recognition that they will not have an opportunity to develop fluency.

The text your students practice rereading orally should also be relatively short—probably 50–200 words, depending on the age of the students. You should also use a variety of reading materials, including stories, nonfiction, and poetry. Poetry is especially well suited to fluency practice because poems for children are often short and they contain rhythm, rhyme, and meaning, making practice easy, fun, and rewarding.

How to Have Your Students Read Aloud Repeatedly.   There are several ways that your students can practice orally rereading text, including student–adult reading, choral (or unison) reading, tape-assisted reading, partner reading, and readers' theatre.

• **Student–adult reading.** In student–adult reading, the student reads one-on-one with an adult. The adult can be you, a parent, a classroom aide, or a tutor. The adult reads the text first, providing the student with a model of fluent reading. Then the student reads the same passage to the adult with the adult providing assistance and encouragement. The student rereads the passage until the reading is quite fluent. This should take approximately three to four rereadings.

• **Choral reading.** In choral, or unison, reading, students read along as a group with you (or another fluent adult reader). Of course, to do so, students must be able to see the same text that you are reading. They might follow along as you read from a big book, or they might read from their own copy of the book you are reading. For choral reading, choose a book that is not too long and that you think is at the independent reading level of most students. Patterned or predictable books are particularly useful for choral reading, because their repetitious style invites students to join in. Begin by reading the book aloud as you model fluent reading. Then reread the book and invite students to join in as they recognize the words you are reading. Continue rereading the book, encouraging students to read along as they are able. Students should read the book with you three to five times total (though not necessarily on the same day). At this time, students should be able to read the text independently.

- **Tape-assisted reading.** In tape-assisted reading, students read along in their books as they hear a fluent reader read the book on an audiotape. For tape-assisted reading, you need a book at a student's independent reading level and a tape recording of the book read by a fluent reader at about 80–100 words per minute. The tape should not have sound effects or music. For the first reading, the student should follow along with the tape, pointing to each word in her or his book as the reader reads it. Next, the student should try to read aloud along with the tape. Reading along with the tape should continue until the student is able to read the book independently, without the support of the tape.

- **Partner reading.** In partner reading, paired students take turns reading aloud to each other. For partner reading, more fluent readers can be paired with less fluent readers. The stronger reader reads a paragraph or page first, providing a model of fluent reading. Then the less fluent reader reads the same text aloud. The stronger student gives help with word recognition and provides feedback and encouragement to the less fluent partner. The less fluent partner rereads the passage until he or she can read it independently. Partner reading need not be done with a more and less fluent reader. In another form of partner reading, children who read at the same level are paired to reread a story that they have received instruction on during a teacher-guided part of the lesson. Two readers of equal ability can practice rereading after hearing the teacher read the passage.

- **Readers' theatre.** In readers' theatre, students rehearse and perform a play for peers or others. They read from scripts that have been derived from books that are rich in dialogue. Students play characters who speak lines or a narrator who shares necessary background information. Readers' theatre provides readers with a legitimate reason to reread text and to practice fluency. Readers' theatre also promotes cooperative interaction with peers and makes the reading task appealing.

What Should I Do about Silent, Independent Reading in the Classroom?   Reading fluency growth is greatest when students are working directly with you. Therefore, you should use most of your allocated reading instruction time for direct teaching of reading skills and strategies. Although silent, independent reading may be a way to increase fluency and reading achievement, it should not be used in place of direct instruction in reading.

Direct instruction is especially important for readers who are struggling. Readers who have not yet attained fluency are not likely to make effective and efficient use of silent, independent reading time. For these students, independent reading takes time away from needed reading instruction.

Rather than allocating instructional time for independent reading in the classroom, encourage your students to read more outside of school. They can read with an adult or other family member. Or, they can read on their own with books at their independent reading level. Of course, students might also read on their own during independent work time in the classroom—for example, as another small group is receiving reading instruction, or after they have completed one activity and are waiting for a new activity to begin.

When Should Fluency Instruction Begin? When Should It End? Fluency instruction is useful when students are not automatic at recognizing the words in their texts. How can you tell when students are not automatic? There is a strong indication that a student needs fluency instruction

- if you ask the student to read orally from a text that he or she has not practiced and the student makes more than ten percent word recognition errors;
- if the student cannot read orally with expression; or
- if the student's comprehension is poor for the text that she or he reads orally.

Is Increasing Word Recognition Skills Sufficient for Developing Fluency? Isolated word recognition is a necessary but not sufficient condition for fluent reading. Throughout much of the twentieth century, it was widely assumed that fluency was the result of word recognition proficiency. Instruction, therefore, focused primarily on the development of word recognition. In recent years, however, research has shown that fluency is a separate component of reading that can be developed through instruction. Having students review and rehearse word lists (for example, by using flash cards) may improve their ability to recognize the words in isolation, but this ability may not transfer to words presented in actual texts. Developing reading fluency in texts must be developed systematically.

Should I Assess Fluency? If So, How? You should formally and informally assess fluency regularly to ensure that your students are making appropriate progress. The most informal assessment is simply listening to students read aloud and making a judgment about their progress in fluency. You should, however, also include more formal measures of fluency. For example, the student's reading rate should be faster than 90 words a minute, the student should be able to read orally with expression, and the student should be able to comprehend what is read while reading orally.

Probably the easiest way to formally assess fluency is to take timed samples of students' reading and to compare their performance (number of words read correctly per minute) with published oral reading fluency norms or standards. Monitoring your students' progress in reading fluency will help you determine the effectiveness of your instruction and set instructional goals. Also, seeing their fluency growth reflected in the graphs you keep can motivate students.

Other procedures that have been used for measuring fluency include Informal Reading Inventories (IRIs), miscue analysis, and running records. The purpose of these procedures, however, is to identify the kinds of word recognition problems students may have, not to measure fluency. Also, these procedures are quite time-consuming. Simpler measures of speed and accuracy, such as calculating words read correctly per minute, are more appropriate for monitoring fluency.

Vocabulary Instruction

Vocabulary refers to the words we must know to communicate effectively. In general, vocabulary can be described as oral vocabulary or reading vocabulary. Oral vocabulary refers to words that we use in speaking or recognize in listening. Reading vocabulary refers to words we recognize or use in print.

Vocabulary plays an important part in learning to read. As beginning readers, children use the words they have heard to make sense of the words they see in print. Consider, for example, what happens when a beginning reader comes to the word *dig* in a book. As she begins to figure out the sounds represented by the letters *d, i, g,* the reader recognizes that the sounds make up a very familiar word that she has heard and said many times. Beginning readers have a much more difficult time reading words that are not already part of their oral vocabulary. Researchers often refer to four types of vocabulary:

- *Listening vocabulary:*   the words we need to know to understand what we hear.
- *Speaking vocabulary:*   the words we use when we speak.
- *Reading vocabulary:*   the words we need to know to understand what we read.
- *Writing vocabulary:*   the words we use in writing.

What Does Scientifically Based Research Tell Us about Vocabulary Instruction?

The scientific research on vocabulary instruction reveals that (1) most vocabulary is learned indirectly, and (2) some vocabulary must be taught directly. The following conclusions from the National Reading Panel (2000) about indirect vocabulary learning and direct vocabulary instruction are of particular interest and value to classroom teachers.

Children Learn the Meanings of Most Words Indirectly, through Everyday Experiences with Oral and Written Language.   Children learn word meanings indirectly in three ways.

- **They engage daily in oral language.** Young children learn word meanings through conversations with other people, especially adults. As they engage in these conversations, children often hear adults repeat words several times. They also may hear adults use new and interesting words. The more oral language experiences children have, the more word meanings they learn.

• **They listen to adults read to them.** Children learn word meanings from listening to adults read to them. Reading aloud is particularly helpful when the reader pauses during reading to define an unfamiliar word and, after reading, engages the child in a conversation about the book. Conversations about books help children to learn new words and concepts and to relate them to their prior knowledge and experience.

• **They read extensively on their own.** Children learn many new words by reading extensively on their own. The more children read on their own, the more words they encounter and the more word meanings they learn.

Although a Great Deal of Vocabulary Is Learned Indirectly, Some Vocabulary Should Be Taught Directly.   Direct instruction helps students learn difficult words, such as words that represent complex concepts that are not part of the students' everyday experiences. Direct instruction of vocabulary relevant to a given text leads to a better reading comprehension, and includes providing students with specific word instruction and teaching students word-learning strategies.

Specific Word Instruction.   Specific word instruction, or teaching individual words, can deepen students' knowledge of word meanings. In-depth knowledge of word meanings can help students understand what they are hearing or reading. It also can help them use words accurately in speaking and writing.

• **Teaching specific words before reading helps both vocabulary learning and reading comprehension.** Before students read a text, it is helpful to teach them specific words they will see in the text. Teaching important vocabulary before reading can help students both learn new words and comprehend the text.

• **Extended instruction that promotes active engagement with vocabulary improves word learning.** Children learn words best when they are provided with instruction over an extended period of time and when that instruction has them work actively with the words. The more students use new words and the more they use them in different contexts, the more likely they are to learn the words.

• **Repeated exposure to vocabulary in many contexts aids word learning.** Students learn new words better when they encounter them often and in various contexts. The more children see, hear, and work with specific words, the better they seem to learn them. When teachers provide extended instruction that promotes active engagement, they give students repeated exposure to new words. When the students read those same words in their texts, they increase their exposure to the new words.

Word Learning Strategies.   Of course, it is not possible for teachers to provide specific instruction for all the words their students do not know. Therefore, students also need to be able to determine the meaning of words that are new to them but not taught directly to them. They need to develop effective word-learning strategies. Word-learning strategies include the following.

- How to use dictionaries and other reference aids to learn word meanings and to deepen knowledge of word meanings
- How to use information about word parts to figure out the meanings of words in text
- How to use context clues to determine word meanings

Students must learn how to use dictionaries, glossaries, and thesauruses to help broaden and deepen their knowledge of words, even though these resources can be difficult to use. The most helpful dictionaries include sentences providing clear examples of word meanings in context.

Examples of Classroom Instruction

Teaching Specific Words. A teacher plans to have his third-grade class read the novel *Stone Fox,* by John Reynolds Gardiner. In this novel, a young boy enters a dogsled race in hopes of winning prize money to pay the taxes on his grandfather's farm. The teacher knows that understanding the concept of taxes is important to understanding the novel's plot. Therefore, before his students begin reading the novel, the teacher may do several things to make sure that they understand what the concept means and why it is important to the story. For example, the teacher may engage students in a discussion of the concept of taxes and read a sentence from the book that contains the word *taxes* and ask students to use context and their prior knowledge to try to figure out what it means. To solidify their understanding of the word, the teacher might ask students to use *taxes* in their own sentences.

Extended and Active Engagement with Vocabulary. A first-grade teacher wants to help her students understand the concept of *jobs,* which is part of her social studies curriculum. Over a period of time, the teacher engages students in exercises in which they work repeatedly with the meaning of the concept of jobs. The students have many opportunities to see and actively use the word in various contexts that reinforce its meaning.

The teacher begins by asking the students what they already know about jobs and by having them give examples of jobs their parents have. The class might have a discussion about the jobs of different people who work at the school.

The teacher then reads the class a simple book about jobs. The book introduces the idea that different jobs help people meet their needs, and that jobs either provide goods or services. The book does not use the words *goods* and *services,* rather it uses the verbs *makes* and *helps.* The teacher then asks the students to make up sentences describing their parents' jobs by using the verbs *makes* and *helps* (e.g., "My mother is a doctor. She helps sick people get well.").

Next, the teacher asks students to brainstorm other jobs. Together, they decide whether the jobs are "making jobs" or "helping jobs." The job names are placed under the appropriate headings on a bulletin board. They might also suggest jobs that do not fit neatly into either category.

The teacher might then ask the students to share whether they think they would like to have a making or a helping job when they grow up. The teacher next asks the students to talk with their parents about jobs. She tells them to try to bring to class two new examples of jobs—one making job and one helping job. As the students come across different jobs throughout the year (for example, through reading books, on field trips, through classroom guests), they can add the jobs to the appropriate categories on the bulletin board.

Repeated Exposure to Words.   A second-grade class is reading a biography of Benjamin Franklin. The biography discusses Franklin's important role as a scientist. The teacher wants to make sure that her students understand the meaning of the words *science* and *scientist,* both because the words are important to understanding the biography and because they are obviously very useful words to know in school and in everyday life.

At every opportunity, therefore, the teacher draws her students' attention to the words. She points out the words *scientist* and *science* in textbooks and reading selections, particularly in her science curriculum. She has students use the words in their own writing, especially during science instruction. She also asks them to listen for and find in print the words as they are used outside of the classroom—in newspapers, magazines, at museums, in television shows or movies, or on the Internet. Then, as they read the biography, she discusses with students in what ways Benjamin Franklin was a scientist and what science meant in his time.

Using Word Parts.   Knowing some common prefixes and suffixes (affixes), base words, and root words can help students learn the meanings of many new words. For example, if students learn just the four most common prefixes in English (*un-, re-, in-, dis-*), they will have important clues about the meaning of about two-thirds of all English words that have prefixes. Prefixes are relatively easy to learn because they have clear meanings (for example, *un-* means "not" and *re-* means "again"); they are usually spelled the same way from word to word; and, of course, they always occur at the beginnings of words.

Learning suffixes can be more challenging than learning prefixes. This is because some suffixes have more abstract meanings than do prefixes. For example, learning that the suffix *-ness* means "the state or quality of" might not help students figure out the meaning of kindness. Other suffixes, however, are more helpful—for example, *-less,* which means "without" (hopeless, thoughtless) and *-ful,* which means "full of" (hopeful, thoughtful).

Latin and Greek word roots are found commonly in content-area school subjects, especially in the subjects of science and social studies. As a result, Latin and Greek word parts form a large proportion of the new vocabulary that students encounter in their content-area textbooks. Teachers should teach the word roots as they occur in the texts students read. Furthermore, teachers should teach primarily those root words that students are likely to see often.

Using Dictionaries and Other Reference Aids.   As his class reads a text, a second-grade teacher discovers that many of his students do not know the meaning of the word *board,* as in the sentence, "The children were waiting to board the buses." The teacher demonstrates how to find *board* in the classroom dictionary, showing students that there are four different definitions for the word. He reads the definitions one at a time, and the class discusses whether each definition would fit the context of the sentence. The students easily eliminate the inappropriate definitions of *board,* and settle on the definition, "to get on a train, an airplane, a bus, or a ship."

The teacher next has students substitute the most likely definition for *board* in the original sentence to verify that it is "The children were waiting to get on the buses" that makes the best sense.

Word Parts.   Word parts include *affixes* (prefixes and suffixes), *base words,* and *word roots. Affixes* are word parts that are "fixed to" either the beginnings of words (prefixes) or the ending of words (suffixes). The word *disrespectful* has two affixes, a prefix (*dis-*) and a suffix (*-ful*). *Base words* are words from which many other words are formed. For example, many words can be formed from the base word *migrate: migration, migrant, immigration, immigrant, migrating, migratory. Word roots* are the words from other languages that are the origin of many English words. About 60% of all English words have Latin or Greek origins.

> A second-grade teacher wants to teach her students how to use the base word *play* as a way to help them think about the meanings of new words they will encounter in reading. To begin, she has students brainstorm all the words or phrases they can think of that are related to *play.* The teacher records their suggestions: *player, playful, playpen, ballplayer,* and *playing field.* Then she has the class discuss the meaning of each of their proposed words and how it relates to *play.*
>
> A third-grade teacher identifies the base word *note.* He then sets up a "word wall," and writes the word *note* at the top of the wall. As his students read, the teacher has them look for words that are related to *note* and add them to the wall. Throughout their reading, they gradually add to the wall the words *notebook, notation, noteworthy,* and *notable.*

Using Context Clues.   Context clues are hints about the meaning of an unknown word that are provided in the words, phrases, and sentences that surround the word. Context clues include definitions, restatements, examples, or descriptions. Because students learn most word meanings indirectly, or from context, it is important that they learn to use context clues effectively.

Not all contexts are helpful, however. Some contexts give little information about a word's meaning. An example of an unhelpful context is the sentence, "We heard the back door open, and then recognized the buoyant footsteps of Uncle

Larry." A number of possible meanings of buoyant could fit this context, including heavy, lively, noisy, familiar, dragging, plodding, and so on. Instruction in using context clues as a word-learning strategy should include the idea that some contexts are more helpful than others.

In a third-grade class, the teacher models how to use context clues to determine word meanings as follows.

> *Student (reading the text):* When the cat pounced on the dog, the dog jumped up, yelping, and knocked over a lamp, which crashed to the floor. The animals ran past Tonia, tripping her. She fell to the floor and began sobbing. Tonia's brother Felix yelled at the animals to stop. As the noise and confusion mounted, Mother hollered upstairs, "What's all that *commotion?*"

> *Teacher:* The context of the paragraph helps us determine what *commotion* means. There's yelping and crashing, sobbing, and yelling. And then the last sentence says, "as the *noise* and *confusion* mounted." The author's use of the words *noise* and *confusion* gives us a very strong clue as to what *commotion* means. In fact, the author is really giving us a definition there, because *commotion* means something that's noisy and confusing—a disturbance. Mother was right; there was definitely a *commotion!*

Questions about Teaching Vocabulary to Students with Reading Disabilities

How Can I Help My Students Learn Words Indirectly?   You can encourage indirect learning of vocabulary in two main ways. First, read aloud to your students, no matter what grade you teach. Students of all ages can learn words from hearing texts of various kinds read to them. Reading aloud works best when you discuss the selection before, during, and after you read. Talk with students about new vocabulary and concepts and help them relate the words to their prior knowledge and experiences.

The second way to promote indirect learning of vocabulary is to encourage students to read extensively on their own. Rather than allocating instructional time for independent reading in the classroom, however, encourage your students to read more outside of school. Of course, your students also can read on their own during independent work time in the classroom—for example, while you teach another small group or after students have completed one activity and are waiting for a new activity to begin.

What Words Should I Teach?   You won't be able to directly teach your students all the words in a text that they might not already know. In fact, there are several reasons why you should not directly teach all unknown words.

- The text may have a great many words that are unknown to students—too many for direct instruction.

- Direct vocabulary instruction can take a lot of class time—time that you might better spend on having your students read.
- Your students can understand most texts without knowing the meaning of every word in the text.
- Your students need opportunities to use word-learning strategies to learn on their own the meanings of unknown words.

You will probably to be able to teach thoroughly only a few new words (perhaps eight or ten) per week, so you need to choose the words you teach carefully. Focus on teaching important words, useful words, and difficult words.

When you teach words before students read a text, directly teach those words that are important for understanding a concept or the text. Your students might not know several other words in the selection, but you will not have time to teach them all. Of course, you should prepare your students to use word-learning strategies to figure out the meanings of other words in the text.

Focus on teaching words that students are likely to see and use again and again. For example, it is probably more useful for students to learn the word *fragment* than the word *fractal;* likewise, the word *revolve* is more useful than the word *gyrate.* Don't forget to provide some instruction for words that are particularly difficult for your students.

Words with multiple meanings are particularly challenging for students. Students may have a hard time understanding that words with the same spelling or pronunciation can have different meanings, depending on their context. Looking up words with multiple meanings in the dictionary can cause confusion for students. They see a number of different definitions listed, and they often have a difficult time deciding which definition fits the context. You will have to help students determine which definition they should choose.

Idiomatic expressions also can be difficult for students, especially for students who are English language learners. Because idiomatic expressions do not mean what the individual words usually mean, you often will need to explain to students expressions such as "hard hearted," "a chip off the old block," "drawing a blank," or "get the picture."

How Well Do My Students Need to "Know" Vocabulary Words?

Students do not either *know* or *not know* words. Rather, they know words to varying degrees. They may never have seen or heard a word before. They may have heard or seen it, but have only a vague idea of what it means. Or they may be very familiar with the meaning of a word and be able to use it accurately in their own speech and writing. These three levels of word knowledge are called *unknown, acquainted,* and *established.*

As they read, students can usually get by with some words at the unknown or acquainted levels. If students are to understand the text fully, however, they need to have an established level of knowledge for most of the words that they read.

Are There Different Types of Word Learning? If So, Are Some Types More Difficult Than Others?   Four different kinds of word learning have been identified:

- Learning a new meaning of a known word
- Learning the meaning of a new word representing a known concept
- Learning the meaning of a new word representing an unknown concept
- Clarifying and enriching the meaning of a known word

These types vary in difficulty. One of the most common, yet challenging, is the third type: learning the meaning of a new word representing an unknown concept. Much of learning in the content areas involves this type of word learning. As students learn about deserts, hurricanes, and immigrants, they may be learning both new concepts and new words. Learning words and concepts in science, social studies, and mathematics is even more challenging because each major concept often is associated with many other new concepts. For example, the concept *deserts* is often associated with other concepts that may be unfamiliar, such as *cactus, plateau,* and *mesa.*

What Else Can I Do to Help My Students Develop Vocabulary?   Another way you can help your students develop vocabulary is to foster word consciousness—an awareness of and interest in words, their meanings, and their power. Word-conscious students know many words and use them well. They enjoy words and are eager to learn new words—and they know how to learn them.

You can help your students develop word consciousness in several ways. Call their attention to the way authors choose words to convey particular meanings. Encourage students to play with words by engaging in word play, such as puns or palindromes. Help them research a word's origin or history. You can also encourage them to search for examples of a word's usage in their everyday lives.

Text Comprehension Instruction

Comprehension is the reason for reading. If readers can read the words but do not understand what they are reading, they are not really reading. As they read, good readers are both purposeful and active.

Good readers are purposeful. They have a purpose for reading. They may read to find out how to use a food processor, read a guidebook to gather information about national parks, read a textbook to satisfy the requirements of a course, read a magazine for entertainment, or read a classic novel to experience the pleasures of great literature.

Good readers are active. They think actively as they read. To make sense of what they read, good readers engage in a complicated process. Using their experiences and knowledge of the world, their knowledge of vocabulary and language structure, and their knowledge of reading strategies (or plans), good readers make sense of the text and know how to get the most out of it. They know when they have problems with understanding and how to resolve these problems as they occur.

Research over thirty years has shown that instruction in comprehension can help students understand what they read, remember what they read, and communicate with others about what they read.

What Does Scientifically Based Research Tell Us about Effective Text Comprehension Instruction?

The scientific research from The National Reading Panel (2000) on text comprehension instruction reveals important information about what students should be taught about text comprehension and how it should be taught. The following key findings are of particular interest and value to classroom teachers.

Text Comprehension Can Be Improved by Instruction That Helps Readers Use Specific Comprehension Strategies.   Comprehension strategies are conscious plans—sets of steps that good readers use to make sense of text. Comprehension strategy instruction helps students become purposeful, active readers who are in control of their own reading comprehension. The following six strategies appear to have a firm scientific basis for improving text comprehension.

Monitoring Comprehension.   Students who are good at monitoring their comprehension know when they understand what they read and when they do not. They have strategies to "fix up" problems in their understanding as the problems arise. Research shows that instruction, even in the early grades, can help students become better at monitoring their comprehension.

Comprehension monitoring instruction teaches students to be aware of what they do understand, identify what they do not understand, and use appropriate "fix-up" strategies to resolve problems in comprehension.

Students may use several comprehension monitoring strategies. Some of these include:

- Identify where the difficulty occurs ("I don't understand the second paragraph on page 76.")
- Identify what the difficulty is ("I don't get what the author means when she says, 'Arriving in America was a milestone in my grandmother's life.'")
- Restate the difficult sentence or passage in their own words ("Oh, so the author means that coming to America was a very important event in her grandmother's life.")
- Look back through the text ("The author talked about Mr. McBride in Chapter 2, but I don't remember much about him. Maybe if I reread that chapter, I can figure out why he's acting this way now.")
- Look forward in the text for information that might help them to resolve the difficulty ("The text says, 'The groundwater may form a stream or pond or create a wetland. People can also bring groundwater to the surface.' Hmm, I don't understand how people can do that . . . Oh, the next section is called 'Wells.' I'll read this section to see if it tells how they do it.")

Using Graphic and Semantic Organizers.   Graphic organizers illustrate concepts and interrelationships among concepts in a text, using diagrams or other pictorial devices. Graphic organizers are known by different names, such as maps, webs, graphs, charts, frames, or clusters. Semantic organizers (also called semantic maps or semantic webs) are graphic organizers that look somewhat like a spider web. In a semantic organizer, lines connect a central concept to a variety of related ideas and events.

Regardless of the label, graphic organizers can help readers focus on concepts and how they are related to other concepts. Graphic organizers help students read to learn from informational text in the content areas, such as science and social studies textbooks and trade books. Used with informational text, graphic organizers can help students see how concepts fit common text structures. Graphic organizers are also used with narrative text, or stories, as story maps. Graphic organizers can help students focus on text structure as they read, provide students with tools they can use to examine and visually represent relationships in a text, and help students write well-organized summaries of a text.

Answering Questions.   Teachers have long used questions to guide and monitor students' learning. Research shows that teacher questioning strongly supports and advances students' learning from reading. Questions appear to be effective for improving learning from reading for the following reasons.

- Give students a purpose for reading
- Focus students' attention on what they are to learn
- Help students to think actively as they read
- Encourage students to monitor their comprehension
- Help students to review content and relate what they have learned to what they already know

Question-answering instruction encourages students to learn to answer questions better and, therefore, to learn more as they read. One type of question-answering instruction simply teaches students to look back in the text to find answers to questions that they cannot answer after the initial reading. Another type helps students understand question–answer relationships—the relationships between questions and where the answers to those questions are found. In this instruction, readers learn to answer questions that require an understanding of information that is text explicit (stated explicitly in a single sentence), text implicit (implied by information presented in two or more sentences), or scriptal (not found in the text at all, but part of the reader's prior knowledge or experience).

Generating Questions.   Teaching students to ask their own questions improves their active processing of text and their comprehension. By generating questions, students become aware of whether they can answer the questions and if they understand what they are reading. Students learn to ask themselves questions that require them to integrate information from different segments of text. For example, students can be taught to ask main idea questions that relate to important information in a text.

Recognizing Story Structure.   Story structure refers to the way the content and events of a story are organized into a plot. Students who can recognize story structure have greater appreciation, understanding, and memory for stories. In story structure instruction, students learn to identify the categories of content (setting, initiating events, internal reactions, goals, attempts, and outcomes) and how this content is organized into a plot. Often, students learn to recognize story structure through the use of story maps. Story maps, a type of graphic organizer, show the sequence of events in simple stories. Instruction in the content and organization of stories improves students' comprehension and memory of stories.

Summarizing.   A summary is a synthesis of the important ideas in a text. Summarizing requires students to determine what is important in what they are reading, to condense this information, and to put it into their own words. Instruction in summarizing helps students identify or generate main ideas, connect the main or central ideas, eliminate redundant and unnecessary information, and remember what they read.

Students Can Be Taught to Use Comprehension Strategies.   In addition to identifying which comprehension strategies are effective, scientific research provides guidelines for how to teach comprehension strategies.

Effective Comprehension Strategy Instruction Is Explicit, or Direct.   Research shows that explicit teaching techniques are particularly effective for comprehension strategy instruction. In explicit instruction, teachers tell readers why and when they should use strategies, what strategies to use, and how to apply them. The steps of explicit instruction typically include the following.

- **Direct explanation.** The teacher explains to students why the strategy helps comprehension and when to apply the strategy.
- **Modeling.** The teacher models, or demonstrates, how to apply the strategy, usually by "thinking aloud" while reading the text that the students are using.
- **Guided practice.** The teacher guides and assists students as they learn how and when to apply the strategy.
- **Application.** The teacher helps students practice the strategy until they can apply it independently.

Effective Comprehension Strategy Instruction Can Be Accomplished through Cooperative Learning.   Cooperative learning (and the closely related concept, collaborative learning) involves students working together as partners or in small groups on clearly defined tasks. Cooperative learning instruction has been used successfully to teach comprehension strategies in content-area subjects. Students work together to understand content-area texts, helping each other learn and apply comprehension strategies. Teachers help students learn to work in groups. Teachers also provide demonstrations of the comprehension strategies and monitor the progress of students.

Effective Instruction Helps Readers Use Comprehension Strategies Flexibly and in Combination.   Although it can be helpful to provide students with instruction in individual comprehension strategies, good readers must be able to coordinate and adjust several strategies to assist comprehension.

Multiple-strategy instruction teaches students how to use strategies flexibly as they are needed to assist their comprehension. In a well-known example of multiple-strategy instruction called *reciprocal teaching,* the teacher and students work together so the students learn four comprehension strategies.

- Asking questions about the text they are reading
- Summarizing parts of the text
- Clarifying words and sentences they don't understand
- Predicting what might occur next in the text

Teachers and students use these four strategies flexibly as they are needed in reading literature and informational texts.

Improving Reading Comprehension for Students with LD

Whereas twenty years ago research on the reading comprehension problems of students with learning disabilities focused on difficulties with decoding text, researchers today view such problems as arising from difficulties across a wide range of language and thinking activities (Swanson & Hoskyn, 1998). They recognize that some students have mastered the mechanics of reading but still have comprehension problems. This type of problem may not be evident until the higher grades when comprehension challenges increase.

Although students with LD may have the ability to process information, they do so with great inefficiency. It is typical for students with LD to be unaware of basic strategies that good readers use as a matter of course, such as re-reading passages they don't understand.

These are difficulties of strategic processing and metacognition (Gersten, Williams, Fuchs, & Baker, 1998). Strategic processing is the ability to control and manage one's own cognitive activities in a reflective, purposeful fashion, and involves metacognition, the ability to evaluate whether one is performing successfully. Research shows that instruction can improve students' strategic processing of text.

The next section of this chapter summarizes relevant research and promising practices in the strategic processing of text, focusing first on the strategic processing of narrative and then expository text.

Narrative Text.   Generally speaking, narrative text is easier to comprehend and remember than expository text (i.e., factual and informational material). For one thing, the content of a narrative is usually more familiar than the content of an exposition. Most research on narrative text has focused on teaching students to utilize story structure as an organizing framework for understanding critical aspects of the stories they read. Even preschool children use story structure to aid their comprehension. As they get older, children improve in their ability to use it. However, students with LD are slower to develop this ability. They may not be good at certain tasks, such as picking out important story information, making inferences, and identifying story themes.

Research studies from the 1980s initially addressed the question of how to improve the ability of students with learning disabilities to use narrative structure. For example, Idol-Maestas (1985) developed a strategy that consisted of the following steps: (T) study story titles, (E) examine and skim pages for clues, (L, L) look for important and difficult words, and (S) think about the story settings. Using this strategy, called TELLS, students improved their performance on comprehension questions and raised their scores on a standardized reading test. However, when the intervention was removed, student performance declined. Maintenance of performance levels after teacher guidance or other external support has been removed is a common concern in these studies.

Maintenance of performance is addressed directly in work on comprehension monitoring. For example, Chan and Cole (1986) trained 11-year-old students with LD to remember what they read by learning to ask a question about the text and/or underline interesting words in the text. The comprehension of all the trained groups improved equally, suggesting that it was not any specific strategy that led to the improvement. Rather, all of the students had been actively engaged with the struggle to understand the texts, which triggered the use of strategies that the students possessed but rarely used.

Probably the most effective strategy has been teaching story grammar to use as an organizational guide when reading. Story grammar refers to the principal components of a story: main character, action, and outcome. This technique has been applied by using story maps and by asking generic questions based on story grammar. It has also been used to move beyond the plot level of stories to teach students with disabilities to identify story themes, a more abstract comprehension level than is typically taught to students with LD. An important question in intervention research is the extent to which one can generalize from the experimental situation to the ordinary classroom. Only a few studies have focused on teacher delivery within naturally occurring classroom settings. One interesting approach is the work of Fuchs and Fuchs (Fuchs, Fuchs, Mathes, & Simmons, 1997), who designed an effective classwide peer-tutoring program (Peer Assisted Learning Strategies—PALS). Overall in these interventions, the effects occur mainly on measures that closely mirror the skills taught. Transfer effects—the students' ability to transfer the skills to a different situation—are seen, but they are often small and sometimes difficult to achieve among students with learning disabilities.

Expository Text.　The comprehension of expository text is more difficult for virtually all students. Exposition usually deals with less familiar content and involves more complex and varied structures (e.g., compare and contrast, cause and effect).

Most classroom instruction does not provide enough guidance for students with learning disabilities to be successful with expository text. Early studies of strategy training focused on teaching one strategy at a time. As in the research on narrative text, teaching the use of generic structural components has been proven effective, but the range and complexity of the various expository text structures means that students need to master several different text structures (e.g., description, sequence, compare–contrast, pro–con, cause–effect, and problem–solution). Moreover, while these single-strategy interventions have been effective in improving performance, there is little evidence that strategy use is maintained over time or transferred to other situations.

Later interventions involved a combination of strategies. Several studies have combined summarization and self-monitoring. These studies, while promising, have not yielded strong maintenance or transfer effects. They have, however, demonstrated that the teacher must play a substantial role in guiding students step-by-step through the instructional procedures.

A Focus on Teacher Training

The growing awareness that the teacher is a potent ingredient in any of these programs has led to a research focus on developing instruction for the teachers themselves. Pressley's Transactional Strategy Instruction demonstrated the feasibility of training teachers in strategy instruction (Pressley, El-Dinary, Gaskins, Schuder, Bergman, Almasi, & Brown, 1992). The goal of such training is to enable a teacher to teach strategies to students in a flexible, opportunistic manner. Such training has been shown to lead not only to better teaching skills but also superior student reading achievement. To be successful, this type of teacher education takes a substantial amount of time and effort.

Questions about Teaching Text Comprehension to Students with Reading Disabilities

Is Enough Known about Comprehension Strategy Instruction for Me to Implement It in My Classroom?   Yes. Scientific study of text comprehension instruction over the past 30 years has suggested instructional approaches that are ready to be implemented in classrooms.

When Should Text Comprehension Instruction Begin?   Even teachers in the primary grades can begin to build the foundation for reading comprehension. Reading is a complex process that develops over time. Although the basics of reading—word recognition and fluency—can be learned in a few years, reading to learn subject matter does not occur automatically once students have "learned to read." Teachers should emphasize text comprehension from the beginning, rather than wait until students have mastered "the basics" of reading. Instruction at all grade levels can benefit from showing students how reading is a process of making sense out of text, or constructing meaning. Beginning readers, as well as more advanced readers, must understand that the ultimate goal of reading is comprehension.

You can highlight meaning in all interactions with text. Talk about the content, whether reading aloud to students or guiding them in reading on their own. Model, or "think aloud," about your own thinking and understanding as you read. Lead students in a discussion about the meaning of what they are reading. Help students relate the content to their experience and to other texts they have read. Encourage students to ask questions about the text.

Has Research Identified Comprehension Strategies Other Than the Six Described Here? The six strategies described have received the strongest scientific support. The following strategies, however, have received some support from research. You may want to consider them for use in your classroom.

Making Use of Prior Knowledge. Good readers draw on prior knowledge and experience to help them understand what they are reading. You can help your students make use of their prior knowledge to improve their comprehension. Before your students read, preview the text with them. As part of previewing, ask the students what they already know about the content of the selection (for example, the topic, the concept, or the time period). Ask them what they know about the author and what text structure he or she is likely to use. Discuss the important vocabulary used in the text. Show students some pictures or diagrams to prepare them for what they are about to read.

Using Mental Imagery. Good readers often form mental pictures, or images, as they read. Readers (especially younger readers) who visualize during reading understand and remember what they read better than readers who do not visualize. Help your students learn to form visual images of what they are reading. For example, urge them to picture a setting, character, or event described in the text.

Which Comprehension Strategies Should Be Taught? When Should They Be Taught? Comprehension strategies are not ends in themselves; they are means of helping your students understand what they are reading. Help your students learn to use comprehension strategies in natural learning situations—for example, as they read in the content areas. If your students are struggling to identify and remember the main points in a chapter they are reading in their social studies textbook, teach them how to write summaries. Or, if students have read a chapter in their science textbook but are unable to answer questions about the chapter, teach them question-answering strategies. When your students find that using comprehension strategies can help them to learn, they are more likely to be motivated and involved actively in learning.

Keep in mind that not all comprehension strategies work for all types of text. Obviously, you can only teach story structure when students are reading stories, not informational text or poetry.

Future Research

What is likely to be the focus of future research in this area? The emphasis on helping students develop effective strategies for reading comprehension is likely to continue, albeit with a strong focus on teacher preparation rather than on direct teaching of strategies to students.

More and more investigators will conduct their studies in real classroom settings, arguing that the results of studies conducted in a more contrived setting, though they may be subjected to better controls, are not generalizable to other settings and situations. In fact, one main research question will be how more substantial transfer effects can be assured.

Interest in peer-mediated learning is likely to continue. One reason for the success of many peer-tutoring programs may well be their ability to generate interest and motivation among students and thus to increase task persistence and achievement.

With the focus on teacher preparation and the realization that teaching specific strategies is less promising than taking a more fluid approach, attention is likely to turn away from trying to improve students' generic thinking strategies. The field is beginning to ask questions about how reading comprehension can be fostered and improved via content-area instruction. Past research on the role of background knowledge and on strategy instruction will be of great value in this endeavor.

One additional topic that seems ripe for attention concerns the assessment of comprehension. What tasks are most appropriate for evaluating whether students really comprehend what they read? Are these tasks the same as those that are most appropriate for instructional purposes? All in all, at the beginning of a new century, we seem to be poised to make major progress in our understanding of the immensely complex nature of reading comprehension.

Student Groupings for Reading Instruction in the Inclusive Classroom

Increasing diversity in the classroom has presented teachers with the challenge of providing appropriate reading instruction for all students in their classes, who may represent a variety of ability levels and cultures. In contrast to past practices, more of today's students with learning disabilities are receiving reading instruction in a general education classroom instead of a special education classroom. This practice can be expected to increase, since the reauthorization of the 1997 Individuals with Disabilities Education Improvement Act (IDEA 2004) provides support for educating students with disabilities in the general education classroom and ensuring their right to access the general education curriculum.

Under these conditions, teachers need to know the best ways of organizing their classrooms and grouping students for instruction in order to maximize student achievement. Ability grouping, long a standard practice in reading instruction, has been criticized for lowering self-esteem and motivation among students with reading problems, and for widening the gap between high and low achievers.

Research funded by the U.S. Office of Special Education Programs (OSEP) identified a number of alternatives to whole-class instruction and ability grouping and provided information about their effectiveness. Such grouping formats include peer (same-age) tutoring, cross-age tutoring, small learning groups, and combined grouping formats. Some of these studies have employed meta-analysis, a way of looking at many research studies on a specified topic. The research shows that these alternative groupings produce better reading outcomes for students with and without disabilities than whole-class instruction.

Peer Tutoring

Peer tutoring has repeatedly been found to be an effective method of teaching reading to students with learning disabilities. While one meta-analysis (Mathes & Fuchs, 1994) found that students with disabilities made greater gains in reading when they served as tutors, another (Elbaum, Vaughn, Hughes, & Moody, 1999) found no difference between the students who served as tutors and those who were tutees. Furthermore, research has shown that students with disabilities can perform effectively either as tutors or tutees, as well as in a reciprocal tutoring role. Reciprocal-role tutoring may offer an additional benefit of boosting students' self-esteem through the teaching role. Use of this technique requires an understanding of the process, organizational planning, training of tutors, and careful monitoring.

Cross-Age Tutoring

The results from a meta-analysis on the benefits of tutoring done by Elbaum, Vaughn, Hughes, and Moody (1999) revealed that students with disabilities derive considerable benefit from tutoring younger students. However, it shows less benefit for tutees, whether or not the tutors have disabilities. Students with disabilities who were tutored by older students did not appear to benefit academically from this type of tutoring. Using this technique requires more planning, because students tutor children who are at least one grade level lower. Like peer tutoring, this technique involves tutor training and careful monitoring to ensure that both tutors and tutees are benefiting from the tutoring.

Small Learning Groups

Small group reading instruction has been shown by many research studies to be more effective than whole-class instruction, but most of these studies did not include students with disabilities. Breaking the class into teacher-led groups of three to ten students helps students learn significantly more than when they are taught using whole-class instruction. Smaller groups appear to be better—groups of three to four students are usually more efficient than groups of five to seven students in terms of teacher and student time, lower cost, increased instructional time, increased peer interaction, and improved generalization of skills.

This practice requires teachers to plan and organize groups and to adapt instruction, methods, and materials for small group use. Benefits are greater when the materials are tailored to the needs of different students. Students with disabilities may require different materials and more direct instruction than students without disabilities.

Combined Grouping Formats

Using a combination of formats produces measurable reading benefits for students with disabilities. For example, a teacher may use whole-class instruction for a part of each period, and have students work in pairs for two days and in small groups for two days. Although combined formats have not yet been studied extensively, they appear to offer promise for inclusive teachers and their students.

General Strategies for Teaching Reading to Students with Learning Disabilities

Reading is the single most important educational skill your students will learn. Understanding the organization and meaning of text and instruction in both phonics and literature is essential to helping young children read. By understanding the prerequisite skills for reading, teachers can build a solid foundation for their students to learn and succeed in school.

Create Appreciation of the Written Word.

- Share stories with children and invite them to explore a story's magic.
- Share informational texts and invite children to wonder about the new ideas presented.
- Take every opportunity to point out the ways in which reading is essential to the communications of everyday life (e.g., on labels, instructions, and signs).

Develop Awareness of Printed Language and the Writing System.

- Teach students how books are organized—that books in English are read from left to right and top to bottom, that print may be accompanied by pictures or graphics, that the pages are numbered, and that the purpose of reading is to gain meaning from the text and understand ideas that words convey.
- Read to children from books with easy-to-read, large print. Use stories that have predictable words in the text.
- Use "big books" to help children notice and learn to recognize words that occur frequently, such as *a, the, is, was,* and *you.*
- Label objects in your classroom.

Teach the Alphabet.   A strong predictor of the ease with which a child learns to read is his or her familiarity with letters of the alphabet. This familiarity is a critical building block for learning to read. It is important to go beyond knowing the names of letters. Students must also develop a sense of the purpose of letters.

- Help students notice the letters in the print that surrounds them and that you share with them every day.
- Engage students in activities that will help them learn to recognize letters visually.
- Help students learn to form letters and encourage them to embellish their work with their names and with other first attempts at writing.

Develop the Students' Phonological Awareness.   In listening and speaking, we pay attention to the meaning of language rather than to its sound. To learn to read, however, students must be taught to attend to the sounds, or phonology, of language. This is necessary for them to understand how speech is represented by print. Children with learning disabilities need special help in learning to develop phonological awareness.

- Model and demonstrate how to break short sentences into individual words. For example, use the sentence *Frogs eat bugs,* and demonstrate with chips, cards, or other manipulatives how the sentence is made up of three words and how the order of the words matters. Using manipulatives to make sentences, play with each word and put it in order.
- Develop students' awareness of the sounds of individual words by asking them to clap out syllables and to listen for and generate rhymes.
- Once children are comfortable in playing games with words, syllables, and rhymes, move on to phonemic awareness.

Develop Phonemic Awareness.   Phonemic awareness refers to an understanding that words and syllables are comprised of a sequence of elementary speech sounds. This understanding is essential to learning to read an alphabetic language. The majority of children with reading disabilities fail to grasp this idea. In teaching phonemic awareness, the focus of all activities should be on the sounds of words, not on letters or spellings.

- Use strategies that make phonemes prominent in children's attention and perception. For example, model specific sounds, such as /s/ in the word *sat,* and ask children to produce each sound in isolation and in many different words until they are comfortable with the sound and understand its nature.
- Begin with simple words and simple challenges. For example, listen for initial /s/ in *sat, sit, sip,* and *sad* or for long /e/ in *me, see, bee,* and so on.
- Teach students to blend phonemes into words. Begin by identifying just one phoneme, for example, /m/-*ilk,* /s/-*at,* working gradually toward blending all the phonemes in words (e.g., /s/-/a/-/t/).

- Teach students to identify the separate phonemes within words. For example, what is the first sound of *soup*? What is the last sound of *kiss*? Beginning phonemes are easier to identify than final phonemes.
- Once students are comfortable listening for individual phonemes, teach them to break words into component sounds, for example, /m/-/oo/-/s/ = *moose*.
- Create a sequence of segmenting and blending activities to help students develop an understanding of the relationship between sounds in words.

Provide children with more support when first teaching a task. For example, model a sound or strategy for making the sound, and have the children use the strategy to produce the sound. Model and practice several examples. Prompt the children to use the strategy during guided practice, and gradually add more examples. As the students master these skills, provide less teacher-directed instruction and more practice and challenge.

Make teaching phonological awareness a top priority. Opportunities to engage in phonological awareness activities should be plentiful, frequent, brief, and fun. Phonemic awareness is essential for learning to read, but it is not enough by itself. It must be coupled with instruction and practice in learning the relationship between letters and sounds.

Teach the Relation of Sounds and Letters.   Students should learn the letters of the alphabet and discriminate each letter from the other, because each stands for one or more of the sounds that occur in spoken words. When presenting each letter, model its corresponding sound and have children produce the sound themselves. For children with learning disabilities, the teaching activities must be explicit and unambiguous. At first, teach and work with only a few letter–sound correspondences that have high utility in many words (e.g., /m/ in *man, mad, him,* and *ham*). Postpone teaching less frequently occurring letters until students have a firm understanding of how left-to-right spellings represent first-to-last sounds (alphabetic understanding).

Teach Children How to Sound Out Words.   After students have mastered a few letter–sound correspondences, teach them to decode words or sound them out. Begin with small, familiar words.

- Teach children to sound out the letters, left to right, and blend them together, searching for the word in memory.
- Model sounding out the word, blending the sounds together and saying the word. The ability to sound out new words allows children to identify and learn new words on their own.
- Give children stories containing words that reflect the letter-sound patterns that have been taught, and encourage them to sound out words whenever they are uncertain.
- Help children learn spelling conventions, such as the use of final /e/'s to mark long vowels, by comparing and contrasting lots of examples.

Teach Children to Spell Words.

- Teach children to spell words by sounding their letters one by one. Model the sounding and spelling process for children as they spell.
- Begin with short words children can sound out, because these words follow regular spelling conventions, for example, *cap, bat,* and *sit* instead of *cape, bait,* and *sight.*
- Begin with simple words that do not contain consonant blends—*ham* and *pan* instead of *slam* and *plan.*
- Encourage students to use spelling knowledge and strategies regularly in their own writing.
- Introduce spelling conventions systematically. Begin with words that exemplify the most frequent and basic conventions, and provide support and practice to help students generalize from these words to others. The goal is to help them see the spelling conventions in the words.
- Use words in which letter–sound correspondences represent their most common sounds (e.g., *get* instead of *gem*).
- Develop a sequence and schedule of opportunities that allow children to apply and develop facility with sounds and words at their own pace. Specify what skills to assess and when to assess them so you will know when to move on. Take into account each student's background knowledge and pace in moving from sounding out to blending words to reading connected text.

Help Children Develop Fluent, Reflective Reading.

- Help children learn to read fluently by requiring them to read new stories and reread old stories every day.
- Help children extend their experience with the words, language, and ideas in books by interactively reading harder texts with them and to them every day.
- Relate information in books to other events of interest to children, such as holidays, pets, siblings, and games. Engage children in discussion of the topics.
- In both stories and informational texts, encourage wondering. For example, *I wonder what Pooh will do now? How do you think the father feels?* or *I wonder what frogs do in the winter? Do you think that's a problem? Why?*
- Model comprehension strategies and provide students with guided assistance.
- Point out how titles and headings tell what a book is about.
- Help students identify the main ideas presented in the text, as well as the supporting detail. Graphics help to reveal main ideas, and the relationship between text and graphics helps students understand what they are reading.
- Point out unfamiliar words and explore their meaning. Revisit these words frequently and encourage students to use them in their own conversations.
- Show children how to analyze contextual clues to figure out the meaning of an unfamiliar word. Research shows that most vocabulary growth comes from learning new words in reading.

Conclusion

We are living at a pivotal time in the history of U.S. education. More than ever before, schools are being asked to deliver a higher level of education and to do so for all students. Meeting this challenge requires that the process of "learning to read" be securely underway for virtually all students by the end of the third grade.

No U.S. school would knowingly withhold a vaccine from students that would prevent a childhood disease like measles. Yet this is, in effect, what is happening when it comes to the teaching of reading. Recent gains in our knowledge of the reading process have given us the tools to help a majority of students, including those with learning disabilities, to learn to read at the level required to function as effective individuals, workers, parents, and citizens in today's world. The challenge is to put this new knowledge in the hands of teachers, parents, and school administrators so that millions of U.S. students who otherwise would fail to learn to read will gain access to this important skill.

Strategies and Instructional Practices for Students with Learning Disabilities in Mathematics

The bar on what students with disabilities are expected to learn was raised by the 1997 Amendments to the Individuals with Disabilities Education Act (IDEA), which emphasized students' participation and progress in the general education curriculum. Navigating the general education math curriculum has become a key to student success.

The mathematics curriculum has changed over the last twenty years due to educational reforms driven by standards. A significant element driving this change is the National Council of Teachers of Mathematics (NCTM) Principles and Standards for School Mathematics (first published in 1989 and revised in 2000), which focus on conceptual understanding and problem solving rather than procedural knowledge or rule-driven computation. Most states and districts have used the NCTM Standards to some degree in revamping their mathematics curricula. (For more information, visit the NCTM web site at http://standards.nctm.org.)

The challenge for teachers is to provide effective math instruction to students with learning disabilities so they can meet the high standards set for what all students must be able to know and do mathematically. Unfortunately, many students with disabilities experience difficulties with the reformed math curriculum. As University of Maryland researchers Paula Maccini and Joe Gagnon have found, students may have difficulty processing and distinguishing relevant information, have deficits in computational skills, or lack reasoning and problem-solving skills. But with the right support, students with learning disabilities can succeed in a higher level math curriculum.

Review of Dyscalculia

Chapter 3 detailed information pertaining to mathematics learning disabilities, referred to as dyscalculia. To summarize, a student with dyscalculia often

- Shows difficulty understanding concepts of place value, quantity, number lines, positive and negative value, and carrying and borrowing

- Has difficulty understanding and doing word problems
- Has difficulty sequencing information or events
- Exhibits difficulty using steps involved in math operations
- Shows difficulty understanding fractions
- Is challenged making change and handling money
- Displays difficulty recognizing patterns when adding, subtracting, multiplying, or dividing
- Has difficulty putting language to math processes
- Has difficulty understanding concepts related to time such as days, weeks, months, seasons, quarters, and so on
- Exhibits difficulty organizing problems on the page, keeping numbers lined up, and following through on long division problems

To understand more about the basics of dyscalculia, please review Chapter 3.

Mathematical Disabilities: What We Know and Don't Know*

Over the past several decades important advances have been made in the understanding of the genetic, neural, and cognitive deficits that underlie reading disability (RD), and in the ability to identify and remediate this form of learning disability (LD). Research on learning disabilities in mathematics (MD) has also progressed over the past ten years, but more slowly than the study of RD. One of the difficulties in studying children with MD is the complexity of the field of mathematics. In theory, MD could result from difficulties in the skills that comprise one or many of the domains of mathematics, such as arithmetic, algebra, or geometry. Moreover, each of these domains is very complex, in that each has many subdomains and a learning disability can result from difficulties in understanding or learning basic skills in one or several of these subdomains.

As an example, to master arithmetic, children must understand numbers (e.g., the quantity that each number represents), counting (there are many basic principles of counting that children must come to understand), and the conceptual (e.g., understanding the base-10 number system) and procedural (e.g., borrowing from one column to the next, as in 43 − 9) features involved in solving simple and complex arithmetic problems. A learning disability in math can result from difficulties in learning any one, or any combination, of these more basic skills. To complicate matters further, it is possible, and in fact it appears to be the case, that different children with MD have different patterns of strengths and weakness when it comes to understanding and learning these basic skills.

So, how does one approach the study of MD? Researchers in this area have narrowed the search for the deficits associated with MD by taking the theories and techniques used to study normal mathematical development and using them to

*By David C. Geary, Professor of Psychology at the University of Missouri at Columbia. Reprinted by permission of LD Online, www.LDOnLine.org.

study children with low achievement scores in mathematics, despite an average or better intelligence (IQ). Nearly all of these studies have focused on elementary-school children and the domains of number, counting, and arithmetic; unfortunately, not enough is know[n] about the normal development of algebraic and geometric skills to provide the foundation necessary to systematically study learning disabilities in these mathematical domains. Because of this research, we now understand some of the deficits that contribute to MD, at least in these basic areas. Before we get to the description of these deficits, the more basic issues of how many children have MD and the diagnose of MD are addressed. The final section presents [a] brief discussion of future directions.

How Common Are Math Disabilities?

There have only been a few large-scale studies of children with MD and all of these have focused on basic number and arithmetic skills. As a result, very little is known about the frequency of learning disabilities in other areas of mathematics, such as algebra and geometry. In any case, the studies in number and arithmetic are very consistent in their findings: Between 6 and 7% of school-age children show persistent, grade-to-grade, difficulties in learning some aspects of arithmetic or related areas (described below). These and other studies indicate that these learning disabilities are not related to IQ, motivation, or other factors that might influence learning.

The finding that about 7% of children have some form of MD is misleading in some respects. This is because most of these children have specific deficits in one or a few subdomains of arithmetic or related areas (e.g., counting) and perform at grade-level or better in other areas of arithmetic and mathematics. The confusion results from the fact that standardized math achievement tests include many different types of items, such as number identification, counting, arithmetic, time telling, geometry, and so [forth]. Because performance is averaged over many different types of items, some of which children with MD have difficulty on and some of which they do not, many of these children have standardized achievement test scores above the 7th percentile (though often below the 20th).

In other words, the mixing of many different types of items on math achievement tests makes the identification of the learning disability of many of these children difficult at best, and, at the same time, results in an impression that they are generally poor at mathematics. In fact, many of these children have average or better skills in some areas of mathematics and very poor skills in more specific areas. The averaging of performance over different types of test items gives the false impression of generally poor performance in all areas of mathematics when, in fact, the difficulty may be confined to one or a few specific areas. To complicate matters further, recent studies suggest that children with MD are a heterogeneous group, with different children showing different patterns of knowledge and learning strengths and deficits. For instance, two children with math achievement scores at the 10th percentile, and average IQ scores (i.e., children with MD), may have different forms of MD, that is, different types of deficits.

To more reliably diagnose MD and to better understand the cognitive strengths and weaknesses of these children, tests that provide information on very specific arithmetical and related skills, such as counting knowledge, arithmetic facts, and so forth are needed. Unfortunately, such tests are not currently available.

What Are the Common Features of MD?

As stated above, there has been very little research on learning disabilities in mathematical domains outside of the areas of number, counting, and arithmetic. Thus, little can be said, at this time, about whether learning disabilities exist in the areas of geometry and algebra, for instance and, if they do exist, what their form or developmental course is. Some general conclusions can, however, be made about the basic number, counting, and arithmetic skills of children with MD and these are briefly discussed in the respective sections below. The final section presents a discussion of the relation between RD and MD.

Number.   The learning of basic number skills is much more complicated than many adults would assume. Children must learn English number words and their correct sequence (i.e., "one, two, three"), as well as the associated Arabic numbers and sequence (i.e., "1, 2, 3"). Children must learn the quantities associated with these number words and Arabic numbers (e.g., that "three" and "3" are symbols that represent a collection of any three things) and learn to translate numbers from one form to another, as in translating "thirty seven" into "37." Equally important, children must develop an understanding of the structure of numbers, for instance, that numbers can be decomposed into smaller numbers or combined to create larger numbers. The most difficult feature of the number system is [its] base-10 structure, that is, the basic sequence of numbers repeats in series of 10 (e.g., 1, 2, 3, 4, 10 is repeated 10 + 1, 10 + 2, that is, 11, 12). Coming to really understand the base-10 system is difficult for all children, but is essential, as this conceptual knowledge is important for the mastery of other domains (e.g., complex arithmetic).

The base-10 knowledge of children with MD has not been studied, but most of the remaining basic number skills have been assessed, at least for smaller numbers (e.g., 3, 4, 23, 67; but not more complex numbers, such as 1,222,976). Although definitive conclusions cannot be drawn at this point, the available evidence suggests that most children with MD do not have a basic deficit in the ability to understand or learn number concepts. This is not to say that they don't have some difficulties along the way, they do (e.g., learning that teen numbers are composed of 1 "10" and × "1s", e.g., 12 = 10 + 2). Rather, the difficulties these children have with learning number sequences and number concepts do not appear to be any different than the difficulties experienced by children without MD.

Counting.   Learning the basic counting sequence, "one, two, three, four" is not difficult; almost all children learn this sequence. What is important is that children learn the basic concepts or rules that underlie the ability to count effectively. The basic rules are as follows:

One–one correspondence. One and only one word tag (e.g., "one," "two") is assigned to each counted object. Counting the same item twice and tagging the item, "one, two" violates this rule.

Stable order. The order of the word tags must be invariant across counted sets. Many preschool children do not yet know the standard sequence of number words, that is, "one, two, three," but still appear to intuitively understand this rule. For instance, they may count two sets of three objects, "A, B, C."

Cardinality. The value of the final word tag represents the quantity of items in the counted set. One way to test knowledge of this rule is to ask children to count a series of objects and then ask them "how many are there?" If the child understands cardinality then she will just repeat the last number word (e.g., "three" if 3 objects were counted). Children who don't understand cardinality will recount the set.

Abstraction. Objects of any kind, such as rocks, toys, and people, can be collected together and counted.

Order-irrelevance. Items within a given set can be tagged in any sequence, from left to right or right to left, or skipping around.

The principles of one–one correspondence, stable order, and cardinality define the "how to count" rules, which, in turn, provide the skeletal structure for children's emerging counting competencies. While this skeletal knowledge appears to be in-born, it is also known that children make inductions about the basic characteristics of counting by observing standard counting behavior. For instance, because counting typically proceeds from left to right, many young children believe that you must count from left to right; right to left counting would be deemed as wrong. Many children also believe that you must count adjacent items, that skipping around is wrong; in fact, skipping around is OK, as long as each item is counted only once—this belief is call the adjacency rule. These beliefs suggest that many young children don't fully understand counting concepts.

As noted above, having children count from 1 to 20, for instance, provides virtually no information on their understanding of counting rules, as nearly all children can do this, and is thus of no value in diagnosing MD. However, the use of more subtle techniques that tap children's intuitive understanding of the just described counting rules does provide a fine-grained assessment of their counting knowledge. Several studies have now used these techniques in the study of children with MD. The results indicate that 1st and 2nd grade children with MD understand the concepts of one–one correspondence, stable order, and cardinality just as well as children without MD—there have been no studies of older MD children's counting knowledge. Many children with MD have difficulties with tasks that assess the order irrelevance principle, or, in other words, believe that only adjacent items can be counted, suggesting that they understand counting as a fixed, mechanical activity.

Although children with MD understand one–one correspondence, they sometimes make mistakes on tasks that assess this concept. In one of these tasks, the child is asked to help a puppet who is just learning how to count. Sometimes the puppet counts correctly and at other times the puppet violates one of the counting rules. The child's task is simply to state whether the puppet's count was "OK and right" or "not OK and wrong." As an example, on some trials, the puppet counts six toys from left to right but double counts, "six, seven," the last toy. Double counting violates the one–one rule and children with MD almost always detect this error. However, when the first toy is double counted, "one, two," many children with MD state that this count is "OK"—the child has to wait until the puppet has finished the count before deciding if the count was "OK" or "not OK." This pattern, and studies using different techniques, suggests that many children with MD have difficulty keeping information (the error notation in this example) in mind while monitoring the counting process. In other words, they understand most of the counting rules, but often forget numerical information during the act of counting.

Arithmetic.   The basic arithmetic skills of children with MD have been extensively studied in the United States, several European nations, and in Israel. These studies have largely focused on the strategies used to solve simple arithmetic problems, such as finger counting or remembering the answer, and the associated reaction times (i.e., speed of problem solving) and error patterns. These studies have revealed several very consistent patterns with children with MD, patterns that are not related to IQ.

First, many children with MD have difficulties remembering basic arithmetic facts, such as the answers to $5 + 3$ or 3×4. It is not that children with MD do not remember any arithmetic facts, but rather they don't remember as many facts as other children do and appear to forget facts rather quickly. Certain patterns in how quickly they remember facts, when they do remember facts, and in the associated error patterns suggest that this is a fundamental memory problem, that is, not something that these children will "grow out of."

Although a definitive conclusion cannot be drawn at this time, there appear to be two sources of this memory problem—some children with MD show both types of memory problem, while other children show one form but not the other.

First, it appears that many MD children have difficulties getting basic facts into long-term memory and difficulties remembering, or accessing, the facts that are eventually stored in long-term memory. It appears that these difficulties are very similar to word finding difficulties that are common in some children with RD.

Second, it appears that some children with MD can get facts into and out of long-term memory without too much difficulty but have trouble inhibiting other facts when they try to remember the answers to specific problems, such as $2 + 3$. These children will not only remember 5, they might also have 4 (the number following 2, 3 in the counting sequence) and 6 (the answer to 2×3) pop into their heads at the same time. With too many facts being remembered, these children take longer to remember the correct answer—they may have to consider all of the answers that they remembered and then pick one of these—and they make more errors.

The other consistent finding is that many children with MD use immature problem-solving procedures to solve simple arithmetic problems, that is they use procedures that are more commonly used by younger children without MD. As an example, the most basic—least mature—strategy for solving simple addition problem is called counting-all. To solve 5 + 3, most younger children will uplift five fingers on one hand, counting "one, two, three, four, five, " and then uplift three fingers on the other hand, counting "one, two, three." They will then recount all of the uplifted fingers starting from one. A quicker and more mature procedure is to simply state the largest number, five in this example, and then count-on a number of times equal to the value of the smaller number, as in "five, six, seven, eight."

As a group, children with MD use less mature counting strategies more frequently and for a longer period of time than do other children; children with MD also tend to make more errors when using counting procedures to solve arithmetic problems. This delay in the adoption of mature counting procedures to solve arithmetic problems appears to be related to the earlier described difficulties in keeping track of information during the counting process and to their rather rigid conceptualization of counting. Although the results are mixed, it appears that many children with MD catch up to their peers in their ability to effectively—in terms of the maturity of the procedure and error rate—use counting procedures to solve arithmetic problems by the middle of the elementary-school years. In other words, for many children with MD this appears to be a developmental delay and not a more fundamental deficit. Nonetheless, there appears to be a subset of children with MD who show difficulties in the use of counting procedures throughout the elementary school years and sometimes later.

Finally, there has been some research on the ability of children with MD to solve more complex arithmetic problems, such as 45 + 97, but considerably less research than with simple arithmetic. The research to date suggests that some of these children have difficulties sequencing the component steps needed to solve these problems. For 45 + 97, the first few steps involve adding 5 + 7, noting the 2 in the appropriate column and then carrying the 10 to the next column. Although many children with MD may understand and be skilled at executing each individual step, "putting them all together in the right order" is often difficult.

Are RD and MD Related?   It appears that many—perhaps more than ½—children with MD also have difficulties learning how to read and that many children with RD also have difficulties learning basic arithmetic. In particular, children and adults with RD often have difficulties retrieving basic arithmetic facts from long-term memory. The issue is whether the co-occurrence of RD and difficulties in remembering arithmetic facts are due to a common underlying memory problem. The answer to this question is by no means resolved. Nonetheless, some evidence suggests that the same basic memory deficit that results in common features of RD, such as difficulties making letter–sound correspondences and retrieving words from memory, is also responsible for the fact-retrieval problems of many children with MD. If future research confirms this relationship, then a core memory problem that is independent of IQ, motivation and other factors, may underlie RD and at least one form of MD.

Where Do We Go from Here?

There is much that needs to be done is this area, in terms of basic research, assessment and diagnosis, and, of course, remediation.

Basic Research.   There are more unanswered than answered questions in the MD area. Some examples of issues that need to be addressed: We need to know more about the basic counting and arithmetic skills of children with MD, their developmental course—which of these deficits are simply delays and which are more fundamental problems—and the basic memory and other cognitive systems that support these skills. We need to begin studies of potential learning disabilities in other areas of mathematics, such as algebra and geometry, although much of this research must await research on normative development in these areas. A few studies suggest that certain forms of MD, such as the fact-retrieval deficit, may represent an inherited risk, although little is actually known about these risks. In other words, we need to learn more about the genetics of MD and the neurological systems that support mathematical cognition and that might be involved in MD. We need to know more about the co-occurrence of RD and MD.

Assessment and Diagnosis.   As described earlier, current standardized achievement tests are too general—they include too many different types of items—to provide useful diagnostic information on the source of poor math learning. To be sure, low performance on such tests suggest that a learning problem may exist, but these tests do not provide information on the exact source of the poor achievement. The poor scores could be due to problems remembering arithmetic facts, poor counting knowledge, and so on. A standardized diagnostic test that provides more precise information on the counting knowledge, counting procedures used to solve arithmetic problems, ability to remember facts, and so forth is needed.

Remediation.   Of course the ultimate goal of learning disabilities research is to develop instructional techniques that remediate, or at least compensate for, the learning difficulty. Perhaps it is needless to say, but, in comparison to remediation studies in the RD area, very little research has been done on remediation in the MD area. Part of the difficulty stems from the fact that, except for the areas described above, little is really known about the nature and course of math disabilities—it is hard to develop effective remedial techniques for a disorder that is not well understood. Nonetheless, this is an area of great need and an area in which we can probably begin to develop remedial programs, at least for basic counting and arithmetic.

Adapting Mathematics Instruction in the General Education Classroom for Students with Mathematics Disabilities*

Students with learning disabilities (LD) are increasingly receiving most of their mathematics instruction in general education classrooms. Studies show that these students benefit from general education mathematics instruction if it is adapted and modified to meet the individual needs of the learners (Salend, 1994). Adapta-

*By Robin H. Lock, the University of Texas at Austin. Reprinted with permission from LD Online, www.LDOnLine.org.

tions and modifications come in many forms. They can be as simple as using graph paper to help student[s] with mathematics disabilities keep columnar addition straight or as complex as solving calculus equations with calculators. To ensure effective instruction, adaptations and modifications for instruction are necessary in the areas of lesson planning, teaching techniques, formatting content, adapting media for instruction, and adapting evaluation (Wood, 1992).

In general education classrooms, adaptations and modifications in mathematics instruction are appropriate for all students, not just students with LD. Teachers of mathematics will find that simple changes to the presentation of mathematical concepts enable students to gain a clearer understanding of the process rather than a merely mechanically correct response. Additionally, adapting and modifying instruction for students creates a more positive atmosphere that encourages students to take risks in problem-solving, which strengthens student understanding of the concept (McCoy & Prehm, 1987).

For many teachers with limited or no preparation for working with students with LD, inclusion of students with mathematics disabilities may create concern. This article provides information on how to adapt and modify mathematics instruction to promote success and understanding in the areas of mathematical readiness, computation, and problem-solving for students with math disabilities. It also presents techniques that promote effective mathematics instruction for these students.

How Can General Education Teachers Facilitate the Learning of Mathematical Skills?

Ariel (1992) stresses the need for all students to develop skill in readiness, computation, and problem-solving skills. As illustrated below, adaptations and modifications can be implemented to help students succeed in all three areas.

Readiness. According to Ariel (1992), students with LD must acquire (a) general developmental readiness, and (b) conceptual number readiness. General developmental readiness includes ability in the areas of classification, one-to-one correspondence, seriation, conservation, flexibility, and reversibility. Knowledge of the student's level of general readiness allows the teacher to determine how adaptations and modifications must be enacted to allow for the student to progress. For some students, mathematics readiness instruction may need to include the development of language number concepts such as big and small and smallest to largest; and attributes such as color, size, or shape. Instruction, review, and practice of these concepts must be provided for longer time periods for students with mathematics disabilities than for other students.

Conceptual number readiness is essential for the development of addition and subtraction skills (Ariel, 1992). Practice and review with board games or instructional software are effective ways to develop conceptual number readiness for students with mathematics disabilities. Manipulatives, such as Cuisenaire rods and Unifix math materials (e.g., 100 block trays) allow students with math disabilities to visualize numerical concepts and engage in age-appropriate readiness skills.

Computational Skills.   Adaptations and modifications in the instruction of computational skills are numerous and can be divided into two areas: memorizing basic facts and solving algorithms or problems.

Basic Facts.   Two methods for adapting instruction to facilitate recall of basic facts for students with math disabilities include (a) using games for continued practice, and (b) sequencing basic facts memorization to make the task easier. Beattie and Algozzine (cited in McCoy & Prehm, 1987) recommend the use of dice rolls, spinners, and playing cards to give students extra practice with fact memorization and to promote interest in the task by presenting a more game-like orientation. Further, McCoy and Prehm (1987) suggest that teachers display charts or graphs that visually represent the students' progress toward memorization of the basic facts. Sequencing fact memorization may be an alternative that facilitates instruction for students with LD. For example, in teaching the multiplication facts, Bolduc (cited in McCoy & Prehm, 1987) suggest[s], starting with the ×O and ×1 facts to learn 36 of the 100 multiplication facts. The ×2 and ×5 facts are next, adding 28 to the set of memorized facts. The ×9s are introduced next, followed by doubles such as 6×6. The remaining 20 facts include 10 that are already known if the student is aware of the commutative property (e.g., $4 \times 7 = 7 \times 4$). New facts should be presented a few at time with frequent repetition of previously memorized facts for students with LD.

Solving Algorithms.   Computation involves not only memorization of basic facts, but also utilization of these facts to complete computational algorithms. An algorithm is a routine, step-by-step procedure used in computation (Driscoll, 1980 cited in McCoy & Prehm, 1987). In the addition process, McCoy and Prehm (1987) present three alternatives to the standard renaming method for solving problems, including expanded notation [see Figure 11.1] partial sums [see Figure 11.2], and Hutchings's low-stress algorithm [see Figure 11.3]. Subtraction for students with mathematics disabilities is made easier through the use of Hutchings' low-stress subtraction method (McCoy & Prehm, 1987) [see Figure 11.4] where all renaming is done first. Multipli-

---

FIGURE 11.1   Expanded Notation

$29 =$	2 tens and 9 ones
$+43 =$	4 tens and 3 ones
Step one: Add the ones and tens.	6 tens and 12 ones
Step two: Regroup the ones, if necessary	6 tens and (1 ten 2 ones)
Step three: Put the tens together.	(6 tens and 1 ten) and 2 ones
Step four: Write the tens in a simpler way.	7 tens and 2 ones
Step five: Write the answer in number form.	72

FIGURE 11.2 Partial Sums

$$
\begin{array}{r}
39 \\
+65 \\
\hline
\end{array}
$$

(sum of the ones)

14

(sum of the tens)

90

___

104

---

cation and division (McCoy & Prehm, 1987) can be illustrated through the use of partial products [see Figure 11.5]. Further, arrays that use graph paper to allow students to plot numbers visually on the graph and then count the squares included within the rectangle they produce. Arrays can be used in combination with partial products to modify the multiplication process, thereby enabling students with math disabilities to gain further insight into the multiplication process.

Providing adaptations is often very effective for helping students with mathematics disabilities successfully use facts to solve computational problems. Salend

---

FIGURE 11.3 Hutchings' Low-Stress Algorithm

Problem: 45 + 77 + 56 + 83 + 27 + 39 =

45

77	1)	Add 5 + 7 and record 12, put the "1" above the tens.
56	2)	Add 2 + 6 and record 8, no tens to carry.
83	3)	Add 8 +3 and record 11, put the "1" above the tens.
27	4)	Add 1 +7 and record 8, no tens to carry.
39	5)	Add 8 + 9 and record 17, put the "1" above the tens.
	6)	Add 3 + 4 and record 7, no tens to carry.
	7)	Add 7 + 7 and record 14, put the "1" in the hundreds
	8)	Add 4 + 5 and record 9, no hundreds to carry.
	9)	Add 9 + 8 and record 17, put the "1" in the hundreds.
	10)	Add 7 + 2 and record 9, no hundreds to carry.
	11)	Add 9 + 3 and record 12, put the "1" in the hundreds.
	12)	Add the hundreds place.

FIGURE 11.4	Hutchings' Low-Stress Subtraction Algorithm

3247	3247	3247	3247	3247
−1736	47	1247	21247	21247
	−1736	−1736	−1736	−1736
				1 511

1) Rewrite the tens and ones places.

2) Determine if renaming is necessary.

3) Rewrite the hundreds, tens, and ones places.

4) Determine if renaming is necessary.

5) Renaming is necessary to complete subtraction in the hundreds place. Rewrite the number in the hundreds place.

6) Complete subtraction with renaming already accomplished.

(1994) lists suggestions for modifying mathematics assignments in computation. These suggestions are shown in [Figure 11.6].

Further adaptations and modifications in computational instruction include color coding of the desired function for the computation problem (Ariel, 1992), either ahead of time by the teacher or during independent practice by the student. This process serves as a reminder to the student to complete the desired function and also may be used as an evaluation device by the teacher to determine the student's knowledge of the mathematical symbols and processes they represent.

Matrix paper allows students a physical guide for keeping the numbers in alignment (Ariel, 1992), thus decreasing the complexity of the task and allowing the teacher and student to concentrate on the mathematical process. In simplifying the task, the teacher then can identify problems in the student's understanding of the process rather than in the performance of the task.

Finally, modeling is another effective strategy for helping students solve computational problems. For example, Rivera and Deutsch-Smith (cited in Salend,

FIGURE 11.5	Partial Products

1) $2 * 3 = 6$

23
$*12$

2) $2 * 20 = 40$

3) $10 * 3 = 30$

4) $10 * 20 = 200 / 276$

FIGURE 11.6	Tips for Modifying Mathematics Computational Assignments

1. Reduce the number of problems on worksheets for independent practice.

2. Increase the amount of time students have to complete the assignment.

3. Provide adequate space for students to write out solutions.

4. Follow a standard format for developing worksheets.

5. Cut the worksheet in halves or fourths requiring students to complete one section at a time.

6. Assign only odd or even problems.

7. Highlight the operation to be performed.

8. Move gradually to increasing the number of problems (not more than twenty problems) and decreasing the amount of time to complete the assignment.

1994) recommend the use of the demonstration plus permanent model strategy, which includes the following three steps designed to increase skill in comprehending the computation process: (a) the teacher demonstrates how to solve a problem while verbalizing the key words associated with each step in solving the computation problem; (b) the student performs the steps while verbalizing the key words and looking at the teacher's model; and (c) the student completes additional problems with the teacher's model still available. Other modeling examples provided by Salend (1994) include the use of charts that provide definitions, correct examples, and step-by-step instructions for each computational process.

Problem-Solving. Problem-solving can be adapted and modified for students with mathematics disabilities in several different ways. Polloway and Patton (1993) note that students with math disabilities improve their problem-solving skills through teacher-directed activities that include (a) having students read or listen to the problem carefully; (b) engaging students in focusing on relevant information and/or significant words needed to obtain the correct answer while discarding the irrelevant by writing a few words about the answer needed (e.g., number of apples), by identifying aloud or circling the significant words in the problem, and by highlighting the relevant numbers; (c) involving students in verbalizing a solution for the problem using a diagram or sketch when appropriate; (d) developing strategies for working through the story problem by writing an appropriate mathematical sentence; and (e) performing the necessary calculations, evaluating the answer for reasonableness, and writing the answer in appropriate terms.

Lack of critical thinking skills compounds problem-solving difficulties. Several cognitive and meta-cognitive strategies can be used effectively. For example, (1992) recommends the use of six problem-solving strategies that students can monitor on an implementation sheet. Students verbalize the steps while completing the problem and note their completion of the steps on the monitoring sheet. The six steps are:

1. Read and understand the problem.
2. Look for the key questions and recognize important words.
3. Select the appropriate operation.
4. Write the number sentence (equation) and solve it.
5. Check your answer.
6. Correct your errors.

Further, Mercer (1992) identifies the components necessary for students to engage in successful problem solving. According to [Mercer], the problem-solving process involves 10 steps, which can be expanded into learning strategies to enable students with math disabilities to be more effective in solving word problem[s]. The 10 steps are:

1. Recognize the problem.
2. Plan a procedural strategy (i.e., identify the specific steps to follow).
3. Examine the math relationships in the problem.
4. Determine the math knowledge needed to solve the problem.
5. Represent the problem graphically.
6. Generate the equation.
7. Sequence the computation steps.
8. Check the answer for reasonableness.
9. Self-monitor the entire process.
10. Explore alternative ways to solve the problem.

Hammill and Bartel (in Polloway & Patton, 1993) offer many suggestions for modifying mathematics instruction for students with LD. They encourage teachers to think about how to alter instruction while maintaining the primary purpose of mathematics instruction: Competence in manipulating numbers in the real world. Their suggestions include:

1. Altering the type or amount of information presented to a student such as giving the student the answers to a story problem and allowing the student to explain how the answers were obtained.
2. Using a variety of teacher-input and modeling strategies such as using manipulatives during the instructional phase with oral presentations.

Techniques to Enhance Mathematics Instruction

For students with math disabilities, effective mathematics instruction is the difference between mathematics as a paper-and-pencil/right-answer type of task and an important real-life skill that continues to be used throughout their lifetime. This section examines effective instructional techniques that the general educator can incorporate into the classroom for all learners, and especially for students with math disabilities.

Increasing Instructional Time.   Providing enough time for instruction is crucial. Too often, "math time" according to Usnick and McCoy (cited in McCoy & Prehm, 1987) includes a long stretch of independent practice where students complete large numbers of math problems without feedback from the teacher prior to completion. Instructional time is brief, often consisting of a short modeling of the skill without a period of guided practice. By contrast, small-group practice where students with math disabilities complete problems and then check within the group for the correct answer, use self-checking computer software programs, and receive intermittent teacher interaction are positive modifications for increasing time for mathematics instruction. Additionally, time must be provided for students to engage in problem-solving and other math "thinking" activities beyond the simple practice of computation, even before students have shown mastery of the computational skills. Hammill and Bartel (cited in Polloway & Patton, 1993) suggest slowing down the rate of instruction by using split mathematics instructional periods and reducing the number of problems required in independent practice.

Using Effective Instruction.   Polloway and Patton (1993) suggest that the components of effective instruction play an important role in the success of students with disabilities in general education mathematics instruction. One suggested schedule for the class period includes a period of review of previously covered materials, teacher-directed instruction on the concept for the day, guided practice with direct teacher interaction, and independent practice with corrective feedback. During the guided and independent practice periods, teachers should ensure that students are allowed opportunities to manipulate concrete objects to aid in their conceptual understanding of the mathematical process, identify the overall process involved in the lesson (i.e., have students talk about "addition is combining sets" when practicing addition problems rather than silent practice with numerals on a worksheet), and write down numerical symbols or mathematical phrases such as addition or subtraction signs.

Teaching key math terms as a specific skill rather than an outcome of basic math practice is essential for students with LD (Salend, 1994). The math terms might include words such as "sum," "difference," "quotient," and "proper fraction," and should be listed and displayed in the classroom to help jog students' memories during independent assignments.

Varying Group Size.   Varying the size of the group for instruction is another type of modification that can be used to create an effective environment for students with math disabilities. Large-group instruction, according to McCoy and Prehm (1987), may be useful for brainstorming and problem-solving activities. Small-group instruction, on the other hand, is beneficial for students by allowing for personal attention from the teacher and collaboration with peers who are working at comparable levels and skills. This arrangement allows students of similar levels to be grouped and progress through skills at a comfortable rate. When using grouping as a modification, however, the teacher must allow for flexibility in the groups so that students with math disabilities have the opportunity to interact and learn with all members of the class.

Using Real-Life Examples.   Salend (1994) recommended that new math concepts be introduced through everyday situations as opposed to worksheets. With everyday situations as motivators, students are more likely to recognize the importance and relevance of a concept. Real-life demonstration enables students to understand more readily the mathematical process being demonstrated. Further, everyday examples involve students personally in the instruction and encourage them to learn mathematics for use in their lives. Changing the instructional delivery system by using peer tutors; computer-based instruction; or more reality-based assignments such as "store" for practice with money recognition and making change also provide real life math experiences (Hammill & Bartel cited in Polloway & Patton, 1993).

Varying Reinforcement Styles.   Adaptations and modifications of reinforcement styles or acknowledgment of student progress begin with teachers being aware of different reinforcement patterns. Beyond the "traditional" mathematical reinforcement style, which concentrates on obtaining the "right answer," students with mathematics disabilities may benefit from alternative reinforcement patterns that provide positive recognition for completing the correct steps in a problem regardless of the outcome (McCoy & Prehm, 1987). By concentrating on the process of mathematics rather than on the product, students may begin to feel some control over the activity. In addition, teachers can isolate the source of difficulty and provide for specific accommodations in that area. For example, if the student has developed the ability to replicate the steps in a long division problem but has difficulty remembering the correct multiplication facts, the teacher should reward the appropriate steps and provide a calculator or multiplication chart to increase the student's ability to obtain the solution to the problem.

Summary

The mathematical ability of many students with LD can be developed successfully in the general education classroom with proper accommodations and special education instructional support. To this end, teachers should be aware of the necessity for adapting and modifying the environment to facilitate appropriate, engaging instruction for these students. Use of manipulatives is encouraged to provide realistic and obvious illustrations of the underlying mathematical concepts being introduced. Reliance on problem-solving strategies to improve students' memories and provide a more structured environment for retention of information also is appropriate. Finally, teachers must evaluate the amount of time spent in instruction, the use of effective instructional practices, student progress, and the use of Real-life activities that encourage active, purposeful learning in the mathematics classroom.

10 Tips for Software Selection for Math Instruction*

Are you excited about the potential technology may have in assisting students with learning disabilities in mathematics? We know that many students with learning disabilities struggle to learn mathematics. Students have trouble understanding mathematical concepts, recalling and carrying out mathematical procedures, and solving a range of mathematical problems. Importantly, researchers have identified a range of effective mathematics interventions for students with disabilities. Computer-aided instruction has been shown to be an effective tool for mathematics instruction (Goldman & Pellegrino, 1987; Okolo, Bahr, & Reith, 1993). Students who use appropriate technology persist longer, enjoy learning more, and make gains in math performance. The potential of hypermedia to improve mathematical performance (Babbitt & Miller, 1997) is being realized in today's software design. There seems to be many good reasons to celebrate technology's use.

On the other hand, are you overwhelmed by the many math software programs available? Is there any substance beneath the sound, color, cute characters and animation? To help you effectively select technology for math instruction, I've put together a list of 10 tips to guide teachers and parents in selecting instructional math software. The focus here is on instructional software such as concept development, drill and practice, tutorial and simulation software rather than tool software such as spreadsheets or graphing software. The software mentioned is for illustrative purposes only.

Tip 1: The Less Clutter on the Screen, the Better. Most students with LD are distracted by too much stimuli coming at them at the same time. Moreover, cluttered screens often distract from the math concept or procedure being studied. Choose programs that use simple screen displays.

Tip 2: Procedures Should Match Those Being Taught in School. Many LD students get confused if the same task is presented in different ways particularly in the early stages of learning. Some computation procedures used in software differ from standard classroom presentations. Weigh the other advantages of the software before introducing this conflict into math instruction. If you decide to use software with differing procedures, take the time to carefully point out the differences and be ready to assist if confusion arises.

Tip 3: Choose Modifiable Software. Software in which speed, number of problems, and instructional levels can be modified will serve the needs of a wide range of students in a single classroom or an individual student over a long period of time. Some students are motivated by the necessity of a speedy response while others become frustrated by the time pressure. While some students enjoy the ever increasing speed of Math Munchers Deluxe (MECC) others are very relieved to play

---

*By Beatrice C. Babbitt, Ph.D., Associate Professor of Special Education at the University of Nevada, Las Vegas. Reprinted with permission from LD Online, at www.LDOnLine.org.

this math matching game with the speed element turned off. Having the ability to modify the response speed is very important to effective math instruction. In addition, students vary greatly in their ability to complete a number of problems before they need feedback and a break. Individuals differ within themselves on persistence depending on the time of day and the difficulty of the problems. This variation can best be responded to by being able to adjust the number of problems in any problem set and the starting level for each student.

Tip 4: Choose Software with Small Increments between Levels.   Most math software designed for all students makes rather large jumps in difficulty from one level to the next. This is particularly true of retail math software that purports to cover the entire K–8 math curriculum. Students with LD will often test out of Level 1 but then fail miserably on Level 2 because the problems have gotten too difficult too fast. Special education publishers such as Edmark (http://www.edmark.com) are more aware of this difficulty and incorporate smaller difficulty increments between levels. The other solution is to choose software that allows problem selection or construction to design an intermediate level that fits a particular student.

Tip 5: Choose Software with Helpful Feedback.   Math software should provide clues to the correct answer when a student makes an error. Software might indicate the range within which the answer should lie or show a diagram to indicate the underlying concept that could help the student solve the problem on their own. Software that simply indicates a student is wrong is less helpful. Fraction Fireworks (Edmark) incorporates an interesting and useful feedback technique. The fireworks celebration after a correct answer illustrates the fraction chosen.

Tip 6: Choose Software that Limits the Number of Wrong Answers for a Single Problem.   A sure formula for creating student frustration is to require students to repeatedly guess on a problem they don't know. It's also a sure formula for encouraging random guessing and other non-thinking behavior. The best software will limit the number of attempts, give clues as to the correct answer, provide the correct answer, and then reintroduce that same item at a later time. Test this feature on a software program by making deliberate errors.

Tip 7: Choose Software with Good Record Keeping Capabilities.   We know that informative performance feedback can help students understand their errors and help them set realistic but challenging goals. Software should keep records for each student. Young children might be told how many items out of the total number were correct. Older students can be given percentages correct. Information should be made available on the types of problems or the exact problems that caused difficulties. Most software will include record keeping capabilities but preview software to be sure.

Tip 8: Choose Software with Built-In Instructional Aids.   The ability to accurately represent word problems can increase problem solving performance. Software that incorporates built-in instructional aids such as counters, number lines, base-ten blocks, hundreds charts, or fraction strips can give the student tools to represent a given problem and then go on to solve it. These virtual manipulatives are incorporated in such programs as Equivalent Fractions by Sunburst (http://www.sunburst.com). A colleague and I have done some preliminary work with students using concrete manipulatives with software when built-in instructional aids were not available. Students found the aids very helpful as they solved fraction comparison problems.

Tip 9: Select Software that Simulates Real-Life Solutions. In real life there is usually more than one way to solve a problem. Money, time, and problem- solving software is more effective if it allows multiple roads to problem solution. Making Change by Attainment Company, Inc. (http://www.attainment-inc.com), for example, is a very helpful program because it combines decisions (where can I buy this item on my shopping list?) with multiple solution routes (students can select any combination of bills and coins to pay for items as long as they give the clerk enough money).

Tip 10: Remember Software Is a Learning Tool—Not the Total Solution! Instructional software is a tool in effective math instruction and learning. With color, graphics, animation, sound and interactivity, it can capture and hold the attention of students so that they persist in mathematics tasks. Software can use these same features to present mathematics in imaginative and dynamic ways. When modifiable, it can support learning at the child's pace and on the child's level. It is important, however, to combine direct teacher instruction with technology-assisted instruction. In most instances, concept development with concrete materials and clear procedural instruction should precede software use. Pencil and paper tasks still have a role to play in student learning. Problem solving should occur with and without technology use. While well designed math software can support student learning in a positive manner, software can rarely stand on its own. Instruction must precede software use and then extend beyond the software to apply the math concepts, procedures, and problem solving in many new settings. . . .

By selecting software wisely and using it effectively with other instructional tools, parents, teachers, and more importantly, students with learning disabilities will find learning mathematics can be an interesting and enjoyable experience.

Homework Strategies for Students with Mathematics Difficulties

Homework is one aspect of the general education curriculum that has been widely recognized as important to academic success. Teachers have long used homework to provide additional learning time, strengthen study and organizational skills, and in some respects, keep parents informed of their children's progress. Generally, when students with disabilities participate in the general education curriculum, they are expected to complete homework along with their peers. But, just as students with learning disabilities may need instructional accommodations in the classroom, they may also need homework accommodations.

Many students with learning disabilities in mathematics find homework challenging, and teachers are frequently called upon to make accommodations for these students. What research supports this practice?

Give Clear and Appropriate Assignments. Teachers need to take special care when assigning homework. If the homework assignment is too hard, is perceived as busy work, or takes too long to complete, students might tune out and resist doing it. Never send home any assignment that students with learning disabilities cannot do. Homework should be an extension of what students have learned in class. To ensure that homework is clear and appropriate, consider the following tips from teachers for assigning homework to students with learning disabilities:

- Make sure students and parents have information regarding the policy on missed and late assignments, extra credit, and available adaptations. Establish a set routine at the beginning of the year.
- Assign work that the students can do
- Explain the assignment clearly
- Write the assignment on the chalkboard and leave it there until the assignment is due
- Remind students of due dates periodically
- Coordinate with other teachers to prevent homework overload

Students concur with these tips. They add that teachers can also:

- Establish a routine at the beginning of the year for how homework will be assigned
- Assign homework toward the beginning of class
- Relate homework to classwork or real life (and/or inform students how they will use the content of the homework in real life)
- Explain how to do the homework, provide examples, and write directions on the chalkboard
- Have students begin the homework in class, check that they understand, and provide assistance as necessary
- Allow students to work together on homework

Make Homework Accommodations. Make any necessary modifications to the homework assignment before sending it home. Identify practices that will be most helpful to individual students with learning disabilities and have the potential to increase their involvement, understanding, and motivation to learn. The most common homework accommodations for students with learning disabilities are to:

- Provide additional one-on-one assistance to students
- Monitor students' homework more closely
- Allow alternative response formats (e.g., allow the student to audiotape an assignment rather than handwriting it)
- Adjust the length of the assignment
- Provide a peer tutor or assign the student to a study group

- Provide learning tools (e.g., calculators)
- Adjust evaluation standards
- Give fewer assignments

It is important to check out all accommodations with other teachers, students, and their families. If teachers, students, or families do not find homework accommodations palatable, they may not use them.

Teach Study Skills.   Both general and special education teachers consistently report that homework problems seem to be exacerbated by deficient basic study skills. Many students, particularly students with learning disabilities, need instruction in study and organizational skills. Here is a list of organizational strategies basic to homework.

- Identify a location for doing homework that is free of distractions
- Have all materials available and organized
- Allocate enough time to complete activities and keep on schedule
- Take good notes
- Develop a sequential plan for completing multi-task assignments
- Check assignments for accuracy and completion before turning them in
- Know how to get help when it is needed
- Turn in completed homework on time

Teachers can enhance homework completion and accuracy by providing classroom instruction in organizational skills. They should talk with parents about how to support the application of organizational skills at home.

Use a Homework Calendar.   Students with learning disabilities in mathematics often need additional organizational support. Just as adults use calendars, schedulers, lists, and other devices to self-monitor activities, students can benefit from these tools as well. Students with learning disabilities can monitor their own homework using planning calendars to keep track of homework assignments. Homework planners also can double as home–school communication tools if they include a space next to each assignment for messages from teachers and parents. Here's how one teacher used a homework planner to increase communication with students' families and improve homework completion rates: Students developed their own homework calendars. Each page in the calendars reflected one week. There were spaces for students to write their homework assignments and columns for parent–teacher notes. The covers were a heavy card stock that the children decorated. Students were expected to take their homework planners home each day and return them to class the next day.

In conjunction with the homework planner, students graphed their homework return and completion rates—another strategy that is linked to homework completion and improved performance on classroom assessments. The teacher built a reward system for returning homework and the planners. On a self-monitoring chart in their planner, students recorded each time they completed and returned their homework assignment by coloring the square for the day green if homework was completed and returned, coloring the square for the day red if homework was not done, and coloring one-half of the square yellow and one-half of the square red if homework was late.

If students met the success criterion, they received a reward at the end of the week, such as fifteen extra minutes of recess. The teacher found that more frequent rewards were needed for students with emotional and behavioral disabilities.

Ensure Clear Home–School Communication.   Homework accounts for one-fifth of the time that successful students invest in academic tasks, yet students complete homework in environments over which teachers have no control—which, given the fact that many students experience learning difficulties, creates a major dilemma. Teachers and parents of students with learning disabilities must communicate clearly and effectively with one another about homework policies, required practices, mutual expectations, student performance on homework, homework completion difficulties, and other homework-related concerns. Recommended ways that teachers can improve communications with parents who have children with learning disabilities include

- Encouraging students to keep assignment books.
- Providing a list of suggestions on how parents might assist with homework. For example, ask parents to check with their children about homework daily.
- Providing parents with frequent written communication about homework (e.g., progress reports, notes, letters, forms).
- Sharing information with other teachers regarding student strengths and needs and necessary accommodations.

Ways that administrators can support teachers in improving communications include

- Supplying teachers with the technology needed to aid communication (e.g., telephone answering systems, email, homework hotlines).
- Providing incentives for teachers to participate in face-to-face meetings with parents (e.g., release time, compensation).
- Suggesting that the school district offer after school and/or peer tutoring sessions to give students extra help with homework.

How Parents Can Help

Research shows that the level of parent involvement in a child's education is strongly related to the degree of success in school (Henderson & Berla, 1994). "Families play a vital role in educating children. What families do is more important to student success than whether they are rich or poor, whether parents have finished high school or not, or whether children are in elementary, junior high, or high school" (Robinson, in Paulu, 1995). The importance of family involvement in education led the U.S. Congress to add the following goal to the National Education Goals: "Every school will promote partnerships that will increase parental involvement and participation in promoting the social, emotional, and academic growth of children." The following are ways in which parents can help their children with mathematics learning disabilities (Sutton, 1998).

Set the Example.   One of the most important ways parents can help a child in math is by exhibiting attitudes and values supportive of learning. "All children have two wonderful resources for learning—imagination and curiosity. As a parent, you can awaken your children to the joy of learning by encouraging their imagination and curiosity."

Accept the Struggle.   Struggle is a normal part of doing math, just as you accept the struggle to become better in sports. Help uncover difficulties and offer suggestions for overcoming them.

Encourage Mastery.   Just as it is important to repeat fundamentals again and again in sports until performed automatically, it is important to see practice in mathematics as developing mastery, not a chore or form of punishment.

Look Beyond the Grade.   Math grades are often calculated on percentages of correct answers on tests and assignments accumulated during a grading period, so they may not reflect understanding that has developed over the course of a grading period. Help focus on understanding and being able to identify specific difficulties.

Discover the Textbook.   "Reading" math can be difficult, and math textbooks are often used as collections of assignments and homework problems. Help your child learn how to "read" the math textbook, see the underlying structure, and learn from the examples provided.

Help Children See the Math around Them.   Help children recognize the use of math around them in daily life, and engage them in games and activities that foster familiarity with numbers and mathematical thinking. A guide, "Helping Your Child Learn Math," is available online at www.ed.gov/pubs/parents/Math/index.html. The guide suggests many activities that parents can do with children (grades K–8) at home, at the grocery store, or in transit. The activities generally make use of playing cards, coins, containers, or other simple materials around the house. Here are some other ideas that the guide offers.

- Wrong answers can help!
- Be patient; incorrect answers tell you that you need to look further, ask questions, and figure out what you do not understand.
- Sometimes a wrong answer is the result of misunderstanding the question.
- Ask your child to explain how they solved a problem; responses may clarify whether help is needed with a procedure, the "facts" are wrong, or a crucial concept is not understood.
- You may learn something that the teacher would find helpful. A short note or telephone call will alert the teacher to possible ways of helping your child.
- Help your children become risk takers. Help them examine wrong answers, and assure them that right answers come with understanding.

- Problems can be solved in different ways. Though a problem may have only one correct solution, there are often many ways to get the right answer.
- Doing math in your head is important. Increased use of calculators and computers makes it increasingly important that people be able to determine whether an answer is reasonable.

More activities and games for strengthening specific skills and concepts are provided online in a "Guide to Helping Your Child Understand Mathematics," provided by Houghton Mifflin's Education Place (see www. eduplace.com/parents/index.html); select "Parent's Place," then "Parent's Resources." Suggestions are also provided for things to do in the grocery store, in a restaurant, while shopping, and on the refrigerator door.

Provide a Place and Resources to Study.   Provide children with convenient, quiet, and comfortable work areas, along with whatever resources are needed to study math and complete assignments. Encourage the use of reference materials (such as dictionaries and encyclopedias), and provide a computer and calculator if possible. If a computer is not available in the home, plan regular visits to a public library or community learning center where access is available.

The computer has become a common and essential tool in understanding many school subjects, particularly mathematics and science. You and your children can use the computer to

- Produce reports and assignments using word-processing programs, spreadsheets, and other software.
- Find information from reference materials on CD-ROMs. Many are typically available from school and public libraries.
- Use commercial software packages that teach math skills in interesting and enjoyable ways.
- Access the abundant math and homework resources and assistance freely available on the Internet.

Conclusion

A positive attitude on the part of the child with a mathematics disability is also crucial to the success of the student, both in and outside of the classroom. Teachers and tutors who have worked consistently with these students are very aware of the role of the self in energizing learning, and the potential damage to the sense of self-worth that comes from labeling. Teachers and parents should appreciate children's thinking as the foundation of their abilities, and maintain some flexibility in their expectations regarding their children's development of certain academic skills, such as mathematics. For children to feel successful, they need to become aware of their unique learning strengths, so they may apply them effectively while working to strengthen the lagging areas (Webb, 1992). Each child needs to feel successful and appreciated as an individual, whatever his or her difficulties in school.

12

Strategies and Instructional Practices for Students with Learning Disabilities in Written Expression

Understanding Why Students Avoid Writing*

It is common for students in today's educational system to dislike and/or avoid the writing process. Many students feel writing takes too long. For some, writing is a very laborious task because there are so many subcomponents which need to be pulled together. For others, the reason lies in some processing difficulties, such as dyslexia or dysgraphia. Some educators wonder if students no longer enjoy the slower, more refined process of written communication because they spend so much time watching the faster-paced visual modality of television.

Students with learning problems, even those who read well, frequently submit written work which is brief and/or difficult to read. Such students can be victims of misunderstandings, a problem which becomes much more pronounced at the secondary level. "Accusations of laziness, poor motivation, and a reprehensible attitude are often directed toward deficit writers. The results can be a serious loss of incentive, a generalized academic disenchantment and demoralization" (Levine 1998, 363). There are many reasons students avoid writing. Primary reasons may be one or more of the following:

- They have a hard time getting started and feel overwhelmed by the task.
- They need to concentrate to form letters: it is not an automatic process.
- They struggle to organize and use mechanics of writing.
- They are slow and inefficient in retrieving the right word(s) to express an idea.
- They struggle to develop their ideas fluently (poor ideation).
- They struggle to keep track of their thoughts while also getting them down on paper.
- They feel that the process of writing on paper is slow and tedious.
- They feel that the paper never turns out the way they want.
- They realize that the paper is still sloppy even though substantial time and effort were spent.

*© Regina G. Richards, MA, Educational Therapist, Richards Educational Therapy Center, Inc., www.retctrpress.com. Originally published by LD Online, www.LDOnline.org. Reprinted with permission.

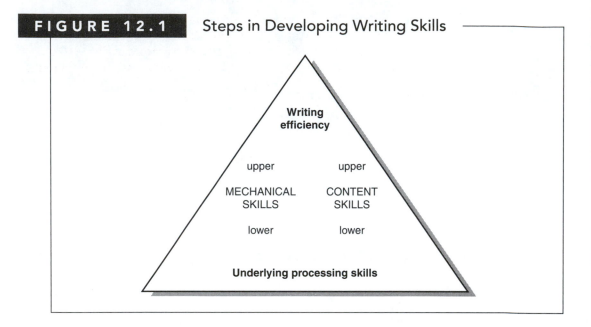

FIGURE 12.1   Steps in Developing Writing Skills

- They are dysgraphic, which causes multiple struggles at the basic processing levels.
- They are dyslexic, which causes very poor spelling and interferes with automatic use of writing mechanics.

As parents and teachers, we can help students deal with their lack of enjoyment of the writing process and also with poor skill development. The techniques are twofold. Students need to (a) develop a greater understanding of and appreciation for the purpose of writing; and (b) develop more efficient skills.

When students have a combination of this understanding and the skills, they are then free to apply techniques and abilities in a wide range of situations. This is especially true and necessary for dyslexic and/or dysgraphic students who are compensating for processing inefficiencies in the language domain.

Skill Development

[Figure 12.1] represents the necessary steps in developing writing skills. These steps are in a hierarchy: if a student has too many gaps in one (or more) of the lower levels, then the top levels may be shaky and unstable.

The underlying processing skills involve development in a variety of memory, motor, and language areas. Examples include:

- Physical components of writing
- Speed of motor performance
- Active working memory
- Language formulation and ideation

The mechanical skills involve lower level tasks such as automatic letter form, use of space, basic spelling, capitalization, and punctuation. More mature mechanics involve speed, clarity of expression, and appropriate grammar.

The content skills relate to organizing and expressing ideas. The upper level skills include:

- Writing using different writing styles
- Being flexible in the writing process
- Understanding the viewpoint of the reader
- Writing with enthusiasm

Overall Guidelines to Help Students Avoid the Avoidance of Writing

There are many reasons a student may avoid writing, but most relate to the concept that writing is not fun or enjoyable. When writing is not meaningful, it is difficult to pull together the variety of skills needed to develop enthusiasm about writing. Students learn to write by writing, which then gives them the confidence to continue to write and continue to develop their skills. Using a variety of modalities can help create enthusiasm for writing and help students view writing as a more meaningful activity.

It is also important to analyze the lower level skills to ensure that the student has appropriately developed automaticity in these skills. When students are frustrated with individual components related to the task of writing and/or when they struggle to get started or to keep track of their thoughts, then the writing process is not fun, and their lack of enthusiasm becomes evident. Writing remains at the level of drudgery no matter how exciting the topic and students may feel threatened by the process of writing.

The goal for these students is to reduce the frustration, struggles, and feeling of threat. Increasing automaticity of skills is required to increase overall writing automaticity for a student. When automaticity, as developed by metacognitive awareness of the writing process and use of specific strategies, is combined with skill development and bypass strategies, the student should be able to deal with the vast majority of written expression tasks. The next step is to integrate purpose and meaning to generate fun and lead to enthusiasm for writing.

Helping Students Who Struggle to Write[*]

There are many reasons students hate to write, the primary of which is that writing is a slow and laborious process. The purpose of this article is to provide suggestions to help students, with emphasis on compensations.

[*]© Regina G. Richards, MA, Educational Therapist, Richards Educational Therapy Center, Inc., www.retctrpress.com. Originally published by LD Online, www.LDOnLine.org. Reprinted with permission. References for this article can be found in the original source.

Students benefit when they compensate for writing problems because so often writing struggles interfere with learning and prevent them from fully demonstrating what they have learned. Compensating helps them bypass the problem area and still accomplish the goal of the activity. Some example classroom compensations include the following:

- **Staging.** Dividing the task into smaller units and performing each subtask independently. Some students become overwhelmed because tasks appear to be too large or have too many steps. Staging helps them focus on each subtask with greater concentration and an emphasis on quality.

- **Decreasing quantity.** Allowing the student to perform fewer math problems, write fewer sentences, or write a shorter story. Some students work so hard for each problem that they find it very difficult to perform an entire assignment or even to concentrate on the concept. Students with writing difficulties sometimes learn more from fewer problems because their concentration is more efficient. Allowing for shorter assignments encourages the student to focus on quality rather than quantity, thus often decreasing the urge to rush through.

- **Increasing time.** Providing the student with more time to finish his work. Many times a student may be capable of completing the work, but unable to do so in the same amount of time as his peers. The extra time decreases the tendency for rushing through and can increase the focus on quality.

- **Copying.** Reducing or eliminating copying demands, such as copying from the chalkboard, or even copying from another paper. Sometimes students with writing difficulties make multiple mistakes when copying information and it is important to insure that they have access to the correct information.

- **Providing structure for math.** Using large graph paper or looseleaf paper turned sideways helps the student alignment numbers properly in multistep math problems. Some students benefit from having their math problems machine copied in enlarged format with additional white space, as this also prevents errors in copying the problem.

- **Adjusting writing format.** Allowing each student to choose the format that is most comfortable. Some students perform better in manuscript whereas other students perform better using cursive. Allowing work to be completed by computer word processing helps the student use staging more efficiently while also bypassing the mechanical difficulties of letter form and space.

- **Spelling.** Allowing for misspelling on in-class assignments. Hold students responsible for correct spelling on final drafts, encouraging use of a phonics-based spell checker, such as one of the Franklin Electronic Resources® with a speaking component.

CAUTION: It is unfair and counterproductive to make a student with writing problems stay in for recess to finish work. These children need *more* movement time, not less.

Keyboarding

The most efficient compensation for any student who struggles with basic letter form and use of spaces [is] to develop efficient word-processing skills. Parents and teachers need to be aware, however, that it is very difficult to go through life totally avoiding use of paper and pencil and, consequently, it is important for each student to develop at least some basic handwriting skills. Specific multisensory strategies designed for dysgraphic students are useful for any student who needs help developing appropriate letter form and automatic motor movements. Specific remedial strategies that incorporate air writing, use of the vertical plane (chalkboard), simultaneous verbal cues, and reinforcement with tactile input, are most effective.

In today's society, keyboarding skills are valuable for all students, but are particularly essential for the student who struggles with writing and/or spelling difficulties. Students are able to learn keyboarding skills at a very young age. However, keyboarding development requires practice and many students complain that the practice is especially *boring*. This can be a problem because consistency and frequency of practice are very important in developing automaticity. Consequently, it is useful to have the student practice keyboarding on a daily basis, but only for [a] very short period of time each day. In early elementary, the student may practice only five to ten minutes a night. In upper elementary, the practice sessions maybe ten to fifteen minutes a night. If the student is just beginning to learn keyboarding as a teenager, it may be necessary to extend the practice sessions to fifteen to twenty minutes a night. The consistency of the practice is critical.

Many fun and efficient software programs are available to help students learn appropriate keyboarding. Access to a variety of programs helps decrease boredom and allows for choice, as the student may select different software each night. Alternate programs have also been developed which teach keyboarding skills based on the alphabetical sequence. One such program starts with the left hand and uses a poem which begins, "little finger a, reach for b, same finger c, d, e."

Initially, as the student is learning, correct finger should not be required when he is typing for content, as this greatly increases the demands on active working memory. For most students, the habits developed during typing practice will eventually integrate with the finger used while concentrating on ideation and content.

Once a student learns word processing skills, she will have the option of progressing to use of voice-activated software, such as Dragon® NaturallySpeaking®. Such software allows the student to dictate into a microphone without the need for direct typing on the keyboard. However, this is a higher level skill which is much more efficient once the student knows and understands basic word processing and writing skills. Clear enunciation, lack of slurring words, and use [of] precise pre-planning and organization are critical for success with voice-activated programs.

Note-Taking

Many students with writing struggles are slow and/or inefficient when taking notes. This is particularly laborious for high school and college-age students. While a laptop computer can be efficient, it can be cumbersome to carry around. Also, it is expensive to fix or replace a vandalized, dropped, or otherwise broken computer. A successful alternative that has become popular with some older students is the use of a personal digital assistant such as the PalmPilot® series or the Visor Handspring® series. These units are quite small (palm size) and easy to transport in a backpack. A nearly standard size keyboard can be attached which greatly facilitates typing and, hence, note-taking. This is especially useful for recording homework assignments and "to do" lists. For note-taking during a lecture, many students still require the assistance of a note-taker, even if the complete notes are only used as a backup.

Spelling

Many students who struggle with writing also have difficulties with spelling. Even if they are able to spell correctly on a weekly spelling test, when they're thinking of content it may be very difficult to also think of the correct spelling of the words they want. Some students then simplify their word usage. Other students just include the incorrectly spelled word.

When such students use a staging approach, they can first focus on pre-organization and then writing (or typing) a draft. A next step would be to go back and work on fixing misspelled words. Sometimes the spell checker on a computer does not help the student because the misspelled word is not close enough to correct. In such situations, the student should be taught to develop strong phonetic analysis skills so that she can learn to spell words phonetically, the way they sound. Then the student will be able to utilize technology such as one of the Franklin® Electronic Resources. In our office, the Language Master 6000 has been found to be very appropriate because of its large font size and speech clarity.

Hand Fatigue

A common complaint of students who struggle to write is that their hand gets tired when writing. This can be due to a variety of factors. Some of the most common factors are inappropriate grip, a very tight pencil grip, or inefficient writing posture. There are many efficient grippers that can be used with the pencil or pen to enhance the efficiency of the students grasp on the pencil. One example, the large Pencil Grip™, is ergonomically developed to work with the natural physiology of the hand to gently place fingers in the proper position for gripping!

Students can be helped to decrease hand fatigue by performing warm-up activities before writing [and] in the middle of the task. Such activities help the student manipulate and relax muscles in the writing hand. Some examples include:

Rubbing palms of hands together
Shaking hands slightly though firmly
Clasping hands together and stretching upwards

For older students who need to take a large number of notes during a class, dividing their paper in half and writing on only one half the [page] helps reduce the drag of the writing instrument across the paper. This too will reduce writing fatigue.

Caution for Teachers

One of the best compensations for a student who struggles with writing is to have a teacher that understands. For some students it is not possible to be neat while also focusing on content. Some students cannot focus on both neatness and use of writing mechanics at the same time. This is why a staging approach is critical. Requiring concentration on only one or two aspects at a time will help reduce the overload for a student.

In the quote below, an elementary school student explains his frustration caused by his struggles in trying to be neat while also thinking.

"So Eli figured it was easier to write just a few sentences. That didn't hurt his hand so much either. His teachers complained, but Eli kept writing very short stories. After all, teachers didn't understand what it was like to struggle and struggle to write, and still have the paper turn out sloppy and full of mistakes. They always told him how messy his papers were. They just couldn't understand how hard he tried. No matter how carefully he worked, the words didn't look like they were supposed to. Sometimes he knew how he wanted the words to look, but they just didn't turn out that way."

Strategies for Dealing with Dysgraphia*

A common teaching technique is to have the students write information to reinforce the material. For example, spelling programs often encourage students to write each spelling word five times or 20 times. For many students, the kinesthetic process of writing reinforces what is to be learned. However, for a small group of students, rather than reinforcing and consolidating information, the process of writing actually interferes with learning. These students struggle to write and consequently spend much more time than their peers on a writing assignment. Even so, they remember less: the act of writing greatly interferes with learning. Cognitively, so much of their energy is spent on the *process* that they often do not learn or some times even process the *content* of what they are working on. Some students with severe dysgraphia may actually complete a writing assignment and then have to reread it to determine what they wrote, especially in a copying task or if they are focusing on neatness.

Educators expect students to learn from the process of writing, yet these students find that the process of writing actually interferes with learning. How, then, can they adequately learn to use the process of writing to express their ideas?

Why does this occur? Dysgraphia is a problem with the writing process. For these students, there is an underlying reason that their papers are messy or that their speed is excessively fast or extremely slow. It is unfair to label them as poorly motivated, careless, lazy, or impulsive. While these interpretations may be true on the surface, they are not the *root* of what is happening. The root for dysgraphia is

*© Regina G. Richards, MA, Educational Therapist, Richards Educational Therapy Center, Inc., www.retctrpress.com. Originally published by LD Online, www.LDOnline.org. Reprinted with permission.

actually found within the processing system involved with sequencing, especially the motor movements which should be sequential and very automatic.

Students with dysgraphia need to develop both compensations and remediation strategies. *Compensations* are techniques to bypass the problem and reduce the negative impact on learning. This is accomplished by avoiding the difficulty, changing the assignment expectations, or using strategies to aid a particular aspect of the task. Compensations can also be termed *bypass strategies* or *accommodations*, the latter term used more frequently in legal situations. *Remediation* provides additional structured practice or re-teaching of the skill or concept using specialized techniques to match the student's processing style and need.

The astute teacher or parent must first determine the point at which the student becomes confused or begins to struggle. Does it begin as soon as the student starts to write? Is it halfway through the paragraph? Is it when the student tries to think about more complex ideas rather than just write a sentence or perform a copying task? When these determinations are made, it is important to identify which components of the task cause the confusions and/or struggles. Is it the use of manuscript, or the use of cursive? Is it the process of dealing with mechanics while writing? Is it the process of trying to think and plan while writing?

Remedial Strategies

It is critical that students do not totally avoid the process of writing, no matter how severe their dysgraphia. Writing is an important life skill necessary for signing documents, filling out forms, writing checks, taking telephone messages or writing a grocery list. Therefore, students need to be able to write, even if they cannot maintain writing for long periods of time.

Young students should receive remediation in letter form, automaticity, and fluency. They need specific multisensory techniques that encourage them to verbalize the motor sequences of the form of letters (for example, *b* is *big stick down, circle away from my body*). Students should also use large air writing to develop a more efficient motor memory for the sequence of steps necessary in making each letter. This is because air writing causes students to use many more muscles than they use when writing with a pencil. Multisensory techniques should be utilized for teaching both manuscript and cursive writing. The techniques need to be practiced substantially so that the letters are fairly automatic before the student is asked to use these skills to communicate ideas.

Some students may be able to copy and write single sentences with a fair degree of ease, but they struggle tremendously with paragraph writing. These students will need to be taught techniques that enable them to perform each subpart prior to pulling together all the parts. Substantial modeling will be necessary at each stage for the student to be successful. For example, when writing a paragraph students can be taught the following eight steps:

1. Think about your ideas and elaborate on each part of the ideas.
2. Organize the ideas you want to express. This type of organization is easily performed using visual graphic organizers. For example, you can create a

mind map so that the main idea is placed in a circle in the center of the page and supporting facts are written on lines coming out of the main circle, similar to the arms of a spider or spokes on a wheel. Many visual organizer formats can be used, with different formats appropriate for different situations.

3. Analyze your graphic organizer to determine if you included all of your ideas. If you have difficulty with spelling, make a list of the more difficult or important words you may want to include in your writing. Having this reference list will help your writing flow more because you will not have to stop to think of how to spell the big words.

4. Now, write a draft of your paragraph (or paper), focusing on the content or ideas. If you have a computer, it is best if you type your draft directly on the keyboard. This will make it much easier to proofread and revise.

5. Proof and editing: you will need specific techniques and strategies to proofread your paper, checking for appropriate use of punctuation, capitalization, and grammar. Then use a spell checker to fix your spelling.

6. Revise your paragraph, incorporating the corrections you determined above.

7. Proofread your paragraph again, editing and revising if necessary.

8. Develop a final product, either in typed or written form.

An easy way to remember these steps is to think of the word *POWER*.

P—plan your paper (step 1)
O—organize your thoughts and ideas (steps 2 and 3)
W—write your draft (step 4)
E—edit your work (steps 5, 6, and 7)
R—revise your work, producing a final draft (step 8)

The student may need substantial modeling at each stage to be successful.

Some dysgraphic students have great difficulty with spelling, especially if sequencing is a major issue for them. Additionally, many dysgraphic students experience dyslexia, a sequential processing problem that affects reading and spelling. These students need very specific remedial assistance in learning to spell phonetically. It is critical that they are able to represent unknown words using good phonetic equivalences. If they are able to spell logically and phonetically, they will be able to use a phonetically-based spell checker, such as a spell checker in one of the Franklin resource products. These handheld devices recognize words using phonetic logic rather than relying on the orthographic sequence, as do most spell checkers on a computer word processing program. . . .

Another vital aspect of remedial assistance that is especially important for young children, involves the student's *pencil grip*. Students should be helped and encouraged to use a consistent and efficient pencil grip right from the beginning of their writing experience. The distance from the student's finger to the pencil point should consistently be between 3/4"–1". Pressure on the pencil should be moderate, not too heavy and not too light. The angle of the pencil should be approximately 45° with the page and slanted toward the student's writing arm. The long edge of the student's paper and his writing arm should be parallel, like *railroad tracks*. With some young students, pencil habits can be changed to a more appropriate form by using a plastic pencil grip (many of which are on the market in a variety of shapes and formats). It is much easier and more efficient to encourage students at the very beginning of their writing experience to develop these appropriate habits through frequent modeling and positive feedback. Older students who have developed firm habits, even if the habits are not efficient, find that it is very time consuming to make changes. Therefore, when making a decision on adapting a student's habits, it is extremely important to consider the time/energy ratio. Is it worth the amount of time necessary to make the change to help the student be more efficient? If not, it is critical to make sure the student has efficient and automatic compensatory strategies.

Many students with dysgraphia are *extremely slow* in their writing performances. When this is the case, it is critical to determine what is causing the slowness. Is it the formulation of ideas? or the organization of ideas? If so, more work needs to be done on pre-organization strategies and this student's language formulation skills need to be thoroughly assessed by a speech and language pathologist. Is the student's slowness a result of slowness in actually making the letters? If this is the case, the student needs much more remedial practice in forming letters independently, without having to think about content. This should be done using multisensory techniques, including saying the letter and/or the sequence of movements while writing the letter; using large air writing techniques (writing the letter in the air using two fingers, with wrist and elbow fairly straight, though not rigid); writing letters in texture, such as on fine sandpaper or in pudding; and writing large letters using a squirt bottle of colored water against an outside wall.

Some students struggle with writing and become readily *fatigued* with the process of writing because of their inefficient pencil grip and poor motor sequencing. Many times an occupational therapist, especially one using a sensory integration philosophy, can help in the remedial process with such students. There are also temporary remedial techniques a teacher or parent can use as warmups or as a writing break. Some suggestions for helping relieve stress and relaxing the writing hand follow. Students can perform any of these for about 10 seconds before writing or in the middle of writing.

- Shake hands fast, but not violently.
- Rub hands together and focus on the feeling of warmth.
- Rub hands on the carpet in circles (or, if wearing clothing with some mild texture, rub hands on thighs, close to knees)
- Use the thumb of the dominant hand to click the top of a ballpoint pen while holding it in that hand. Repeat using the index finger.
- Perform *sitting pushups* by placing each palm on the chair with fingers facing forward. Students push down on their hands, lifting their body slightly off the chair.

Compensatory Strategies

The overall goal of compensations is to help the student perform more automatically and still participate in and benefit from the writing task. The goal is to allow the student to go around the problem so that she can then focus more completely on the content. Some example strategies include:

- **Understanding**—Understand the student's inconsistencies and performance variabilities.
- **Print or cursive**—Allow the student to use either form. Many dysgraphic students are more comfortable with manuscript printing.
- If getting started is a problem, **encourage pre-organization strategies,** such as use of graphic organizers.
- **Computer**—Encourage student to become comfortable using a word processor on a computer. Students can be taught as early as 1st grade to type sentences directly on the keyboard. In doing so, do not eliminate handwriting for the child: handwriting is still important but computer skills will be invaluable for longer and important tasks.
- For older students, encourage use of a **speech recognition** program combined with the word processor so the student can dictate his papers rather than type them. This increases speed and efficiency and allows the student to focus more completely on complex thoughts and ideas.
- Encourage consistent **use of spell checker** to decrease the overall demands of the writing task and encourage students to wait until the end to worry about spelling.
- Encourage **use of an electronic resource** such as the spell check component in a Franklin Language Master® to further decrease the demands. If student has concurrent reading problems, a Language Master® with a speaking component is most helpful because it will read/say the words. This author prefers the Language Master 6000 because of its large font size and speech clarity.
- Do not count off for poor **spelling** on first drafts, in-class assignments, or on tests. However, depending on age, student may be held responsible for spelling in final drafts completed at home.
- Have student **proofread papers after a delay,** using a checklist of the points to check. If students proofread immediately after writing, they may read what they intended rather than what was actually written.
- If necessary, **shorten** writing assignments.
- Allow **extra time** for writing activities.
- **Note taking:** Provide student with copy of completed notes (perhaps through a note taking buddy who can use carbon paper) to fill in missing parts of his own notes.
- **Note taking:** Provide a partially completed outline so the student can fill in the details under major headings. As a variety, provide the details and have student fill in headings while listening.
- Allow student to **tape record important assignments** and/or take oral tests.

- **Staging:** Have students complete tasks in logical steps or increments instead of all at once.
- **Prioritization:** Stress or de-emphasize certain task components during a complex activity. For example, students can focus on using descriptive words in one assignment, and in another, focus on using compound sentences. Also, design assignments to be **evaluated** on specific parts of the writing process (prioritization).
- **Remove neatness** as a grading criteria, except on computer-generated papers.
- **Reduce copying** aspects of tasks, such as providing a math worksheet rather than requiring student to copy problems from the book. A copying buddy can be helpful in copying the problems using carbon paper.
- Have younger students use large **graph paper** for math calculation to keep columns and rows straight. Older student may use loose leaf paper turned sideways to help maintain straight columns.
- Allow and encourage use of **abbreviations** for in-class writing assignments (such as *b/4* for "before" or *b/c* for "because"). Have the student keep a list of appropriate abbreviations in his note book and taped to his desk for easy reference. Begin with only a few and increase as the first few become automatic.
- Reinforce the **positive aspects** of student's efforts.
- Be **patient.**
- **Encourage student to be patient** with himself.

A Note on Creativity

Dysgraphia does not have to limit creativity, as identified by the sample below composed on a computer by a 12-year-old dyslexic and dysgraphic student.

a) First draft of creative story as typed by 12-year-old student:

the way I describe a bumby ride is like wothgan mowtsarts mowsek. eshe bumby rowd is like a song. Eshe bumb is the a note eche uncon at the sam time ste is. that was the mewstere to mowts mowsuk it was vare metereus and unperdekdable.So the next time you drive down a bumby theak of mowtsart.

b) Same story. Student read to teacher using his draft:

The way I describe a bumpy ride is like Wolfgang Mozart's music. Each bumpy road is like a song. Each bump in the road is a note. Each bump is uncontrolled at the same time it still is controlled. That was the magic to Mozart's music. It was very mysterious and unpredictable. So the next time you drive down a bumpy road think of Mozart.

A Note Regarding Development of Word Processing Skills

Many dysgraphic students have difficulty with correct fingering in keyboarding skills. However, it is important to expose students to the correct fingering to develop quick visual locating skills for letters on the keyboard, ideally without having to look each time. One important strategy is to have the student practice keyboarding skills approximately 10 minutes a day (this can be part of a homework assignment). The student should use a variety of child-oriented typing tutor programs and work to develop appropriate skills to the best of her ability. At the same time, whenever the student types for ideas or content, whether a word, a sentence or a whole paragraph, she should be allowed to use whatever fingering she wants. Eventually, the goal is for the student to automatically incorporate at least some correct keyboard fingering when typing content. This author has seen dysgraphic students use a combination of correct keyboard fingering with their own style and reach typing speeds of 60 wpm. With this degree of speed and efficiency, it is unnecessary to *force* a student to use standard keyboarding techniques. However, many students do begin to use the correct techniques, as this is often much more efficient. However, if practice with correct fingering is avoided or not used frequently enough, the student will never have the opportunity to incorporate the correct skills.

Meta-Analysis of Research-Based Instructional Approaches for Teaching Written Expression to Students with Learning Disabilities

Gersten & Baker's (1999) meta-analysis highlighted research-based instructional approaches for teaching written expression to students with learning disabilities, including ways to teach students how to analyze material learned in the classroom and how to write personal narratives, persuasive essays, and other genres. All of the instructional interventions studied improved the quality of students' written products, and there was evidence of positive impact on students' self-efficacy, that is, their senses of being able to write.

Expressive writing was defined as writing for the purpose of displaying knowledge or supporting self-expression (Graham & Harris, 1989a). This analysis asked, "Given a group of studies designed explicitly for the purpose of improving the writing of students with learning disabilities, which interventions and components were found to be most effective, and what is the strength of their effects?" This definition and research question led the analysis to include studies of various interventions. Virtually all of the interventions studied were multifaceted. Three components stood out as ones that reliably and consistently led to improved outcomes in teaching expressive writing to students with learning disabilities: adhering to a basic framework of planning, writing, and revision; explicitly teaching critical steps in the writing process; and providing feedback guided by the information explicitly taught.

Adhering to a Basic Framework of Planning, Writing, and Revision

Teaching students to write requires showing them how to develop and organize what they want to say and guiding them in the process of getting it down on paper.

Most of the interventions used a basic framework based on planning, writing, and revising. These steps are part of a recursive, rather than linear, process, that is, each step may be revisited during the writing process, and the steps do not always proceed in the same order. In these studies, each step was taught explicitly, with several examples and often supported by a "think sheet," a prompt card, or a mnemonic.

Planning. Well-developed plans for writing result in better first drafts. Teachers or peers who write well can verbalize the process they go through to help students develop their own "plans of action." One type of plan of action, called a "Planning Think Sheet," uses a series of sequential, structured prompts. It specifies a topic and asks the questions, *Who (am I writing for)?, Why am I writing?, What do I know?, How can I group my ideas?* and *How will I organize my ideas?* (Englert, Raphael, & Anderson, 1992). Another technique is to use semantic mapping to help students plan their writing.

Creating a First Draft. Using a plan of action helps students create first drafts. The plan serves as a concrete map for engaging in the writing process and provides students with suggestions for what to do when they feel stuck. The plan of action provides a permanent reminder of the content and structure of the writing task.

A well-developed plan of action also gives the student and teacher a common language to use in discussing the writing. The dialogue between teacher and student represents a major advance in writing instruction over traditional methods that required students to work in relative isolation.

Revising and Editing. Revising and editing skills are critical to the writing process. Developing methods to help students refine and edit their work has been difficult, but a few researchers have begun to develop specific strategies that appear promising. For example, Wong, Butler, Ficzere, and Kuperis (1996), in teaching students to write opinion essays, used peer editing as an instructional strategy for the students. Pairs of students alternated their roles as student-writer and student-critic. The student-critic identified ambiguities in the essay and asked the writer for clarification. With help from the teacher, the students made revisions. The teacher also provided the student-writer with feedback on clarity and on the cogency of the supportive arguments. Once the clarity and cogency of the essay met the teacher's standard, the pair moved on to correct capitalization, spelling, and punctuation. Through this process, the student-writer had to explain his or her communicative intent to the peer and revise the essay to faithfully reflect it. These clarifying interactive dialogues led the student-critic and student-writer to understand each other's perspective. In this way the trainees developed a sense of audience for their writing.

Explicitly Teaching Critical Steps in the Writing Process

Explicitly teaching text structures provides a guide for the writing task, whether it is a persuasive essay, a personal narrative, or an essay comparing and contrasting two phenomena. Different types of writing are based on different structures. For example, a persuasive essay contains a thesis and supporting arguments, whereas narrative writing may contain character development and a story climax. Instruction in text structures typically includes numerous explicit models and prompts. Although different writers may proceed with the structures in a different order, good writing involves what Englert and Mariage (1991) called "overlapping and recursive processes." These processes do not proceed in a particular order, and one process may inform another in such a way that the author returns to previous steps to update or revise on a regular basis. Again, a plan of action is helpful. The plan makes text structures more visible to students and helps to demystify the writing process.

Providing Feedback Guided by the Information Explicitly Taught

A third component common to these successful interventions was frequent feedback to students on the overall quality of writing, missing elements, and strengths. When feedback is combined with instruction in the writing process, the dialogue between student and teacher is strengthened. Giving and receiving feedback also helps students to develop "reader sensitivity" and their own writing style. Wong, Butler, Ficzere, and Kuperis (1997) hypothesized that interactive dialogues, which led students through multiple cycles of reflection, realization, and redress of problems, helped students "see" their thoughts and write from another's perspective. Across the studies of successful writing instruction, teachers and students had an organizational framework and language to use in providing feedback on such aspects of writing as organization, originality, and interpretation. Wong and her colleagues modeled procedures, for students and teachers, providing feedback so they would attend to the surface features of writing (e.g., spelling and punctuation) as well as to the presentation of ideas.

Specific Methods

Numerous methods for teaching written expression incorporate these three common principles. Two examples are Self-Regulated Strategy Development (SRSD) (Graham & Harris, 1989b) and Cognitive Strategy Instruction in Writing (Englert et al., 1995; Englert & Mariage, 1991). The SRSD technique involves self-directed prompts that require the students to (a) consider their audience and reasons for writing; (b) develop a plan for what they intend to say using frames to generate or organize writing notes; (c) evaluate possible content by considering its impact on the reader; and (d) continue the process of content generation and planning during the act of writing. Cognitive Strategy Instruction in Writing includes brainstorming strategies for preparing to write, organizing strategies to relate and categorize the ideas, comprehension strategies as students read and gather information for their writing, and monitoring strategies as they clarify their thoughts and the relationships among their items of information. All of these strategies are applied prior to the actual writing.

Conclusion

Gersten and Baker (1999) identified some issues in which research is expected to blossom in coming years. The first group of issues concerns the mechanics versus the content of writing. Early evidence suggested that writing instruction that focused more on content would better capitalize on the strengths of students with learning disabilities. When asked to write about complex ideas, students with learning disabilities often showed conceptual performance beyond that which would be expected on the basis of their performance on lower-level skills such as capitalization, punctuation, and spelling (Goldman, Hasselbring, & The Cognition Technology Group at Vanderbilt, 1977).

More recent research indicates that dictating to a scribe can eliminate mechanical difficulties and result in a longer, higher-quality composition (e.g., De La Paz & Graham, 1997). While students must eventually learn to do their own writing, these findings suggest a possible bridge to higher performance. Gersten and Baker point out that daily writing instruction should include time devoted to both the mechanics and the process of writing. Problems with the mechanics of writing must be addressed in expressive writing instruction; there is a reciprocal relationship between mastery of transcription skills and growth in the quality of writing. When students have mastered the mechanics, their cognitive resources can be devoted to planning, composing, and revising their work.

According to Gersten and Baker, another issue that is likely to be the focus of expressive writing research is the transfer of writing skills and the spontaneous use of the strategies involved in writing to other subject matter areas to raise the student's overall level of academic achievement. In the meta-analysis reported here, few researchers investigated the transfer of writing skills. Those that did found mixed results. Wong called for instruction to promote transfer of skill. When students are provided such opportunities, she says, transfer will be greatly enhanced.

13

Strategies and Instructional Practices for Students with Attention-Deficit Hyperactivity Disorder

What ADHD Is and How It Manifests

Attention-Deficit Hyperactivity Disorder is a neurological condition that involves problems with inattention and hyperactivity-impulsivity that are developmentally inconsistent with the age of the child. We are now learning that ADHD is not a disorder of attention, as had long been assumed. Rather, it is a function of developmental failure in the brain circuitry that monitors inhibition and self-control. This loss of self-regulation impairs other important brain functions crucial for maintaining attention, including the ability to defer immediate rewards for later gain (Barkley, 1998a). Behavior of children with ADHD can also include excessive motor activity. The high energy level and subsequent behavior are often misperceived as purposeful noncompliance when, in fact, they may be a manifestation of the disorder and require specific interventions. Children with ADHD exhibit a range of symptoms and levels of severity. In addition, many children with ADHD often are of at least average intelligence and have a range of personality characteristics and individual strengths.

Children with ADHD typically exhibit behavior that is classified into two main categories: poor sustained attention and hyperactivity-impulsiveness. As a result, three subtypes of the disorder have been proposed by the American Psychiatric Association (APA) in the fourth edition of the *Diagnostic and Statistical Manual of Mental Disorders (DSM-IV):* predominantly inattentive, predominantly hyperactive-impulsive, and combined types (Barkley, 1997). A child expressing hyperactivity commonly will appear fidgety, have difficulty staying seated or playing quietly, and act as if driven by a motor. Children displaying impulsivity often have difficulty participating in tasks that require taking turns. Other common behaviors may include blurting out answers to questions instead of waiting to be called and flitting from one task to another without finishing. The inattention component of ADHD affects the educational experience of these children because ADHD causes them to have difficulty in attending to detail in directions and sustaining attention for the duration of the task, and they misplace needed items. These children often fail to give close attention to details, make careless mistakes, and avoid or dislike tasks requiring sustained mental effort.

> Although these behaviors are not in themselves a learning disability, almost one-third of all children with ADHD have learning disabilities. (National Institute of Mental Health [NIMH], 1999)

Children with ADHD may also experience difficulty in reading, math, and written communication (Anderson, Williams, McGee, & Silva, 1987; Cantwell & Baker, 1991; Dykman, Akerman, & Raney, 1994; Zentall, 1993). Furthermore, ADHD commonly occurs with other conditions. Current literature indicates that approximately 40–60% of children with ADHD have at least one coexisting disability (Barkley, 1990a; Jensen, Martin, & Cantwell, 1997). Although any disability can coexist with ADHD, certain disabilities seem to be more common than others. These include disruptive behavior disorders, mood disorders, anxiety disorders, tics and Tourette's Syndrome, and learning disabilities (Jensen et al., 2001). In addition, ADHD affects children differently at different ages. In some cases, children initially identified as having hyperactive-impulsive subtype are subsequently identified as having the combined subtype, as their attention problems surface.

These characteristics affect not only the academic lives of students with ADHD, they may affect their social lives as well. Children with ADHD of the predominantly hyperactive-impulsive type may show aggressive behaviors, while children of the predominantly inattentive type may be more withdrawn. Also, because they are less disruptive than children with ADHD who are hyperactive or impulsive, many children who have the inattentive type of ADHD go unrecognized and unassisted. Both types of children with ADHD may be less cooperative with others and less willing to wait their turn or play by the rules (NIMH, 1999; Swanson, 1992; Waslick & Greenhill, 1997). Their inability to control their own behavior may lead to social isolation. Consequently, the children's self-esteem may suffer (Barkley, 1990a).

Identifying Children with ADHD

There are an estimated 1.46 to 2.46 million children with ADHD in the United States; together these children constitute 3 to 5% of the student population (Stevens, 1997; APA, 1994). More boys than girls are diagnosed with ADHD; most research suggests that the condition is diagnosed four to nine times more often in boys than in girls (Bender, 1997; Hallowell, 1994; Rief, 1997). Although for years it was assumed to be a childhood disorder that became visible as early as age 3 and then disappeared with the advent of adolescence, the condition is not limited to children. It is now known that, although the symptoms of the disorder may change as a child ages, many children with ADHD do not grow out of it (Mannuzza, Klein, Bessler, Malloy, & LaPadula, 1998).

The behaviors associated with ADHD change as children grow older. For example, a preschool child may show gross motor overactivity—always running or climbing and frequently shifting from one activity to another. Older children may be restless and fidget in their seats or play with their chairs and desks. They frequently fail to finish their schoolwork, or they work carelessly. Adolescents with ADHD tend to be more withdrawn and less communicative. They are often impulsive, reacting spontaneously without regard to previous plans or necessary tasks and homework.

According to the *DSM-IV* (APA, 1994), ADHD can be defined by behaviors exhibited. Individuals with ADHD exhibit combinations of the following behaviors:

- Fidgeting with hands or feet or squirming in their seat (adolescents with ADHD may appear restless)
- Difficulty remaining seated when required to do so
- Difficulty sustaining attention and waiting for a turn in tasks, games, or group situations
- Blurting out answers to questions before the questions have been completed
- Difficulty following through on instructions and in organizing tasks
- Shifting from one unfinished activity to another
- Failing to give close attention to details and avoiding careless mistakes
- Losing things necessary for tasks or activities
- Difficulty in listening to others without being distracted or interrupting
- Wide ranges in mood swings
- Great difficulty in delaying gratification

Children with ADHD show different combinations of these behaviors and typically exhibit behavior that is classified into two main categories: poor sustained attention and hyperactivity-impulsiveness. Three subtypes of the disorder have been described in the *DSM-IV:* predominantly inattentive, predominantly hyperactive-impulsive, and combined types (APA, as cited in Barkley, 1997). For instance, children with ADHD, without hyperactivity and impulsivity, do not show excessive activity or fidgeting but instead may daydream, act lethargic or restless, and frequently do not finish their academic work. Not all of these behaviors appear in all situations. A child with ADHD may be able to focus when he or she is receiving frequent reinforcement or is under very strict control. The ability to focus is also common in new settings or while interacting one-on-one. While other children may occasionally show some signs of these behaviors, in children with ADHD the symptoms are more frequent and more severe than in other children of the same age.

Although many children have only ADHD, others have additional academic or behavioral diagnoses. For instance, it has been documented that approximately a quarter to one-third of all children with ADHD also have learning disabilities (Forness & Kavale, 2001; Robelia, 1997; Schiller, 1996), with studies finding populations where the comorbidity ranges from 7 to 92% (DuPaul & Stoner, 1994; Osman, 2000). Likewise, children with ADHD have coexisting psychiatric disorders at a much higher rate. Across studies, the rate of conduct or oppositional defiant disorders varied from 43 to 93% and anxiety or mood disorders from 13 to 51% (Burt, Krueger, McGue, & Iacono, 2001; Forness, Kavale, & San Miguel, 1998; Jensen, Martin, & Cantwell, 1997; Jensen, Shertvette, Zenakis, & Ritchters, 1993).

National data on children who receive special education confirm this comorbidity with other identified disabilities. Among parents of children age 6 to 13 years who have an emotional disturbance, 65% report their children also have ADHD. Parents of 28% of children with learning disabilities report their children also have ADHD (Wagner & Blackorby, 2002).

When selecting and implementing successful instructional strategies and practices, it is imperative to understand the characteristics of the child, including those pertaining to disabilities or diagnoses. This knowledge will be useful for implementing and evaluating successful practices, which are often the same practices that benefit students without ADHD.

Causes of ADHD

ADHD has traditionally been viewed as a problem related to attention, stemming from an inability of the brain to filter competing sensory inputs such as sight and sound. Recent research, however, has shown that children with ADHD do not have difficulty in that area. Instead, researchers now believe that children with ADHD are unable to inhibit their impulsive motor responses to such input (Barkley, 1997; 1998a).

It is still unclear what the direct and immediate causes of ADHD are, although scientific and technological advances in the field of neurological imaging techniques and genetics promise to clarify this issue in the near future. Most researchers suspect that the cause of ADHD is genetic or biological, although they acknowledge that the child's environment helps determine specific behaviors.

Imaging studies conducted during the past decade have indicated which brain regions may malfunction in patients with ADHD, and thus account for symptoms of the condition (Barkley, 1998a). A 1996 study conducted at NIMH found that the right prefrontal cortex (part of the cerebellum) and at least two of the clusters of nerve cells known collectively as the basal ganglia are significantly smaller in children with ADHD (as cited in Barkley, 1998a). It appears that these areas of the brain relate to the regulation of attention. Why these areas of the brain are smaller for some children is yet unknown, but researchers have suggested mutations in several genes that are active in the prefrontal cortex and basal ganglia may play a significant role (Barkley, 1998a). In addition, some nongenetic factors have been linked to ADHD, including premature birth, maternal alcohol and tobacco use, high levels of exposure to lead, and prenatal neurological damage. Although some people claim that food additives, sugar, yeast, or poor child rearing methods lead to ADHD, there is no conclusive evidence to support these beliefs (Barkley, 1998a; Neuwirth, 1994; NIMH, 1999).

Legal Requirements Relating to Children with ADHD

According to the U.S. Department of Education (2004), two important federal mandates protect the rights of eligible children with ADHD—the Individuals with Disabilities Education Act and Section 504 of the Rehabilitation Act of 1973. The regulations implementing these laws are 34 CFR sections 300 and 104, respectively, which require school districts to provide a "free appropriate public education" to students who meet their eligibility criteria. Although a child with ADHD may not be eligible for services under IDEA, he or she may meet the requirements of Section 504.

The requirements and qualifications for IDEA are more stringent than those of Section 504. IDEA provides funds to state education agencies for the purpose of providing special education and related services to children evaluated in accordance with IDEA and found to have at least one of the 13 specific categories of disabilities, and who thus need special education and related services. ADHD may be considered under the specific category of "Other Health Impairment" (OHI), if the disability results in limited strength, vitality, or alertness, including a heightened alertness to environmental stimuli that results in limited alertness with respect to the educational environment and that is due to chronic or acute health problems.

Under IDEA, each public agency—that is, each school district—shall ensure that a full and individual evaluation is conducted for each child being considered for special education and related services. The child's IEP team uses the results of the evaluation to determine the educational needs of the child. The results of an assessment by a medical doctor, psychologist, or other qualified professional indicating a diagnosis of ADHD may be an important evaluation result, but the diagnosis does not automatically mean that a child is eligible for special education and related services. A group of qualified professionals and the parent of the child determine whether the child is an eligible child with a disability according to IDEA. Children with ADHD also may be eligible for services under the "Specific Learning Disability," "Emotional Disturbance," or other relevant disability categories of IDEA if they have those disabilities in addition to ADHD.

After it has been determined that a child is eligible for special education and related services under IDEA, an IEP is developed that includes a statement of measurable annual goals, including benchmarks or short-term objectives that reflect the student's needs. The IEP goals are determined with input from the parents and cannot be changed without the parents' knowledge. Although children who are eligible under IDEA must have an IEP, students eligible under Section 504 are not required to have an IEP but must be provided regular or special education and related aids or services that are designed to meet their individual educational needs as adequately as the needs of students without disabilities are met.

Section 504 was established to ensure a free appropriate education for all children who have an impairment—physical or mental—that substantially limits one or more major life activities. If it can be demonstrated that a child's ADHD adversely affects his or her learning—a major life activity in the life of a child—the student may qualify for services under Section 504. To be considered eligible for Section 504, a student must be evaluated to ensure that the disability requires special education or related services or supplementary aids and services. Therefore, a child whose ADHD does not interfere with his or her learning process may not be eligible for special education and related services under IDEA or supplementary aids and services under Section 504.

IDEA and Section 504 require schools to provide special education or to make modifications or adaptations for students whose ADHD adversely affects their educational performance. Such adaptations may include curriculum adjustments, alternative classroom organization and management, specialized teaching techniques and study skills, use of behavior management, and increased parent/teacher collaboration. Eligible children with ADHD must be placed in regular education classrooms, to the maximum extent appropriate to their educational needs, with the use of supplementary aids and services if necessary. Of course, the needs of some children with ADHD cannot be met solely within the confines of a regular education classroom, and they may need special education or related aids or services provided in other settings.

Academic Instruction

The first major component of the most effective instruction for children with ADHD is effective academic instruction. Teachers can help their students with ADHD to achieve by applying the principles of effective teaching when they introduce, conduct, and conclude each lesson. The discussion and techniques that follow pertain to the instructional process in general (across subject areas); strategies for specific subject areas are discussed later in this section.

Introducing Lessons

Students with ADHD learn best with a carefully structured academic lesson—one where the teacher explains what he or she wants children to learn in the current lesson and places these skills and knowledge in the context of previous lessons. Effective teachers preview their expectations about what students will learn and how they should behave during the lesson. The following practices have been found especially useful in facilitating this process.

- **Provide an advance organizer.** Prepare students for the day's lesson by quickly summarizing the order of various activities planned. Explain, for example, that a review of the previous lesson will be followed by new information and that both group and independent work will be expected.
- **Review previous lessons.** Review information about previous lessons on this topic. For example, remind children that yesterday's lesson focused on learning how to regroup in subtraction. Review several problems before describing the current lesson.
- **Set learning expectations.** State what students are expected to learn during the lesson. For example, explain to students that a language arts lesson will involve reading a story about Paul Bunyan and identifying new vocabulary words in the story.
- **Set behavioral expectations.** Describe how students are expected to behave during the lesson. For example, tell children that they may talk quietly to their

neighbors as they do their seatwork or they may raise their hands to get your attention.

- **State needed materials.** Identify all materials that the children will need during the lesson, rather than leaving them to figure out on their own the materials required. For example, specify that children need their journals and pencils for journal writing or their crayons, scissors, and colored paper for an art project.
- **Explain additional resources.** Tell students how to obtain help in mastering the lesson. For example, refer children to a particular page in the textbook for guidance on completing a worksheet.
- **Simplify instructions, choices, and scheduling.** The simpler the expectations communicated to an ADHD student, the more likely it is that he or she will comprehend and complete them in a timely and productive manner.

Conducting Lessons

To conduct the most productive lessons for children with ADHD, effective teachers periodically question children's understanding of the material, probe for correct answers before calling on other students, and identify which students need additional assistance. Teachers should keep in mind that transitions from one lesson or class to another are particularly difficult for students with ADHD. When these children are prepared for transitions, they are more likely to respond and to stay on task. The following suggestions may assist teachers in conducting effective lessons.

- **Be predictable.** Structure and consistency are very important for children with ADHD; many do not deal well with change. Minimal rules and minimal choices are best for these children. They need to understand clearly what is expected of them, as well as the consequences for not adhering to expectations.
- **Support the student's participation in the classroom.** Provide students with ADHD with private, discreet cues to stay on task and advance warning that they will be called upon shortly. Avoid bringing attention to differences between ADHD students and their classmates. At all times, avoid the use of sarcasm and criticism.
- **Use audiovisual materials.** Use a variety of audiovisual materials to present academic lessons. For example, use an overhead projector to demonstrate how to solve an addition problem requiring regrouping. The students can work on the problem at their desks while you manipulate counters on the projector screen. Also, many schools are now equipped with SMART boards and other technologically advanced equipment. Learn how to use these and incorporate their use into your lessons, as appropriate.
- **Check student performance.** Question individual students to assess their mastery of the lesson. For example, you can ask students doing seatwork (i.e., lessons completed by students at their desks in the classroom) to demonstrate how they arrived at the answer to a problem, or you can ask individual

students to state, in their own words, how the main character felt at the end of the story.

- **Ask probing questions.** Probe for the correct answer after allowing a child sufficient time to work out the answer to a question. Mentally count at least 15 seconds before giving the answer or calling on another student. Ask followup questions that give children an opportunity to demonstrate what they know.
- **Perform ongoing student evaluation.** Identify students who need additional assistance. Watch for signs of lack of comprehension, such as daydreaming or visual or verbal indications of frustration. Provide these children with extra explanations, or ask another student to serve as a peer tutor for the lesson.
- **Help students correct their own mistakes.** Describe how students can identify and correct their own mistakes. For example, remind students that they should check their calculations in math problems and reiterate how they can check their calculations; remind students of particularly difficult spelling rules and how students can watch out for easy-to-make errors.
- **Help students focus.** Remind students to keep working and to focus on their assigned task. For example, you can provide follow-up directions or assign learning partners. These practices can be directed at individual children or at the entire class.
- **Follow-up directions.** Effective teachers of children with ADHD also guide them with followup directions:

  1. *Oral directions.* After giving directions to the class as a whole, provide additional oral directions for a child with ADHD. For example, ask the child if he or she understood the directions and repeat the directions together.
  2. *Written directions.* Provide followup directions in writing. For example, write the page number for an assignment on the chalkboard and remind the child to look at the chalkboard if he or she forgets the assignment.

- **Lower noise level.** Monitor the noise level in the classroom, and provide corrective feedback, as needed. If the noise level exceeds the level appropriate for the type of lesson, remind all students—or individual students—about the behavioral rules stated at the beginning of the lesson. Also, if the noise is coming from outside the classroom, be sure you have a way of reducing the noise level.
- **Divide work into smaller units.** Break assignments into smaller, less complex tasks. For example, allow students to complete five math problems before presenting them with the remaining five problems.
- **Highlight key points.** Highlight key words in the instructions on worksheets to help the child with ADHD focus on the directions. Prepare the worksheet before the lesson begins, or underline key words as you and the child read the directions together. When reading, show children how to identify and highlight a key sentence, or have them write it on a separate piece of paper, before asking for a summary of the entire book. In math, show children how to un-

derline the important facts and operations; in "Mary has two apples, and John has three," underline *two*, *and*, and *three*.

- **Eliminate or reduce frequency of timed tests.** Tests that are timed may not allow children with ADHD to demonstrate what they truly know due to their potential preoccupation with elapsed time. Allow students with ADHD more time to complete quizzes and tests in order to eliminate "test anxiety," and provide them with other opportunities, methods, or test formats to demonstrate their knowledge.
- **Use cooperative learning strategies.** Have students work together in small groups to maximize their own and each other's learning. Use strategies such as Think-Pair-Share, where teachers ask students to think about a topic, pair with a partner to discuss it, and share ideas with the group (Slavin, 2002).
- **Use assistive technology.** All students, and those with ADHD in particular, can benefit from the use of technology (such as computers and projector screens), which makes instruction more visual and allows students to participate actively.

Concluding Lessons

Effective teachers conclude their lessons by providing advance warning that the lesson is about to end, checking the completed assignments of at least some of the students with ADHD, and instructing students how to begin preparing for the next activity.

- **Provide advance warnings.** Provide advance warning that a lesson is about to end. Announce 5 or 10 minutes before the end of the lesson (particularly for seatwork and group projects) how much time remains. You may also want to tell students at the beginning of the lesson how much time they will have to complete it.
- **Check assignments.** Check completed assignments for at least some students. Review what they have learned during the lesson to get a sense of how ready the class was for the lesson and how to plan the next lesson.
- **Preview the next lesson.** Instruct students on how to begin preparing for the next lesson. For example, inform children that they need to put away their textbooks and come to the front of the room for a large-group spelling lesson.

Individualizing Instructional Practices

In addition to the general strategies listed above for introducing, conducting, and concluding their lessons, effective teachers of students with ADHD also individualize their instructional practices in accordance with different academic subjects and the needs of their students within each area. This is because children with ADHD have different ways of learning and retaining information, not all of which involve traditional reading and listening. Effective teachers first identify areas in which each child requires extra assistance and then use special strategies to provide structured opportunities for the child to review and master an academic lesson that was previously presented to the entire class. Strategies that may help facilitate this goal include the following (grouped by subject area):

Language Arts and Reading Comprehension.   To help children with ADHD who are poor readers improve their reading comprehension skills, try the following instructional practices.

- **Silent reading time.** Establish a fixed time each day for silent reading. Examples include Drop Everything and Read (DEAR), and Sustained Silent Reading (SSR) (Manzo & Zehr, 1998 and Holt & O'Tuel, 1989).
- **Follow-along reading.** Ask the child to read a story silently while listening to other students or the teacher read the story aloud to the entire class.
- **Partner reading activities.** Pair the child with ADHD with another student partner who is a strong reader. The partners take turns reading orally and listening to each other.
- **Storyboards.** Ask the child to make storyboards that illustrate the sequence of main events in a story.
- **Storytelling.** Schedule storytelling sessions where the child can retell a story that he or she has read recently.
- **Playacting.** Schedule playacting sessions where the child can role-play different characters in a favorite story.
- **Word bank.** Keep a word bank or dictionary of new or hard-to-read sight-vocabulary words.
- **Board games for reading comprehension.** Play board games that provide practice with target reading-comprehension skills or sight-vocabulary words.
- **Computer games for reading comprehension.** Schedule computer time for the child to have drill-and-practice with sight vocabulary words.
- **Recorded books.** These materials, available from many libraries, can stimulate interest in traditional reading and can be used to reinforce and complement reading lessons.
- **Backup materials for home use.** Make available to students a second set of books and materials that they can use at home.
- **Summary materials.** Allow and encourage students to use published book summaries, synopses, and digests of major reading assignments to review (not replace) reading assignments.

Phonics.   To help children with ADHD master rules of phonics, the following techniques are effective.

- **Mnemonics for phonics.** Teach the child mnemonics that provide reminders about hard-to-learn phonics rules (e.g., *When two vowels go walking, the first does the talking*) (Scruggs & Mastropieri, 2000).
- **Word families.** Teach the child to recognize and read word families that illustrate particular phonetic concepts (e.g., *ph* sounds, *at-bat-cat*).

- **Board games for phonics.** Have students play board games, such as bingo, that allow them to practice phonetically irregular words.
- **Computer games for phonics.** Use a computer to provide opportunities for students to drill and practice with phonics or grammar lessons.
- **Picture-letter charts.** Use these for children who know sounds but do not know the letters that go with them.

Writing.   In composing stories or other writing assignments, children with ADHD benefit from the following practices.

- **Standards for writing assignments.** Identify and teach the child classroom standards for acceptable written work, such as format and style.
- **Recognizing parts of a story.** Teach the student how to describe the major parts of a story (e.g., plot, main characters, setting, conflict, and resolution). Use a storyboard with parts listed for this purpose.
- **Post office.** Establish a post office in the classroom, and provide students with opportunities to write, mail, and receive letters to and from their classmates and teacher.
- **Visualize compositions.** Ask the child to close his or her eyes and visualize a paragraph that the teacher reads aloud. Another variation of this technique is to ask a student to describe a recent event while the other students close their eyes and visualize what is being said as a written paragraph.
- **Proofread compositions.** Require that the child proofread his or her work before turning in written assignments. Provide the child with a list of items to check when proofreading his or her own work.
- **Tape recorders.** Ask the student to dictate writing assignments into a tape recorder, as an alternative to writing them.
- **Dictate writing assignments.** Have the teacher or another student write down a story told by a child with ADHD.

Spelling.   To help children with ADHD who are poor spellers, the following techniques have been found to be helpful.

- **Everyday examples of hard-to-spell words.** Take advantage of everyday events to teach difficult spelling words in context. For example, ask a child eating a cheese sandwich to spell "sandwich."
- **Frequently used words.** Assign spelling words that the child routinely uses in his or her speech each day.
- **Dictionary of misspelled words.** Ask the child to keep a personal dictionary of frequently misspelled words. Show them one that you keep for your own use, so they understand that checking one's work is something everyone should do.
- **Partner spelling activities.** Pair the child with another student. Ask the partners to quiz each other on the spelling of new words. Encourage both students

to guess the correct spelling, using rules they have learned, when they are not sure of the answer.

- **Manipulatives.** Use cutout letters or other manipulatives to spell out hard-to-learn words.
- **Color-coded letters.** Color code different letters in hard-to-spell words (e.g., "receipt").
- **Movement activities.** Combine movement activities with spelling lessons (e.g., jump rope while spelling words out loud).
- **Word banks.** Use 3" × 5" index cards of frequently misspelled words sorted alphabetically.

Handwriting.   Students with ADHD who have difficulty with manuscript or cursive writing may well benefit from their teacher's use of the following instructional practices.

- **Individual chalkboards.** Ask the child to practice copying and erasing the target words on a small, individual chalkboard. Two children can be paired to practice their target words together.
- **Quiet places for handwriting.** Provide the child with a special "quiet place" (e.g., a table outside the classroom) to complete his or her handwriting assignments.
- **Spacing words on a page.** Teach the child to use his or her finger to measure how much space to leave between each word in a written assignment.
- **Special writing paper.** Ask the child to use special paper with vertical lines to learn to space letters and words on a page.
- **Structured programs for handwriting.** Teach handwriting skills through a structured program, such as Jan Olsen's Handwriting Without Tears program (Olsen, 2003).

Math Computation.   Numerous individualized instructional practices can help children with ADHD improve their basic computation skills. The following are just a few.

- **Patterns in math.** Teach the student to recognize patterns when adding, subtracting, multiplying, or dividing whole numbers. For example, the digits of numbers, that are multiples of 9 (18, 27, 36 . . .) add up to 9.
- **Partnering for math activities.** Pair a child with ADHD with another student and provide opportunities for the partners to quiz each other about basic computation skills.
- **Mastery of math symbols.** If children do not understand the symbols used in math, they will not be able to do the work. For instance, do they understand that the "plus" in 1 + 3 means to add and that the "minus" in 5 − 3 means to take away?
- **Mnemonics for basic computation.** Teach the child mnemonics that describe basic steps in computing whole numbers. For example, "Don't Miss Susie's

Boat" can be used to help the student recall the basic steps in long division (i.e., divide, multiply, subtract, and bring down).

- **Real-life examples of money skills.** Provide the child with real-life opportunities to practice target money skills. For example, ask the child to calculate his or her change when paying for lunch in the school cafeteria, or set up a class store where children can practice calculating change.
- **Color coding arithmetic symbols.** Color code basic arithmetic symbols, such as +, −, and =, to provide visual cues for children when they are computing whole numbers.
- **Calculators to check basic computation.** Ask the child to use a calculator to check addition, subtraction, multiplication, or division.
- **Board games for basic computation.** Ask the child to play board games to practice adding, subtracting, multiplying, and dividing whole numbers.
- **Computer games for basic computation.** Schedule computer time for the child to drill and practice basic computations, using appropriate games.
- **"Magic minute" drills.** Have students perform a quick (60-second) drill every day to practice basic computation of math facts, and have children track their own performance.

Solving Math Word Problems. To help children with ADHD improve their skill in solving word problems in mathematics, try the following.

- **Reread the problem.** Teach the child to read a word problem *two times* before beginning to compute the answer.
- **Clue words.** Teach the child clue words that identify which operation to use when solving word problems. For example, words such as *sum, total,* or *all together* may indicate an addition operation.
- **Guiding questions for word problems.** Teach students to ask guiding questions in solving word problems. For example: What is the question asked in the problem? What information do you need to figure out the answer? What operation should you use to compute the answer?
- **Real-life examples of word problems.** Ask the student to create and solve word problems that provide practice with specific target operations, such as addition, subtraction, multiplication, or division. These problems can be based on recent, real-life events in the child's life.
- **Calculators to check word problems.** Ask the student to use a calculator to check computations made in answering assigned word problems.

Use of Special Materials in Math. Some children with ADHD benefit from using special materials to help them complete their math assignments, including:

- **Number lines.** Provide number lines for the child to use when computing whole numbers.
- **Manipulatives.** Use manipulatives to help students gain basic computation skills, such as counting poker chips when adding single-digit numbers.

- **Graph paper.** Ask the child to use graph paper to help organize columns when adding, subtracting, multiplying, or dividing whole numbers.

Organizational and Study Skills for Children with ADHD.　Many students with ADHD are easily distracted and have difficulty focusing their attention on assigned tasks. However, the following practices can help children with ADHD improve their organization of homework and other daily assignments.

- **Designate one teacher as the student's advisor or coordinator.** This teacher will regularly review the student's progress through progress reports submitted by other teachers and will act as the liaison between home and school. Permit the student to meet with this advisor on a regular basis (e.g., Monday morning) to plan and organize for the week and to review progress and problems from the past week.
- **Assignment notebooks.** Provide the child with an assignment notebook to help organize homework and other seatwork.
- **Color-coded folders.** Provide the child with color-coded folders to help organize assignments for different academic subjects (e.g., reading, mathematics, social science, and science).
- **Work with a homework partner.** Assign the child a partner to help record homework and other seatwork in the assignment notebook and file work sheets and other papers in the proper folders.
- **Clean out desks and book bags.** Ask the child to periodically sort through and clean out his or her desk, book bag, and other special places where written assignments are stored.
- **Visual aids as reminders of subject material.** Use banners, charts, lists, pie graphs, and diagrams situated throughout the classroom to remind students of the subject material being learned.

Time Management for Students with ADHD.　Children with ADHD often have difficulty finishing their assignments on time and can thus benefit from special materials and practices that help them to improve their time management skills. Try the following techniques.

- **Use a clock or wristwatch.** Teach the child how to read and use a clock or wristwatch to manage time when completing assigned work.
- **Use a calendar.** Teach the child how to read and use a calendar to schedule assignments.
- **Practice sequencing activities.** Provide the child with supervised opportunities to break down a long assignment into a sequence of short, interrelated activities.
- **Create a daily activity schedule.** Tape a schedule of planned daily activities to the child's desk.

Helpful Study Skills for Students with ADHD.　Children with ADHD often have difficulty in learning how to study effectively on their own. The following strategies may assist ADHD students in developing the study skills necessary for academic success.

- **Adapt worksheets.** Teach a child how to adapt instructional worksheets. For example, help a child fold his or her reading worksheet to reveal only one question at a time. The child can also use a blank piece of paper to cover the other questions on the page.
- **Venn diagrams.** Teach a child how to use Venn diagrams to help illustrate and organize key concepts in reading, mathematics, or other academic subjects.
- **Note-taking skills.** Teach a child with ADHD how to take notes when organizing key academic concepts that he or she has learned, perhaps with the use of a program such as Anita Archer's Skills for School Success (Archer & Gleason, 2002).
- **Checklist of frequent mistakes.** Provide the child with a checklist of mistakes that he or she frequently makes in written assignments (e.g., punctuation or capitalization errors), mathematics (e.g., addition or subtraction errors), or other academic subjects. Teach the child how to use this list when proofreading his or her work at home and school.
- **Checklist of homework supplies.** Provide the child with a checklist that identifies categories of items needed for homework assignments (e.g., books, pencils, and homework assignment sheets).
- **Uncluttered workspace.** Teach a child with ADHD how to prepare an uncluttered workspace to complete assignments. For example, instruct the child to clear away unnecessary books or other materials *before* beginning his or her seatwork.
- **Monitor homework assignments.** Keep track of how well your students with ADHD complete their assigned homework. Discuss and resolve with them and their parents any problems in completing these assignments. For example, evaluate the difficulty of the assignments and how long the children spend on their homework each night. Keep in mind that the *quality*, rather than the *quantity*, of homework assigned is the most important issue. While doing homework is an important part of developing study skills, it should be used to reinforce skills and to review material learned in class, rather than to present, in advance, large amounts of material, or material that is new to the student.

Behavioral Interventions

The second major component of effective instruction for children with ADHD involves the use of *behavioral interventions*. Exhibiting behavior that resembles that of younger children, children with ADHD often act immaturely and have difficulty learning how to control their impulsiveness and hyperactivity. They may have problems forming friendships with other children in the class and may have difficulty thinking through the social consequences of their actions.

The purpose of behavioral interventions is to assist students in displaying the behaviors that are most conducive to their own learning and that of classmates. Well-managed classrooms prevent many disciplinary problems and provide an environment that is most favorable for learning. When a teacher's time must be spent interacting with students whose behaviors are not focused on the lesson being presented, less time is available for assisting other students. Behavioral interventions should be viewed as an opportunity for teaching in the most effective and efficient manner, rather than as an opportunity for punishment.

Effective Behavioral Intervention Techniques

Effective teachers use a number of behavioral intervention techniques to help students learn how to control their behavior. Perhaps the most important and effective of these is verbal reinforcement of appropriate behavior. The most common form of verbal reinforcement is praise given to a student when he or she begins and completes an activity or exhibits a particular desired behavior. Simple phrases such as "good job" encourage a child to act appropriately. Effective teachers praise children with ADHD frequently and look for a behavior to praise before a child gets off task. The following strategies provide some guidance regarding the use of praise:

> **Define the appropriate behavior while giving praise.** Praise should be specific for the positive behavior displayed by the student: The comments should focus on what the student did right and should include exactly what part(s) of the student's behavior was desirable. Rather than praising a student for not disturbing the class, for example, a teacher should praise him or her for quietly completing a math lesson on time.
>
> **Give praise immediately.** The sooner that approval is given regarding appropriate behavior, the more likely the student will continue or repeat it.
>
> **Vary the statements given as praise.** The comments used by teachers to praise appropriate behavior should vary; when students hear the same praise statement repeated over and over, it may lose its value.
>
> **Be consistent and sincere with praise.** Appropriate behavior should receive consistent praise. Consistency among teachers with respect to desired behavior is important, to avoid confusion on the part of students with ADHD. Similarly, students will notice when teachers give insincere praise, and this insincerity will make praise less effective.

Keep in mind that the most effective teachers focus their behavioral intervention strategies on praise rather than on punishment. Negative consequences may temporarily change behavior, but they rarely change attitudes and may actually increase the frequency and intensity of inappropriate behavior by rewarding misbehaving students with attention. Moreover, punishment may only teach children what not to do; it does not provide children with the skills that they need to do what is expected. Positive reinforcement produces the changes in attitudes that will shape a student's behavior over the long term. In addition to verbal reinforcement, the following set of generalized behavioral intervention techniques has proven helpful with students with ADHD.

Selectively ignore inappropriate behavior. It is sometimes helpful for teachers to selectively ignore inappropriate behavior. This technique is particularly useful when the behavior is unintentional or unlikely to recur or is intended solely to gain the attention of teachers or classmates without disrupting the classroom or interfering with the learning of others.

Remove nuisance items. Teachers often find that certain objects (such as rubber bands and toys) distract the attention of students with ADHD in the classroom. The removal of nuisance items is generally most effective after the student has been given the choice of putting it away immediately and then fails to do so.

Provide calming manipulatives. While some toys and other objects can be distracting for both the students with ADHD and peers in the classroom, some children with ADHD can benefit from having access to objects that can be manipulated quietly. Manipulatives may help children gain some needed sensory input while still attending to the lesson.

Allow for "escape valve" outlets. Permitting students with ADHD to leave class for a moment, perhaps on an errand (such as returning a book to the library), can be an effective means of settling them down and allowing them to return to the room ready to concentrate.

Activity reinforcement. Students receive activity reinforcement when they are encouraged to perform a less desirable behavior before a preferred one.

Hurdle helping. Teachers can offer encouragement, support, and assistance to prevent students from becoming frustrated with an assignment. This help can take many forms, from enlisting a peer for support to supplying additional materials or information.

Parent conferences. Parents have a critical role in the education of students, and this axiom may be particularly true for students with ADHD. Parents must be included as partners in planning for the student's success. Partnering with parents entails including parental input in behavioral intervention strategies, maintaining frequent communication between parents and teachers, and collaborating in monitoring the student's progress.

Peer mediation. Members of a student's peer group can positively impact the behavior of students with ADHD. Many schools now have formalized peer mediation programs, in which students receive training in order to manage disputes involving their classmates.

Effective teachers also use **behavioral prompts** with their students. These prompts help remind students about expectations for their learning and behavior in the classroom. Three prompts may be particularly helpful.

Visual cues. In a private conversation with the student, establish simple, nonintrusive visual cues that you will use to remind the child to remain on task. For example, you can point at the child while looking him or her in the eye, or you can hold out your hand, palm down, near the child.

Proximity control. When talking to a child, move to where the child is standing or sitting. Your physical proximity to the child will help the child to focus and pay attention to what you are saying.

Hand gestures. Set up hand signals so the child can communicate privately with you. For example, ask the child to raise his or her hand every time you ask a question. A closed fist can signal that the child knows the answer; an open palm can signal that he or she does not know the answer. You would call on the child to answer only when he or she makes a fist.

In some instances, children with ADHD benefit from instruction designed to help students learn how to manage their own behavior.

Social Skills Classes.   Teach children with ADHD appropriate social skills using a structured class. For example, you can ask the children to role-play and model different solutions to common social problems. It is critical to provide for the generalization of these skills, including structured opportunities for the children to use the social skills that they learn. Offering such classes and experiences to the general school population can positively affect the school climate.

Problem-Solving Sessions.   Discuss how to resolve social conflicts. Conduct impromptu discussions with one student or with a small group of students when the conflict arises. In this setting, ask two children who are arguing about a game to discuss how to settle their differences. Encourage the children to resolve their problem by talking to each other in a supervised setting.

For many children with ADHD, functional behavioral assessments and positive behavioral interventions and supports, including behavioral contracts and management plans, tangible rewards, or token economy systems, are helpful in teaching them how to manage their own behavior. Because students' individual needs are different, it is important for teachers, along with the family and other involved professionals, to evaluate whether these practices are appropriate for their classrooms. Here are examples of these techniques, along with steps to follow when using them (DuPaul & Stoner, as cited in Shinn, Walker, & Stoner, 2002).

Functional Behavioral Assessment (FBA).   FBA is a systematic process for describing problem behavior and identifying the environmental factors and surrounding events associated with problem behavior. A team works closely with the child exhibiting problem behavior to (1) observe the behavior and identify and define its problematic characteristics, (2) identify which actions or events precede and follow the behavior, and (3) determine how often the behavior occurs. The results of the FBA should be used to develop an effective and efficient intervention and support plan (Gable et al., 1997).

Behavioral Contracts and Management Plans.   Identify specific academic or behavioral goals for the child with ADHD, along with behavior that needs to change and strategies for responding to inappropriate behavior. Work with the child to cooperatively identify appropriate goals, such as completing homework assignments on time and obeying safety rules on the school playground. Take the time to ensure that the child agrees that his or her goals are important to master. Behavioral contracts and management plans are typically used with individual children, as opposed to entire classes, and should be prepared with input from parents.

Tangible Rewards.   Use tangible rewards to reinforce appropriate behavior. These rewards can include stickers, such as "happy faces" or sports team emblems, or privileges, such as extra time on the computer or lunch with the teacher. Children should be involved in the selection of the reward. If children are invested in the reward, they are more likely to work for it.

Token Economy Systems.   Use token economy systems to motivate a child to achieve a goal identified in a behavioral contract (Barkley, 1990). For example, a child can earn points for each homework assignment completed on time. In some cases, students also lose points for each homework assignment not completed on time. After earning a specified number of points, the student receives a tangible reward, such as extra time on a computer or a "free" period on Friday afternoon. Token economy systems are often used for entire classrooms, as opposed to solely for individual students.

Self-Management Systems.   Train students to monitor and evaluate their own behavior without constant feedback from the teacher. In a typical self-management system, the teacher identifies behaviors that will be managed by a student and provides a written rating scale that includes the performance criteria for each rating. The teacher and student separately rate student behavior during an activity and compare ratings. The student earns points if the ratings match or are within one point and receives no points if ratings are more than one point apart; points are exchanged for privileges. With time, the teacher involvement is removed, and the student becomes responsible for self-monitoring.

Classroom Accommodations

The third component of a strategy for effectively educating children with ADHD involves physical *classroom accommodations.* Children with ADHD often have difficulty adjusting to the structured environment of a classroom, determining what is important, and focusing on their assigned work. They are easily distracted by other children or by nearby activities in the classroom. As a result, many children with ADHD benefit from accommodations that reduce distractions in the classroom environment and help them to stay on task and learn.

Special Seating Arrangements for ADHD Students

One of the most common accommodations that can be made to the physical environment of the classroom involves determining where a child with ADHD will sit. Three special seating assignments may be especially useful.

> **Seat the child near the teacher.** Assign the child a seat near your desk or the front of the room. This seating assignment provides opportunities for you to monitor and reinforce the child's on-task behavior.
>
> **Seat the child near a student role model.** Assign the child a seat near a student role model. This seat arrangement provides opportunity for children to work cooperatively and to learn from their peers in the class.
>
> **Provide low-distraction work areas.** As space permits, teachers should make available a quiet, distraction-free room or area for quiet study time and test taking. Students should be directed to this room or area privately and discreetly in order to avoid the appearance of punishment.

Instructional Tools and the Physical Learning Environment

Skilled teachers use special instructional tools to modify the classroom learning environment and accommodate the special needs of their students with ADHD. They also monitor the physical environment, keeping in mind the needs of these children. The following tools and techniques may be helpful.

> **Pointers.** Teach the child to use a pointer to help visually track written words on a page. For example, provide the child with a bookmark to help him or her follow along when students are taking turns reading aloud.
>
> **Egg timers.** Note for the children the time at which the lesson is starting and the time at which it will conclude. Set a timer to indicate to children how much time remains in the lesson and place the timer at the front of the classroom; the children can check the timer to see how much time remains. Interim prompts can be used as well. For instance, children can monitor their own progress during a 30-minute lesson if the timer is set for 10 minutes three times.
>
> **Classroom lights.** Turning the classroom lights on and off prompts children that the noise level in the room is too high and they should be quiet. This practice can also be used to signal that it is time to begin preparing for the next lesson.
>
> **Music.** Play music on a tape recorder or chords on a piano to prompt children that they are too noisy. In addition, playing different types of music on a tape recorder communicates to children what level of activity is appropriate for a particular lesson. For example, play quiet classical music for quiet activities done independently and jazz for active group activities.
>
> **Proper use of furniture.** The desk and chair used by children with ADHD need to be the right size; if they are not, the child will be more inclined to

squirm and fidget. A general rule of thumb is that a child should be able to put his or her elbows on the surface of the desk and have his or her chin fit comfortably in the palm of the hand.

Conclusion

This chapter has outlined a series of instructional strategies that have proven to be successful in educating children with ADHD. However, it should be emphasized again that these techniques are also highly useful for *all* children. The three main components of a successful strategy for educating children with ADHD are *academic instruction, behavioral interventions,* and *classroom accommodations.* By incorporating techniques from these three areas into their everyday instructional and classroom management practices, teachers will be empowered to improve both the academic performance and the behavior of their students with ADHD. In doing so, teachers will create an enhanced learning environment for all students.

IV Practical Considerations for Teachers of Students with Learning Disabilities

Your role as a teacher of children with learning disabilities requires that you become familiar with a wide range of responsibilities, both in general education and special education. In order to do the most effective job possible, you will need to become familiar with all of the requirements that will be asked of you by the school, staff, parents, and students.

The first responsibility of a teacher of children with learning disabilities is having a thorough knowledge base of this particular disability. The topics covered in this book under Theory, Diagnosis, and Assessment should have provided you with that foundation. Once you have a strong working knowledge of those areas, it will be time to move on to more practical concerns. We are sure that you will have many questions, especially when it is your first time teaching children with learning disabilities. Even if you have taught children with special needs, this section of the book may reinforce, enlighten, or educate you further.

Our experience has shown us that new teachers need a great deal of practical guidance, since there is so much about learning disabilities that is unknown. This section of the book will be as practical as possible, and will assume that you have never taught children with learning disabilities. To accomplish this task, we have divided the school year into four stages:

1. The Preliminary Stage: before the start of school
2. The Initiation Stage: the first month of school
3. The Interim Stage: October–March
4. The Culmination Stage: April–June

As you will see, there are very specific and distinct responsibilities that need to be addressed within each section of the school year. We hope that by the end of this book, you will be able to "hit the ground running" if you are offered a job as a teacher of children with learning disabilities.

At first, you will find yourself having numerous questions about what to do, such as:

- Where do I start?
- What will I need to know?
- How do I get started?
- How do I find out about the children I will be working with in the class?
- How do I deal with parents?
- How do I deal with staff?
- What happens if. . .?

These are all very normal concerns. The first section we will deal with is called the Preliminary Stage, which occurs prior to school. As a special education teacher, it will be very important that you know as much about your students before they come to school on the first day. In order to do the best job possible for these children, you will need to be as prepared as you can. An educated and informed teacher is very reassuring to parents and students.

CHAPTER 14

Preliminary Stage: Before the Start of School

The **Preliminary Stage,** which should ideally begin before the first day of school, involves eight steps.

1. *Gather information about your students with LD.*
2. *Read IEPs.*
3. *Contact parents and students.*
4. *Meet with your assistant teacher, paraprofessional, or aide before classes begin.*
5. *Set up your classroom.*
6. *Communicate with related service providers.*
7. *Communicate with classroom teachers.*
8. *Evaluate your resources and order new materials.*

All of the steps should be accomplished before your students enter the classroom on the first day of school. So let's get started and discuss each, one at a time.

Step One—Gather Information about Your Students with LD

Without background information, you will be working in the dark and may possibly hamper your students' potential progress. Most likely, you will be amazed at how much information is available on a child who has been classified with a learning disability—within your school building, at the administration building, and in the child's home environment. This information may not always be easy to gather, but it does exist somewhere. It will require you to be very proactive. Do not assume that someone will provide you with this information. If someone does, then consider yourself fortunate, but there may be more that is not provided. Either way, try to gather the following materials.

   1. A copy of the child's current IEP. This document can be found in several places. First, look in the special education files that may already exist within your room or may have been passed on to you by another special education teacher. Second, a copy should be part of the school psychologist's records. You can ask him/her for a copy. Third, a copy will definitely exist at the district office of the director of pupil personnel services or the chairperson of the IEP Committee (also known as the Committee on Special Education or Eligibility Committee, depending on the state in which you are working). If your district is using a computer-based IEP system, then you will probably need the student's ID number to access the material. Someone at the office of the director of pupil personnel services should have this information.

2. A copy of the student's most recent psychological and educational assessment report. If this is the first time the child has been both classified and receiving services, you should ask for the initial evaluation report. This was part of the information that was used to determine the existence of the learning disability by the IEP Committee. You should be able to get this from the psychologist or district office. If the child has been classified for several years, you will need to get a copy of the most recent triennial review, which is done every three years. This report should also be in the psychologist's office or district office. It will contain very important and specific information on the child's areas of academic strength and weakness, emotional strengths and weaknesses, family background, academic history, recommendations, and other information that will provide a profile of the child.

3. A copy of the child's group achievement test results from as far back as possible. Some school districts require children to take group achievement (e.g., Metropolitan Achievement Test, California Tests of Basic Skills, and Stanford Achievement Tests) tests at different times in their school career. You should be able to find this information in the each child's permanent record folder in the main office. If you are unsure where this information is located, ask someone (most likely a secretary) in the main office where these folders exist, since you will need other information from them later. Group achievement tests can provide additional skill information. However, be careful when interpreting the scores, since children with LD often have great difficulties taking group administration tests (Child Development Institute, 2004). Consequently, the scores may not be as valid as those provided by the individually administered tests and informal assessment measures used for the initial review or triennial review.

4. A copy of past report cards. The pattern of grades on report cards can further your understanding of the areas of disability or struggle a child has experienced over the years. Look for patterns of strengths and weaknesses. This information is usually found in the permanent record folder.

5. Attendance records. In the case of a child with a learning disability, the pattern of school attendance can provide further information regarding the possible level of frustration he or she may be experiencing. A pattern of many sporadic missed single days, frequent absences on Mondays or right after holidays may provide you with valuable information on present stress levels. Children with learning disabilities who are encountering a great deal of stress will often use school avoidance to cope with their tension. All too often, children with severe learning disabilities may be under such stress and tension that physical symptoms begin to appear (Berkowitz, 2004), which may also account for the pattern of absences. If you notice this, speak with the school psychologist for further guidance. Attendance information is usually found in the main office, at the elementary level, and at the attendance office, for secondary students.

6. **Past teacher comments and reports.** Comments from past teachers can provide additional data on a child's strengths and weaknesses. These comments may also provide information on the child's social skills and interaction with peers, which will be important for managing your own class. If you know anything about prior teacher styles, you may want to see which style the child responded to positively and which styles had negative results. Although teacher style did not create the learning disability, it may provide information on what has and has not been effective. This information should be in the permanent record folder as separate reports or as part of the report card comments.

7. **Disciplinary reports.** There may be times when a student with LD has secondary emotional problems. As a result, he or she may get into frequent trouble in school. This information is valuable, since it may offer insight into the types of management tools you may need to utilize in the classroom. At the elementary level, disciplinary reports will probably be in the principal's office. At the secondary level, they will most likely be in the Dean's office or the Assistant Principal's office. However, guidance counselors at the secondary level may also have copies sent to them, so they may be another resource for obtaining this information.

8. **Medical records.** Medical records in schools can provide some very basic as well as significant information. For instance, you should immediately look to vision and hearing test results, see if the child needs glasses or hearing aids, as well as outside test results from a pediatrician, neurologist, and so on. More significant information may include chronic illnesses or medication. If the child is on medication, you will need to know the dosage, who administers it, and possible side effects, in case the child exhibits side effect symptoms in the classroom. Although you are not a medical doctor, you must have some working knowledge of the medications that each child in your classroom is taking. This is imperative, so that when you meet with each parent, you will already appear knowledgeable about his/her child's situation. You can find basic medication information in libraries, book stores, and on the Internet.

IMPORTANT POINT

Always remember that you are *never* to provide any suggestions, medical information, guidance or information to parents concerning medication or medical issues in general. If parents ask you what you think, or if they should cut back or change medications, let them know that this is not your area of expertise and that it is in their best interests to speak to their doctor about this matter as soon as possible.

Step Two—Read IEPs

As a teacher of children with learning disabilities, you must understand and monitor the requirements of each child's Individualized Education Program. The IEP is a written plan containing all the goals that a student should meet in the upcoming academic year. For the child to meet the IEP goals, you will need a very good understanding of his or her IEP. We will now discuss the specific sections of the IEP that you will need to become familiar with so that you can design the most relevant, practical, and effective educational program for each of your students with LD.

There are many sections to any IEP. Some sections pertain only to children in elementary school, some only to middle school or junior high school students, and others (in particular, areas dealing with transition services) to students over the age of 14. Regardless, you should understand all of the following sections.

- **Classification.** There is a high probability that the child's IEP simply uses the label Learning Disability under the category of Classification. Although this narrows down the type of disability to some degree, it by no means gives you the specific type, subtype, or other conditions of that learning disability. You will need to find out the specific type of learning disability the child may have (e.g., dyslexia, dysgraphia, visual processing disorder, etc.). This information may be contained in the assessment reports.

- **Modifications.** The next section to examine on the child's IEP will be classroom and test modifications. You will need to fully understand these modifications, since you will be communicating and explaining them to the child's teachers, parents, and the student. Once you have found this section on the IEP, you will need to determine how these modifications will be implemented in the classroom.

- **Health Alerts.** On the front page of the IEP, you should look for a category titled *Health Alerts*. Health Alerts inform you about medical conditions, medications, and any relevant medical issues pertaining to this child. Whatever is noted under the Health Alerts section must be taken very seriously. You have a responsibility to do as much research as possible so that you have a strong working knowledge of the child's medical condition. This research can be done in libraries, through journals, and even through various Internet resources. Again, although you are not a medical doctor, you need be educated on this topic in order to best understand this child, as well as to have a greater awareness of his medical issues.

- **Accommodations.** Some students are given accommodations on their IEP, such as special furniture, filters for lighting, acoustic enhancements, and so on. Investigate and learn about each accommodation by speaking with your supervisor, director of student services, or the psychologist.

- **Related Services.** The student's IEP will also contain a section indicating each related service provided, as well its length and frequency. Become familiar with the related services and the areas covered under each service. Later, we will discuss contact with the related service provider.

- **Assistive Technology Needs.** Today, technology has become an integral part in all classrooms, including special education classrooms. Some children may be entitled to assistive technology (e.g., word processor, FM trainer, or magnification devices). This should appear on the child's IEP in a section titled something like "Assistive Technology Needs." If there is required assistive technology, find out everything you can regarding the type, its purposes, and any other relevant information pertaining to the child's needs. Research on the latest assistive technology devices can be done in libraries, through journals, and through numerous Internet resources.

- **Ability Levels.** Ability levels refers to the child's current academic level according to the most recent assessment. Look for the section of the IEP that reads something like, "Present Levels of Academic Performance." This section should offer some guidance on the child's current academic strengths and weaknesses.

- **SPAM Needs.** This section of the IEP focuses specifically on the child's **SPAM** (social, physical, academic, and management) needs. This information can be found directly on the IEP, and from it you can learn which needs are mild, moderate, or severe. This information should help you to plan classroom expectations and management. For example, if the child's social needs are severe, you should consider setting up group counseling with the psychologist. If management needs are the most severe issue, then consider very restrictive boundaries, collaboration with the psychologist, behavioral contracts, and so on.

Step Three—Contact Parents and Students

Contacting Parents

We strongly advise you to meet individually with each student with LD, together with the parent(s) before the first day of school begins if it is possible. This will help you get to know the family, reduce their anxiety about the child's starting school, answer their questions and concerns, and let them become confident in you, your teaching, and your knowledge.

If you can begin a week before school starts, we highly recommend that you get the permission of administration to send a letter to each family introducing yourself and inviting the student and parent(s) to come to the school to help you set up the room, or to just come in so you all can get to know each other. A sample letter is shown in Figure 14.1. The letter will be more effective if you use the student's preferred name, so try to learn what that is, either from the documentation you are reviewing or from another staff member who knows the student.

Meeting with Parents and the Students

According to Friend and Cook (2000), your first goal in working with parents is to help them participate in meetings, conferences, and other interactions in a way that is meaningful and respectful. Therefore, in your first meeting with the parent(s) and

FIGURE 14.1   Letter of Introduction

Dear _____ :

My name is _____ and I will be _____'s (*student's first name*) special education teacher (*adjust, if needed*) this year. I am inviting you and _____ (*student's first name*) to a meeting before school begins so we can discuss any questions or concerns that you or _____ (*student's name*) may have about the upcoming academic year. Students and teachers want to start the school year on a positive note, and I feel this meeting will give us that type of beginning. Plus, there will be snacks! (*Arrange to provide a plate of healthy choices, such as nuts, carrots, and dip, or cheese and cut-up fruit.*) The following dates and times are available: (*Insert the available time slots, including some in the evening and early morning, if possible.*) Please call to let me know which date and time would be convenient for you. My number at _____ (*home or school? Decide which you want to give them.*) is _____. If I do not answer, please leave your name and number so I can return your call.

(If you are a new teacher, add the following.)

Since this is my first year here at _____ (*school name*), I would like to give you some background on my professional and educational experiences. (*Here, provide past teaching experiences, schools where you have worked, programs you were involved in, experience with children with disabilities, colleges from which you received your Master's and Bachelor's degrees.*)

(If you are a returning teacher, add the following instead.)

As you may know, I have worked at _____ (*school or district name*) for the past ___ years. I have truly enjoyed my experiences here, and I believe that my students have, too. I know that I can help _____ (*student's first name*) to have a very positive and successful year.

(Close the letter simply.)

I look forward to meeting you soon. Please call soon to set up the appointment, or if you have any questions.

Sincerely,

Note that a "ragged" right margin usually seems friendlier than a letter with right justification.

the child, they suggest that the first part of the meeting be held with the parents alone, and that you have an activity for the student in a nearby, supervised space, such as the school library. With the parent(s) alone, discuss the following issues:

- Parental role and responsibilities
- Parental expectations
- Parental involvement with homework

• Means of communication between home and school and between school and home

After you discuss these issues and address any questions the parents may have, bring the child in to discuss student roles and responsibilities in front of the parents. After some general comments and questions to the student (e.g., hobbies, summer vacation, etc.) you should address the following issues.

- Your expectations for classroom behavior
- Your expectations regarding homework
- Ways for the student to communicate with the teacher, especially if the work is too hard, if the student does not understand something, or has any questions or concerns. Many children with LD do not communicate their fears and feelings and bury them, which leads to more frustration and feelings of low self-esteem.

Friend and Bursuck (2002) also suggest that to learn more about each child from the parent(s), you should enclose a questionnaire, checklist, or both in the initial letter home. Friend and Bursuck provide the following questions which might serve as a structure for such questionnaires or checklists (p. 100):

1. What is your child's favorite class activity?
2. Does your child have any worries about class activities? If so what are they?
3. What are your priorities for your child's education this year?
4. What questions do you have about your child's education in my class this year?
5. How could we at school make this the most successful year ever for your child?
6. Are there any topics you want to discuss which may require a conference? If so please let me know.
7. If a conference is requested, would you like other individuals to participate? If so please give me a list of their names so that I can invite them.
8. If a conference is requested would you like me to have particular school information available? If so please let me know.
9. If you have any questions that I may be able to answer by phone you can reach me between i.e. 7:30 and 8:10 a.m. and between 3:00 and 3:30 p.m. at the following number _____. If you prefer you can reach me by email at _____(Optional)

Step Four—Meet with Your Assistant Teacher, Paraprofessional, or Aide before Classes Begin

As a teacher of children with LD, you may be responsible for their education in a resource room program, inclusion classroom, or special class. In some cases, special educators have one or more paraprofessionals, aides, or assistant teachers to help them. If you are working with one or more of these individuals, try to get a copy of each person's job description from central administration, the director of special education, or the principal. This information should provide you with the roles, responsibilities, and expectations for each one. Pierangelo (2004) suggests that that you consider the following issues in terms of working with assistant teachers, aides, and paraprofessionals:

- Allow them to use their abilities and talents; give them the chance to make and try suggestions.
- Let them see that you appreciate initiative. Make sure they realize that they are essential to the success of the students with whom they work.
- Treat your aides and paraprofessional or assistant teachers as "second teachers" in the classroom. Encourage them to look around, see what needs to be done, and do it. However, be very aware that liability issues may arise if the children are left with an aide, paraprofessional, or assistant teacher who is not a licensed certified teacher. If a child gets hurt or problems arise while you are not in the room, there could be problems. Meet with your supervisor and discuss this matter to see what your guidelines and responsibilities are in these cases.
- Make the aide, paraprofessional, or assistant teacher aware of the IEP goals for each student. These individuals will acquire personal growth when you trust them and appreciate what they do.
- Short written notes of thanks are a really good practice, such as "I want to thank you for being so positive when talking to the students."
- First-year teachers seem very unsure of how to use their aide. If aides are idle, resources are being underutilized. Aides and teaching assistants can perform numerous duties, including assisting with grading, and duplicating worksheets. Working with students, however, whether individually or in small groups, is their most important function.
- If problems arise with your aide, paraprofessional, or assistant, you may want to meet with the school psychologist, your coordinator of special education, or the principal to determine a way to resolve the problems. It is advisable to act promptly in these instances—the longer you wait to talk about a challenging situation, the more difficult it often becomes.

Working with Another Educator in an Inclusion Classroom

Unlike a resource room or special education class (where you are the lead teacher), working in an inclusion setting poses some different issues that need to be addressed. An inclusion classroom is defined as a regular education setting for children with disabilities *and* nondisabled peers. The room normally has a regular education teacher and a special education teacher. An important component to the success of an inclusion classroom is the chemistry and rapport between the special education teacher and the regular education classroom teacher. Many issues need to be discussed to prevent frustration, misconceptions, or dissension from occurring, since the success of the program will definitely be affected by the cooperation of this relationship. Some issues that need to be addressed when collaborating with another educator in an inclusion classroom include the following.

- Clearly define roles and professional responsibilities so that neither person is confused or feels pushed aside.
- Discuss your individual teaching styles to see if they will work together or whether some changes will need to be made. Even if you have different teaching styles, different approaches can complement each other and provide alternatives for students' different learning styles.
- Talk about the various delivery systems to be used in the classroom. Alternative delivery systems are teacher management and presentation systems that provide support for students and maximize learning, while working with the core curriculum in an inclusion setting. These alternative systems are discussed in the next section.

Alternative Delivery Systems

Team Teaching. Cooperative teaching, sometimes known as co-teaching, is an educational approach in which general and special educators, as well as specialists from other categorical programs, are simultaneously present in the general education classroom, sharing responsibility for some specific classroom instruction. This approach allows the integration of the teaching to be successful, since the classroom teacher is teamed with the specialist.

General and special educators jointly plan to teach academic subject content to all students. The general education teacher remains responsible for the entire class, while the special educator is responsible for implementing the IEP goals for students in special education.

Complementary Instruction. In this approach, the general education teacher assumes primary responsibility for teaching specific subject matter. The specialist is responsible for teaching academic survival skills necessary for the student to access and master the core curriculum. The content may be delivered in the classroom and complemented when the special education student is pulled out of the classroom to another setting (Villa, 2004). The critical difference between complementary instruction and the traditional pullout program is that two professionals prepare instruction together and it is delivered in the general classroom. Specific types of complementary instruction include the following.

- **One teach/one observe.** In this approach, one teacher leads the lesson while the other gathers specific predetermined information on certain students. It is important that both teachers switch off roles so that more than one perception is used in making academic decisions for students.
- **One teach/one support.** In this type of delivery system, the regular education teacher is responsible for teaching the curriculum, while the role of the special education teacher is to move from each child with a disability to the

next and assist in answering questions, monitoring class notes, explaining the material and assignments, and working closely with the students to help level the playing field.

Station teaching. In this type of delivery system, one teacher presents half the content to half the students while the other teaches the other half to the rest of the class. The student groups are then switched and each teacher repeats his/her lesson.

Parallel teaching. In this type of delivery system, both teachers divide the class into heterogeneous groups and each teacher presents a lesson to half the class. Sometimes a third, independent study group can be established as well, to reduce the number of students in each group being taught.

Alternate teaching. In this type of delivery system, the two teachers divide the group into one large and one small group. This type of system allows the use of remediation with the small group of students that might require more individual attention.

Step Five—Setting Up Your Classroom

The way you set up your classroom can dramatically affect students' attitudes toward learning, and the habits they form. Students learn best in an environment that is organized, stimulating, and comfortable. Creating such an environment entails arranging a practical physical layout, supplying diverse materials and supplies, and encouraging students to have a sense of belonging and ownership. Setting up the physical structure of your classroom is a personal choice. Depending on the type of setting in which you are employed (such as resource room or inclusion class) and the level (elementary or secondary), room arrangements and designs will differ. However, be logical when determining the layout of your room.

Arrange the Learning Centers

Take the physical features of your classroom into account when planning. As the year progresses, you may find yourself changing the environment, but the room will need to be ready when the children enter it for the first time. A look of readiness is crucial to start the year off, since it will convey a feeling of structure, authority, organization, security, and order—qualities that children with LD need in their learning environment. Keep the following general guidelines in mind when setting up your classroom.

- Face computers away from windows to keep glare from sunlight off the screens.
- Arrange bookshelves to create different areas in the larger room.
- Provide comfortable seating, such as floor pillows or bean bag chairs, in a reading area that students may use at designated times.
- Save space by using walls for posters, display shelves, books, and supplies.

- If you are lucky enough to have the space and administration support for this, build a loft to save space while creating a private spot for independent reading.
- Set aside an area to meet with small groups. Allow seating for about eight students.
- Make sure that all students will have an unrestricted view of the chalkboard.
- Your desk should be out of the way, but in an area where you can view the entire classroom. Set aside an off-limits zone for your records and supplies.

Arrange the Whole-Group Area

Whole-group activities include informal discussion, direct instruction, and student presentations.

- Consider using a rug to mark off the whole-group area if you have a primary-grade classroom.
- Consider what whole-group activities will take place, to determine how to arrange students' desks. Arranging desks in a circle promotes discussions, and small clusters of desks can double as small-group meeting areas.

Arrange Optional Learning Areas

Small-Group Area. Here you can give small-group instruction or allow groups of students to gather for peer-led discussions.

Reading Area. This is a place for students to read independently or quietly with a partner. It should provide comfortable seating, a variety of books, and a quiet, secluded atmosphere.

Writing Center. Here students write independently and collaboratively. The area should contain comfortable space for writing and a variety of supplies.

Cross-Curricular Center. This is an active center where students explore relationships across different curricula, including literature, science, social studies, art, and math.

Computer Station. This area is for computer use in writing, math, reading, keyboard practice, research, telecommunications, and creative games.

Creative Arts Center. This area is where students can get involved in visual art and dramatic play. It should have a variety of art supplies, costumes, and props.

Communication Area/Post Office. This area has mail slots for students and teacher to exchange written messages and suggestions.

Listening Station. Here students listen to tapes of books, stories, songs, and poems.

If you are hired for an elementary inclusion class, the regular education teacher will normally set up the room. In this case assist the teacher, making suggestions if you feel they will better serve the population of children with disabilities. An example is a quiet corner or study carrel, for children who are easily distracted. If you are hired as an inclusion teacher at the high school, then there may be less to do with setting up the room, since various teachers will be using that setting. However, again assist the teacher and suggest anything that you feel might help.

Step Six—Communicate with Related Service Providers

One of the most important support services for your student with a learning disability may be the related service provider(s) listed on the child's IEP. You must maintain close communication with every related service provider involved with your children. You want to maintain the most up-to-date information in case you are questioned by parents, students, or administrators. When you determine the specific related services for each student, you will need to find out the provider for these services. You should be able to get this information from the main office or the director of pupil personnel services. Once you have determined these individuals, send out letters to the related service providers for each child introducing yourself and asking for a time to get together with each of them. Outline the objectives of such a meeting, including coordination of services, avoiding scheduling conflicts, communication, and IEP development. Figure 14.2 is an example of this letter.

At this meeting, discuss schedules, goals of the service, expectations, communication with parents, and collaboration meetings to discuss the child's progress. If you are designated the case manager for the IEP (a strong possibility), discuss the means for communicating information that will be necessary in developing the new IEP at the annual review meeting. Also, learn from the service provider(s) as much as you can about the child's specific problem, etiology (cause), and expected prognosis (outcome).

FIGURE 14.2   Letter to Service Providers

Dear _____,

During this school year I will be _____'s (child's first and last name) special education teacher. It is noted on _____'s (child's first name) IEP that _____ (she or he) is to receive _____ (related service) (frequency [i.e., 1 × a week]) from you beginning on _____ (date to begin services. Be aware that related services should begin as close to the start of school as possible, if not the first day). To coordinate services, I am suggesting that we meet to discuss schedules, communication with parents and teachers, modifications and accommodations, and any other matters that may assist _____'s (child's first name) this year.

I will try to contact you to see what times and days are convenient for you, or if you prefer I can be reached at _____ (phone and extension) between the hours of _____. My room number is _____ at the _____ (name of school) school.

I look forward to meeting with you.

Sincerely yours,

| **FIGURE 14.3** | Resource Room Letter—First-Year Teacher |

Dear _____:

My name is _____ and this school year I will be working with _____(first and last name of child) in the Resource Room. _____ (child's first name) has been assigned this service according to _____ (his or her) IEP for a minimum of _____ a day (designate the frequency and time period for services). These services are being provided to _____ (him or her) for the following reasons:

(State reasons—usually weakness areas determined by an evaluation or IEP team)

To collaborate on the services for _____ (child's first name), I would like to meet with you to discuss _____ (his or her) program, scheduling time, parent communication and modifications that are required as a result of the IEP. I will be stopping by your room to discuss a convenient time for this meeting. If you prefer to call me, I can be reached at _____ (phone and extension) between the hours of _____. My room number is _____.

I look forward to meeting with you.

Sincerely yours,

Step Seven—Communicate with Classroom Teachers

If you are assigned to an auxiliary setting (e.g., resource room) or will have students in a special LD class who will be partially included in the general education classroom, one of your most important responsibilities after assisting your students is to communicate with their classroom teachers. One of your major roles will be to assist in adapting curriculum, monitoring modifications, preparing adapted materials to use in the classroom, provide information and suggestions on each child's disability, and provide alternate curriculum materials suited to each child's skill levels (Pierangelo, 2004).

If you are a new teacher to the school, you should first place a letter in the teacher's mailbox introducing yourself, offering some background information, and listing the name/s of the children you wish to discuss. Figures 14.3 and 14.4 provide examples of this letter.

During the meeting the two of you arrange, you will want to meet the following objectives.

- Discuss your role, responsibilities, and the resources you can provide to the teacher (i.e., information on the disability, the process and availability of adaptive classroom materials, suggestions for more suitable materials for the child's skill levels)
- Discuss scheduling the child's time in the resource room or general education experience to avoid fragmenting the child's day. This occurs when a child leaves the classroom to go to the resource room in the middle of one lesson

FIGURE 14.4   Special Class with Participation in the General Education Program—First-Year Teacher

Dear _____:

My name is _____ and this school year I will be working with _____ (first and last name of child) in a special class for children with learning disabilities (some classes may have names, titles etc). (child's first name) has been assigned to my class and in the general education class in _____ (state subject area) has been strongly suggested by the IEP Team.

To collaborate on the services, I would like to meet with you to discuss _____'s (child's first name) program, scheduling time, parent communication, and modifications that are required as a result of _____ (his or her) IEP. I will be stopping by your room to discuss a convenient time for this meeting. If you prefer to call me, I can be reached at _____ (phone and extension) between the hours of _____. My room number is _____.

I look forward to meeting with you.

Sincerely yours,

and returns in the middle of another lesson. Such fragmentation can be a serious problem for many children, who are already confused by the demands of the curriculum. Try to find a convenient time that will ease the transition for the child to and from the classroom.

- You may need to educate the classroom teacher on the purpose and legality of classroom and test modifications and accommodation on an IEP. Be sure to leave the teacher with a written statement of these modifications. Discuss how they could be implemented in the classroom.
- Go over the child's IEP step-by-step so the teacher is fully aware of what has been determined by the IEP Committee at the initial classification meeting or annual review.
- See if the teacher has any curriculum concerns and offer alternatives and options.
- Discuss the process of coordinating parent communication. Also discuss what kind of communication will be reported to parents, so that there is no overlap.

If one of your students with a learning disability is going to be included in the general education classroom, keep in mind that the regular education teacher may have serious concerns or apprehensions about this type of arrangement. Additional suggestions might include the following.

- Provide the general education teacher with specific information on the child's disability, with Internet sites, and names of books or articles the teacher may want to research

- Provide information and examples on adaptive materials that could be used in the classroom to increase the child's chances of completion and success and to avoid frustration
- Provide information and examples on finding more suitable materials for the child's skill levels
- Provide suggestions and examples of forms that can be used to monitor progress
- Assure the teacher that you will be available, both for scheduled meetings and when the need arises, to alleviate any concerns that may develop
- Reassure the teacher that you are always available to answer any questions and solve any issues that need to be addressed
- Discuss specific goals that you may have for the child and how you will go about determining whether the situation is working for the child and/or the teacher (i.e., academic, behavioral, social, and emotional goals)

Step Eight—Evaluate Your Resources and Order New Materials

Do not be surprised, when you enter your room for the first time, if you find few materials available for use. What you need to do is "hope for the best and prepare for the worst." In the worst-case scenario, you will need to catalog what is available to you. The checklist in Box 14.1 will help you determine what you have available, what you may need to order, and what you may need to improvise or "do without."

If you are lucky to have money to spend, then use the Internet to find special education classroom materials. The following sites may be helpful in starting out.

Assistive Technology
http://dmoz.org/Shopping/Health/Disabilities/Assistive_Technology/

Audiovisual and Multimedia Products
http://dmoz.org/Reference/Education/Products_and_Services/Technology/Audiovisual_and_Multimedia/Special_Education/

Computers and Software
http://dmoz.org/Computers/Software/Educational/

Daily Living
http://dmoz.org/Shopping/Health/Disabilities/Assistive_Technology/Daily_Living/

Dyslexia
http://dmoz.org/Reference/Education/Special_Education/Learning_Disabilities/Dyslexia/Technology/

BOX 14.1

FURNITURE

_____Chairs
_____Tables
_____Round table
_____Computer table or cart
_____Bookshelves
_____Blackboard
_____Portable blackboard
_____Book carts
_____Filing cabinets
_____Children's mailboxes or cubby holes
_____Closets or freestanding cabinets for storage
_____Teacher's desk
_____Teacher's chair

CLASSROOM SUPPLIES

_____Writing, drawing, and construction paper
_____Pencils/pens
_____Crayons
_____Paste/glue
_____Stapler/staples
_____Paper clips
_____Rubber bands
_____Straight and safety pins
_____Transparent tape
_____Manila file folders
_____Marking pens
_____Rulers
_____Art supplies
_____Grade book
_____Lesson plan book
_____Attendance materials
_____Textbooks/workbooks
_____Boxes for keeping units
_____Calculator
_____Sticky notes
_____Tissues
_____Hole punch
_____Pencil sharpener
_____Lined & blank paper
_____Scissors
_____Chalk board erasers

_____Graph paper in several sizes
_____Pencil grips
_____Markers
_____12" and 3' rulers
_____Gummed reinforcements for 3-holed paper
_____Pencil erasers
_____Pencil holder
_____Key ring
_____Personal coffee cup or beverage mug
_____5 × 8 index cards
_____Hanging files
_____Push tacks
_____Calendar
_____Small size legal pads
_____Small screwdriver for glasses repair
_____Safety pins
_____Small sewing kit and tool kit

ACADEMIC MATERIALS

_____Textbooks at several levels
_____Workbooks
_____Worksheets
_____Reading programs
_____Math programs

TECHNOLOGY

_____Computer
_____Printer
_____Color printer
_____Scanner
_____Cable hook up to the Internet
_____Internet access
_____Word processing program
_____Reading software
_____Math software
_____Spelling software
_____Writing software
_____Voice recognition software and devices
_____Magnification devices

Software
http://dmoz.org/Computers/Software/Educational/Special_Education/

Special Education
http://dmoz.org/Reference/Education/Products_and_Services/
Special_Education/

Technology Sites
http://dmoz.org/Reference/Education/Products_and_Services/
Technology/

In conclusion, there is a great deal to accomplish before school begins. However, "a strong foundation allows for a very sturdy house," and how you prepare for the start could affect the rest of the year. Be as prepared as possible so that you will have a successful year.

CHAPTER

15 Initiation Stage: The First Month of School

Now that you have established the preliminary but important foundation require-ments for your students with LD, you can focus on the classroom and your stu-dents' adjustment to the room. This stage, the **initiation stage,** will provide you with guidelines for creating a comfortable, logical, attractive, and exciting learning environment within which your students will flourish. The specific suggestions may be somewhat different for elementary and secondary environments, as well as for resource rooms and inclusion classes. However, we have provided general suggestions that will apply to all the different options, and offer specific sugges-tions that apply to particular settings, when necessary.

Create an Attractive and Useful Classroom

The following suggestions provide guidelines when creating an atmosphere con-ducive to students with learning disabilities and pertain to any type of setting. Since we spoke about room arrangement in the preliminary stage, this section will focus more on environmental factors rather than structural ones.

A comfortable learning environment begins with the feelings children get when they first enter your room. You can create a very attractive setting without having a room that contains too many distractions. When working with children with learning disabilities it is far better to have a few very beautiful areas that are decorated than many. You may want to add the decorative touches that make the room feel more cozy—an easy chair or two, a table lamp and pictures on your desk, and plants around the room.

The room should be well organized. Therefore, it should not seem cluttered or contain too many things lying around. Initially have labeled places for all class-room items, books, paper, pencils, jackets so that the students begin to develop a sense of organization. Work with a buddy system so that each student checks the other in terms of if they put their coat away, cleaned out their desk before school starts each day of all not important items and clutter, have their books and pens and pencils ready, have their homework ready and so on. Use a checklist so that each student becomes aware of what is expected. Have them sign off on each other when everything is ready. Eventually you hope that each student will automatically do what is expected. Listed below are some specific suggestions.

- Provide quiet, reflective areas, such as the library corner, writing center, or independent work areas which should take place away from the more active areas.
- If the bulletin boards are old and dirty, cover them with new colored paper or wallpaper or cloth. However, first check with the principal concerning fire codes.
- Provide reference boards for questions the students may frequently ask and train them to go there first before coming to you. Many times children with learning disabilities develop "learned helplessness," which you do not want to reinforce. The language used on the reference boards should be simple and should not contain too many steps or explanations. These boards may contain rules for book reports, rules for homework submission, Funny Rules, and so on.
- Allow the students to bring cushions to make the chairs softer. This may enhance the learning environment and reduce fatigue. If there are some students who cannot afford cushions, try to have a few "extra" cushions on hand.
- Provide a library center where you have all the books that are necessary for the activities in the classroom. Include extra textbooks, reference books, and reading books, so a student can borrow one, if necessary.

Develop Classroom Rules

The next very important step is to set classroom rules as soon as possible. In fact, make this a priority from the start. The first week will be a period of familiarizing students with classroom rules. Not having these rules and then trying to enforce them is more difficult than having them there from the start. What rules a teacher chooses to have is a personal issue based on his/her tolerances, personality style, and teaching style.

Students with learning disabilities may require more structure than other children. This structure allows these students the opportunity to focus on their work and not be concerned about controlling their own behavior. Keep the following general ideas in mind.

1. All rules will need to be publicized to the students. This should be done whether they are presented in writing or verbally.
2. Keep the number of rules to a minimum and always place them in priority order. The more rules you have, the greater the chance that someone will always be breaking at least one—which leads to a punitive environment.

INITIATION STAGE

3. Students must understand what is expected of them right at the beginning. The rules should be discussed in a positive way. Reinforce the concept that following the rules is a choice and following them will allow for everyone to learn and feel comfortable. Emphasize that choosing not to follow the rules means that they will have to be responsible for their own behavior and the consequences that result.

4. The meaning of the rules must be reasonably clear. Do not get into long explanations; just simply state the expected behavior.

5. The rule must be sufficiently narrow, to be something you can enforce.

6. During the first week or so you should take a few minutes at the beginning of the class and discuss the rules, indicating to students what you expect from them during this class. You can mention that you expect them to follow the rules and if there is any concern to see you immediately. During the first week, be kind but firm about your expectations. *Judy, this is a quiet work time. You may not talk to Alex right now. Which rule are you violating?* (Wait for the student to answer, *Rule x.*) Listed here are examples of rules from which you can choose.

- Raise your hand and wait to be called on to speak.
- Follow directions the first time they are given.
- Keep your hands and feet to yourself.
- Treat others with kindness and respect.
- Use inside voices in the classroom and hallways.
- Listen to the teacher and follow directions.
- Use a quiet voice in the classroom.
- Walk in the classroom and hallway.
- Treat others as you would want to be treated.
- If someone is addressing the class, you're not to talk.
- Show respect to your classmates, your instructor and yourself.
- No working on assignments for other subjects.
- No sleeping.
- If it's not yours, don't touch it.
- Properly turn off the lights and equipment before leaving the room.
- Food and drinks are not allowed at the computers. Remember, this equipment is not yours and should be treated accordingly.
- Leave the room clean every day. (Yes, it bears repeating.)

Basic Classroom Management for the First Month

When teaching children with LD, it is important to manage your classroom with logic, commonsense, and fairness. How you choose to manage your room will dictate what kind of year both you and your students may have in terms of comfort and performance. Classroom management style is also a personal choice, but there are several issues which you should keep in mind when working with students with learning disabilities.

Foster Completion and Accomplishment

When working with students with LD, you should always remember that the two most important goals to foster are the sense of completion and the sense of accomplishment. You should never take it for granted that an assignment is "easy." This is a relative term and may be perceived very differently by a student with serious learning problems. If a student is unable to complete an assignment, your first response should be to make sure you were realistic when you designed the assignment. If your first response is to think of the child as lazy or stubborn, then you run the risk of not meeting the needs of the child. Fostering a sense of accomplishment and the sense of success may require you to make adjustments, such as giving shorter assignments, presenting the task in a different fashion, or requiring a different mode of response.

Create a Positive Tone

It is very important to create a positive feeling or tone in the classroom. You want a classroom where both you and the students feel comfortable. Students report they prefer teachers who "don't yell, who listen to us and care how we feel, who reward us for good work, who have a sense of humor, and who like us." It is important that the students see you as fair and logical in your concerns and resolutions of issues and problems. It is very important to the management of any class that all the rules apply to all the students. While students may not like consequences, they usually accept the consequences better if they feel they are being treated equally.

Since children with learning disabilities are under a great deal of academic stress all day, it is very important that you appear calm and relaxed. Speaking in a soothing and confident voice will tend to calm the children's anxiety. Move slowly and frequently around the room from one student to the next. Proximity usually provides students with external controls and helps to limit problems.

Give Students "Advance Organizers"

A schedule on the board that shows the progression of activities is reassuring, but avoid listing specific time periods. Give yourself the option to extend or shorten the time depending on how the activity is going. Remember that children with LD may need more time to process the information that is required for the completion of tasks. Have your students list the activities that they will need to accomplish and then cross off activities as they are completed. This gives the students a feeling of accomplishment.

Before starting a quiet activity, let students know what they can do when they are finished. Suggested ideas include:

- Draw or work on a project or a puzzle
- Listen to tapes
- Use the computer

- Choose and work on activity papers that you keep on hand
- Work on homework or unfinished assignments
- Read a favorite book

Offer Feedback and Support

Credible and genuine positive feedback is a must for children with learning disabilities. Don't be phony about what you are saying. Children are very perceptive and know when their work is terrible, but it is always possible to find something positive in any child.

In the beginning of the year, when students raise their hands, try to recognize them as quickly as possible and thank the student for remaining quiet until recognized. Go over to students even when they are not in need of your help, just to give them a sense of availability and caring. Reprimands should be delivered very quietly. If you need to speak with a student, try leaning down to the student's ear or ask them to come with you outside where there is no audience. This will allow the child to save face and provide you with a much better atmosphere for setting boundaries. Giving a student a look or standing next to them while teaching usually results in compliance.

Deal with Inappropriate Behavior

Along with a management plan must come a plan of action if misbehavior does occur. Any management plan should originate from a positive point of view. In this way your emphasis will be on catching students doing the right thing and reward them for it. The reward will range from a simple acknowledgment of their effort to a system of ongoing value. When dealing with inappropriate behavior, always give the student an opportunity to self-correct before moving into a plan of action. However, inappropriate behavior must be dealt with immediately and decisively. Make it very clear to the student the consequences he/she may face if a better choice is not made.

Think twice about sending a student to the office as a means of controlling behavior except in very serious situations, since all it does is give the message that you are unable to deal with situations, feel overwhelmed, feel helpless, and (worst of all) feel powerless. However, if the student is a threat to himself/herself or others, then immediately seek guidance from the principal.

Some teachers use a gradient plan or one with levels that disburse consequences in stages depending on the number of times the incident occurs. See the following example

A Step System with Three Levels.

> **Level 1**—A verbal warning to change behavior will be issued, either quietly to the student or as a general announcement to the class, depending on the situation and infraction.

> Level 2—Student will be moved to a desk in the rear of the room facing a wall while completing the work. After a certain length of time, student will be asked to rejoin the group.
>
> Level 3—Parent will be called and a notice sent home.

Twenty Tips for Successful Classroom Management. The most effective special education teacher is one who remains calm under all circumstances, is patient, and who counsels students on better ways to handle life's frustrations. The following is a list of tips for successful classroom management.

1. Make no more than five rules and consistently enforce them.
2. Be sure students understand they are in school to learn. Insist on work production. Working students are less likely to misbehave. As students begin to feel successful, they make gains in self-esteem.
3. Watch for and intervene to prevent frustration and stress. Take stretch breaks to relax.
4. Before beginning an activity, set parameters for behavior. *You may . . . , You may not . . . , When you finish your work, you may . . . , You may not . . .*
5. Reduce clatter and noise during working sessions. Have students practice whispering. Use white music or earphones to cover noise. Restrict movement.
6. Use signals instead of yelling. Sometimes you can get students to reduce noise by *lowering* rather than raising your voice. If you yell, students may interpret it as a signal you do not have things under control.
7. Move parts of the group instead of the entire group. *Table Four may line up* (order) instead of *Everybody line up* (chaos).
8. Plan for transitions. When students enter the room, give a short 5- to 10-minute activity or review worksheet so students are occupied while you do essential things before starting class.
9. Keep directions short, clear, and supported by notes on the board and other visuals.
10. Make efficient use of your classroom aide. Enlist parent help.
11. When walking down a hallway with a group of students, put three trustworthy students in front to lead. Walk at the back of the line so that from there you can see what the students in front of you are doing. If a student is not doing what is expected, call that student to the end of the line to be near you.
12. When you are going to do a class activity, be sure you either have enough materials for everyone or explain how they are to share.
13. Vary the activities: rest/activity; individualized/group; inside/outside.
14. Offer students some choice in the activities: where to work, with whom to work, what to do.
15. When you ask a question, tell students who put their hands up immediately that you are going to wait a minute so everybody has time to think of their answer.
16. Be sure you call on *all* students. Students need equal opportunities to answer questions. Research has shown that LD students are called on less frequently. Sometimes it is necessary to keep a chart to ensure you are not overlooking anyone.

17. Classrooms need to be colorful, inviting, and reflect what is going on. Display lots of student work.

18. Team-teach with another teacher at your grade level, and share ideas. Work together on academic preparations and disciplinary problems. Two heads *are* better than one!

19. If a student needs a reprimand, go to him or her, form eye contact, and *quietly* deliver your message. One extremely effective message is to say, *Your behavior is inappropriate. Can you fix it?* (Wait for an answer.) Students almost always say they can, and almost always do. Return to that student later and thank him or her.

20. Do not allow grading and record-keeping chores to pile up. It is far better to occasionally risk that students may not grade their own paper accurately than to hold onto papers for several days. By that time, the returned assignment is no longer meaningful to the student.

The First Week of School

Plan the First Week's Activities

The first week is a good time to get to know your students better. You may want to have some private meetings with them to see what kinds of concerns, thoughts, goals, fears, and so on they have. You may also want to create a list of what they would like to accomplish this year. You may need to provide them with examples to start off, or offer them a checklist from which they can choose their goals.

Developing a sense of confidence will be crucial right from the start. Children with LD too often lack a sense of confidence in their academic ability. Further, this lack of confidence may have a direct effect on their perception, cooperation, willingness to try, and so on. Children with low confidence tend to be more rigid, more sensitive, over-reactive, more insecure, and more vulnerable. How do teachers expect children with low self-confidence to absorb anything, when most of their energy is going into self-protection? Therefore, you may want to consider the concept of Positive Restructuring, developed by Pierangelo and Giuliani (2001).

Creating a classroom environment to ensure successful experiences is referred to as *Positive Restructuring*. There is no doubt that Positive Restructuring requires a great deal of work. However, the long-term effects and benefits greatly outweigh any amount of work. Why would any teacher not want to guarantee success and develop a child's overall sense of confidence? As educators, we have an obligation to question any teaching style that frustrates children, makes them feel like failures, reinforces their inadequacy, promotes negative self-worth, exposes them to ego-deflating experiences, and promotes teacher "ego" at the expense of student failure (belittling students in front of others).

Positive Restructuring.   There are twenty principles involved in Positive Restructuring that need to be conveyed to students and parents right from the start of the school year.

1. **Empowerment.** Empowerment says, *It is not as important to use power, as it is to know we have it when we need it.* Providing students with educational tools (e.g., calculator, dictionary) that he/she can turn to at times of doubt can enhance their feelings of security.

2. **Hope.** Hope is the genuine belief that we have a direct effect on the outcome of a situation. When students feel hopeless they feel powerless. By having hope, students will tend to take more risks and chances, because they believe they can succeed.

3. **Resiliency.** Resiliency is the student's ability to bounce back from an unsuccessful experience. For example, a student with high resiliency who fails a test would be more willing to look at the factors as to why he/she may have failed rather than giving up.

4. **Security.** A classroom is a child's second home. As a teacher, it is your responsibility to create the warmest and most comforting environment so that the children in your classroom can work to their potential without worry.

5. **Recognition.** Everyone needs to be validated. This need is normally provided by parents. However, teachers are second to parents in the child's desire to please and attain validation for performance and effort. Validation provides motivation and incentive to continue working. A lack of recognition and validation inhibits desire since the belief is that "no one cares what I do anyway."

6. **A sense of completion.** The feeling one gets from a completion of a task is crucial to the development of confidence. Confidence is reinforced by the belief that one's behavior will for the most part play a crucial role in leading to completion of some task, project, etc. In Positive Restructuring this sense of completion is enhanced by control over the assigned work to ensure success.

7. **Develop decision making skills.** You will need to teach your students the concepts of delay before making decisions so that they learn to consider all possible consequences. Many times children with learning disabilities act impulsively and add to their problematic situation with poor judgment and a lack of awareness of consequences.

8. **A sense of accomplishment.** You will need to provide tasks that every child will be able to finish with a feeling of success. Do not be afraid to limit the assignments, or the level of difficulty in favor of a sense of completion. Once confidence is developed, the student will have more motivation if you offer more lengthy assignments with a different level of difficulty.

9. **A sense of initiation without fear.** Children who are more confident will be more willing to ask questions and clarify issues with the teacher thereby preventing problems or failures. Providing an atmosphere of acceptance, tolerance, and reassurance will allow children to approach without fear or concern.

10. **An enjoyment of school.** Children who feel more confident will look forward to coming to school. Keep in mind that success breeds success and everyone likes being in a place that reinforces their feelings of self worth.

11. The belief that every child is capable of being successful. Students need to believe from the start that they are all capable of success in some or all areas of school. What prevents many students from this belief is the amount, type, and level of work that is presented to them, coupled with the definition of "success" used by many educators. When "success" is defined as a group comparison, tests such as SATs, then failure will always occur. Why do schools need failure by some students? What purpose to the system is really served by students' failing grades? Other than a reduction of confidence, setting them off from other students who scored higher, feelings of inadequacy, parental anger and frustration, resentment, avoidance, there is nothing served. The belief that children learn by failure is really a tragedy to the educational system. Schools really practice what we call triage education that is the belief that one has to accept a certain amount of "casualties by failure." Do we really believe that society would tolerate a medical system of a hospital that suffered a 25% death rate? There would be a public outcry and immediate change. But no such outcry exists in today's schools. You must decide within yourself whether or not you believe that all students are capable of succeeding in school, and if not, why? Schools tend to accept failure and point to unmotivated or trouble youth as the cause. We believe that we need to look at the delivery system used by schools. Don't always look at the high death rate in a hospital as an indication of how unhealthy people are getting, the real problem may be the delivery system of medical attention.

12. The belief that every child has potential that may not have been exhibited up to this point. It is not realistic to believe that all schools provide the opportunity for all children to express their true potential. The only thing that schools may offer is the opportunity for some to exhibit their academic potential, limited sports potential through gym activities, creative ability in a few areas, such as art and music, and that is about it. The areas of potential may include—but are not limited to—the following:

- Creative
- Intellectual
- Recreational
- Physical
- Academic
- Sports
- Social

Schools need to explore every area possible to see where a child's true potential may lie. It is true that potential may not appear until certain ages; however, it is never too early to start exploring. Potential is an area that adds to a child's identity both in and out of school.

Through the use of interest inventories geared to potential, discussion, interviews with students and parents, observation and so on, the teacher needs to develop a mentality that believes that everything good about a child does not always happen in school.

13. Confidence is the necessary foundation for feeling good about yourself and your ability. Building a house on top of water is not as reliable as one built on land.

Children have to be taught that building confidence is a process that develops from successful experiences and not overnight.

14. There is definite hope, even though the student may not have felt successful up to this point. Failure forces children into closets labeled failure or inadequate. Coaxing a child out of this "closet" is not easy but can occur with recognition of the difficulty he/she has faced, coupled with the hope of change. Children who lack confidence in schools tend to "cocoon," that is pull in within themselves.

15. That you, the teacher, are in charge and know what you are doing. Conveying a strong leadership message to children will provide the structure that someone knows how to get the most out of them. Being a good lifeguard is a crucial step in having children feel secure and confident.

16. It will not take forever to build confidence. Children need to be informed that there is a light at the end of a tunnel and that if they work with you, they will see results within 30 days.

17. Once you have confidence, you will be motivated to try other experiences. Success breeds success. A child who lacks confidence will have a very small safety zone, the area in which he/she feels adequate or comfortable. However, small safety zones also carry along the following:

- Unwillingness to try new experiences
- Giving up easily
- Rigidity
- Low frustration tolerances
- Lack of new experiences
- Self-doubt
- Boredom
- Social isolation
- Loneliness
- Avoidance
- Lack of tolerance for others
- And many more!

Have a discussion on what life would be like living in a closet versus outdoors. The limitations of a small safety zone and the excitement of increasing the zone need to be presented.

18. There are reasons for not feeling confident. Children need to understand how inadequacy and a lack of confidence occur. They need to know that inadequacy does not just appear, that it is a process, just like regaining confidence. A discussion about why children lose confidence needs to be discussed. Some examples may include:

- School failure
- Socially unpopular

- Family issues
- Physical limitations
- Few feelings of success
- No one to believe in them
- Lack of recognition

19. All children will not become confident at the same time, but that does not mean it cannot happen. Children will need to know that, like growing, confidence grows in individuals at different rates. Therefore it is important for them to realize that some children will gain confidence more quickly, but that does not mean they will not. Reaching confidence is not a competition, but a process that can exist in all children.

20. Feeling confident and good about yourself is always better than feeling inadequate. Children who lack confidence and feelings of inadequacy learn to function in a state of unnaturalness. This may be a long-standing issue for some children. They have to learn that feeling good about yourself in any way is always better than feeling inadequate, even if it is the only feeling they know. Teaching children who lack confidence that feeling good is a better place to be may be like convincing a feral child that there is more to life than the forest. They have no frame of reference but with work, will begin to feel the results of confidence, a more natural state for the human condition.

Observing students habits while they are working will give you further insight into their learning styles. You want to be free to circulate among your students, provide positive feedback, recognize talents, observe work habits, solve problems that arise, and teach classroom rules. During the first week it will be important to choose activities that:

- Are simple to do
- Appeal to a variety of interests
- Involve reinforcement of previously learned material
- Build feelings of belonging to the group
- Allow students to be successful

Communicate IEP Modifications to Other Teachers

One of your responsibilities will be to make sure that every teacher involved with your students with LD is notified of the modifications listed on their IEPs. The responsibility for this notification lies with you and should be in written form, followed up by a personal meeting. This will be necessary so that you can protect yourself with a paper trail in case a teacher forgets or does not see the necessity of such modifications. While educational modifications are legally mandated and must be followed, having the paper trail will protect you if a colleague says that you never notified them, or if a complaint is filed by a parent.

Curriculum Considerations

General Curriculum Areas Seen in IEPs

The Required Core Curriculum.   Most schools require all children with LD to fulfill the required core curriculum courses taken by all students. These courses might include the following.

English language arts	Health/physical education
Other languages, to the extent possible	Fine arts
Mathematics	Social studies
Science	Physical sciences

The Expanded Core Curriculum.   When dealing with students with LD, be aware of a secondary curriculum: the expanded core curriculum. These courses are offered to ensure that the child has the best chance of success while in school and when they age out or leave school. The expanded core curriculum the following areas might include:

Compensatory or Functional Academic Skills, Including Communication Modes. Compensatory skills are those skills needed by students with LD in order to access all areas of the core curriculum. Mastery of compensatory skills will usually mean that the student has access to learning in a manner equal to that of his/her nondisabled peers. Functional skills refers to the skills that students with learning disabilities learn that provide them with the opportunity to work, play, socialize, and take care of personal needs to the highest level possible.

Compensatory and functional skills include such learning experiences as concept development, spatial understanding, study and organizational skills, speaking and listening skills, and adaptations necessary for accessing all areas of the existing core curriculum. Communication needs will vary, depending on degree of the learning impairment, effects of additional disabilities, and the task to be done. Regardless, each student will need instruction from a teacher with professional preparation to instruct students with LD in each of the compensatory and functional skills they need to master. These compensatory and functional needs of the child with a learning disability are significant, and are not addressed with sufficient specificity in the existing core curriculum.

Social Interaction Skills.   Many children with LD lack the social perception for adequate social response. As a result, many of these children may lack the social skills necessary for appropriate interaction with their peers. Therefore, social skills must be carefully, consciously, and sequentially taught either by you, with a social skills program, or in coordination with the school psychologist. Nothing in the existing core curriculum addresses this critical need in a satisfactory manner. Thus, instruction in social interaction skills becomes a part of the expanded core curriculum as a need so fundamental that it can often mean the difference between social isolation and a satisfying and fulfilling life as an adult.

Independent Living Skills.   This area of the expanded core curriculum is often referred to as "daily living skills." It consists of all the tasks and functions persons perform, in accordance with their abilities, in order to lead lives as independently as possible. These curricular needs are varied, as they include skills in personal hygiene, food preparation, money management, time monitoring, organization, etc. Some independent living skills are addressed in the existing core curriculum, but they often are introduced as splinter skills, appearing in learning material, disappearing, and then re-appearing. This approach will not adequately prepare some students with learning disabilities for adult life. Traditional classes in home economics and family life are not enough to meet the learning needs of most of these students, since they assume a basic level of knowledge, acquired incidentally through an intact information processing system.

Recreation and Leisure Skills.   Skills in recreation and leisure are seldom offered as a part of the existing core curriculum. Rather, physical education in the form of team games and athletics are the usual way in which physical fitness needs are met for children with LD. Many of the activities in physical education are excellent and appropriate for these students, while other students may require adaptive physical education due to coordination limitations. In addition, however, students with LD need to develop recreation and leisure activities that they can enjoy throughout their adult lives. Many children with learning disabilities who have problems in gross motor coordination shy away from leisure activities, out of a fear of inadequacy and failure. Teaching recreation and leisure skills to students with learning disabilities must be planned and deliberately undertaken, and should focus on the development of life-long skills.

Career Education.   There is a need for general vocational education, as offered in the traditional core curriculum, as well as the need for career education offered specifically for students with LD. Many of the skills and knowledge offered to all students through vocational education can be of value to these students. Those skills will not be sufficient, however, to prepare students for adult life, since such instruction assumes a basic knowledge of the world of work based on prior experiences. Career education in an expanded core curriculum provides students of all ages with LD the opportunity to learn first-hand the work done by the bank teller, the gardener, the social worker, the artist, and so on. Career education will provide the student opportunities to explore strengths and interests in a systematic, well-planned manner.

Because unemployment and underemployment have been the leading problem facing adult persons with disabilities in the United States, this portion of the expanded core curriculum is vital to students, and should be part of the expanded curriculum for even the youngest of these individuals.

Technology.   Technology is a tool to unlock learning and expand the horizons of students. It is not, in reality, a curriculum area. However, it is added to the expanded core curriculum because technology occupies a special place in the education of students with learning disabilities. Technology can be a great equalizer.

Technology enhances communication and learning, as well as expands the world of persons with disabilities in many significant ways. Thus, technology is a tool to master, and is essential as a part of the expanded core curriculum.

Factors Affecting Curriculum

Academic Factors. At times, academic deficits impair a child's ability to function in the classroom. Factors that can contribute to academic dysfunction include, but are not limited to, the following.

Developmental reading disorders	Lack of basic skills
Developmental math disorders	Inconsistency during critical periods
Developmental writing disorders	of skill development
Developmental spelling disorders	Problems in concept formation
Poor prior teaching	Lack of reinforcement

Whatever the cause, academic factors need to be remedied as quickly as possible because there are critical stages of skill development. Underachievement due to academic factors, in spite of adequate intelligence, is very frustrating to students, teachers, and parents. Many times, these problems can be resolved with extra help, tutors, reinforcement, and so on. However, if problems are unrecognized or unidentified for a long period of time, then psychological problems are likely to develop, as well.

Environmental Factors. Environmental factors are defined as those factors that the child may be exposed to at home or in the community that may have a profound impact on the child's ability to function in school. These factors may include home issues such as the ones listed here.

Parental abuse	Moving into a new neighborhood
Fighting among parents	Serious sibling rivalry
Separation	Family mental illness
Divorce	Relatives residing in the home
Family illness	Alcoholism
Economic hardships	Drug abuse
Loss of parent's job	

Environmental factors may also originate from community issues, such as these.

Problems with neighbors	Poor reputation in the neighborhood
Isolation of the family from neighbors	Problems with the law

These factors tend to cause a child great stress which may manifest in school symptoms. Be aware of the possibility that classroom symptoms resulting in dysfunction may actually have their roots in issues outside of school.

Intellectual Factors. There may be times when a child's difficulties in school may be the result of intellectual factors. When these factors are present, a child's stress may be manifested in a variety of symptoms. The factors that fall under this category include undetected limited intellectual ability and undetected gifted intellectual capacity. Limited intellectual ability can cause a great deal of stress in a child for fear of social ridicule, teacher reaction and disappointment, parental reaction and disappointment, and so on. This problem may not always be detected early. Some teachers may misinterpret this factor as immaturity, stubbornness, or a lack of motivation. When this factor is not quickly identified, the child deals with the stress of the situation through many symptoms (i.e., avoidance and procrastination).

Language Factors. Language provides the foundation upon which communication, problem solving, integrating, analyzing, and synthesizing knowledge takes place. Therefore, deficits in language can have a profound impact on an individual's ability to learn and function competently and confidently in the world. Difficulties may arise in a child's language development that result in classroom symptoms. Language issues may arise from difficulties in the following areas.

Nonverbal language	Audiology
Oral language (listening and speaking)	Word retrieval
Written language (reading and writing)	Articulation
Pragmatic language (using language	Receptive aphasia
for a specific purpose, such as	Expressive aphasia
asking for help)	Bilingualism

How quickly a person can access words or ideas in memory further influences his or her use of language. A child who must struggle to find an appropriate term is at a great disadvantage in a learning and social environment. As he grapples to retrieve a word, others have moved on. The student may miss critical pieces of knowledge, connect incorrect bits of information in memory, and have an ineffective means of showing others all that he knows. Such problems can result in lowered levels of achievement and in feelings of confusion, helplessness, and frustration.

Before embarking upon an extensive (and expensive) battery of tests, examiners should ensure that any apparent speech or language impairment is not actually the result of a hearing impairment that, in effect, prevents the child from hearing words clearly and learning to use or understand them.

Similarly, many children with physical disabilities may not be able to speak clearly enough to be understood, but, when provided with assistive technology (e.g., speech synthesizers, computers), may show themselves to be competent users of language.

Medical Factors. Medical factors that may contribute to a child's academic dysfunction can be numerous. While teachers are not asked to be doctors, certain medical conditions may manifest certain symptoms in the classroom. For the most part, one would assume that any serious medical condition may have already been identified by the child's pediatrician or parent. Medical problems that may impair a child's ability to function adequately in the classroom may include but are not limited to the following.

Attention deficit disorder	Neurological problems
Vision problems	Muscular problems
Hearing problems	Coordination problems

Perceptual Factors.   There are times when perceptual issues can impair a child's ability to function in the classroom. Perceptual deficits are often misunderstood or undiagnosed, but they do account for the problems experienced by a large number of high-risk children. Being able to identify the symptoms that may be caused by serious perceptual deficits can reduce a child's frustration, both in and out of the classroom.

The learning process is like an assembly line, through which the information that has been received travels. Therefore, teachers and other professionals must identify those areas that may have a direct impact on a child's ability to adequately process information and possibly interfere in his academic achievement. This identification must occur as soon as possible for the child to have a good chance of overcoming the deficit.

Psychological Factors.   Psychological factors which may be contributing to a child's dysfunction in school may include the following (but note that this list is not exhaustive).

Clinical depression	Psychosexual dysfunction
Mental illness	Substance abuse
Anxiety	Sleep disorders
Eating disorders	Brief situational disturbances or
Personality disorders	adjustment reactions
Schizophrenia	Conduct disorders
Phobias	Separation anxiety
Obsessive compulsive disorders	Oppositional defiant disorders

If serious enough, these factors will create an inordinate amount of tension and subsequent behavioral symptoms. Once the problem is identified, then a useful treatment plan can be devised which includes the home, the school psychologist or outside therapist, medication (if necessary) and classroom management techniques to reduce the secondary effects of the symptoms generated by these problems.

Social Factors.   Social factors may contribute to a child's stress and consequently interfere with learning. While social status is a crucial factor at many ages, it becomes more of a factor as one approaches adolescence. Social pressures and peer influence sometimes create an imbalance in a child's functioning. This imbalance may often result in lower available energy for school-related issues because of the intense need for energy to cope with the social world or social conflicts. Social factors which may lower a child's available energy and result in academic dysfunction include the following.

Peer rejection
Preoccupation with boyfriend
   or girlfriend
Low social status
Social victimization
Scapegoat status
Difficulty with social intimidation

Victim of bully behavior
Social control issues—the need to be
   in control
Peer competition
Social isolation
Social overindulgence

When children have serious social concerns, their thoughts may be obsessive and may preoccupy much of their energy. These symptoms can be intense, and if not identified quickly, can lead to numerous secondary issues.

Modifying General Instructional Conditions for Children with LD

Be aware that not all techniques will work with all students, but you should try as many of them as possible until you find one that works. These techniques should create a better learning environment for children with learning disabilities.

Adjust the Type, Difficulty, Amount, and Sequence of Materials.   Here are suggestions that can enhance the classroom growth of students with LD. As a bonus, these techniques are helpful to many nondisabled students, as well, though not all of the methods would be practiced with an entire classroom.

1. Give shorter but more frequent assignments.
2. Copy chapters of textbooks so that the child can use a highlighter pen to underline important facts.
3. Make sure that the children's desks are free of all unnecessary materials.
4. Correct the students' work as soon as possible to allow for immediate gratification and feedback. This way, if they are doing the assignment incorrectly you can provide additional instruction or direct their energy to more manageable tasks.
5. Allow students several alternatives in both obtaining and reporting information—tapes, interviews, and so on.
6. Break assignments down to smaller units. Allow the children to do five problems at time, or five sentences, so that they can feel some accomplishment.
7. Hold frequent, even if short, private conferences with students to allow for questions, to discuss sources of confusion, to give them a sense of connection, and to avoid the development of a sense of isolation, which often occurs if the work is too difficult.

Adjust Space, Work Time, and Grouping.

1. Permit the child who is easily distracted to work in a quiet corner or a study carrel, when requested or necessary. This should not be all the time, because isolation may have negative consequences.
2. At first, seat a distractible or disruptive child closer to you for more immediate feedback.
3. Try to separate a child from other students who may be distracting.
4. Alternate quiet and active time to maintain levels of interest and motivation among the entire class.
5. Make up a work contract with specific times and assignments so that a child with problems focusing has a structured idea of his or her responsibilities.
6. Keep work periods short and gradually lengthen them as the student begins to cope.
7. Try to match the student with a peer helper to help with understanding assignments, reading important directions, doing oral practice drills, summarizing important textbook passages, and working on long-range assignments.

Adjust Presentation and Evaluation Modes. Some students learn better by seeing (visual learners), some by listening (auditory learners), some by feeling (tactile learners), some through movement (kinesthetic learners), and some by a combination of approaches. Adjust your presentations and assignments to accommodate the learning needs of children with limited learning repertoires, which will probably include your students with LD. The necessary adjustments will vary from child to child and are usually specified in the IEPs.

Auditory Learners. For children who are primarily auditory learners, offer adjustments in the mode of presentation by use of the following techniques.

1. Give verbal as well as written directions to assignments.
2. Place assignment directions on tape so that students can replay them when they need to.
3. Give students oral rather than written tests.
4. Have students drill on important information using tape recorder, reciting information into the recorder and playing it back.
5. Have students drill aloud to themselves or to other students.
6. Have children close their eyes to try and hear words or information.

Visual Learners. For children who are primarily visual learners, offer the following adjustments in your mode of presentation.

1. Have students use flash cards printed in bold bright colors.
2. Let students close their eyes and try to visualize words or information in their heads, to "see things in their minds."
3. Provide visual clues on the chalkboard for all verbal directions.
4. Encourage students to write down notes and memos to themselves concerning important words, concepts, and ideas.

Tactile and Kinesthetic Learners.   To help the students who learn best through touch and action, incorporate the following techniques and aids.

1. Provide "manipulatives" when appropriate, such as counting blocks, geometric shapes, and so on.
2. Include educational board games as "reward" or "rainy recess" activities.
3. Teach the class rhythmic mnemonics that they can call out, "shoot baskets" to, clap to, jump rope to, and so on.

Adapting and Modifying the Curriculum

What Are Curriculum Adaptations?   There are several factors that you will need to consider in adapting the curriculum. Adaptive instructional programs are characterized by combined teaching strategies, flexible scheduling, individualized instruction, mastery learning, large and small group instruction, individualized tutorials, and cooperative learning. Further, while we will need to adapt the form of instruction to meet the individual needs of children with learning disabilities, we will also need to adapt the delivery and response factors that will face the child in school.

ORCLISH, a statewide federally funded project under the direction of the Ohio Department of Education Division of Special Education, put together a checklist of suggestions for adapting instruction. This checklist offers specific areas to focus on when you work with your students with learning disabilities.

What to Adapt?

- Curriculum materials (textbook assignments, workbook, tests)
- Instruction (grouping strategies, learning centers, audio visuals)
- Classroom organization and behavior management (daily schedules and routines, classroom rules, seating arrangements, and individualized behavior plans)

Consider these areas, as well as others, and consider adaptations in several areas at one time to maximize results.

Create Alternate Goals.

Change the Expected Outcome or Goal for the Student Using the Same Materials or Curriculum as Other Students.   For example, the student will only copy the spelling words, while others will spell from memory; the student will match state names to the map while others will locate state capitals; the student will participate in science by building the DNA model while others build the model, label it, and answer questions.

Substitute Curriculum.   Provide different instruction, materials and goals for a student. For example, a student may learn computer/keyboarding skills while others are taking a language test; a student may cut out food items from a magazine and create a picture book of favorite foods while others are writing a creative story;

a student will create his personal schedule for the day while others are doing group circle or calendar time.

Tricks for Staying On Task.

- Break assignments down into small units
- Provide frequent teacher feedback and redirection
- Provide time in resource room for completion of classwork
- Use a buddy system to remind child to stay on task
- Lessen homework expectations (if necessary)

Homework Adaptations.

- Individualize
- Shorten
- Allow more time
- Provide more help

Presentation of Material.

- Present visually written demonstration pictured objects
- Use consistent expectations
- Divide instruction into small steps
- Provide opportunities to teach and practice skills needed
- Provide needed prompts and cues

Assessment and Assignments.

- Shorten
- Modify difficulty
- Alter activity
- Highlight text
- Provide a choice (when appropriate)
- Teach format ahead of time
- Modify question format
- Allow extra time
- Link learning to real situations

Communicating with the Student.

- Be concrete and specific
- Avoid using terms like "later" and "maybe"
- Do not use sarcasm yourself, or allow students to do so
- Slow down the pace, allow student time to process (3 to 6 sec)
- If necessary, break tasks into smaller steps
- Use gestures, modeling, and demonstrations with verbalizations
- Provide warnings about change
- Provide information about expectations

Encouraging Communication with the Student.

- Pause, listen, and wait
- Watch and listen to attempts to respond
- Respond positively to attempts
- Model correct format without corrections
- Encourage input and choice when possible

Social Supports.

- Create cooperative learning situations where student may share proficiencies
- Establish a buddy system
- Practice specific skills through natural activities with one or more peers
- Structure activities with set interaction patterns and roles when appropriate
- Praise classmates when they treat student properly, discourage teasing
- Focus on social process rather than end product
- Develop social stories
- Teach, rehearse, practice, model and reinforce the following skills: turn-taking, responding, waiting, greeting, joining others, taking the lead, joking and teasing, and complimenting

Environment and Routine.

- Provide a predictable and safe environment
- Minimize transitions
- Offer a consistent daily routine
- Avoid surprises, prepare student in advance
- Recognize distractions and sensory overloads (noise, vision, smell, tactile)
- Allow modifications to sensory problems when necessary

Self Management/Behavior.

- Teach use of visual schedule, cues, and timer
- Provide reinforcement that is individualized, immediate, and concrete
- Incorporate strengths and interests into daily activities
- Encourage choices, when appropriate
- Determine why behavior is occurring and develop behavior plan
- Avoid punitive measures; use positive and natural consequences
- Avoid disciplinary actions for behaviors that may be part of their disability

Strategies for Adapting Tests and Quizzes

Preparing for Tests and Quizzes.

- Teach students strategies to prepare for a test or quiz
- Teach students what to look for in test questions; how to read a test
- Use a variety of formats to thoroughly review for several days before tests or quizzes, including quiz bowls, small-group review, question-and-answer periods, and study buddies

- Provide students with examples of test content and format
- Provide study guides in advance of the test
- Provide review time during or outside of the class, emphasizing key points to study

Writing Tests or Quizzes.

- Write clear, concise directions
- Vary the test format (e.g., written, oral, short answer, essay, multiple choice, matching, yes/no, demonstration testing, open book/notes, take home, co-operative group testing)
- Underline or highlight important words in the test directions or on test items
- Give more objective than subjective items
- Increase allowable time for test completion
- Review orally to ensure comprehension of essay questions
- Give shorter tests, covering less information, more frequently
- Avoid penalizing for grammar, handwriting, or spelling
- Reduce the test items by starring those that are the most important concepts
- Give the same test to all students, but score some students on the priority items only, giving extra credit for any additional questions answered correctly

Administering and Scoring Tests and Quizzes.

- Provide students with the opportunity to have tests read orally
- Read test instructions aloud to any student who would prefer them read aloud
- Allow students to take the test in the classroom during the scheduled time, then give opportunities to have it read to them orally and average the two scores
- Tape record tests, using assistants, tutors, parent volunteers and others
- Allow students to tape record answers
- Allow students to use charts, calculators, or manipulatives that they have used on assignments
- Create a modified grading scale or consider a pass/fail, satisfactory/unsatis-factory grade on the test
- Grade student effort and individual ability in addition to test scores
- Allow students to retake the test and give credit for improvement
- Provide feedback to students via teacher/student conferences
- Encourage students to chart their progress
- Take time to review corrected tests and allow students to make corrections on their test or a clean copy of the test
- Provide partial credit for various correct steps in a problem-solving process
- Correct tests immediately and reteach in skill groups
- Give students opportunity to critique their own work based on your criteria before they hand it in
- Allow students to grade their own tests immediately upon completion in a designated area; the teacher does the final scoring
- Allow students to take the test in small groups; students may use a group an-swer or their own

Provide Alternatives to Tests and Quizzes.   Provide a menu of options for students to demonstrate knowledge other than, or in addition to, tests. Allow students to demonstrate their knowledge and skills by doing some of the following activities.

- Design collages, posters, timelines of events, story boards
- Conduct interviews of individuals who have something to say about the unit of study
- Find a guest speaker
- Develop and conduct a survey
- Create maps, graphs, diagrams
- Design and play simulation game activities
- Write and perform skits
- Complete a packet of activities relating to the unit that the teacher has provided
- Keep a journal
- Participate in discussions
- Point to a picture cue system for test or quiz responses
- Design their own project or demonstration
- Provide information on the standard report card indicating adaptations have been made

In terms of evaluating nontraditional alternatives such as those just listed, consider using the following means.

- Vary the grading system; grade on items other than the tests, such as homework, special projects
- Offer extra credit activities throughout the grading period
- Use a grading contract, detailing the basis for grades
- In secondary programs, consider an audit system to allow students to take classes that provide knowledge but do not result in a credit or grade
- Allow test partners as a student option. Each student has his own set of notes and his own copy of the test. Student partners are allowed to read and discuss questions, then if there is disagreement each can write her own answer. Both partners must be present on the day of the test or the test is taken alone.

Adapting Response Mode.   Another very important factor in adapting the curriculum is to consider the use of a variety of response modes for the child with a learning disability. Providing many different options will increase the likelihood of success. Some options for changing response mode include the following.

Animated movie	Game board
Commentary	Poster
Book	Speech
Display	Mobile
Scavenger hunt	Tape
Panel discussion	Tour

Interview	Charades
Portrait	Television show
Pantomime	Invention
Play	Radio
Model	Radio commercial
Skit	Puppet show
Song	Slide presentation
Report	Bulletin board
Poem	Cookbook
Puzzle	Telephone talk
Map	Maze
Cartoon	Show case
Magazine	Banner
Comic strip	Visual art form
Diorama	Script
Brochure	Brainteasers
Collage	Diary
Newspaper	Time capsule
Blueprint	Video tape recording
Survey	Mural
Sculpture	Timeline

Choosing Materials

Choosing the right materials for your students with LD is something that you will need to consider within the first month of school. If your district provides new teachers a mentor or "buddy teacher," that person can be a wonderful resource in helping you think out your curriculum and choose materials. Districts often provide new teachers valuable in-service meetings and a multitude of educational materials to use. Courses of study for regular classes are also available. Do not be afraid to ask. Most veteran teachers are eager to help you—they remember how it felt to be new.

Grading Procedures and the Use of Informal Assessments

When grading students, a number of concepts serve as guiding principles. Christianson (1997) put it as follows.

Teachers should keep in mind that grades communicate a spectrum of information:

- The relative quality (not quantity) of an individual's work
- The student's readiness for future instruction
- The status of a student's work

- The student's level of competence/skill mastery (IEP conditions)
- Progress and effort (p. 9)

This range of information is important in communicating the achievements of all students, with or without disabilities. The reliable reporting of such information is also a critical component in measuring the impact of educational programming.

During the first month it will be very important to obtain some informal assessments on each child with a learning disability. These informal assessments will provide further insight into each child's strengths and weaknesses and provide a better assessment of performance, skill development, and areas in need of attention. According to Project Choices (2004), if instruction is to be adapted to address the identified IEP needs of a student with a disability, then assessment and grading must also be adapted. The general education teacher, the parents, the student, and the special education support staff should review the curriculum and objectives for each class and determine appropriate student outcomes based on the IEP of the student with a disability. Outcomes for the student are then identified and instructional strategies developed. Based on these individualized outcomes, student performance will be assessed and grades assigned. Because many important outcomes cannot be adequately measured by paper-and-pencil tests alone, one or more of the following alternative measurement strategies may need to be considered.

- **Portfolios.** A collection of the student's work over time that demonstrates his/her understanding of the competencies identified
- **Checklists.** A criterion-based measurement system which has the instructor check the student's progress against a predetermined list of needed skills or the completion of specific tasks. Competencies can be derived from the course outline or from the student's IEP
- **Class participation and discussion**
- **Class projects.** This includes cooperative learning activities.
- **Verbal reports** from students
- **Anecdotal records** of student performance
- **Daily logs** of student activities
- **Modified tests,** such as verbal answer, performance, shortened checklists

Determine Readability Levels of Textbooks and Other Materials

When working with students with LD, it is crucial to match the materials presented with their reading ability levels to reduce their frustration. To accomplish this task you should understand the readability factors of the books the child will be exposed to during the school day. According to Stone (2000), readability is a measure of the ease with which a given passage of text can be read and understood. The only complete way to test readability is to give people a passage to read and then follow up with a test to see if they understood it. If a significant number of people do understand the passage, it may be generalized that many other people with about the same level of reading skills will understand it too. After finding a way to predict reading levels that agree with how people actually score on standardized passages, one should also be able to predict how well they will understand other reading material of similar difficulty. This is the rationale behind readability estimates.

Almost all readability estimates use some measure of word difficulty and syntactic complexity as their main predictors. Examples of word difficulty predictors are word length, syllable counts, and the number of unfamiliar words. Examples of sentence difficulty predictors are the number of dependent clauses and average sentence length. Of these, the number of unfamiliar words and average sentence length have proven to be the best predictors.

Many factors contribute to the readability of a passage. Size of print, illustrations, and inherent difficulty of the subject matter are but a few. While readability estimates can be lowered by breaking long sentences into shorter ones and by using more common synonyms of unfamiliar words, most studies show that very little, if any, increases in comprehension are gained by this practice. In addition, it is important to understand what the various readability estimate formulas will *not* do. They do not take into account many of the most important aspects of the material and its relationship to the reader. They do not take into account the interest areas and interest level of the material. They do not deal with style and syntax. Perhaps most important of all, they do not relate to the background of experience and interest on the part of the reader, and are unrelated to personal and ethnic variables.

Readability Formulas

According to Precononline (2004), nine formulas can be used to determine the readability of materials. Internet addresses have been provided for several of these systems so that you can read about how to use the formula.

1. **Dale-Chall:** A vocabulary-based formula, normally used to assess upper-elementary through secondary materials. Available at www.interventioncentral .org/htmdocs/tools/okapi/okapimanual/dale_challWorksheet.PDF
2. **Flesch Grade Level:** Most reliable when used with upper-elementary and secondary materials.
3. **Flesch Reading Ease:** Normally used to assess adult materials; shows scores on a scale between 0 and 100.
4. **FOG:** Widely used in the health care and general insurance industries for general business publications. www.tasc.ac.uk/sdev1/drobis/profcom/fog.htm
5. **FORCAST:** Focuses on functional literacy. Used to assess nonrunning narrative, such as questionnaires, forms, and tests. http://agcomwww.tamu.edu/ market/training/power/readabil.html
6. **Fry Graph:** Used over a wide grade range of materials, from elementary through college and beyond.

7. **Powers-Sumner-Kear:** Used in assessing primary through early elementary level materials.
8. **SMOG:** Unlike any of the other formulas, SMOG predicts the grade level required for 100 percent comprehension. www.med.utah.edu/pated/authors/readability.html
9. **SPACHE:** A vocabulary-based formula, widely used in assessing primary through fourth-grade materials. www.interventioncentral.org/htmdocs/tools/okapi/okapimanual/spachedir1.shtml

Conduct Positive Parent Conferences

An important skill for special educators is their ability to hold positive parent conferences. Many times parents will leave a conference having been bombarded with jargon and statistics and will feel that they understand nothing. Pierangelo (2004) suggests the following ways to report results of classroom activities, experiences, performances, and so on so that they are understood.

1. When setting up the appointment with a parent, never allow yourself to begin the explanation of the results over the phone, even if the parent requests a quick idea of how their child is performing. If the parent does request this, mildly say that this type of information is better explained and understood in person. If you sense further anxiety, try to reassure the parent that you will meet as soon as possible. It is important to visually see the parent(s) so you can further explain areas in which they seem confused or uncomfortable. The face-to-face contact also makes the conference a more human approach. Hearing results from a doctor over the phone may not be as comforting as in person. This is also true when dealing with students with learning disabilities, as the parents may already have a great deal of academic anxiety.
2. Make parents feel comfortable and at ease by setting up a receptive environment. If possible, hold the meeting in a pleasant setting. If possible, use a round table, or any table instead of the teacher's desk, and offer some type of refreshment to ease the possible tension of the situation.
3. It may be helpful to refresh the parent's memory about the areas on the student's IEP that have been identified as being in need of attention.
4. Go over strength areas first, no matter how few there may be. You can also report positive classroom comments, and any other information that may help set the tone for their acceptance of problem areas.
5. Provide a typed outline of each student's classroom test scores, grades, group achievement test results, and so on for parents to take with them. It looks more professional if this information is typed and may help alleviate problems that may occur when parents go home and share the information with their spouse.
6. If you are discussing test results, explain in simple terms any statistical terms you may be using, such as percentiles, stanines, mental ages, and so on. In

fact, it may be a good idea to define these on the same sheet with the scores so that parents have a key when they go back and review the scores.

7. Offer parents a pad and pen so that they can write down information, terms, or notes on the meeting. Further indicate that they should feel free to call you with any questions or concerns they may have.

8. Put aside a sufficient amount of time for difficult conferences. This is not the type of situation in which you want to run out of time. The parents should leave in a natural manner, not rushed.

9. Take time to explain the differences between symptoms and problems. This explanation can go a long way in alleviating parent's frustration.

10. It is helpful for parents to hear how the problems or deficiencies now identified have been contributing to the symptoms in the classroom and at home. It is reassuring for parents to know that what they were seeing were only symptoms, even though they may have been quite intense, and that the problems have been identified and recommendations are available. Offer them as much realistic hope as possible.

11. Be as practical and specific as possible when offering suggestions on how parents can help at home. Offer them printed sheets with step-by-step procedures for any recommendation that you make. Parents should not be teachers and should never be given general recommendations that require their interpretation. This may aggravate an already tense situation at home. Offer parents supportive materials that they can use with their child. On the other hand, while a parent working with a child can be positive, in some cases, such as low parental frustration thresholds, you may not want to encourage this type of interaction.

Prepare for Open School Night and Parent–Teacher Conferences

Holding successful parent meetings and conferences is a valuable experience when you are working with parents of students with LD. It is in the best interest of the child for the parents and teachers to work hand in hand to help the child deal with the responsibilities and pressures of school. You will always want to be an advocate for your students and their parents. Parent meetings and conferences can improve the communication between school and home and alleviate many fears and misinformation the parents have.

You may want to consider the following suggestions for Open School Night meetings.

1. Provide a comfortable environment when parents first walk in the room. Soft classical music or quiet jazz is suggested and some form of food or drinks is suggested to provide a nurturing atmosphere.

2. Make sure all your students have their names on their desks so the parents know where to look.

3. Hand out index cards and ask parents to write any questions they would like you to address. For parents of students with LD, it may be easier to ask questions anonymously. This way, you will have a chance to see the questions first, allowing you to formulate better answers.

Parent–Teacher Conferences

According to Teachervision (2004), professionally conducted parent–teacher conferences can prove a most valuable strategy for improving student classroom behavior as well as enhancing learning. Here are some ideas used by successful teachers to reap the maximum benefit from parent–teacher conferences.

- Before the conference, plan what you hope to accomplish. What information do you want to share with the parent? What problems need solving? Do not overwhelm the parent. Settle on no more than two or three concerns to be addressed. A laundry list of complaints will only discourage or alienate them.
- If you are requesting the conference in response to a specific problem with the child, allow some time to cool off before meeting with the parent. You'll be less emotionally charged and more objective after a couple of days. Remember, you are a professional educator.
- When a student begins to misbehave in class, begin to keep an index card recording specific disturbances noted. Include the name, date, description of problem behavior, and action taken. Make your notes as soon after an incident as possible.

Shalaway (2004) indicates that, as with teaching, planning is critical to an effective conference. Here are some important steps to include.

- Prepare a note to send home that invites parents to meet with you, states the purpose of the conference, and lists potential times, including both afternoon and evening slots. Have parents call or send a note to reserve a time slot. **Note:** When divorced parents share custody, don't forget to invite both.
- Decide on the goals for the conference (one or two will do).
- Prepare an agenda that you share with parents before the conference. Agenda topics should include your general impression of the child, his or her progress in each academic area, standardized test scores, your goals for the child in each content area, and strategies you will use to meet goals.
- Plan (and write down) questions to ask, points to make, and suggestions to offer.
- Ask parents to bring to the conference a list of their child's strengths and weaknesses as they perceive them.
- Fill out a form listing the child's strengths and weaknesses and proposing action to be taken.
- Collect samples of the student's work to display.
- Prepare to explain your goals and teaching strategies.

- Schedule enough time for questions and discussion. If you expect a difficult load, this should be a minimum of 10–15 minutes.
- Pull together necessary materials such as a daily schedule of classroom activities, a checklist of skill areas and notes on student progress, sample work, test scores, and reports from other teachers, where appropriate.

Arrange the Setting.   First, try making the conference area as comfortable as possible. Experienced teachers report that such amenities as adult-sized chairs, soft, relaxing music, and refreshments put parents at ease. Also, try to greet parents at the door and sit with them at a table or in chairs facing each other. (Never put the teacher's desk between yourself and parents.) If you provide paper and pens, parents can take notes to follow up on at home. And make sure you have a few activities for the younger siblings who invariably tag along.

Many teachers find it helpful to hang a "Conference in Progress" sign on the door to prevent interruptions. Further, many suggest setting a table of materials that parents can take home—for example, information on homework and grading policies, newsletters, suggestions for how to help children at home and at school, and invitations to school activities or parent-group meetings.

Conducting the Conference.   First off, briefly review the agenda you prepared in advance. Then, communicate the specific information you have gathered about the child. Listen carefully to parents' responses, answer their questions, explain each point, and ask them if they can confirm your impressions. Set goals together for the child's future progress.

When you are delivering news about an academic or behavioral problem, author Susan Swap and others suggest certain strategies.

- Focus your comments and efforts only on things that can be changed.
- Limit the number of suggestions for improvements so that parents are not overwhelmed.
- Speak plainly and avoid jargon and euphemistic language.
- Be tactful, but not so tactful that you don't adequately communicate the problem.
- Ask for and listen to parents' reactions.

INITIATION STAGE

Interim Stage: October–March

Once your class has settled down after the first month of school and IEP goals, classroom goals, and classroom rules have been established, it is now time to consider the interim months between October and March. During this period there are many things we need to do to ensure that the students in your class have a very positive and productive year. Doing this involves working with the following issues.

- Clarify each student's learning needs
- Establish educational plans for each child and his/her parent(s)
- Determine your instructional design for working with students with learning disabilities
- Grade the work of students with learning disabilities
- Report to parents
- Meet district requirements for determining academic growth
- Understand parents' rights
- Work with difficult parents
- Call special meetings of the IEP Committee
- Work throughout the year with the parents of students with learning disabilities

There are many specific areas of learning that need to be explored when teaching students with learning disabilities. While district policies and requirements may vary from district to district or state to state, the areas we will consider should cover the ones you will face in most settings. Each student in your class will have a unique set of issues when it comes to learning. Raymond (2000) outlines a variety of specific deficit areas (developmental and academic) that children with learning disabilities will possess.

Developmental Learning Disabilities

Some children will have deficits or delays involving skills that normally develop at early ages. These skills, which affect later learning, may include attention, perception, and memory, as well as thinking (or cognitive skills) and oral language (Kirk, 1987, cited in Raymond, 2000). Specifically Raymond explains these developmental disabilities in the following manner.

Attention refers to two skills: selective attention, or the skill of selecting and focusing on relevant stimuli, and sustained attention, or the skill of maintaining that attention over time.

Perception involves the interpretation of sensory stimuli and the labeling of those stimuli with meaningful names.

Thinking or cognitive disorders affect the child's ability to solve problems, to develop conceptual knowledge, and to store and retrieve information in long-term memory.

Oral language skills include children's abilities to listen effectively and to express themselves orally.

Academic Learning Disabilities

Academic learning disabilities manifest themselves in school-age youngsters who have normal learning capacity but who fail to develop age-appropriate skills in reading, written expression, spelling, handwriting, and mathematics. You will need to focus much of your attention on working with each child on weaknesses in these areas.

Instructional Design for Students with Learning Disabilities

Teaching students with learning disabilities will require you to "think out of the box" when it comes to traditional teaching methods. Students with learning disabilities will require a varied approach to teaching that will take into account the diverse needs of each student. One of the main goals should be to develop an environment, teaching style, materials, outcome expectations, and curriculum adaptations that are as usable as possible by a diverse range of individuals. By focusing on these diverse methods and strategies you hope to develop an inclusionary approach that enables students with disabilities to overcome some of their barriers to learning.

The concept of Universal Design for Instruction (UDI) while geared to students with learning disabilities at college, contains 9 general principles that can be adapted for any age level of student with this type of disability. According to Scott, McGuire, and Shaw (2001), the UDI framework consists of general principles to guide faculty in thinking about and developing instruction for a broad range of students with disabilities.

1. **Equitable use.** Instruction is designed to be useful to and accessible by people with diverse abilities. It provides the same means of use for all students,

identical whenever possible, equivalent when not. Example: Using web-based courseware products with links to online resources so all students can access materials, regardless of varying academic preparation, distance from campus, and so on.

2. **Flexibility in use.** Instruction is designed to accommodate a wide range of individual abilities. It provides choice in methods of use. Example: Using varied instructional methods (lecture with a visual outline, group activities, use of stories, or web-based discussions) to support different ways of learning.

3. **Simple and intuitive instruction.** Instruction is designed in a straightforward and predictable manner, regardless of the student's experience, knowledge, language skills, or current concentration level. It eliminates unnecessary complexity. Example: Providing a grading scheme for papers or projects to clearly state performance expectations.

4. **Perceptible information.** Instruction is designed so that necessary information is communicated effectively, regardless of ambient conditions or the student's sensory abilities. Example: Selecting textbooks, reading material, and other instructional supports in digital format so students with diverse needs can access materials through print or by using technological supports (e.g., screen reader, text enlarger).

5. **Tolerance for error.** Instruction anticipates variation in individual student learning pace and requisite skills. Example: Structuring a long-term course project with the option of turning in individual project components separately for constructive feedback and for integration into the final product.

6. **Low physical effort.** Instruction is designed to minimize nonessential physical effort in order to allow maximum attention to learning. Note: This principle does not apply when physical effort is integral to essential requirements of a course. Example: Allowing students to use a word processor for writing and editing papers or essay exams.

7. **Size and space for approach and use.** Instruction is designed with consideration for appropriate size and space for approach, reach, manipulations, and use regardless of a student's body size, posture, mobility, and communication needs. Example: Using a circular seating arrangement in small class settings to allow students to see and face speakers during discussion. This is important for students with attention problems.

8. **A community of learners.** The instructional environment promotes interaction and communication among students and between students and faculty. Example: Fostering communication among students in and out of class by structuring study and discussion groups, email lists, or chat rooms.

9. **Instructional climate.** Instruction is designed to be welcoming and inclusive. High expectations are espoused for all students. Example: Creating a statement on the syllabus affirming the need for students to respect diversity, underscoring the expectation of tolerance, and encouraging students to discuss any special learning needs with the instructor.

Examples of UDI Adapted to Your Classroom

Equitable Use. If you have students who have serious issues with visual motor problems that severely interfere with writing, you may want to alleviate this problem by posting class notes on the class web site, making the notes available in the same form to all students. Any student with a learning disability would have immediate access to a complete set of notes and assignments and would no longer need a note taker or worry about missing assignments. This may also help students whose primary language is not English, students with attention deficits, and students wanting to preview the day's instruction.

Flexible Use. When giving an assignment that requires term papers, long-range projects, book reports, and so on, allow students to set their own due dates for the assignments (within a reasonable boundary). Since students will set their own schedules and adjust the submission dates to fit other demands on their time, they will learn to work within their learning styles and more frequently feel a sense of completion and a sense of accomplishment. Also, in this way you will be able to get feedback to your students more promptly while being responsive to other demands on students' time.

A Community of Learners. Set up an environment that promotes interaction and communication among your students and between students and you. As many students with learning disabilities may have difficulties talking about their feelings concerning frustrations in learning, you may want to start a classroom chat room on the computer that is open only to your students. This technique may allow more students to interact since they do not have to have eye-to-eye contact. On these chat rooms you can post questions such as, *What works for you when something is difficult,* or *What helped me with last night's assignment,* or *What gets me frustrated.* You may also want to foster email interaction between your students to encourage communication skills, but set very clear guidelines about what is acceptable. Further, you may want to limit the amount of time and the specific period of time that such interaction will be available. You should speak to parents before you begin to use any computer-based interaction. You also must be sensitive to students who may not have access to this equipment.

Educational Plans

The educational plan for your students with learning disabilities should be a triangular one. Coordination of services and techniques between the school, the child, and home will increase the chances of success in school for a child with learning disabilities. Many times it is only the school that is involved with the child, while the child is a passive recipient and the parents are onlookers. To increase the chances of success for the child you will need to coordinate the three sides of the educational plan.

Responsibilities of the School and Teacher. One side of the triangle is the school's responsibilities to help the child learn to his potential. The school's responsibilities include the following.

RESPONSIBILITIES OF THE SCHOOL AND TEACHER

Setting academic goals and objectives	Providing and monitoring related services
Determining and monitoring modifications	Collaborating with the child's other teachers
IEP development	Maintaining communication with the home
Adaptations to the curriculum	Writing year-end reports
Determination of the child's learning style	Teaching the required curriculum

Parental Responsibilities.   You will need to communicate and instruct the parents so that they are very clear as to their role in this process. The side of the educational plan that contains the responsibilities of the parents includes the following.

1. Making sure that homework is checked every night so that the child comes to school every day feeling a sense of accomplishment and avoiding a sense of embarrassment or failure.
2. Contacting you through mail, email, or phone if the child has had difficulty with an assignment and needs to go over it again.
3. Reading to the child every night before bed, if in elementary school. Having the child read for 15 minutes every night, if in secondary school. The reading should be of the child's choice, although stress-free reading before bedtime is advisable. You do not want the child to go to sleep frustrated.
4. Attending all conferences.
5. Working with child on homework in ways described further in this section.
6. Helping their child study for tests by following learning and studying guidelines set forth by you. Here you will have to carefully instruct the parents through specific directions in the appropriate study support procedures that will not frustrate the child.
7. Ensure that the child begins studying for tests on the study start date indicated to them by you. This should take into account the child's learning style.
8. Returning all progress reports on time with signatures indicating their awareness of the progress or concerns. Keep these in your files for accountability if there should ever be a concern.

Student Responsibilities.   The child makes up the third side of the triangle and his or her involvement in this process is equally important. Student responsibilities can be outlined in the form of a contract or letter to the child. It should include the following points.

- Finishing homework every night or trying as much as he/she understands.
- Allowing his/her parent to check homework and suggest corrections. Note that you will have to work with parents on constructive suggestions verses criticism.

- Following class rules
- Beginning to study for tests when you inform the parents of the study start date for an upcoming test.
- Being able to approach the teacher when he or she is unable to do an assignment or does not understand a topic.

Grading Students with Learning Disabilities

Grading students with learning disabilities presents a dilemma for all educators. If we use traditional competitive grading systems, then students who try, participate, and finish assignments—but because of their disability fail tests—will receive a failing grade when compared to their peers. This type of approach may lead to frustration, loss of motivation, parent frustration, and a "why bother" attitude on the part of the child. On the other hand, grading students solely on attitude, effort, accountability, responsibility, and so on despite failing grades may mislead both parents and students into setting unrealistic goals. Salend (2001) describes a variety of student grading systems that you may want to consider when determining your students' grades.

Numeric/Letter Grades. Teachers assign numeric or letter grades based on students' performance on tests or specific learning activities.

Checklists/Rating Scales. Teachers develop checklists and rating scales that delineate the benchmarks associated with their courses and evaluate each student according to mastery of these benchmarks. Some school districts have revised their grading systems by creating rating scales for different grade levels. Teachers rate students on each skill, using a scale that includes "Not yet evident," "Beginning," "Developing," and "Independent."

Anecdotal/Descriptive and Portfolio Grading. Teachers write descriptive comments regarding students' skills, learning styles, effort, attitudes, and growth, and suggest strategies to improve student performance. These comments can be included with examples of students' work as part of portfolio grading.

Pass/Fail Systems. Minimum course competencies are specified and students who demonstrate mastery receive a "P" grade, while those who fail to meet the minimum standards are given an "F" grade. Some schools have modified the traditional pass/fail grading system to include such distinctions as honors (Honor-P), high pass (HP), pass (P), and low pass (LP).

Mastery Level/Criterion Systems. Students and teachers meet to divide the material into a hierarchy of skills and activities based on an assessment of individual needs and abilities. After completing the learning activities, students take a posttest or perform an activity to demonstrate mastery of the content. When students demonstrate mastery, they receive credit for that accomplishment and repeat the process with the next skill to be mastered.

Progressive Improvement Grading. Students take exams and engage in learning activities, and receive feedback and instruction based on their performance throughout the grading period. Only performance on cumulative tests and learning activities during the final weeks of the grading period, however, are used to determine students' grades.

Multiple Grading. Teachers grade students in the areas of ability, effort and achievement. Students' report cards can then include a listing of the three grades for each content area or grades can be computed by weighting the three areas.

Level Grading. Teachers use a numeric subscript to indicate the level of difficulty at which the students' grades are based. For example, a grade of B6 can be used to note that a student is working in the B range at the sixth-grade level. Subscript systems can also be devised to indicate whether students are working at grade level, above grade level, or below grade level.

Contract Grading. Teachers and students agree on a contract outlining the learning objectives; the amount, nature, and quality of the products students must complete; and the procedures for evaluating student products and assigning a grade.

IEP Grading. Teachers assign grades that acknowledge students' progress in meeting the students' IEP goals and performance criteria.

Reporting to Parents

Parents place a higher priority on receiving information about their children's progress than any other type of information they receive from schools (Cuttance & Stokes, 2000). They further indicated that parents identified a number of concerns and improvements required in the reporting process.

- Parents consider there is a tendency, more common in primary schools, to avoid facing or telling hard truths. Parents understand how difficult it may be for teachers to convey "bad" news, but nevertheless they indicate that they want a "fair and honest" assessment, in plain language, of the progress of their children.
- There is a lack of objective standards that parents can use to determine their children's attainment and rate of progress. Many parents specifically asked for information that would enable them to compare their child's progress with other students or with agreed state/territory-wide or national standards.
- Parents indicated they would like more interpretative and constructive reporting. Parents want something more substantial from reports than simple statements of achievement levels. They also want advice on what the report means in terms of the future learning goals for their child, and how parents can support their children's learning.
- Most systems that report test results to parents do not require schools to incorporate these results in their reports to parents. Parents express a degree of

confusion when they receive test reports in one style and metric, and school reports in another, unrelated style using a different metric.

- Parents want more comprehensible reports when they are based on outcomes reporting. Some education systems have adopted approaches that use criterion-based outcomes reporting, but many parents are finding it difficult to understand the reports because of changes in assessment practices.
- Parents require more appropriate timing of reports. They indicated a clear preference for reports earlier each year when they are in a better position to support their children with any learning improvement. Parents appreciated reports during Term 1, where these were provided, and find that an end-of-year report is too late for any constructive use.
- There is a mistrust of computer-generated reports in the parent community. Parents indicate that they find computer reports to be impersonal and limited. Parents want reports that are tailored to their individual children.
- Parent–teacher meetings need to be more useful to parents. Parents are dissatisfied with meetings that are poorly organized and lack focus and purpose. They consider meetings of 5 to 10 minutes to be too limited to be useful and believe such meetings are organized mainly for ceremonial purposes. The timing of most meetings does not encourage an interactive discussion.
- The detection and prompt reporting of learning and behavioral problems is of major concern to parents. Many parents are concerned that they had not been advised as early as they could have been of their children's learning problems.
- Parents would like an enhanced role for their children in the reporting process. Parents believe that their children are an integral part of the reporting process and seek to involve them in parent–teacher meetings as well as in other aspects of assessment and reporting.

In light of the above information you may want provide a variety of opportunities to convey information home to parents. Keep in mind that informed parents usually mean supportive parents. Noninformed parents may have a tendency to assume, write negative scripts, interrogate their child, and be defensive. We suggest you try the following steps.

1. Hold individual interviews with the parent(s) at the beginning of the year. This allows parents to give teachers first-hand information that will assist them in planning to meet the specific individual needs of each child.
2. Use a variety of progress reports that focus on the specific needs or concerns of the child instead of a general one which focuses on too many areas. For instance, if the parents are not aware if homework has been given and need to know that it was turned in the next day use the form in Figure 16.1. At the secondary level, you may want to use the form in Figure 16.2. This type of daily record will reinforce the child's accountability and assist the parents in working with the child at home. When you meet with the parents at the beginning of the year explain that they should expect this form to be brought home every night.

| FIGURE 16.1 | Progress Report for Elementary Grades |

Name:

Date

_____ Monday

Homework tonight   yes _____   no _____

Homework handed in   yes _____   no _____

Comments:

_____ Tuesday

Homework tonight   yes _____   no _____

Homework handed in   yes _____   no _____

Comments:

_____ Wednesday

Homework tonight   yes _____   no _____

Homework handed in   yes _____   no _____

Comments:

_____ Thursday

Homework tonight   yes _____   no _____

Homework handed in   yes _____   no _____

Comments:

_____ Friday

Homework tonight   yes _____   no _____

Homework handed in   yes _____   no _____

Comments:

Such Progress Reports are important sources of information on the child's learning at school. Do not be afraid to tailor such reports to specific behaviors if they are required and necessary to facilitate positive outcomes. More detailed reports focusing on academic achievement, social abilities, cooperation, etc. should be done monthly with children with learning disabilities. However, have a policy that allows parents to request an interview with you at any time throughout the school year.

Provide a system of communication home on regular basis providing positive information, suggestions, solutions to issues you have noticed, or just to see if the

FIGURE 16.2	Progress Report for Secondary Level Student

Name:

Date: Monday _____

Subject

Math

Homework tonight	yes _____	no _____
Homework handed in	yes _____	no _____

Comments:

Social Studies

Homework tonight	yes _____	no _____
Homework handed in	yes _____	no _____

Comments:

English

Homework tonight	yes _____	no _____
Homework handed in	yes _____	no _____

Comments:

Science

Homework tonight	yes _____	no _____
Homework handed in	yes _____	no _____

Comments:

This form would be sent home for Monday, Tuesday, Wednesday, Thursday, and Friday school days.

parents have any concerns. Using this type of approach will facilitate the closeness with the school and facilitate your educational plans discussed later in this section.

Measuring Academic Growth–District Requirement

You may be asked by your district or supervisor to determine levels of academic growth over the coming school year. Depending on the district, this may be determined through informal assessment measures or formal assessment measures (see Chapter 5). You will need to become familiar with the different types of tests used, and how to administer and score the tests.

While the emphasis in today's schools is to move away from the use of standardized testing to determine a child's strengths and weaknesses, some districts may still require special education teachers to assess their student's present academic levels through the use of standardized testing for developing the following year's IEPs. This will require a pretest, usually administered in October, and a posttest, usually administered in May or June of the same school year. In this way, it is assumed that academic growth can be measured for that school year. For some districts this is accomplished through the use of group achievement tests (norm-referenced tests) such as the Stanford Achievement Tests, Metropolitan Achievement tests, or California Tests of Basic Skills.

Some school districts may require you to administer individual achievement tests to determine areas of growth. Although these tests may take longer to administer they tend to be more reliable, more valid, and provide more useful information. Examples of these tests include the Wechsler Individual Achievement Test, Woodcock Johnson Achievement Battery, or the Wide Range Achievement Test.

Understanding Parents' Rights

One of the first things you should do at the beginning of the Interim Stage is to sit down with your state's copy of *A Parent's Rights in Special Education.* This booklet, put out by every state, completely outlines the rights parents have in the special education process. In today's world, parents are becoming their own child's advocate, and rightfully so, and as a result are very familiar with their rights and your role and responsibilities in ensuring those rights. You never want to be in a position of doing something that may impair, diminish, or exclude the rights of any student or parent in the special education process. Become very familiar with this book and do not be afraid to offer every parent a copy, or the address to obtain a copy, since many states may offer them free of charge. Your district should have provided a copy of this booklet to the parents when their child was first classified as learning disabled. If you have any concern about obtaining one, first ask your district supervisor of special education for one. If he or she is out of them, then contact your state education department. You can start by going to the following site and choosing your state: http://nichcy.org/states.htm. Then look on the list of state resources for the State Department of Education: Special Education. Give them a call and they will be happy to send you copies.

Calling Special Meetings of the IEP Committee

There may be times when you are working with a student with LD and feel that she may benefit from further modifications, accommodations, change in diploma track, or assistive technology. Since these may not appear on the child's IEP, any changes to that document must involve a meeting with the IEP Committee (Eligibility Committee, Committee on Special Education, etc., depending on the state in which you reside). In this case you will need to contact the chairperson of the IEP Committee and ask for a special meeting in order to make your recommendations for changes to the child's IEP. The parent must also attend any meeting where the IEP is changed or recommendations to change are suggested. Consider the following points if you make such a request:

1. Make sure you read the child's present IEP thoroughly to see if it contains your suggestions in different terminology. For example, you are recommending someone to take notes for the child because of visual motor problems, but the child already receives the services of a scribe (an individual whose job it is to takes notes for a student).

2. Speak with the child's former teachers to see if similar problems have occurred in the past. For instance, if you are suggesting extended time for a fifth grade student in your class but he has never had a history of needing such a modification, you may want to explore other reasons for the child's difficulties. Modifications, unless certain variables have changed, should never be given as a crutch, but rather as assistance if the child needs such help.

3. You may want to try the suggested modification or accommodation for a short period to see if it has any effect on the child's performance. Then when you are asked by the members of the team you will be able to provide experiences from trial exposures that the child benefited from such a modification or accommodation.

4. Make sure that the modification or accommodation that you are suggesting falls within the guidelines of what is acceptable in the law.

5. If you are suggesting some assistive technology device, you are better off first suggesting an assistive technology evaluation. This evaluation, often contracted out to agencies, evaluates the child's need for certain types of technology, evaluates the child on several different types of the same technology, and makes recommendations as to which specific piece of equipment works best for the child. It is usually a very thorough evaluation and will better serve the child in the long run.

Working throughout the Year with Parents

Help Parents Understand—What You Can Do

One of the most important things you will need to do is to make sure that all the parents of the children with LD fully understand the disability. Never assume that parents are educated in this area. Further, even if they are educated or informed, it is important to know what they do know and what they do not. To accomplish this you may want to meet with all the parents and hold mini workshops or get-togethers before, during, or after school. The purpose of these meetings is to make sure that everyone understands all the necessary information about LD so that everyone is working from the same frame of reference. This coordinated knowledge base will facilitate your job by having the parents fully understand what is going on in school and what you are trying to accomplish. It will also prevent faulty assumptions, unrealistic expectations, and unnecessary pressure on the children. You will need to make sure that all the parents have a good understanding of the following topics concerning learning disabilities. You may want to coordinate your efforts for some of these topics with the school psychologist.

- What can be done in school to help a child with learning disabilities
- How the goals are determined for each child
- Understanding IEPs
- Communication and collaboration with the school and the classroom teacher
- What parents can do at home to help their children with learning disabilities
- Handling the siblings of children with learning disabilities—What to tell, what to do.
- Organizations for parents
- Family adjustment to learning disabilities

These are just examples of what can be offered to parents. You may want to ask them for their specific needs and add to this list as the suggestions are provided.

Help Parents Help with Homework

You will find that one of the most difficult periods of time for parents working with their children with LD comes at homework time. This period of time can be very stressful and problematic for both children and their parents if it is not handled properly. Parents need direction. Offering them concrete, practical things to do for the homework period will be appreciated. Pierangelo (2004) suggests several things that parents can do to facilitate homework with children with learning disabilities.

1. **Set up a homework schedule.** For some children, the responsibility of deciding when to sit down and do homework may be too difficult. Children may decide to do their homework after school or after dinner. This is a personal choice and has to do with learning style. However, once the time is determined, the schedule should be adhered to as closely as possible.
2. **Rank order assignments.** For some children, the decision as to what to do first becomes a major chore. They may dwell over this choice for a long period of time because everything takes on the same level of importance. Rank ordering assignments means that the parent determines the order in which the assignments are completed.
3. **Do not to sit next to your child while he or she does homework.** Employing this technique may create learned helplessness because the same "assistance" is not imitated in the classroom. Parents serve their children better by acting as a resource person to whom the child may come with a problem. After the problem is solved or question answered, the child should return to his

work area without the parent.

4. **Check correct problems first.** When the child brings the parent a paper to check, have the parent mention how well she did on the correct problems, spelling words, and so on. For the ones that are incorrect say, *I bet if you go back and check these over you may get a different answer.*

5. **Never let homework drag on all night.** The only thing accomplished by allowing a child to linger on his homework hour after hour with very little performance is increased feelings of inadequacy. If this occurs, end the work period after a reasonable period of time and write the teacher a note explaining the circumstances.

6. **Discuss homework questions before your child reads the chapter.** Suggest that the parent discuss the questions to be answered before the child reads the chapter. In this way the child will know what important information to look for while reading.

7. **Check small groups of problems at a time.** Many children can benefit from immediate gratification. Suggest to the parents that they have the child do five problems and then come to check them. This way, if she is doing the assignment incorrectly, the error can be detected and explained, preventing her child from doing the entire assignment incorrectly.

8. **Place textbook chapters on tape.** Research indicates that the more sensory input children receive, the greater the chance the information will be retained. For instance, parents can place science or social studies chapters on tape so that the child can listen while reading along.

9. **Be aware of negative nonverbal messages during homework.** Many messages, especially negative ones, can be communicated easily without your awareness (for example, deep sighs, raised eyebrows, inattentiveness). If children are sensitive, they will pick up these messages, which only adds to their tension.

10. **Avoid finishing assignments for your child.** Children tend to feel inadequate when a parent finishes their homework. If children cannot complete an assignment and they have honestly tried, write the teacher a note explaining the circumstances.

11. **Be aware of possible signs of more serious learning problems.** Parents should always be aware of symptoms indicating the possibility of more serious learning problems. Many of these symptoms may show up during homework. If these symptoms present a pattern, contact the psychologist or resource room teacher for further assistance. Such symptoms may include constant avoidance of homework, forgetting to bring home assignments, taking hours to do homework, procrastination of class work, low frustration tolerance, labored writing, poor spelling, and so on.

12. **Check homework assignments at the end of the night.** This will reduce the child's concerns over the thought of bringing incorrect homework to school. This also offers children a feeling of accomplishment, a source of positive attention, and a sense of security that the work is completed.

INTERIM STAGE

Working with Difficult Parents

One of the most upsetting experiences for new teachers may be working with difficult parents.These parents may exhibit themselves as angry, confrontational, needy, helpless, or questioning everything you do. While this topic could be a book in itself, there are several things you should remember.

Moore (2004) provides a list of suggestions when working with difficult parents. He adds that you need to remember that you can't change "toxic" parents, principals, or fellow staff members, but you can learn to cope with them and neutralize their impact on your life. Here are some effective strategies to try.

- Always stand at eye level with the person you are confronting. Never have them standing over you, looking down.
- Respect the toxic person and always expect respect in return. Settle for nothing less.
- Remain calm. A calm cool response to an angry verbal barrage can neutralize a toxic experience.
- Listen attentively. Don't argue or interrupt, just listen.
- Don't accuse or judge, just state how you feel about the situation.
- If the toxic person tries to verbally bully you, just say, *I'm sorry but I don't allow people to treat me this way. Perhaps we can continue this when you have calmed down.* Then slowly and calmly walk away.
- When someone is being toxic to you, here is a powerful response and one that is easy to use because you don't have to say a word. In the midst of a toxic attack just . . . *pause . . . look at the person, without emotion . . . turn, and walk away.* It works!
- While anger is sometimes a valid response it has to be used as a last resort. Anger doesn't usually accomplish anything with a difficult parent and can actually cause further alienation.
- Put your qualifications on display. Whether people like to admit it or not, they are impressed by paper qualifications. When you enter a doctor's office you see on the wall behind the desk all the degrees, diplomas, and additional courses taken in various medical fields. Seeing this gives most people more confidence in the doctor's expertise. Teachers should do the same. Behind your desk have copies of your degrees, teacher's certificates, professional courses taken, and so on mounted on the wall for all to see.
- When interviewing a difficult parent, never sit behind your desk. Move your chair out from behind the desk and place it close to and in front of the parent. This sends a strong assertive message to the one being interviewed. It says, *I am comfortable and confident in this situation.* That's just the message you want to send.
- Never underestimate the power of a stern, disapproving look. It certainly saves you words and allows you to assert yourself with minimum risk. If someone is doing or saying something that puts you down or tries to over-

power you, give them a look of disapproval which says loudly and clearly, *Back off.*

- Selective silence is one of the most effective ways of working with difficult people. It is easy to use, and very low-threat. When people are being difficult, they are often seeking attention and power. When you respond verbally to their toxic attack you are giving them the attention and power they desire. When you use selective silence you deny them both attention and power.
- When you are being harassed by a fellow staff member or fellow teacher with your board, in the interest of professional ethics, you must have the courage to confront. You can do this verbally, face-to-face, or in writing. Stay calm and professional. You can say something like this. *It has come to my attention that you have some concern about my teaching. Is this true?* Listen calmly and carefully to their response. Follow up with, *Perhaps you could put your concerns in writing. I will study them and get back to you with my written response.* Great harm is done to a teacher's reputation and well-being by a fellow teacher acting unprofessionally. Challenge them.

Now that we have taken into consideration many of the issues that you may encounter in the interim stage, we can move on to the culmination stage, which encompasses the last few months of school.

Culmination Stage: April–June

Even though we are coming down to the end of the school year, there will be several important issues that need to be the focus of your attention. This is a very crucial part of the year, since it will define what you have accomplished with parents and students. Many legal requirements occur during this time of year, depending on the school district in which you are employed. So let's take these topics one at a time so that you are prepared for each one. The topics covered in this stage will include:

- Teacher reports for triennial evaluations
- Preparing for annual review meetings
- Declassification or decertification of students with learning disabilities
- Extended school year recommendations
- Writing end-of-year reports to parents

Teacher Reports for Triennial Evaluations

Every three years, beginning from when the child was initially classified by the IEP Committee, a reevaluation takes place in order to assess the child's current strengths and weaknesses, determine if the variables that determined the classification are still present to the level of significant impairment, and to make recommendations based on the outcomes of the assessment. This assessment is very thorough as defined in the law and the results must be shared with the parents and the IEP Committee. This is sometimes done at the annual review for that year.

While a triennial review can occur at any time of the year, many school districts share triennial results at the annual review meeting held at the end of the school year. As the child's classroom teacher you will be asked by the Multidisciplinary Team to provide information on the child that will assist in these recommendations. This information, in the form of a report, should include the following.

- The child's present academic levels in reading, math, spelling, and writing. These may be available as a result of recent individual or group achievement tests, informal evaluations that you may have administered, observation, class tests, and so on
- The child's present pattern of classroom behavior. Write this up in behavioral terms (factual, observable, and descriptive notes of behavior that do not include analysis or judgment)
- The child's present levels of social interaction and social skills
- The child's interest areas and areas of strength
- Samples of the child's work
- Grade level, if it is possible to determine, and where the child falls in comparison to others in the class
- Outline of parent conferences, phone conversations or meetings, and the purpose and outcome of each. These notes should be kept on an ongoing basis.
- Your opinion as to whether the child is benefiting from the current placement
- Any physical limitations noted and their implication for the learning process
- Any pertinent comments made by the child that may have an impact on the current situation
- A copy of the child's current schedule

Preparing for Annual Review Meetings

Beginning in March or April, depending on the school district, you will be asked to participate in annual review meetings. These meetings which are required by law are held by the IEP Committee to review the child's progress over the past school year and make recommendations for the following school year. The parent or parents of the child usually attend this meeting, so being prepared is crucial. There are many things you will need to consider.

As with a regular IEP Committee meeting, there are several people who may attend this meeting. This may vary from district to district, but will likely include the director of special education services or assignee, school psychologist, parent member, parent of the child, guidance counselor (secondary level), assigned teacher (at the secondary level this may be the classroom teacher in a self-contained class, resource room teacher if this is the only service provided, or one of the child's special education teachers in a special education departmentalized program) classroom teacher (elementary level), speech and language therapist (if the child classification requires this service), the child (if over a certain age and the professionals feel that the child could benefit from the discussion or may be able to shed light on a concern or recommendation being considered), and any other individual deemed necessary.

This meeting should be taken very seriously, since it will determine the child's educational direction and objectives for the coming year. As a result you should be prepared and familiar with the following materials.

CULMINATION STAGE

- Any pre- and post-standardized test scores indicating the child's academic progress for the year
- A copy of the child's report card clearly outlining grades and attendance for the year
- Suggested goals and objectives for the coming year
- An evaluation indicating whether or not the child benefited from the modifications allowed on the IEP, and the reasons why they may or may not have been beneficial
- If applicable, recommendations for additional test modifications
- If applicable, recommendations for additional related services and the reasons
- If applicable, recommendations for reduction of related services and the reasons
- Samples of the child's work over the course of the year
- A review of the student's overall social progress for the year

The information listed above should be sufficient to present a professional judgment of the child's progress and needs for the coming year (Pierangelo, 2004).

Declassification of a Student with a Learning Disability

A major component of special education reform is the decertification of students no longer in need of special education services and, where necessary, providing support services and transitional services in general education. If declassification or decertification is determined to be appropriate, you will be an active participant in this process.

During periodic reviews of the student's IEP (i.e., annual reviews, requested reviews, and triennial reviews), the IEP Committee should determine whether the student no longer requires special education services because the student's needs can be met in the general education program. For students who no longer require special education services, this committee should also determine whether the student requires temporary services to facilitate transition to general education (in other words, declassification support services). Students who continue to require ongoing special education services for more than a year are not yet ready for decertification.

Decisions regarding decertification must be made on an individual, case-by-case basis by the IEP Committee, based on the needs of the student. The decertification process must comply with federal IDEA regulations and the Board of Education procedures for your district. This includes the active participation of the student's parents and the student, as appropriate, in the decision-making process. Under the reauthorized IDEA, parents also have the right to request that assessments be conducted.

Declassification Support Services are temporary services (not to exceed twelve months) designed to assist students who have been declassified from a special education service and who are recommended for a general education program with no other special education services. Declassification Support Services provide temporary direct support to students and the receiving teacher to facilitate transition to the general education classroom and maintain appropriate student functioning. Declassification support services may include individual or group counseling, individual or group speech and language service, small group instruction, modified curricula, or other strategies that have demonstrated success with students.

Extended School Year Recommendations

One of the issues that you may need to consider is whether any of your students with LD will need services over the summer to ensure that they do not lose what they have gained. Such services are provided to maintain continuity of learning and make sure that the student does not fall behind before the coming school year. These services are called Extended School Year (ESY) services and are determined appropriate by the IEP Committee. However, again you will play a very crucial role in this determination and should be aware of the requirements.

As part of the IEP process, a multidisciplinary team must determine if a child needs a program of special education and related services extending beyond the normal school year. For such a child, restricting services to a standard number of school days per year does not allow development of an education program that is truly individualized. A child may require ESY services in order to receive FAPE (Free and Appropriate Public Education).

Reasons why ESY services may be needed vary from child to child, but the end result is that some children may suffer severe losses of social, behavioral, communication, academic, or self-sufficiency skills during interruptions in instruction. This is particularly true during long breaks such as summer vacations. Losses suffered by a child may be so extensive that when school resumes, unreasonable amounts of time are needed to recover (recoup) lost skills. Other children may experience losses because they reach critical learning stages at the end of a school year and need ESY services to avoid irreparable loss of learning opportunity. For some children, skills that support continued placement in the least restrictive environment can be maintained only by ESY services.

The determination of whether a child with a disability needs ESY services must be made on an individual basis following the IEP process. The critical question that each IEP team must ask regarding ESY services is whether the learning that occurred during the regular school year will be significantly jeopardized if ESY services are not provided.

Your role will include providing documentation to the committee. The primary criteria in determining a child's need for ESY services are the likelihood of significant regression of previously learned skills during a break in service, and limited or delayed recoupment of these skills after services resume. The courts have found that the regression/recoupment measures are an integral part of the determination of need for ESY services, although they are not the only measures.

In determining significant regression and limited recoupment, it is important to consider the distinction between generalization and maintenance. A loss of skills over time could be due to failure to maintain performance or failure to generalize acquired skills to new settings. Many children do not easily generalize acquired skills to environmental conditions beyond those under which initial learning took place. In terms of interventions, the distinction between maintenance and generalization is essential. Regression may be an indication of either or both.

Regression can be defined as a decline to a lower level of functioning demonstrated by a decrease of previously learned skills which occurs as a result of an interruption in educational programming. Recoupment can be defined as the ability to recover or regain skills at the level demonstrated prior to the interruption of educational programming.

School districts should use regression/recoupment criteria in determining the need for ESY services, but a broad range of relevant factors must also be considered. The factors to be considered in making ESY placement decisions shall include, but are not limited to, the following.

Category of Disability.   Children with disabilities requiring consistent, highly structured programs may be predisposed to regression when their services are interrupted. These children may also have limited recoupment capacity.

Severity of Disability.   Although limited recoupment capacity can occur among children with moderate disabilities, it is more likely to be a learning characteristic of children with severe disabilities. Children with the most severe emotional disturbance, for example, are more likely to revert to lower functioning levels or to exhibit inappropriate behaviors, such as extreme withdrawal or anxiety reactions, when their programs are interrupted. For many of these children, each successive interruption in programming and consequential regression also reduces the level of motivation and trust and may lead to an irreversible withdrawal from the learning process. Finally, children with severe disabilities are more likely to have difficulty attaining the goals of self-sufficiency and independence from caretakers, and may need additional help and support to reach those goals.

Parents' Ability to Provide an Educational Structure at Home.   A parent or guardian may be unable to maintain a child's level of performance during a break in programming because of the complexity of the program, time constraints, lack of expertise, or other factors. This consideration is relevant to whether a child can be expected to regress. Also relevant is the child's stage of mastery of crucial skills or behavioral controls at the point of interruption in programming.

When appropriate, school districts should consider offering training to parents to help them maintain their child's level of performance during interruptions in programming. School districts may also consider offering support services in the home, either directly or in cooperation with other agencies, if such services will prevent the child's regression during breaks in programming.

School districts are free to utilize the resources of other public or private agencies in order to meet the child's needs, so long as there is no cost or financial liability to the child's parents or guardians.

Child's Rate of Progress.   Just as every child's rates of learning, regression, and recoupment are different from that of other children, an individual's rate of learning specific skills or behaviors may differ from his or her rate of attaining other skills. Certain skills or behaviors are particularly essential to meeting the goals of self-sufficiency. For example, basic self-help skills, such as toileting or eating, are essential for minimal independence; stable relationships, impulse control and appropriate peer interaction are necessary for community living. Therefore, if a child would suffer significant regression in a skill or behavior which is particularly crucial to reaching the goal of self-sufficiency and independence from caretakers, the child requires continuous education programming in that skill or behavior area.

Keep in mind that not all your students will require these services. However, closely evaluate each child's needs and do not be afraid to make this suggestion if you feel it might benefit him/her. If you make this recommendation, you are offering the committee your professional judgment and if you provide support for the above criteria you should make a very professional presentation.

Writing Year-End Reports to Parents

If your school district requires you to write year-end reports to parents you will need to take several things into consideration. In general, you will want to use plain language, because special education jargon may not be readily understood by most parents. You may want to hold your own year-end meeting with each child's parent(s), even though you may have just seen them at an annual review meeting. At this meeting you will want to discuss summer plans, extended school year services if applicable, the parent's role in maintaining learning over the summer, suggested materials and readings, and discussion about what to expect next year. At this meeting you can go over your report, but make sure they also have a neat, typed copy to take with them. When writing this report, keep the following points in mind.

- The written report will provide information on what students have learned as a result of the school's teaching programs in each of the key learning areas.
- Information provided in the report should be consistent with syllabuses in each key learning area. Written reports may also provide additional information about student achievement in relation to school programs that extend beyond syllabus requirements or where students have special needs.
- The written report will identify student strengths and areas that need further development or assistance.
- The written report will provide information about the student's attendance at school.

- Information about the student's social skills and development and commitment to learning should be in the report.
- The written report may include information about student participation in other school programs, such as sports, music, and clubs.
- The written report should track the child's progress toward the annual goals.

Try to keep the report to one page if possible. This can be a lot of information for parents to grasp.

This brings us to the end of the four stages that we hope will prepare you for what lies ahead in the teaching of students with learning disabilities. We are sure that there may be other aspects you will encounter that we did not cover. We have tried to provide you with a framework of issues that are normally experienced by teachers in your field. We hope this makes a difference for you in your job as a special education teacher.

Frequently Asked Questions about IDEA 2004

General

What is the Individuals with Disabilities Education Act (IDEA)?

The Individuals with Disabilities Education Act (IDEA) is the nation's special education law. First enacted three decades ago, IDEA provides billions of dollars in federal funding to assist states and local communities in providing educational opportunities for approximately six million students with varying degrees of disability who participate in special education.

In exchange for federal funding, IDEA requires states to provide a free appropriate public education (FAPE) in the least restrictive environment (LRE). The statute also contains detailed due process provisions to ensure the provision of FAPE. Originally enacted in 1975, the Act responded to increased awareness of the need to educate children with disabilities and to judicial decisions requiring states to provide an education for children with disabilities if they provide an education for children without disabilities.

Part A of IDEA contains the general provisions, including the purposes of the Act and definitions. Part B, the most frequently discussed part of the Act, contains provisions relating to the education of school-aged and preschool children, the funding formula, evaluations for services, eligibility determinations, Individualized Education Programs (IEPs) and educational placements. It also contains detailed requirements for procedural safeguards (including the discipline provisions) as well as withholding of funds and judicial review. Part B also includes the Section 619 program, which provides services to children aged 3 through 5 years old.

Part C of IDEA provides early intervention and other services for infants and toddlers with disabilities and their families (from birth through age 3). These early intervention and other services are provided in accordance with an Individualized Family Service Plan developed in consultation between families of infants and toddlers with disabilities and the appropriate state agency. Part C also provides grants to states to support these programs for infants and toddlers with disabilities. Part D provides support for various national activities designed to improve the education of children with disabilities, including personnel preparation activities, technical assistance, and special education research.

Key Definitions

What is a free appropriate public education (FAPE)?

IDEA recognizes that, to the extent possible, children with disabilities are entitled to the same educational experience as their non-disabled peers. IDEA further recognizes that the expenses associated with providing for the special needs of children with disabilities are a public responsibility. Therefore, the centerpiece of the law is the FAPE concept. Generally, FAPE means that children with disabilities are entitled to a publicly financed education that is appropriate to their age and abilities. Specifically, FAPE means special education and related services that are available to all children with disabilities in a state that

- are provided at public expense, under public supervision and direction, and without charge;
- meet the standards of the state educational agency (SEA);
- include an appropriate preschool, elementary school, or secondary school in the state; and
- are provided in conformity with the Individualized Education Program established for the child.

What is the least restrictive environment (LRE)?

When IDEA was originally enacted in 1975, Congress recognized that many children with disabilities were unnecessarily separated from their peers and educated in alternative environments. Therefore, IDEA requires that states provide a free appropriate public education (FAPE) to children with disabilities in the least restrictive environment (LRE). The general goal is to allow children with disabilities to be educated with their peers in the regular classroom to the extent possible.

IDEA recognizes that there is an array of placements that meet the general requirements of providing FAPE in the least restrictive environment. LRE may change from child to child, school to school, and district to district. In developing the IEP, parents and the local educational agency are empowered to reach appropriate decisions about what constitutes LRE for the individual child, including placements that may be more or less restrictive in order to maximize the child's benefit from special education and related services.

What is an Individualized Education Program (IEP)?

The Individualized Education Program, or IEP, is the key document developed by the parent and his or her child's teachers and related services personnel that lays out how the child receives a free appropriate public education in the least restrictive environment. Among other components, the IEP lays out the child's academic achievement and functional performance, describes how the child will be included in the general education curriculum, establishes annual goals for the child and describes how those goals will be measured, states what special education and related services are needed by the child, describes how the child will be appropriately assessed including through the use of alternate assessments, and determines what accommodations may be appropriate for the child's instruction and assessments.

What is an Individualized Family Service Plan (IFSP)?

An IFSP is the Part C (formula program for infants and toddlers with disabilities) equivalent of an IEP. It is developed through an assessment and evaluation process, identifies the child's present levels of development and performance, establishes goals for future development and performance, and outlines how the child will receive early intervention and other services. Unlike an IEP, the IFSP explicitly integrates the needs of the family with those of the child and presents a comprehensive plan that enables the family to meet its goals.

Highly Qualified Teachers

Are special education teachers required to be "highly qualified" under the No Child Left Behind Act?

Yes. IDEA aligns "highly qualified" requirements for special education teachers with those requirements established under the No Child Left Behind Act (NCLB). This means that all special education teachers who teach core academic subjects must meet the "highly qualified" definition in NCLB by the end of the 2005–2006 school year. The core academic subjects, as defined in NCLB, are English, reading or language arts, mathematics, science, foreign languages, civics and government, economics, arts, history, and geography.

However, IDEA clarifies the definition of a highly qualified teacher in NCLB to address the unique needs of special education teachers. IDEA requires that special education teachers obtain certification as a special education teacher or pass the state special education teacher licensing exam, and hold a license to teach in the state as a special education teacher. In addition, special education teachers may not have had their certification or licensure requirements waived on an emergency, temporary, or provisional basis, and they must hold at least a bachelor's degree.

Special education teachers can fall into one of several categories depending on whether they teach one or more core academic subject areas, and whether they teach students who are assessed using alternate achievement standards. Requirements for specific types of special education teachers are discussed in greater detail below.

What requirements apply to special education teachers who teach core academic subjects exclusively to children who are assessed against alternate achievement standards?

All teachers have the ability to demonstrate that they are highly qualified by meeting the requirements of NCLB. However, Congress recognized that these requirements did not completely reflect the needs of some special education teachers, and to assist special education teachers working to become highly qualified, added greater flexibility and modified those requirements in IDEA.

Special education teachers who teach exclusively to children who are assessed against alternate achievement standards (those children with the most significant cognitive disabilities) may demonstrate subject knowledge and teaching skills in the areas of the basic elementary school curriculum by passing a rigorous state test, or demonstrate competence in those core academic subject areas he or she teaches based on a high objective uniform state standard of evaluation (HOUSSE) as defined in NCLB. At the state's discretion, teachers who provide instruction above the elementary school level may demonstrate subject matter knowledge appropriate to the level of instruction provided, as defined by the state.

What requirements apply to special education teachers who teach multiple core academic subjects?

Special education teachers who teach multiple core academic subjects may simply meet the requirements of NCLB that apply to any new or veteran elementary, middle, or secondary school teacher for each academic subject they teach. Or, special education teachers may take advantage of new flexibility that was added in the 2004 IDEA reauthorization. Under IDEA, veteran teachers may demonstrate their competence in all of the core academic subjects they teach through the state-developed high objective uniform state standard of evaluation (HOUSSE) option. Also, new special education teachers who are highly qualified in mathematics, language arts, or science may demonstrate competence in the other core academic subjects they teach by also completing the HOUSSE option for those subjects within two years of their initial date of employment.

What requirements apply to special education teachers who do not teach core academic subjects?

IDEA recognizes the important contributions of special education teachers who do not teach core academic subjects, but who provide special education services to students with disabilities. Such services may include adjustments to the learning environment, modifications of instructional methods, adaptation of curricula, the use of positive behavioral supports and interventions, supporting a regular education teacher in the classroom, or applying appropriate accommodations to meet the needs of individual children. Such teachers can meet the "highly qualified" requirement by obtaining special education certification as defined by the state and holding at least a Bachelor's degree.

Individualized Education Program

What is the timeline for getting a child evaluated for a disability?

In order for a child to be eligible for special education and related services, the child must first be determined to have a disability. Parents, teachers, or other school officials who suspect that the child may have a disability would request that the child be evaluated by a multi-disciplinary team to determine if the child has a disability and needs special education or related services as a result of the disability. Generally speaking, IDEA requires that a child be evaluated within 60 days once the parent has given consent for the evaluation. States may establish shorter or longer timeframes in their own state legislation or regulation, and those state-developed timelines would be binding.

Exceptions to the timeline exist if the child moves from one district or state to another district or state after the evaluation was requested or if the parent refuses to make the child available for the evaluation. Under those circumstances, districts are required to make sufficient progress to ensure that a timely evaluation is conducted.

If a child moves from one district to another within the state, does the IEP follow the child?

No. The new local educational agency (LEA) is required to continue to provide a free appropriate public education to the child with a disability including providing services that are comparable to those services outlined in the child's original IEP. The new LEA is not required to implement the pre-existing IEP, but may choose to do so at its own discretion. If the new LEA does not implement that IEP, the new LEA must work with the parent through the IEP Team process to develop an IEP that is consistent with federal and state law.

If a child moves from one state to another, does the IEP follow the child?

No. The new LEA in the new state is required to provide a free appropriate public education to the child with a disability including providing services that are comparable to those services outlined in the child's original IEP. The new LEA in the new state is not required to implement the pre-existing IEP, but may choose to do so at its own discretion. If the new LEA does not implement that IEP, the new LEA in the new state must work with the parent through the IEP Team process to develop an IEP that is consistent with federal and state law.

Additionally, because definitions of disability and eligibility vary from state to state, the new LEA in the new state may require the child to be evaluated to determine whether the child is eligible to be identified as a child with a disability under state law. If the child is eligible for services under IDEA in the new state, an IEP must be developed and implemented for the child.

What if a parent doesn't provide consent for evaluation or for services?

If a parent does not provide their consent for an evaluation, the LEA does have the authority to use the due process procedures to seek an order from a hearing officer requiring an evaluation. LEAs should use this authority sparingly.

If both parents do not provide their consent for the provision of services, no special education or related services may be provided. The rights of parents to decide what educational services their child receives cannot be overturned using IDEA's due process procedures. If a parent indicates that he or she will refuse both consent for evaluations and consent for services, nothing in IDEA requires that an LEA use the due process procedures to proceed through the evaluation phase.

What methods are local educational agencies (LEAs) allowed to use to identify a child as having a specific learning disability?

Almost half of the students identified as being disabled under IDEA are placed in the category of "specific learning disability." In order to eliminate out-dated methods of determining whether a child actually has a specific learning disability, and to respond to the need to identify children before they start to fail academically because of their disability, IDEA allows local districts significant new flexibility in developing appropriate methods of determining whether a child has a specific learning disability.

However, IDEA does prohibit states from requiring that LEAs routinely use an IQ test as a part of the determination of specific learning disabilities. This means that the IQ-achievement discrepancy model in which a specific learning disability is identified when there is a discrepancy between achievement and intellectual ability cannot be mandated. States and LEAs are encouraged to look to research-based practices, especially models using response-to-intervention strategies, to determine whether a child has a specific learning disability. The Department of Education will develop guidance and provide technical assistance to states and LEAs using effective, scientifically based research to help states and LEAs develop effective models of identification practices.

Must all children with disabilities participate in state assessments?

Yes. Under the No Child Left Behind Act (NCLB), for the first time ever states and local schools are held accountable for ensuring all children—including children with disabilities—are learning. Children with disabilities must be included in the assessment system required under the No Child Left Behind Act and schools must report their results through NCLB's adequate yearly progress structure. IDEA requires that the IEP Team determine how the child with a disability is assessed, not whether the child is assessed. IDEA recognizes that children learn in different ways, with different methods of instruction and assessment. The IEP Team is required to determine which accommodations are necessary, how to instruct the child, and how to assess the child.

The IEP Team can have a child with a disability take the regular state assessment; the regular state assessment with appropriate accommodations such as Braille, additional time, or having the instructions read to the child multiple times; an alternate assessment aligned to grade level standards; or an alternate assessment aligned to alternate achievement standards. This array of assessment opportunities ensures that all students with disabilities can be assessed appropriately for individual and systemic accountability efforts.

Should all states have alternate assessments?

Yes. IDEA builds on the education reforms of the past decade by allowing states to develop appropriate alternate assessments aligned to grade level standards for students with disabilities so that they can demonstrate what they know. Since 1997, IDEA has required that all states have alternate assessments. In 2004, IDEA was updated to allow states to develop alternate assessments tied to alternate achievement standards to allow for maximum flexibility in appropriately assessing students with disabilities. However, all decisions about which assessment a child with a disability should take are to be made by the IEP Team.

Is there a conflict between IDEA and NCLB on assessments for students with disabilities?

No. IDEA and NCLB work in concert to ensure that students with disabilities are included in assessments and accountability systems. While IDEA focuses on the needs of the individual child, NCLB focuses on ensuring improved academic achievement for all students.

Is the IEP required to include benchmarks and short term objectives for all students with disabilities?

No. IDEA was updated to be aligned carefully with NCLB to ensure that parents of students with disabilities get access to the same level of information about their children's academic performance as all other students. For most students with disabilities, the IEP Team will include a statement of the child's current performance, establish annual goals, describe how those goals will be measured, and establish a reporting cycle similar to all other students.

However, for those students with disabilities taking an alternate assessment aligned to alternate achievement standards, the IEP Team will be required to include benchmarks and short-term objectives. Since these students will typically not perform at or near grade-level, measuring their progress requires a different approach that can be accommodated through the use of benchmarks and short-term objectives.

Who has to be part of the IEP Team?

The IEP Team is responsible for developing the IEP and ensuring its effective implementation so that the child can receive special education and related services. The IEP Team must include the parents of the child with a disability, a regular education teacher (if the child is participating in the regular education environment), a special education teacher, and a representative of the school district. In addition, the parent and the school district can agree to add other members knowledgeable about related services or with expertise about the child.

Do IEP Team members need to be at every meeting?

To provide efficient and effective use of IEP Team meetings, the parent and the LEA may agree to excuse any member of the IEP Team from the IEP Team meeting if their area of curriculum or related services is not being addressed.

The parent and the LEA may also agree to excuse any member of the IEP Team from the IEP Team meeting if their area of curriculum or related services is being addressed, but the Team member will be required to submit his or her input in writing to the parent and the LEA prior to the IEP Team meeting.

The parent must provide written consent to the excusing of any IEP Team member.

Can the IEP be amended without reconvening the whole IEP Team?

Yes. To provide greater flexibility for parents and schools, IDEA allows the parent and the LEA to agree to amend or modify the IEP without reconvening the whole IEP Team. Such an amendment or modification must be in writing to clearly lay out what has been modified or amended.

Can IEP Teams use modern technology to develop the IEP and conduct meetings?

Yes. In order to facilitate the meeting process, reduce paperwork, and make meetings more efficient, IDEA allows IEP Teams to use computers to develop an IEP for a child with a disability instead of using typewriters or written documents. Additionally, to better accommodate busy work schedules for parents and school personnel, IDEA allows the parents to agree to use conference calls, video conferencing, or other alternative means of participation to conduct IEP meetings and other meetings required under IDEA, including resolution session meetings.

Procedural Safeguards

The procedural safeguards of IDEA provide the foundation for ensuring access to a free appropriate public education. Procedural safeguards provide the ability of parents to understand the rights of their child, facilitate communication between parents and schools, and detail the due process procedures if a complaint about the implementation of the Act as it relates to an individual child is registered. The procedural safeguards section of the Act also includes the discipline provisions.

What is the procedural safeguards notice? When must it be provided?

The procedural safeguards notice is a copy of the procedural safeguards available to parents and children with disabilities. IDEA requires state and local educational agencies to provide parents with this notice. Generally, the agency is only required to provide the notice once a year. However, the notice must also be provided when parents request an initial evaluation or when a child is initially referred to the agency, the first time parents file any complaint, and whenever parents request the notice.

Does IDEA place a statute of limitations on when a due process complaint can be filed?

Yes. While parents are permitted under IDEA to file due process complaints when they feel that their child's rights under IDEA have been violated, any complaints must be filed no later than two years after the violation is alleged to have occurred.

Are there exceptions to the statute of limitations?

Yes. IDEA provides a number of exceptions to the two year statute of limitations. First, if a state's law provides a different time limit on the presentation of a complaint, that state-imposed limit prevails.

IDEA also provides exceptions to protect the rights of children and their families. If a local educational agency falsely claims that it has resolved the complaint, or withholds information it was required to provide, then the two year statute of limitation does not apply.

What is the due process notice?

The due process notice is an official complaint from the parent about their child's individualized education program or services provided under IDEA. A party alleging a due process violation under IDEA is required to provide a due process complaint notice to the other party and the state educational agency (SEA). The notice must include the name and home address of the child, the name of the school the child attends, a description of the nature of the problem, and a proposed resolution. The party presenting the complaint must file this notice before a due process hearing can occur.

What actions must the LEA take when it receives a due process notice?

If the LEA has not provided a prior written notice to the parents regarding the subject matter of the complaint, the LEA must provide a response to the parents within ten days of receiving the due process notice that contains the following:

- an explanation of why the agency proposed or refused to take the action raised in the complaint;
- a description of other options that the IEP Team considered and the reasons those options were rejected;
- a description of each evaluation procedure, assessment, record, or report the agency used as the basis for the proposed or refused action; and
- a description of the relevant factors in the LEA's proposal or refusal.

What if the LEA believes the due process notice is not sufficient?

If the LEA believes that the due process notice fails to meet the requirements for such a notice, the LEA must notify the hearing officer in writing within fifteen days of receiving the complaint. Hearing officers then have up to five days to determine if the notice meets the requirements. Upon making a determination, the officer must immediately notify all parties in writing of the decision.

If the hearing officer determines that the complaint is sufficient, the LEA must respond to the complaint. If the hearing officer determines that the complaint is not sufficient, the parent has the opportunity to resubmit a new complaint and the timelines start over.

Does IDEA allow a party to amend its due process notice after the notice has been delivered to the hearing officer and other party?

The due process complaint notice may be amended if the other party consents to the amendment in writing and is given the opportunity to resolve the complaint through the resolution session. The hearing officer may also allow a due process notice to be amended, but only if the amendment is made more than five days before the due process hearing. When a due process complaint is amended, the applicable timeline for a due process hearing begins again when the party files the amended notice.

What requirements apply to a complaint?

When a parent files a complaint the parent must describe the nature of the problem, relevant facts relating to the problem, and a proposed resolution to the problem.

If the LEA feels that the complaint is not sufficient to inform them about the problem, the LEA has fifteen days from when the parent filed their complaint to ask a hearing officer to decide whether the complaint was sufficient.

The hearing officer has five days to make a determination that the complaint is sufficient. If the hearing officer decides that the complaint is not sufficient, the complaint is returned to the parent, and the parent is able to file a new complaint with greater specificity and the timeline starts over once a new complaint is filed.

When is mediation allowed?

To discourage unnecessary and costly litigation, IDEA requires states to establish and implement procedures to allow parties to resolve disputes through a mediation process. Any dispute, including matters that arise prior to the filing of a formal complaint, are eligible for mediation.

Mediation is defined as an attempt to bring about a peaceful settlement or compromise between parties to a dispute through the objective intervention of a neutral party. Mediation is an opportunity for parents and school officials to sit down with an independent mediator and discuss a problem, issue, concern, or complaint in order to resolve the problem amicably without going to due process. Mediation can be initiated at any time, if both parties agree, to expedite the development of a solution.

What requirements must states meet in developing mediation procedures?

To ensure that the mediation process is a valuable alternative to litigation, IDEA contains guidelines states must follow in developing a mediation program. First, mediation must be voluntary for both parties. Second, mediation may not be used to deny or delay a parent's right to a due process hearing, or to deny other rights guaranteed under IDEA. And, third, mediation must be conducted by a qualified and impartial mediator who is trained in effective mediation techniques.

Can state educational agencies (SEAs) or local educational agencies (LEAs) actively encourage parents and schools to participate in mediation?

Yes. IDEA allows state and local educational agencies to provide parents and schools that choose not to participate in mediation the option of meeting with a disinterested party who may encourage the use and explain the benefits of mediation. Such a meeting must be convened at a time and location that is convenient for the parents. The disinterested party must be under contract with a parent training and information center, community parent resource center, or an appropriate alternative dispute resolution entity.

How does IDEA make mediation a viable alternative to parents and schools?

IDEA requires states to pay for the mediation process and to maintain a list of qualified mediators who are knowledgeable about the laws and regulations pertaining to the provision of special education and related services. The state must also ensure that each mediation session is scheduled in a timely manner and held in a location that is convenient for the parties involved.

Does mediation produce a legally binding resolution?

Yes. If the parties resolve the complaint, they must execute a legally binding agreement. The agreement explains the resolution and states that all discussions that occurred during the mediation process will remain confidential and may not be used as evidence in any subsequent due process hearing or civil proceeding; contains signatures from both the parent and a representative of the state or local educational agency who has the authority to legally bind the agency; and is enforceable in any state court of competent jurisdiction or in a U.S. district court.

What is the impartial due process hearing?

Whenever parents or the local educational agency (LEA) file a complaint related to the provision of special education and related services to a child with a disability, the party filing the complaint has the opportunity for this hearing. The hearing is conducted by the state educational agency (SEA) or LEA, depending on state law, and is meant to provide the parties a fair, impartial venue for resolving the issues contained in the complaint.

What is the resolution session?

A resolution session is a new provision created under the 2004 IDEA reauthorization, which provides an opportunity for parents and local educational agencies (LEAs) to resolve any issues in the complaint in an efficient and effective manner so that parents and LEAs can avoid due process hearings and provide immediate benefit to the child. Within 15 days of when a complaint is filed, and prior to a due process hearing, the LEA must convene a resolution session between the parents and the relevant members of the IEP Team who have specific knowledge of the facts contained in the complaint (as determined by the LEA and the parents).

The resolution session must include a representative of the LEA who has decision making authority on behalf of the agency, but may not include an attorney for the LEA unless the parent is also accompanied by an attorney. The session provides an opportunity for the party who filed the complaint to discuss that complaint and the facts forming the basis of it, and an opportunity for the responding party to resolve the complaint.

If the parties reach agreement through this process, they must execute a legally binding agreement that is signed by the parents and a representative of the LEA with the authority to legally bind the LEA, and that is enforceable in any state court of competent jurisdiction or district court of the United States. Either party may void the agreement up to three days after its execution.

In the event the complaint is not resolved through this process, the parties may then proceed to a due process hearing. The parties may agree not to conduct the resolution session if both agree in writing or decide to use mediation.

What topics may be covered during the due process hearing?

The due process hearing is limited to those issues covered in the complaint. The party requesting the hearing can only raise other issues if the other party agrees. The party filing the complaint should consolidate multiple issues into one complaint when possible.

Who presides over the due process hearing? What qualifications must he or she meet?

An impartial hearing officer presides over the due process hearing. The hearing officer must not be an employee of the state or local educational agency involved in the education of the child and must not have a professional or personal interest that conflicts with his or her objectivity in the hearing. The hearing officer must know and understand IDEA, federal and state regulations pertaining to IDEA, and legal interpretations of IDEA by the courts. The hearing officer must also be able to conduct hearings and render decisions in accordance with standard legal practice.

On what does a hearing officer base his or her decisions?

In general, a hearing officer's decision should be made on substantive grounds based on a determination of whether the child received a free appropriate public education (FAPE). If the complaint alleges procedural violations, the hearing officer may find that the child did not receive a FAPE only if the procedural violations impeded the child's right to a FAPE, significantly impeded the parents' opportunity to participate in the decision making process regarding the provision of a FAPE for the child, or deprived the child of educational benefits. However, a hearing officer can order the LEA to comply with procedural requirements even if noncompliance does not result in a failure to provide a FAPE.

When a parent files a complaint, how long does the LEA or SEA have to resolve the complaint?

The LEA must convene the resolution session within 15 days of receiving a complaint. If the LEA has not otherwise resolved the complaint within 30 days of receiving it, the due process hearing may then occur.

Once the LEA has failed to resolve the complaint within 30 days and a due process hearing is required, the SEA must conduct the hearing and mail a written copy of the hearing officer's final decision to all parties involved.

How long does a party have to request a hearing after the alleged violation occurs?

The party requesting the hearing must submit the request within two years of when the alleged violation occurred. If state law provides for a different timeline, the state law prevails. The timeline does not apply to parents if the LEA falsely claims that it has resolved the complaint or withholds information it was required to provide.

Are there avenues for appeal when a party disagrees with the hearing officer's decision?

Yes. When the hearing is conducted by the LEA, either party may appeal the decision to the SEA. The hearing officer conducting the review on behalf of the SEA must conduct an impartial review of the findings and decision and make an independent judgment upon the completion of the review. The SEA must reach a final decision and mail a copy of that decision to both parties.

Does the due process hearing preclude a party from filing a civil action in court?

No. Any party who disputes the final decision of the hearing officer may bring a civil action in any state court of competent jurisdiction or in a U.S. district court. The party bringing the civil action has 90 days from the date of the hearing officer's final decision to file the claim. If state law provides for a different timeline, the state law prevails.

Can a court award attorneys' fees to the prevailing party in a civil action?

Yes. U.S. district courts may award reasonable attorneys' fees to prevailing parties (parents, SEAs, or LEAs) as part of any settlement of a due process complaint or civil action. Attorneys' fees granted to SEAs or LEAs may only be granted under certain guidelines. First, the parents' attorney may be forced to pay the agency's attorneys' fees when that attorney files a complaint or civil action that is frivolous, unreasonable, or without foundation, or continues to pursue a civil action after the litigation clearly became frivolous, unreasonable, or without foundation. Second, the parents, or their attorney, may be forced to pay the SEA's or LEA's attorneys' fees if the parents' complaint or subsequent civil action was presented for any improper purpose, such as to harass, cause unnecessary delay, or needlessly increase the cost of litigation.

For what services may a prevailing party not be awarded attorneys' fees?

Not all legal and administrative proceedings and services are eligible for reimbursement. A court may not award attorneys' fees for any services performed subsequent to the time a written offer of settlement is made to the parents if:

- the offer is made in accordance with Rule 68 of the Federal Rules of Civil Procedure;
- in the case of an administrative proceeding, the offer is made more than 10 days prior to the hearing;
- the offer is not accepted within ten days; and
- the court or administrative hearing officer finds that the relief finally obtained by the parents is not more favorable than the offer of settlement.

However, attorneys' fees may be awarded to parents who were substantially justified in rejecting the settlement offer. Also, IEP Team meetings are not eligible for reimbursement unless the meeting is convened as a result of an administrative proceeding or judicial action, or, at the discretion of the state, for a mediation session. And, attorneys' fees for resolution session meetings are also ineligible for reimbursement.

Can the court reduce the amount of attorneys' fees eligible for reimbursement under certain circumstances?

Yes. The court is required to reduce the amount of fees eligible for reimbursement when the court finds that any of the following apply:

- the parents, or the parents' attorney, unreasonably protracted the final resolution of a complaint during the course of the administrative proceeding or civil action;
- the amount of the attorneys' fees otherwise authorized to be awarded unreasonably exceeds the hourly rate prevailing in the community for similar services by attorneys of reasonably comparable skill, reputation, and experience;
- the time spent and legal services provided were excessive considering the nature of the administrative proceeding or civil action; or
- the attorney representing the parents did not provide to the LEA the appropriate information in the due process complaint notice.

However, if the court finds that the SEA or LEA unreasonably protracted the final resolution of the administrative proceeding or civil action or violated any of the procedural safeguards provisions, then the above requirements do not apply.

Discipline

Disciplinary procedures under IDEA have been a source of concern among parents, schools, and disability advocates for years. At issue are concerns about the protection of rights for students, which must be fairly balanced with the ability of school personnel to maintain safety and order in schools for the benefit of all students. The 2004 IDEA reauthorization resulted in significant improvements to discipline provisions in order to add significant clarity and common sense to the discipline provisions within IDEA.

In what circumstances do the discipline procedures apply?

In reauthorizing IDEA, the bipartisan conference committee sought to ensure that schools would be safe for students and teachers, and that discipline problems would be addressed with common sense. The new IDEA helps school personnel ensure school safety and hold students responsible for their actions, while protecting the rights of children with disabilities. The discipline procedures only apply where the discipline infraction results in a change in placement for longer than 10 school days, and was a direct result of the child's disability. Unless a disciplinary infraction is the direct result of a child's disability, the child will be disciplined in the same manner and for the same duration as a non-disabled student.

Does a school have to discipline a child with a disability in every instance?

No. When a student has violated a code of conduct, school personnel may consider any unique circumstances on a case-by-case basis to determine whether a change of placement for discipline purposes is appropriate.

Do IDEA discipline procedures apply if the child with a disability will be disciplined for less than 10 school days?

No. Where the discipline infraction would result in a change in placement for less than 10 school days, the discipline procedures do not apply.

If the discipline infraction of the child relates to drugs, weapons, or serious bodily injury, will that child's discipline be handled differently?

Yes. If the disciplinary infraction involves the serious safety issues of drugs, weapons, or serious bodily injury, the child will automatically be removed from the classroom for up to 45 school days. The child will be placed in an interim alternative educational setting, but will continue to receive educational services to make progress on his or her IEP. Also during this time, a determination will be made as to whether the disciplinary infraction was the direct result of a child's disability.

What process will determine whether the disciplinary infraction was the direct result of a child's disability?

In order to determine whether the disciplinary infraction was the direct result of a child's disability, the LEA, the parent, and the relevant members of the IEP Team must determine whether the conduct in question was a "manifestation of the child's disability." This process is called a manifestation determination. The manifestation determination will analyze the child's behavior as demonstrated across settings and across time when determining whether the discipline infraction is a direct result of the child's disability.

Previously, the LEA had to prove that the child's action resulting in the discipline infraction was not caused by the child's disability. The new IDEA places the obligation on the parent to show that the child's action resulting in the discipline infraction was the direct result of the child's disability.

What does the term *manifestation of a child's disability* mean?

This term has been significantly changed in this reauthorization. Previously any tangential or attenuated relationship between the discipline infraction and the child's disability was sufficient to determine that the infraction was a "manifestation" of the child's disability. In the new IDEA, the bipartisan consensus acknowledged that "[i]t is the intention of the Conferees that the conduct in question was caused by, or has a direct and substantial relationship to, the child's disability, and is not an attenuated association, such as low self-esteem, to the child's disability." Accordingly, it is now clear in the new IDEA that the disciplinary infraction must be caused by or be the direct result of a child's disability, and not a mere correlation or attenuation.

Who are the relevant members of the IEP Team when conducting a manifestation determination?

Depending on the type of discipline infraction, when the infraction occurred and who was present, some members of the IEP Team may not be relevant to the discussion of the discipline event. For example, although transportation is an important issue, if the discipline infraction occurred during the school day, the transportation member would not be relevant to the discussion of the discipline event. Conversely, if the discipline infraction occurred on the school bus, the transportation member may be the relevant member of the IEP Team. Nonetheless, in each instance the relevant members should be determined in collaboration by the parents and LEA.

What services and placement would then be available to the child if the actions are determined to be a manifestation of the child's disability?

In situations where the local educational agency, the parent and the relevant members of the IEP Team determine that the discipline infraction was the direct result of the child's disability, a child with a disability would not be subject to discipline in the same manner as a non-disabled child. However, such determination is not to say that the child should not be subject to any discipline.

In these situations, the IEP Team shall determine whether a functional behavioral assessment has been conducted and a behavioral intervention plan has been implemented for such child. If the IEP Team finds either that such assessment has not been conducted or a behavioral intervention plan has not been implemented for such child, then both should be completed. Where a behavioral intervention plan has been developed, the IEP Team must review the behavioral intervention plan and modify it, as necessary, to address the behavior. Additionally, unless the parent and the LEA agree to a change of placement, the child must be returned to the placement from which the child was removed.

What services and placement are available to the child if the actions are determined not to be a manifestation of the child's disability?

Unless a disciplinary infraction is the direct result of a child's disability, the child will be disciplined in the same manner and for the same duration as a non-disabled student. The child may be placed in an interim alternative educational setting. However, if the suspension is for longer than 10 school days, the child will continue to receive educational services to make progress on his or her IEP.

Can a parent appeal the decision regarding manifestation?

Yes, if the parent of a child with a disability disagrees with the manifestation determination or placement, the parent may request a hearing. At such hearing (as for the manifestation determination), the obligation is on the parent to show that the child's action resulting in the discipline infraction was the direct result of the child's disability.

Where will the child receive services while the appeal is pending?

Previously during appeals, a child with a disability remained in the original placement. This was called the "stay put" requirement. The new IDEA eliminates the "stay put" requirement. Now during the time that an appeal is pending, the child will remain in the interim alternative educational setting until the appeal is resolved or until the expiration of the suspension, whichever occurs first. However, the placement can be changed during this time if the parent and LEA agree.

Do any of these procedures apply to children who have not been identified as having a disability?

A child who has not been determined to be eligible for special education services and who has a discipline infraction that violates a code of student conduct, may assert the discipline protections if the LEA had "knowledge" that the child was a child with a disability before the discipline infraction occurred. However, if the LEA does not have knowledge that a child is a child with a disability, the child may be disciplined in the same manner and to the same extent as non-disabled students.

An LEA is deemed to have "knowledge" if, before the discipline infraction occurred, one of the following happened.

- The parent of the child expressed concern in writing to supervisory or administrative personnel of the LEA, or a teacher of the child, that the child is in need of special education services;
- The parent of the child has requested an evaluation of the child pursuant to IDEA; or
- The teacher of the child, or other LEA personnel, has expressed specific concerns directly to the director of special education or to other supervisory personnel.

If the parent of the child has not allowed an evaluation of the child or has refused services, or the child has been evaluated and it was determined that the child was not a child with a disability then an LEA will not be deemed to have "knowledge" that the child is a child with a disability.

Funding

How has spending for IDEA Part B increased since Republicans won control of the House in 1994?

When Congress first passed IDEA in 1975, many believe Congress committed to pay up to 40 percent of the national average per pupil expenditure to offset the excess cost of educating children with disabilities; talk about reaching "full funding" means reaching this 40 percent funding goal. Since taking control of Congress in 1994, Republicans have dramatically increased spending for the IDEA Part B Grants to States program, which funds direct services to students. Funding has increased by nearly 360 percent, and the federal share of funding has increased from 7.3 percent of the average per pupil expenditure in FY 1996 to 18.7 percent in FY 2005. Under Republican leadership, Congress has increased its rate of progress toward finally reaching the 40 percent level many believe Congress sought in 1975.

What is the level of funding for IDEA for fiscal year '05?

For FY 2005, IDEA Part B Grants to States are funded at nearly $10.6 billion, the largest amount ever allocated for special education. This figure represents an increase of nearly 360 percent in special education state grant funding since FY 1995, the last year of a Democratic-controlled Congress.

The bulk of federal special education funding is contained in the part B Grants to States program, which provides much of the federal funding for direct special education and related services for children with disabilities.

What does the President's '06 budget include for IDEA?

Under President Bush's FY 2006 budget proposal, the IDEA Part B Grants to States program would receive $11.1 billion, a $508 million increase over FY 2005 levels. By devoting a significant amount of federal funds to IDEA, local schools will have greater discretion over how to spend local education funds, including how to fund school construction, teacher hiring, professional development, and the many other needs facing most local school districts.

Are local educational agencies (LEAs) allowed to reduce their own spending?

Yes. As a result of the significant increases in federal funding for IDEA and the maintenance of effort requirements, local educational agencies (LEAs) have been required to maintain artificially high levels of funding on special education, even as the federal share has increased. Accordingly, the reauthorized IDEA allows LEAs to reduce their own local spending on special education by an amount equal to 50 percent of the increase in federal funding from one year to the next. This will give local communities greater control over how their own, local dollars are spent on education.

For example, if the LEA receives an increase of $5,000 in federal funds over its allocation from the previous year, the LEA will be able to reduce its own local funding by $2,500. However, if the LEAs allocation of federal funds does not increase, then the LEA will not be able to reduce its local spending in that year.

Any reduction in the maintenance of effort level is permanent, so LEAs will be able to plan accordingly in making decisions about whether to use this authority and how to develop their own budgets and spending decisions. It is important to note, however, that the LEA still has the obligation to provide a free appropriate public education to students with disabilities.

Can schools provide additional services to children before they are identified as needing special education? What activities can local educational agencies (LEAs) support with early intervening funds? Are LEAs required to support these activities?

IDEA allows local educational agencies (LEAs) to use up to 15 percent of their total federal IDEA funding to provide services to students before they are identified as having a disability. This will allow LEAs to use their funds with flexibility and creativity to address difficulties young children may have; prevent a disability from developing; reduce the severity of any potential disability; or identify children earlier as needing to undergo the evaluation process of IDEA.

This is an optional activity at the local level. LEAs can choose whether to conduct this activity, and the authority and responsibility is intentionally broad and expansive. LEAs can use early intervening funds to support professional development activities, educational supports and services, positive behavioral supports and evaluations, or other activities to help children succeed in the general education curriculum.

Private Schools

What rights are provided to children with disabilities, and their parents, who voluntarily enroll in private schools?

Children with disabilities should not be excluded from special education evaluations or services simply because their parents choose to place them in private schools. Therefore, under IDEA, children with disabilities who are enrolled in private schools by their parents are entitled to evaluations and, if necessary, special education and related services from the local educational agency (LEA) with jurisdiction over the district in which the private school is located. Such special education and related services must be equitable to what is provided to the LEA's public school children. In addition, the LEA must consult with representatives of the parents and the private schools to ensure that the design and delivery of evaluations and special education and related services meet the children's needs.

What are the obligations of local educational agencies (LEAs) in providing for children with disabilities who are enrolled by their parents in private schools?

Local educational agencies (LEAs) are required to provide special education and related services for children with disabilities who are enrolled by their parents in private schools located in the school district served by the LEA. LEAs can provide services, including direct services, such as professional development for teachers, physical therapy, occupational therapy, and provide educational materials in specialized formats. Funds for these services must be equal to a proportionate amount of the federal funds made available to the LEA under Part B of IDEA as related to the number of private school students located in the LEA. State and local funds may be used to supplement federal funds, but may not be used in place of federal money to comply with this requirement.

Special education and related services may be provided to children with disabilities on the premises of private schools to the extent consistent with state and federal law or, when appropriate, at a location and in a manner deemed appropriate by the LEA in consultation with representatives from the private schools and the parents. Special education and related services must be provided by employees of a public agency or through contract by the public agency with another entity, and be secular, neutral, and non-ideological. The funds used to provide the special education and related services must be controlled and administered by a public agency. In addition, the LEA must provide the state educational agency (SEA) the number of children enrolled by their parents in private schools evaluated by the LEA, the number of such children determined to be children with disabilities, and the number of children served.

Charter Schools

Are charter schools required to serve students with disabilities?

Yes. Charter schools are required to serve children with disabilities in accordance with IDEA, state law, and the state's charter school statute.

How and when must charter schools that are part of a local educational agency (LEA) receive funds?

A local educational agency (LEA) must provide charter schools in its district with IDEA funds on the same basis that it provides funds to its other public schools, including proportional distribution based on the relative enrollment of children with disabilities. These funds must be distributed by the LEA at the same time as it distributes other federal funds to its other public schools.

Must a local educational agency (LEA) provide services to students with disabilities that are attending charter schools within the LEA?

If the local educational agency (LEA) has a policy or practice of providing supplementary services, including related services, to its other public schools, then the LEA must also serve children with disabilities attending its charter schools in the same manner and to the same extent, including direct services.

New State Policies

What are the new requirements to address over-identification of children, particularly minority children, for special education?

Based on numerous studies and reports, Congress concluded that some students are being inappropriately identified as having a disability, or being identified in the wrong disability category, largely due to their race or ethnicity. This is an unacceptable practice, and states and school districts should take positive steps to eliminate this problem. Accordingly, IDEA requires states to develop policies and procedures to prevent the inappropriate over-identification or disproportionate representation by race and ethnicity of children as having a disability, or as having a particular disability. States are also required to collect and report data on this issue.

Based on these policies and data, states will be required to help LEAs reduce inappropriate identification and over-identification, or disproportionate identification, by reviewing their policies and procedures, updating evaluation and referral procedures, and potentially requiring school districts to use early intervening funds to address the problem. It is important that the Department of Education and the states use their significant flexibility to develop appropriate policies to reduce inappropriate identification and over-identification, or disproportionate identification, without resorting to quotas. For example, states can examine historical trends in districts and review records to ensure that a pattern of over-identification does not inappropriately place a larger number of students of a particular ethnic or racial background in special education.

What are the new requirements about medication for children?

Parents should not be forced to medicate their children as a condition of the child attending school, and school personnel should not attempt to make medical diagnoses that should rightly be made by trained medical personnel. To ensure the rights of parents are protected, the law requires that each state prohibit state and local educational agency personnel from requiring a child to obtain a prescription for a controlled substance as a condition of attending school, receiving services, or receiving an evaluation for a disability. This requirement was included to ensure that parents are not coerced into placing their children on certain drugs (e.g., Ritalin) so that their children can go to school. School personnel are not licensed medical practitioners, and should not be making medical decisions or imposing such decisions on parents.

The law does allow school personnel to continue to share observations about a child's academic achievement, functional performance, or behavior management with parents so that parents are aware of the child's performance during the school day. Parents can then use that information and consult with appropriate medical practitioners for more information if they feel medication is necessary or beneficial to helping improve their child's academic achievement.

Does IDEA create a national special education curriculum?

No. IDEA clearly prohibits the Department from mandating, directing, or controlling the curriculum decisions of state or local educational agencies or the specific instructional content, academic achievement standards, assessments, or programs of instruction. The federal government plays a supporting role in funding education and shaping overall policy goals, but these important decisions are appropriately left to states and local school districts.

Monitoring and Enforcement

The U.S. Department of Education is tasked with ensuring that states are effectively implementing the law and providing a free appropriate public education to students with disabilities. In order to ensure that this happens, IDEA 2004 includes major changes to the monitoring system by laying out a clear set of priorities for the Secretary to adhere to when developing a monitoring and enforcement system. The Secretary will then use data gathered by monitoring visits and state reports to determine whether states are fulfilling their obligations under the law, and take appropriate compliance actions based on that information.

Who will develop the indicators used for the new monitoring and enforcement provisions?

The U.S. Department of Education will develop a framework of the data sets the department will use to develop the monitoring system included in IDEA. This system must focus on key components of the law designed to improve educational results and functional outcomes for children with disabilities. The Secretary will publish these indicators in the Federal Register for public comment and review.

Primarily, the Secretary will focus on indicators that examine the provision of a free appropriate public education in the least restrictive environment, state exercise of general supervisory authority, and the disproportionate representation of racial and ethnic groups in special education and related services. The Secretary may establish additional areas of focus at her discretion.

Can the Secretary force a state to change its targets or establish specific targets?

No. States develop their own plans for monitoring and enforcement, which include targets for performance. The Secretary has the authority to approve or disapprove of the state plan. During the approval process the Secretary may work with states to ensure that the plan is sufficiently rigorous. If the Secretary disapproves the plan, the state has the ability to appeal the Secretary's decision and have the Secretary review the decision to reject the plan. The Secretary does not have the authority under IDEA to impose a specific target or targets for the indicators.

Does the Secretary have to impose sanctions?

Yes, the Secretary has an obligation to enforce the law. IDEA provides an array of enforcement options to the Secretary if a determination is made that a state is not meeting the requirements and purposes of the Act. The Secretary has considerable latitude to work with states to ensure that they meet the requirements and purposes of the Act, but once the need for an enforcement action is necessary, the Secretary must take action.

Are states required to monitor LEA progress in implementing the Act?

Yes. IDEA requires that states monitor and enforce the provisions of the Act as implemented by LEAs. States are required to take appropriate enforcement actions when necessary to ensure that all students with disabilities have access to a free appropriate public education in the least restrictive environment.

Questions and Answers about State and District-Wide Assessments

Overview

Requirements for including all children in assessments are based on a number of federal laws, including Section 504 of the Rehabilitation Act of 1973 (Section 504), Title II of the Americans with Disabilities Act of 1990 (ADA), Title I of the Elementary and Secondary Education Act (Title I), and the Individuals with Disabilities Education Act Amendments of 1997 (IDEA). Assessment is often associated with direct individual benefits such as promotion, graduation, and access to educational services. In addition, assessment is an integral aspect of educational accountability systems that provide valuable information which benefits individual students by measuring individual progress against standards or by evaluating programs.

Title I and IDEA include a number of specific requirements for including all children in assessments. In adding these requirements, Congress recognized that many students were not experiencing levels of achievement in school that would enable them to successfully pursue postsecondary educational or competitive work opportunities. Students with disabilities, minority children, migrant and homeless children, children with limited English proficiency and children in poverty were especially at risk. Many of these children's educational programs were marked by low expectations, limited accountability for results, and exposure to a poorer curriculum than that offered to other children.

Congress's findings for the IDEA 1997 amendments noted that "the implementation of this Act has been impeded by low expectations. . . . Over twenty years of research and experience has demonstrated that the education of children with disabilities can be made more effective by having high expectations for such children and ensuring their access in the general curriculum to the maximum extent possible."

According to the Report from the Committee on Labor and Human Resources of May 9, 1997, IDEA provided parents and educators with tools to "promote improved educational results for children with disabilities through early intervention, preschool, and educational experiences that prepare them for later educational challenges and employment." The Report further notes that:

- The new focus is intended to produce attention to the accommodations and adjustments necessary for disabled children to access the general education curriculum and the special services which may be necessary for appropriate participation.

- Children with disabilities must be included in State and district-wide assessments of student progress with individual modifications and accommodations as needed. Thus, the bill requires that the IEP include a statement of any individual modifications in the administration of State and district-wide assessments.

This next section is provided in response to frequently asked questions submitted to the Office of Special Education Program by parents, teachers, assessment coordinators, State education agency staff, and other policy makers. In some cases, the responses provided are clarifications of legal issues. In other instances, the responses are intended to stimulate reflection about the implications of policies and practices for students with disabilities. Clearly, high expectations for students entail high expectations for teachers and schools. This document is intended not only to provide guidance in meeting specific legal requirements, but also to help achieve the benefits of these provisions for students with disabilities.

Accountability

Question: Are students with disabilities required to participate in a State's accountability system?

Although IDEA makes no specific reference as to how States include children with disabilities in the State accountability system, IDEA requires States to establish performance goals and indicators for children with disabilities—consistent to the maximum extent appropriate with other goals and standards for all children established by the State—and to report on progress toward meeting those goals.

Under Title I of the Elementary and Secondary Education Act, in the 2000–01 school year, each State must have a State assessment system that serves as the primary means for determining whether schools and districts receiving Title I funds are making adequate yearly progress toward enabling all students in Title I schools to reach high standards. All students with disabilities in those schools must be included in the State assessment system, and the scores of students with disabilities must be included in the assessment system for purposes of public reporting and school and district accountability. Under Title I, State assessment systems must assign a score, for accountability purposes, to every student who has attended school within a single school district for a full academic year. And, States must explain how scores from alternate assessments are integrated into their accountability systems.

Question: How do States and LEAs use their assessment results?

Under IDEA, States must use information about the performance of children with disabilities in State and district-wide assessment programs to revise their State Improvement Plans as needed to improve their performance. Under Title I, States and LEAs also use the results to review the performance of LEAs and schools, respectively, and to identify LEAs and schools in need of improvement. States and LEAs also use results for rewards and sanctions for schools and districts, and some for decisions about student promotion or graduation. Assessment results can also be used in planning teacher training, summer school and after school programs, and in reviewing alignment between assessments and curriculum. These are State and local district decisions. In addition, IEP teams can consider individual assessment results as they develop programs for students with disabilities.

IEP Processes

Question: What is the role of the IEP team in determining whether the child will participate in general or alternate assessments?

The IEP team determines *how* the child participates in State and district-wide assessments of student achievement. The IEP team determines if any individual modifications in administration are needed in order for the student to participate in the assessment. If the IEP team determines that the child will not participate in a particular State or district-wide assessment of student achievement (or part of an assessment), the IEP team states why the assessment is not appropriate for the child and how the child will be assessed. IEP teams should have the level of expertise needed to make these decisions in an effective manner.

Question: May IEP teams exempt children with disabilities from participating in the State or district-wide assessment program?

No. The IEP team determines HOW individual students with disabilities participate in assessment programs, NOT WHETHER. The only students with disabilities who are exempted from participation in general State and district-wide assessment programs are students with disabilities convicted as adults under State law and incarcerated in adult prisons (34 CFR §300.311(b)(1)). With this statutory exception, there should be no language in State or district assessment guidelines, rules, or regulations that permits IEP teams to exempt students from State or district-wide assessment programs.

Section 504 prohibits exclusion from participation of, denial of benefits to, or discrimination against, individuals with disabilities on the basis of their disability in federally assisted programs or activities. Title II of the ADA provides that no qualified individual with a disability shall, by reason of such disability, be excluded from participation in or be denied the benefits of the services, programs, or activities of a public entity or be subjected to discrimination by such an entity.

Inclusion in assessments provides valuable information which benefits students either by indicating individual progress against standards or in evaluating educational programs. In some States, participation in assessments is a means to access benefits such as promotion and graduation. Given these benefits, exclusion from assessment programs based on disability would potentially violate Section 504 and Title II of the ADA.

Question: Can the IEP statement of how the child will participate in State and district-wide assessments of student achievement be changed without reconvening the IEP team?

No. If the IEP team wishes to modify a provision of the IEP, it must meet again to make the change.

Parental Permission

Question: Is parental permission required for children with disabilities to participate in State and district-wide assessment programs if parental permission is not required for the participation of non-disabled students?

No. If parental permission is not required for participation in the State and district-wide assessment programs for non-disabled children, it is not required for children with disabilities. However, parents of children with disabilities as members of the IEP team will be involved in IEP team decisions on how an individual child will participate in such assessment programs.

Question: If a State permits parents of non-disabled children to choose not to have their child participate in State or district-wide assessments, do parents of children with disabilities have the same right in regard to assessments and alternate assessments?

Yes. Parents of a child with a disability should have the same right to "opt out" as parents of non-disabled students consistent with any allowable justification criteria established by the SEA or LEA. Denying parents of children with disabilities the same rights afforded parents of non-disabled children would raise concerns about discrimination on the basis of disability. However, parents and students should be informed of the consequences of participation and non-participation in State or district-wide assessments. For example, parents should know that State and district-wide assessments can improve accountability and promote services that better meet the needs of the participating students, while non-participation may limit opportunities for promotion, graduation and access to programs. Parents should not be pressured to "opt out" of assessment programs.

Most States already keep track of students who are "opted out" of assessment programs by parents. States and districts should keep track of parent-requested "opt out" exemptions for students with disabilities disaggregated from those for students without disabilities. This should help the State to determine if "opting out" pressure is occurring.

Accommodations and Modifications

Question: Can the SEA or LEA limit the authority of the IEP team to select individual accommodations and modifications in administration needed for a child to participate in the assessment?

No. 34 CFR §300.347(a)(5)(I) requires that the IEP team have the responsibility and the authority to determine what, if any, individual modifications in the administration of State or district-wide assessments of student achievement are needed in order for a particular child with a disability to participate in the assessment. If the IEP Team determines that individual modifications in the administration of State or district-wide assessments of student achievement are needed, the Team must include a statement of any such modifications in the IEP. In addition, §300.138(a) requires that appropriate accommodations and modifications in administration of State or district-wide assessments must be provided if necessary to ensure the participation of children with disabilities in those assessments. As part of each State's general supervision responsibility under §300.600, it must ensure that these requirements are carried out. States that have developed a comprehensive policy governing the use of testing accommodations (including the conditions and instructions for appropriate use of specific accommodations and how scores are to be reported and used) need to ensure that they are consistent with this IDEA requirement.

At the same time, IEP teams need to understand and consider the implications of SEA/LEA policies on the reporting and use of scores in addressing what individual modifications and accommodations are appropriate for an individual child with a disability. SEAs and LEAs should carefully consider the intended and unintended consequences of accommodation policies that may impact on student opportunities such as promotion or graduation (e.g., receipt of a regular diploma, a certificate of attendance, etc.). Parents and students need to be fully informed of any consequences of such policies.

A major challenge for assessment programs is how to maintain assessment rigor (reliability and validity of assessments), implement and protect the individual rights of students, and simultaneously ensure that schools teach all children what they need to know and to do (knowledge and skills). Much of the current research on accommodations and modifications is inconclusive, so in many cases the impact of specific accommodations is not known. Continued research is underway, and more is needed.

A number of legal principles and concerns apply if a student may be denied benefits such as promotion or graduation because of questionable validation of accommodations. One solution suggested by the National Center on Educational Outcomes (NCEO) at the University of Minnesota is to collect and use additional evidence that allows the student to demonstrate competency in lieu of a single test score. Further information is available from the NCEO (612-626-1530; www.coled.umn.edu/NCEO).

Alternate Assessments

Question: What is an alternate assessment?

Generally, an alternate assessment is understood to mean an assessment designed for those students with disabilities who are unable to participate in general large-scale assessments used by a school district or State, even when accommodations or modifications are provided. The alternate assessment provides a mechanism for students, including those with the most significant disabilities, to participate in and benefit from assessment programs.

Alternate assessments need to be aligned with the general curriculum standards set for all students and should not be assumed appropriate only for those students with significant cognitive impairments. The need for alternate assessments depends on the individual needs of the child, not the category of the child's disability. Although it is expected that the number of students participating in alternate assessments will be relatively small, participation in alternate assessments should not, in and of itself, preclude students from access to the same benefits available to non-disabled students for their participation. Thus, the alternate assessment is sufficiently flexible to meet the needs of difficult-to-assess students with disabilities who may need the alternate assessment to demonstrate competency for benefits such as promotion or a diploma. It may also enable IEP teams, including informed parents, to make choices about appropriate participation that may lead to an IEP diploma or other type of certification.

Question: Do the requirements to establish participation guidelines for alternate assessments and to develop alternate assessments apply to both SEAs and LEAs?

Yes. 34 CFR §300.138 specifically requires inclusion of children with disabilities in both State and district-wide assessment programs and requires both the SEA and the LEA, as appropriate, to develop guidelines for the participation of children with disabilities in alternate assessments for those children who cannot participate in State and district-wide assessments, and develop alternate assessments.

Of course, if an LEA does not conduct district-wide assessments other than those that are part of the State assessment program, then the LEA would follow SEA guidelines and use the SEA alternate assessment(s). The requirements apply to district-wide assessments regardless of whether or not there is a State assessment.

Question: If the SEA has developed guidelines for participation in State alternate assessments, can the LEA use those guidelines to meet its LEA responsibility?

There is nothing that prohibits the LEA from adopting the SEA guidelines if the SEA guidelines are consistent with the assessment program objectives of LEA district-wide assessments. However, if the district-wide assessment is used for significantly different purposes than the State assessment, the LEA should ensure that the participation guidelines developed for the State assessment are consistent with the purposes of the district-wide assessment, or should develop guidelines consistent with the purposes of its district-wide assessment.

Question: Does a State need to have an alternate assessment for each content area assessed in the regular assessment program?

The number of alternate assessments is a State decision. As in many State and district-wide assessment programs, the assessment may consist of multiple components or batteries. The alternate assessment(s) should at a minimum assess the broad content areas such as communication, mathematics, social studies, science, etc., assessed in the State or district-wide assessment. The alternate assessment may assess additional content, including functional skills, as determined necessary by the State or local district. Functional skills can also be aligned to State standards as real world indicators of progress toward those standards. Title I requires that at a minimum reading/language arts and math are assessed, but Title I also requires that if other subject areas are assessed by the State for Title I purposes, then all students in Title I schools in the grades assessed need to be assessed in those content areas as well. The purpose of an alternate assessment should match at a minimum the purpose of the assessment to which it is intended to serve as an alternate.

Question: Can LEAs use the State alternate assessment to meet its obligation to develop an alternate to its district-wide assessment?

The issue is alignment between the alternate assessment and the large-scale assessment. Whether an alternate assessment developed by the State for use with a State-wide assessment is also an appropriate alternate assessment to the local district-wide assessment depends upon the type of alternate assessment selected, the nature of the district-wide assessment, the content measured, and the purposes for which the results will be used. The purpose of an alternate assessment should match at a minimum the purpose of the assessment to which it is intended to serve as an alternate.

Question: Can LEAs use their own alternate assessment or must they use the State's alternate assessment?

In States with statewide assessment programs, local districts must administer the State alternate assessment. Moreover, local districts must develop and conduct alternate assessments if they have district-wide assessments, or use the State alternate if appropriate.

Out-of-Level Testing

Question: Is out-of-level testing by States acceptable?

"Out-of-level testing" means assessing students in one grade level using versions of tests that were designed for students in other (usually lower) grade levels. Some States allow out-of-level testing in an effort to limit student frustration and provide appropriate assessment levels. Although IDEA does not specifically prohibit its use, out-of-level testing may be problematic for several reasons when used for accountability purposes. 34 CFR §300.137 requires that the performance goals for children with disabilities should be consistent, to the maximum extent appropriate, with other goals and standards for all children established by the State. The purpose is to maintain high expectations and provide coherent information about student attainment of the State's content and student performance standards.

Out-of-level testing may not assess the same content standards at the same levels as are assessed in the "grade-level" assessment. Thus, unless the out-of-level test is designed to yield scores referenced to the appropriate grade-level standards, out-of-level testing may not provide coherent information about student attainment of the State or LEA content and student performance standards. Also, many assessment experts argue that out-of-level testing produces scores that are (even using transformation formulations) insufficiently comparable to allow aggregation, as required by 34 CFR §300.139. If out-of-level tests are used, IEP teams need training and clear information about the statistical appropriateness of administering such tests at each possible level different from the student's grade level.

Out-of-level tests may lower expectations for students, prevent them from demonstrating their full competence, subject them to a lower-level curriculum, and restrict their access to the general curriculum. Important goals of both IDEA and Title I are to maintain high expectations for all children and to ensure that teachers and schools are able to teach diverse learners. Students with disabilities are entitled to the same rich curriculum as their non-disabled peers.

One source for additional information about out-of-level testing is the National Center on Educational Outcomes (NCEO) at the University of Minnesota (612-626-1530; www.coled.umn.edu/NCEO).

Question: Can an out-of-level test be considered an "alternate" assessment?

Out-of-level tests are considered modified administrations of the State or district-wide assessments rather than alternate assessments, and scores on out-of-level tests should be converted to reflect performance at grade level and reported as performance at the grade level at which the child is placed unless such reporting would be statistically inappropriate.

Reporting

Question: IDEA refers to children with disabilities being included in "general State and district-wide assessment programs," but only requires that State education agencies report to the public on the participation and performance of children with disabilities on assessments. Are local education agencies also required to report to the public in a similar fashion?

The IDEA requirement is for reporting by the State education agency. Many States have similar requirements for local education agencies to report similarly on local assessment programs. Under IDEA, this is a State decision.

Question: What are the requirements for aggregation and disaggregation of data? Are aggregation and disaggregation required at the State level only? State level and district level only? Or State level, district level, and site level?

Under IDEA, States must report aggregated data that include the performance of children with disabilities together with all other children and disaggregated data on the performance of children with disabilities. There is no requirement for disaggregation by category of disability, just disaggregation of the performance of children with disabilities separate from the performance of non-disabled children. These reports must be made with the same frequency and in the same detail as reports on the assessment of non-disabled children. For example, if school level results are reported, then school level results for students with disabilities generally must be disaggregated. It is the SEA's decision how to collect sufficient data from LEAs to meet the Federal SEA reporting requirement consistent with these provisions.

Question: What is meant by "statistically sound" in 34 CFR 300.139?

There are at least two issues for consideration. One has to do with the sample size. In some instances, for example if a State chooses to disaggregate by disability categories (not a federal requirement) or report on the performance of students with disabilities in small school districts, the relatively small number of students in that category or district might raise questions about statistical soundness if generalizations are to be made about student performance. A second issue centers around the reporting of performance for students who take non-standard or modified administrations of an assessment. In such cases, there may be questions about the validity of the assessment and its comparability to the standard assessment.

Question: Can a State or local education agency provide individual performance results to its schools, or would this violate the requirement to avoid disclosure of performance results identifiable to individual children?

The reference to disclosure simply refers to the inappropriateness of public reports that deal with samples so small as to publicly disclose the performance of individual students, not to providing results to schools for students served by the school.

Question: To avoid publicly disclosing performance results identifiable to individual students, can a State or local education agency adjust the administrative levels at which it reports these results? For example, can it report the alternate assessment at the district level even though the general assessment is reported at the school level?

Yes, but only if necessary to avoid publicly disclosing results identifiable to individual students.

Bibliography

Acosta, S., & Richards, R. G. (1999). Cursive writing: A multisensory approach. So. California Consortium *Resource directory,* International Dyslexia Association, www.retctrpress.com.

Adams, M. J. (1990). *Beginning to read.* Cambridge, MA: MIT Press.

Alarcón-Cazares, M. (1998). Neuroanatomical correlates of reading disability: A twin study: Dissertation Abstracts International: Section B. *The Sciences and Engineering, 58*(10-B), 5662.

Allardice, B. S., & Ginsburg, H. P. (1983). Children's psychological difficulties in mathematics. In Ginsburg, H. P. (Ed.), *The development of mathematical thinking.* New York: Academic Press.

Alley, G., & Deshler, D. (1979). *Teaching the learning disabled adolescent: Strategies and methods.* Denver: Love.

American Academy of Pediatrics. (2000). Diagnosis and evaluation of the child with attention-deficit/hyperactivity disorder (AC0002). *Pediatrics, 105*(5), 1158–1170.

American Academy of Special Education Professionals. (in press). *Educator's Diagnostic Manual of Disabilities and Disorders.* San Francisco, CA: Jossey-Bass.

American Institutes for Research (2005). *Addressing student problem behavior.* Retrieved on May 19, 2005, from www.air.org.

American Psychiatric Association. (1994). *Diagnostic and statistical manual of mental disorders* (4th ed.). Washington, DC: Author.

American Psychiatric Association. (2000). Diagnostic and statistical manual of mental disorders, text revision: DSM-IV-TR (4th ed.). Washington, DC: Author.

Anderson, R. C., Hiebert, E. H., Scott, J. A., & Wilkinson, I. A. (1985). *Becoming a nation of readers. The report of the commission on reading* (p. 7). Washington, DC: National Institute of Education.

Archer, A., & Gleason, M. (2002). *Skills for school success: Book 5.* North Billerica, MA: Curriculum Associates, Inc.

Ariel, A. (1992). *Education of children and adolescents with learning disabilities.* NY: Merrill.

Arnold, L. E., Christopher, J., Huestis, R. D., & Smeltzer, D. J. (1978). Megavitamins for minimal brain dysfunction: A placebo controlled study. *Journal of the American Medical Association, 240,* 2642–2643.

Ascher, M. (1990, February). A river-crossing problem in cross-cultural perspectives. *Mathematics Magazine, 63*(1), 26–29.

Ashbaker, M. H., & Swanson, H. L. (1996). Short-term memory and working memory operations and their contributions to reading in adolescents with and without learning disabilities. *Journal of Abnormal Child Psychology, 18,* 29–45.

Babbitt, B. C., & Miller, S. P. (1997). Using hypermedia to improve the mathematics problem-solving skills of students with learning disabilities. In K. Higgins & R. Boone (Eds.), *Technology for students with learning disabilities* (pp. 91–108). Austin, TX: PRO-ED.

Barkley, R. A. (1997). Behavioral inhibition, sustained attention, and executive functions: Constructing a unifying theory of ADHD. *Psychological Bulletin, 121*(1), 65–94.

Barkley, R. A. (1990). *Attention deficit hyperactivity disorder: A handbook for diagnosis and treatment.* New York: Guilford.

Bateman, B. (1965). An educator's view of a diagnostic approach to learning disorders. In J. Hellmuth (Ed.), *Learning disorders* (Vol. 1, 217–239). Seattle, WA: Special Child.

Behrmann, M., & Schaff, J. (2001). Assisting educators with assistive technology: Enabling children to achieve independence in living and learning. *Children and Families 42*(3), 24–28.

Bender, W. (1997). *Understanding ADHD: A practical guide for teachers and parents.* Upper Saddle River, NJ: Merrill/Prentice Hall.

Bender, W. N. (1992). Learning disabilities. In P. J. McLaughlin & P. Wehman (Eds.), *Developmental Disabilities.* Boston: Andover Medical Publishers.

Bender, W. N. (2001). *Learning disabilities: Characteristics, identification, and teaching strategies* (4th ed.). Boston: Allyn & Bacon.

Bender, W. N. (2002). *Differentiating instruction for students with learning disabilities: Best practices for general and special educators.* Thousand Oaks, CA: Corwin Press.

Berdine, W. H., & Meyer, S. A. (1987). *Assessment in special education.* Boston: Little, Brown.

Bigge, J. L. (1990). *Teaching individuals with physical and multiple disabilities* (3rd ed.). Columbus, OH: Merrill.

Bigge, J., & Stump, C. (1999). *Curriculum, assessment, and instruction for students with disabilities.* Belmont, CA: Wadsworth.

Birsch, J. R. (Ed.). (1999). *Multisensory teaching of basic language skills.* Baltimore, MD: Paul H. Brookes Publishing.

Blair, C., & Scott, K. G. (2002). Proportion of LD placements associated with low socioeconomic status: Evidence for a gradient? *Journal of Special Education, 36,* 14–22.

Bloom, L., & Lahey, M. (1978). *Language development and language disorders.* New York: John Wiley.

Borkowski, J. G., Estrada, M. T., Milstead, M., & Hale, C. A. (1989). General problem-solving skills: Relations between metacognition and strategic processing. *Learning Disability Quarterly, 12,* 57–70.

Bos, C. S., & Filip, D. (1984). Comprehension monitoring in learning disabled and average students. *Journal of Learning Disabilities, 17,* 229–233.

Bowe, F. (2005). *Making inclusion work.* Upper Saddle River, NJ: Merrill/Prentice Hall.

Bradley, L., & Bryant, P. (1985). *Rhyme and reason in reading and spelling.* Ann Arbor, MI: University of Michigan Press.

Bradshaw, J. (2001). *Developmental Disorders of the Fronto-Striatal System.* Philadelphia: Psychiatric Press.

Brown, A. L., & Palincsar, A. S. (1982). Including strategic learning from texts by means of informed, self-control training. *Topics in Learning and Learning Disabilities, 2*(1), 1–17.

Bryan, T. (1997). Assessing the personal and social status of students with learning disabilities. *Learning Disabilities Research & Practice, 12,* 63–76.

Bryan, T., Bay, M., Lopez-Reyna, N., & Donahue, M. (1991). Characteristics of students with learning disabilities: A summary of the extant data base and its implications for educational programs. In J. W. Lloyd, N. N. Singh, & A. C. Repp (Eds.), *The regular education initiative: Alternative perspectives* (pp. 121–131). Sycamore, IL: Sycamore.

Bryan, T. A., & Sullivan-Burstein, R. (1998). Teacher selected strategies for improving homework completion. *Remedial and Special Education, 19,* 263–273.

Burt, S. A., Krueger, R. F., McGue, M., & Iacono, W. G. (2001). Sources of covariation among attention-deficit/hyperactivity disorder, oppositional defiant disorder, and conduct disorder: The importance of shared environment. *Journal of Abnormal Psychology, 110,* 516–525.

Candler, A. C., & Hildreth, B. L. (1990). Characteristics of language disorders in learning disabled students. *Academic Therapy, 25*(3), 333–343.

Castellani, J., & Jeffs, T. (2001). Emerging reading and writing strategies using technology. *Teaching Exceptional Children, 33*(5), 6–67.

Castles, A., Datta, H., Gayan, J., & Olson, R. K. (1999). Varieties of developmental reading disorder: Genetic and environmental influences. *Journal of Experimental Child Psychology, 72,* 73–94.

Cawley, J. F., & Frazita, R. R. (1996). Arithmetic computation abilities of students with learning disabilities: Implications for instruction. *Learning Disabilities Research, 11,* 230–237.

Center for Disease Control (2004). *General lead information: Questions and answers.* Retrieved on July 8, 2005, from www.cdc.gov/nceh/lead/faq/about.htm.

Chan, L. K. S., & Cole, P. G. (1986). The effects of comprehension monitoring training on the reading competence of learning disabled and regular class students. *Remedial and Special Education, 7,* 33–40.

Chard, D. J., & & Dickson, S. V. (1999). Phonological awareness: Instructional and assessment guidelines. *Intervention in Clinic and School, 34*(5), 261–270.

Christianson, J. (1997). Try this framework for grading. *The Special Educator, 12*(22), 9.

Cirino, P. T., Morris, M., & Morris, R. (2002). Neuropsychological concomitants of calculation skills in college students referred for learning disabilities. *Developmental Neuropsychology, 21*(2), 201–218.

Clements, S. D. (1966). *Minimal brain dysfunction in children* (NINDS Monograph No. 3, Public Health Service Bulletin No. 1415). Washington, DC: U.S. Department of Health, Education and Welfare.

Codina, G. E., Yin, Z., Katims, D. S., and Zapata, J. T. (1998). Marijuana use and academic achievement among Mexican American school-age students: Underlying psychosocial and behavioral characteristics. *J. Child & Adolescent Substance Abuse, 7*(3), 79–96.

Coles, C. D. (1991). Reading test scores lower in children whose mothers drank alcohol during last trimester of pregnancy. *Neurotoxicology & Teratology, 13,* 357–367.

Conte, R. (1991). Attention disorders. In B. Wong (Ed.), *Learning about learning disabilities* (pp. 60–103). San Diego, CA: Academic Press.

Corral, N., & Antia, S. D. (1997, March/April). Self-talk: Strategies for success in math. *TEACHING Exceptional Children, 29*(4), 42–45.

Cott, A. (1972). Megavitamins: The orthomolecular approach to behavioral disorders and learning disabilities. *Academic Therapy, 7*(3), 245–258.

Council for Children with Learning Disabilities. (2000). What are some common signs of learning disabilities? Available at www.ldonline.org/ccldinfo/2.html.

Council for Learning Disabilities (2004). What are Learning Disabilities? Retrieved on May 19, 2005, from www.cldinternational.org/c/@oVxSISRR8S1uo/Pages/scienceP2.html.

Cox, L. S. (1975). Diagnosing and remediating systematic errors in addition and subtraction computations. *The Arithmetic Teacher, 22,* 151–157.

Culbertson, J. L. (1998). Learning disabilities. In T. H. Ollendick & M. J. Herson (Eds.), *Handbook of Child Psychopathology* (3rd ed., pp. 117–155), New York: Plenum Press.

Cullinan, D. (2002). *Students with emotional and behavioral disorders: An introduction for teachers and other helping professionals.* Upper Saddle River, NJ: Merrill/Prentice Hall.

Cuttance, P., & Stokes, S. (2000, January). *Reporting on student and school achievement: The University of Sydney: A research report prepared for the Commonwealth Department of Education, Training and Youth Affairs: Department of Education, Training and Youth Affairs.* Retrieved May 19, 2005, from www.dest.gov.au/schools/publications/2000/cuttance.htm#Ex-3.

Day, V. P., & Elksnin, L. K. (1994). Promoting strategic learning. *Intervention in School and Clinic, 29*(5), 262–270.

De La Paz, S., & Graham, S. (1997). Strategy instruction in planning: Effects on the writing performance and behavior of students with learning difficulties. *Exceptional Children, 63*(2), 167–183.

DeFries, J. C., Gills, J. J., & Wadsworth, S. J. (1993). Genes and genders: A twin study of reading disability. In A. M. Galaburda (Ed.), *Dyslexia and development: Neurobilogical aspects of extra-ordinary brains* (pp. 187–294). Cambridge, MA: Harvard University Press.

Denson, R., Nanson, J. L., & McWatters, M. A. (1994). Smoking mothers more likely to have hyperactive children (ADHD). *Children Canadian Psychiatric Association Journal, 20,* 183–187.

Deshler, D. D., Shumaker, J. B., Alley, G. R., Clark, F. L., & Warner, M. M. (1981). Paraphrasing strategy. University of Kansas, Institute for Research in Learning Disabilities (Contract No. 300-77-0494). Washington, DC: Bureau of Education for the Handicapped.

Deutsch-Smith, D. (2004). *Introduction to special education: Teaching in an age of opportunity* (5th ed.). Boston: Allyn & Bacon.

DuPaul, G. J., & Stoner, G. (1994). *ADHD in the schools: Assessment and intervention strategies.* New York: Guilford Press.

DuPaul, G. J., & Stoner, G. (2002). Interventions for attention problems. In M. R. Shinn, H. M. Walker, & G. Stoner (Eds.), *Interventions for academic and behavior problems II: Preventive and remedial approaches* (pp. 913–938). Bethesda, MD: National Association of School Psychologists.

Elbaum, B. E., Vaughn, S., Hughes, M., & Moody, S. W. (1999). Grouping practices for reading outcomes for students with disabilities. *Exceptional Children, 65*(3), 399–415.

Elliott, R. (1987). *Litigating intelligence: IQ tests, special education, and social science in the courtroom.* Dover, MA: Auburn House.

Ellis, E., Deshler, D., Lenz, B., Schumaker, J., & Clark, F. (1991). An instructional model for teaching learning strategies. *Focus on Exceptional Children, 23*(6), 1–23.

Ellis, E. S. (1994). Integrating writing strategy instruction with content-area instruction: Part II-writing process. *Intervention in School and Clinic, 29,* 219–228.

Engelmann, B. (1977). Sequencing cognitive and academic tasks. In R. Kneedler & S. Tarver (Eds.), *Changing perspectives in special education* (pp. 46–61). Columbus, OH: Merrill.

Englert, C. S., & Mariage, T. V. (1991). Shared understandings: Structuring the writing experience through dialogue. *Journal of Learning Disabilities, 24*(6), 330–342.

Englert, C. S., Raphael, T. E., & Anderson, L. M. (1992). Socially mediated instruction: Improving students' knowledge and talk about writing. *Elementary School Journal, 92,* 411–449.

Englert, C. S. (1984). Measuring the teacher's effectiveness from the teacher's point of view. *Focus on Exceptional Children, 17*(2), 1–14.

Englert, C. S., Garmon, A., Mariage, T., Rozendal, M., Tarrant, K., & Urba, J. (1995). The early literacy project: Connecting across the literacy curriculum. *Learning Disability Quarterly, 18,* 253–275.

Feingold, B. (1975). Hyperkinesis and learning disabilities linked to artificial food flavors and colors. *American Journal of Nursing, 75,* 797–803.

Field, S., & Hoffman, A. (1994). Development of a model for self-determination. *Career Development for Exceptional Individuals, 17,* 159–169.

Field, S., Hoffman, A., & Spezia, S. (1998). *Self-determination strategies for adolescents in transition.* Austin, TX: PRO-ED.

Finland Department of Public Health (1994). *Children age 14 still show harmful effects if mothers smoked during pregnancy.* Retrieved May 19, 2005, from www.droit-air-pur.com.

Fletcher, J., & Forman, B. (1994). Issues in definitions and measurement of learning disabilities. In G. Lyon (Ed.), *Frames of reference for the assessment of children with learning disabilities* (pp. 185–202). Baltimore, MD: Paul H. Brookes.

Forness, S. R., & Kavale, K. A. (2001). ADHD and a return to the medical model of special education. *Education and Treatment of Children, 24*(3), 224–247.

Forness, S. R., Kavale, K. A., & San Miguel, S. (1998). The psychiatric comorbidity hypothesis revisited. *Learning Disability Quarterly, 21,* 203–207.

Forness, S. R., & Kavale, K. A. (2002). Impact of ADHD on school systems. In P. Jensen & J. R. Cooper (Eds.), *NIH consensus conference on ADHD.*

Foss, B. (2004). *Non verbal learning disorders.* Retrieved on July 8, 2005, from www.nldline.com/.

Franklin Electronic Publishers, 800/BOOKMAN.

Frechtling, J. A. (1991). Performance assessment: Moonstruck or the real thing? *Educational Measurement: Issues and Practices, 10*(4), 23–25.

Fried, P., & Watkinson, B. (1992). Marijuana use increases symptoms of attention deficit disorder in first grade children. *Neurotoxicology and Teratology, 14,* 299–311.

Friend, M. (2005). *Special education: Contemporary perspectives for school professionals.* Boston: Allyn & Bacon.

Fuchs, D. M., Fuchs, L. S., Mathes, P. G., Lipsey, M. W., & Roberts, P. H. (2001). *Is "learning disabilities" just a fancy term for low achievement: A meta-analysis of reading differences between low achievers with and without the label.* Retrieved May 19, 2005, from www.air.org/ldsummit.

Fuchs, D., Fuchs, L., Mathes, P. H., & Simmons, D.C. (1997). Peer-assisted strategies: making classrooms more responsive to diversity. *American Educational Research Journal, 34,* 174–206.

Fuchs, L. S., & Fuchs, D. (1997). Use of curriculum-based measurement in identifying students with learning disabilities. *Focus on Exceptional Children, 30,* 1–16.

Fuchs, L. S., & Fuchs, D. (2001). Principles for the prevention and intervention of mathematics difficulties. *Learning Disabilities Research & Practice, 16,* 85–95.

Fulk, B. M., Brigham, F. J., & Lohman, D. A. (1998). Motivation and self-regulation: A comparison of students with learning and behavior problems. *Remedial and Special Education, 19*(5), 300–309.

Gable, R. A., Sugai, G. M., Lewis, T. J., Nelson, J. R., Cheney, D., Safran, S. P., & Safran, J. S. (1997). *Individual and systemic approaches to collaboration and consultation.* Reston, VA: Council for Children with Behavioral Disorders.

Gargiulo, R. (2004). *Special education in contemporary society: An introduction to exceptionality.* Belmont, CA: Thompson.

Garnett, K. (1998). *Math learning disabilities.* Retrieved May 19, 2005, from http://ldonline .org/ld_indepth/math_skills/garnett.html.

Gearheart, C., & Gearheart, B. (1990). *Introduction to special education assessment: Principles and practices.* Denver, CO: Love.

Gersten, R., & Baker, S. (1999). *Teaching expressive writing to students with learning disabilities: a meta-analysis.* Eugene, OR: University of Oregon.

Gersten, R., Carnine, D., & Woodward, J. (1987). Direct instruction research: The third decade. *Remedial and Special Education, 8*(6), 48–56.

Gersten, R., Williams, J., Fuchs, L., & Baker, S. (1998). *Improving reading comprehension for children with learning disabilities.* Final Report: Section 1, U.S. Department of Education Contract HS 921700. Washington, DC: U.S. Department of Education.

Gilger, J. (2001, December). Current issues in the neurology and genetics of learning-related traits and disorders: Introduction to the special issue. *Journal of Learning Disabilities, 34,* 490–491.

Gill, M. (2001). *Define and explain task analysis.* EDUC 6254 Bulletin Board. Retrieved May 19, 2005, from http://education.uncc.edu/galloway/_disc15/00000042.htm.

Glasgow City Council (2003). *Devloping literacy in early stages: Phonological awareness.* Glasgow Literacy Imporvement Program.

Goldman, S. R., Hasselbring, T. S., & The Cognition Technology Group at Vanderbilt (1977). Achieving meaningful mathematics literacy for students with learning disabilities. *Journal of Learning Disabilities, 30*(2), 198–208.

Goldman, J., & Pellegrino, J. W. (1987). Information processing and microcomputer technology: Where do we go from here? *Journal of Learning Disabilities, 20,* 336–340.

Goodman, Y., & Burke, C. (1972). *Reading miscue inventory manual: Procedure for diagnosis and evaluation.* New York: Macmillan.

Government of British Columbia. (2004). *BC Performance Standards.* Retrieved May 19, 2005, from www.bced.gov.bc.ca/perf_stands/.

Graham, S., & Harris, K. (1989a). Cognitive training: Implications for written language. In J. Hughes & R. Hall (Eds.), *Cognitive behavioral psychology in the schools: A comprehensive handbook* (pp. 247–279). New York: Guilford.

Graham, S., Harris, K. R., & Reid, R. (1992). Developing self-regulated learners. *Focus on Exceptional Children, 24*(6), 1–16.

Gresham, F. M. (1982). Misguided mainstreaming: The case for social skills training with handicapped children. *Exceptional Children, 48*(5), 422–431.

Grossman, H. J. (Ed.). (1983). *Manual on terminology and classification in mental retardation* (3rd ed., rev.). Washington, DC: American Association on Mental Deficiency.

Gusella, J. L., & Fried, P. A. (1984). Language skills damage easily from light social drinking. *Neurobehavioral Toxicology & Teratology, 6,* 13–17.

Hallahan, D. P. (1998). Teach. Don't flinch. *DLD Times, 16*(1), 1, 4.

Hallahan, D. P., & Kauffman, J. M. (2003). *Exceptional children: Introduction to special education* (9th ed.). Boston: Allyn & Bacon.

Hallahan, D. P., Kauffman, J. M., & Lloyd, J. W. (1999). *Introduction to learning disabilities* (2nd ed.). Boston: Allyn & Bacon.

Hallowell, E. (1994). *Driven to distraction: Recognizing and coping with attention deficit disorder from childhood through adulthood.* Tappan, NJ: Simon & Schuster.

Haney, W., & Madaus, G. (1989). Searching for alternatives to standardized tests: Whys, whats, and whitlers. *Phi Delta Kappan, 70*(9), 683–687.

Hardman, M. L., Drew, C. J., & Egan, M. W. (2003). *Human exceptionality: Society, school and family* (7th ed.). Boston: Allyn & Bacon.

Hardman, M. L., Drew, C. J., & Egan, M. W. (2005). *Human exceptionality: Society, school and family* (8th ed.). Boston: Allyn & Bacon.

Hart, D. (1994). *Authentic assessment: A handbook for educators.* Menlo Park, CA: Addison-Wesley.

Heath Resource Center. (2004). *College freshmen with disabilities: A biennial statistical profile.* Retrieved May 19, 2005, from www.heath .gwu.edu.

Heaton, S., & O'Shea, D. J. (1995). Using mnemonics to mkake mnemonics. *Teaching Exceptional Children, 28*(1), 34–36.

Henderson, A. T., & Berla, N. (Eds.) (1994). *A new generation of evidence: The family is critical to student achievement* (ED 375 968). Washington, DC: National Committee for Citizens in Education.

Henderson, E. (1985). *Teaching spelling.* Boston: Houghton Mifflin.

Henry, L. A. (2001). How does the severity of a learning disability affect working memory performance? *Memory, 9*(4–6), 233–247.

Heward, W. L. (2003). *Exceptional children: An introduction to special education* (8th ed.). Englewood Cliffs, NJ: Prentice Hall.

Heward, W. L., & Orlansky, M. D. (1992). *Exceptional children: An introductory survey of special education* (4th ed.). New York: Merrill.

Holt, S. B., & O'Tuel, F. S. (1989). The effect of sustained silent reading and writing on achievement and attitudes of seventh and eighth grade students reading two years below grade level. *Reading Improvement, 26,* 290–297.

Hoy, C., & Gregg, N. (1994). *Assessment: The special educator's role.* Pacific Grove, CA: Brookes/Cole.

Hunt, N., & Marshall, K. (2002). *Exceptional children and youth* (3rd ed.). Boston: Houghton Mifflin.

Hunt, N., & Marshall, K. (2005). *Exceptional children and youth* (4th ed.). Boston: Houghton Mifflin.

Hutchinson, N. L., Freeman, J. G., & Bell, K. (2002). Children and adolescents with learning disabilities: Case studies of social relations in the inclusive classrooms. In B. Y. L. Wong & M. Donahue (Eds.), *The social dimension of learning disabilities* (pp. 189–214), Mahwah, NJ: Lawrence Erlbaum Associates.

Idol, L. (1987). Group story mapping: A comprehensive strategy for both skilled and unskilled readers. *Journal of Learning Disabilities, 20,* 196–205.

Idol-Maestas, L. (1985). Getting ready to read: Guided probing for poor comprehenders. *Learning Disability Quarterly, 8,* 243–254.

Individuals with Disabilities Education Act. (2004). Washington, DC: U.S. Government Printing Office.

Jenkins, J., & O'Connor, R. (2001). *Early identification and intervention for young children with reading/learning disabilities.* Paper presented at the 2001 LD Summit: Building a Foundation for the Future. Retrieved July 1, 2003, from www.air.org/ldsummit.

Jensen, P. S., Martin, D., & Cantwell, D. P. (1997). Comorbidity in ADHD: Implications for research, practice, and DSM-IV. *Journal of the American Academy of Child and Adolescent Psychiatry, 36,* 1065–1079.

Jensen, P. S., Shertvette, R. R., Zenakis, S. N., & Ritchters, J. (1993). Anxiety and depressive disorders in attention deficit disorder with hyperactivity: New findings. *American Journal of Psychiatry, 150,* 1203–1209.

John, J. L. (1985). *Basic reading inventory* (3rd ed.). Boise, Iowa: Kendall-Hunt.

Johnson, D. J., & Myklebust, H. R. (1967). *Learning disabilities: Educational principles and practices* (Report No. EC-001-107). New York: Grune & Stratton, Inc. (ERIC Document Reproduction Service No. ED 021 352).

Jordan, N. C., & Hanich, L. B. (2003). Mathematical thinking in second-grade children with different forms of LD. *Journal of Learning Disabilities, 33,* 567–578.

Kamphaus, E. W. (1993). *Clinical assessment of children's intelligence.* Boston: Allyn & Bacon.

Kavale, K., & Forness, S. (1983) Hyperactivity and diet treatment: A meta-analysis of the Feingold hypothesis. *Journal of Learning Disabilities, 16*(6), 324–330.

Kavale, K., and Forness, S. (1996). Social skill deficits and learning disabilities. A meta-analysis. *Journal of Learning Disabilities, 29*(3), 226–237.

Keogh, B., & Margolis, T. (1976). Learn to labor and wait: Attentional problems of children with learning disorders. *Journal of Learning Disabilities, 9,* 276–286.

King-Sears, M. E. (1994). *Curriculum based assessment in special education.* San Diego, CA: Singular.

Kirk, S. A. (1962). *Educating exceptional children.* Boston: Houghton Mifflin.

Kirk, S. A. (1963). Behavioral diagnosis and remediation of learning disabilities. In *Proceedings of the Conference on the Exploration into the Problems of the Perceptually Handicapped Child.* Evanston, IL: Fund for the Perceptually Handicapped Child.

Kirk, S., Gallagher, J., & Anastasiow, N. (2005). *Educating exceptional children* (11th ed.). Boston: Houghton Mifflin.

Klinger, J., Vaughn, S., Hughes, M., Schumm, J., & Erlbaum, B. (1998). Outcomes for students with and without learning disabilities in inclusive classrooms. *Learning Disabilities Research and Practice, 13,* 153–161.

Kluwe, R. (1987). Executive decisions and regulation of problem-solving behavior. In F. Weinert & R. Kluwe (Eds.), *Metacognition, motivation and understanding* (pp. 31–64). Hillsdale, NJ: Erlbaum.

Kotkin, R. A., Forness, S. R., & Kavale, K. A. (2001). Comorbid ADHD and learning disabilities: Diagnosis, special education, and intervention. In D. P. Hallahan & B. K. Keogh (Eds.), *Research and global perspectives in learning disabilities: Essay in honor of William M. Cruickshank* (pp. 43–63). Mahwah, NJ: Lawrence Erlbaum Associates.

Kruger, K., Kruger, J., Hugo, R., & Campbell, N. (2001). Relationship patterns between CAPD and language disorders, learning disabilities, and sensory integration dysfunction. *Communication Disorders Quarterly, 22,* 87.

Lahm, E., & Morrissette, S. (1994, April). *Zap 'em with assistive technology.* Paper presented at the annual meeting of The Council for Exceptional Children, Denver, CO.

Lam, T. C. M. (1995). Fairness in performance assessment. College Park, MD: ERIC Clearinghouse on Assessment and Evaluation. (ERIC Document Reproduction Service No. ED 391982)

Lantoff, J. P. (2004). *Dynamic assessment of L2 development.* Retrieved May 19, 2005, from http://calper.la.psu.edu/dyna_assess.php.

LD Online. (2001). www.ldonline.org.

Lenz, B., Ellis, E. S., & Scanlon, D. (1996). *Teaching learning strategies to adolescents and adults with learning disabilities.* Austin, TX: PRO-ED.

Leonard, C. M. (2001). Imaging brain structure in children: Differentiating language disability and reading disability. *Learning Disability Quarterly, 24,* 158–176.

Lerner, J. (1988). *Learning disabilities: Theories, diagnosis, and teaching strategies* (3rd ed.). Boston: Houghton Mifflin.

Lerner, J. (2000). *Learning disabilities: Theories, diagnosis, and teaching strategies* (8th ed.). Boston: Houghton Mifflin.

Lerner, J. (2003). *Learning disabilities: Theories, diagnosis, and teaching strategies* (9th ed.). Boston: Houghton Mifflin.

Levine, M. D. *Developmental variation and learning disorders* (2nd ed.). www.epsbooks.com.

Levine, M. D. *Educational care: A system for understanding and helping children with learning problems at home and in school.* www.epsbooks.com.

Levine, M. D. *Keeping a head in school.* www.epsbooks.com.

Lewis, B., & Thompson, L. (1992). A study of the development of speech and language disorders in twins. *Journal of Speech and Hearing Research, 35,* 1086–1094.

Liberman, I. Y., & Liberman, A. M. (1990). Whole language versus code emphasis. *Annals of Dyslexia, 40,* 51–75.

Liberman, I., & Shankweiler, D. (1994). Phonology and the problems of learning to read and write. In H. L. Swanson (Ed.), *Advances in learning and behavioral disabilities.* Greenwich, CT: Jai Press.

Linn, R. E., Baker, E. L., & Dunbar, S. B. (1991). Complex, performance-based assessment: Expectations and validation criteria. *Educational Assessment, 20*(8), 15–21.

Lovitt, T. (1978). The learning disabled. In N. Haring (Ed.), *Behavior of exceptional children* (2nd ed., pp. 155–191). Englewood Cliffs, NJ: Prentice Hall.

Lundberg, I., et al. (1988). Effectiveness of an extensive program for stimulating phonological awareness in preschool children. *Reading Research Quarterly, 23*(3), 263–84.

Lyon, G., & Moats, L. (1997). Critical conceptual and methodological considerations in reading intervention research. *Journal of Learning Disabilities, 29*(4), 344–354.

Maker, C. J. (1993). Creativity, intelligence, and problem solving: A definition and design for cross-cultural research and measurement related to giftedness. *Gifted Education International, 9*(2), 68–77.

Makin, M., & Fried, M. (1991). Math, language, & behavior problems elevated in children of smoking parents. *Neurotoxicology and Teratology, Vol. 13.* Retrieved May 19, 2005, from www.droit-air-pur.com.

Majesky, D. (2004). *Assessment to inform: Authentic assessment as a diagnostic tool.* Retrieved May 19, 2005, from www.ohiorc.org/features/spotlight/1,4196,0401_splus,00.shtm.

Mandernach, J. (2003). *Incorporating authentic assessment.* Retrieved May 19, 2005, from http://captain.park.edu/facultydevelopment/authentic_assessment.htm.

Mannuzza, S., Klein, R. G., Bessler, A., Malloy, P., & LaPadula, M. (1998). Adult psychiatric status of hyperactive boys as grown up. *American Journal of Psychiatry, 155,* 493–498.

Manzo, K. K., & Zehr, M. A. (1998). Take note. *Education Week, 18*(3), 3.

Marshall, K., & Hunt, N. (2005). *Exceptional children and youth* (5th ed.). Boston: Houghton Mifflin.

Mathes, P. G., & Fuchs, L. S. (1994). The efficacy of peer tutoring in reading for students with mild disabilities: A best-evidence synthesis. *School Psychology Review, 23*(1), 59–80.

Mathes, P. G., Fuchs, D., Fuchs, L. S., Henley, A. M., & Sanders, A. (1994). Increasing strategic reading practice with Peabody classwide peer tutoring. *Learning Disabilities Research and Practice, 9*(1), 44–48.

McCartney, B. (1994). Auditory processing reduced in school age children exposed to cigarette smoke. *Neurotoxicology and Teratology, Vol. 16*(3). Retrieved May 19, 2005, from www.droit-air-pur.com.

McCoy, E. M., & Prehm, H. J. (1987). *Teaching mainstreamed students. Methods and techniques.* Denver, CO: Love Publishing Company.

McGloughlin, J., & Lewis, R. (1990). *Assessing special students* (3rd ed.). Columbus, OH: Merrill.

McGrady, H. J., Lerner, J. W., & Boscardin, M. L. (2001). The educational lives of students with learning disabilities. In P. Rodis, A. Garrod, & M. L. Boscardin (Eds.), *Learning disabilities and life stories* (pp. 177–193). Boston: Allyn & Bacon.

McIntyre, T. (2004). *Task analysis.* Retrieved on July 8, 2005, from http://maxweber.hunter.cuny.edu/pub/eres/EDSPC715_MCINTYRE/TaskAnalysis.html.

McLoughlin, J. A., & Lewis, R. B. (1990). *Assessing special students* (3rd ed.). Columbus, OH: Merrill.

Mercer, C. D. (1992). Students with learning disabilities (4th ed.). NY: Merrill.

Mercer, C. (1997). *Students with learning disabilities* (5th ed.). Upper Saddle River, NJ: Prentice Hall.

Mercer, C. D., Campbell, K. U., Miller, M. D., Mercer, K. D., and Lane, H. B. (2000). Effects of a reading fluency intervention for middle-schoolers with specific learning disabilities. *Learning Disabilities Research and Practice, 15*(4), 179–189.

Mercer, C. D., Jordan, L., Allsopp, D. H., & Mercer, A. R. (1996). Learning disabilities definitions and criteria used by state education departments. *Learning Disabilities Quarterly, 19*, 217–231.

Merriam-Webster (2005). *Merriam Webster online dictionary.* Retrieved May 19, 2005, from www.m-w.com.

Michaels, C. (1994). *Transition strategies for persons with learning disabilities.* San Diego, CA: Singular.

Montague, M. (1997). Student perception, mathematical problem solving, and learning disabilities. *Remedial and Special Education, 18,* 46–53.

Moore, M. (2004). *How to deal with toxic parents/principals/staff members.* Inspiring Teachers Publishing Inc.: Garland, Texas. Retrieved May 19, 2005, from www.inspiringteachers.com/tips/parents/difficult.html.

Murphy-Brennan, M. G., & Oei, P. S. (1999). Is there evidence to show that fetal alcohol syndrome can be prevented? *Journal of Drug Education, 29*(1), 5–24.

Myers, P. I., & Hammill, D. D. (1990). *Learning disabilities: Basic concepts, assessment practices, and instructional strategies* (3rd ed.). Austin, TX: PRO-ED.

National Academy of Sciences–National Research Council. (1993). *Pesticides in the diets of infants and children.* Washington, DC: National Academy Press.

National Advisory Committee on Handicapped Children to the Bureau of Education for the Handicapped, Office of Education, Department of Health, Education, and Welfare. (1968). *First Annual Report on Handicapped Children.* Washington, DC: Author.

National Center for Addiction and Substance Abuse. (1999). *Fast facts from Schwab Learning.org on learning disabilities.* Retrieved May 19, 2005, from www.schwablearning.org/articles.asp?g=1&r=627.

National Center for Education Statistics. (1999). *Digest of educational statistics.* Washington, DC: U.S. Department of Education, Office of Research and Improvement.

National Center on Educational Outcomes. (1999). Students with Disabilities in Postsecondary Education: A Profile of Preparation, Participation, and Outcomes. Retrieved from www.coled.umn.edu/NCEO.

National Council of Teachers of Mathematics. (2000). *Principles and Standards for School Mathematics.* Reston, VA: Author.

National Dissemination Center for Children and Youth with Disabilities (2004). *Learning disabilities (Fact Sheet #7).* Washington, DC: Author.

National Joint Committee on Learning Disabilities. (1981). As reported in Hammill, D. D., Leigh J. E., McNutt, G., & Larsen, S. C. (1981). A new definition of learning disabilities. *Learning Disability Quarterly, 4,* 336–342.

National Joint Committee on Learning Disabilities. (2000). Professional development for teachers. *Learning Disability Quarterly, 23,* 2–6.

National Joint Committee on Learning Disabilities. (2001). Learning disabilities: Issues on definition. In *Collective perspectives on issues affecting learning disabilities* (2nd ed.). Austin, TX: PRO-ED.

National Joint Committee on Learning Disabilities (1994). *Secondary to postsecondary education transition planning for students with learning disabilities.* Austin, TX: PRO-ED.

National Longitudinal Transition Study (1994). *A summary of findings.* Retrieved May 19, 2005, from www.schwablearning.org/articles.asp?g=1&r=627.

National Longitudinal Transition Study (2003). *The Achievements of Youth with Disabilities During Secondary School.*

Neill, D. M., & Medina, W. J. (1989). Standardized testing: Harmful to educational health. *Phi Delta Kappan, 70*(9), 688–697.

NLD online. (2004). *NLD on the Web.* Available at: www.nldontheweb.org/.

Nowacek, E. J., McKinney, J. D., & Hallahan, D. P. (1990). Instructional behaviors of more and less effective beginning regular and special educators. *Exceptional Children, 57,* 140–149.

Okolo, C. M., Bahr, C. M., & Reith, H. J. (1993). A retrospective view of computer-based instruction. *Journal of Special Education Technology, 12*(1), 1–27.

Okolo, C., Cavalier, A., Feretti, R., & MacArthur, C. (2000). Technology, literacy, and disabilities: A review of the research. In R. Gersten, E. Schiller, & S. Vaughn (Eds.), *Contemporary special education research* (pp. 179–250). Mahwah, NJ: Erlbaum.

Olsen, J. (2003). *Handwriting without tears.* Retrieved May 23, 2003, from http://hwtears.com.

Olson, J. L., & Platt, J. M. (1996). *Teaching children and adolescents with special needs* (2nd ed.). Englewood Cliffs, NJ: Merrill.

Ortiz, S. (2004). Learning Disabilities: A primer for parents about identification. *NASP Communiqué, 32*, (5). Retrieved May 19, 2005, from www.nasponline.org/publications/cq325ldinsert.html.

Osman, B. B. (2000). Learning disabilities and the risk of psychiatric disorders in children and adolescents. In L. Greenhill (Ed.), *Learning disabilities in children with a psychiatric disorder* (pp. 33–57). Washington, DC: American Psychiatric Association.

O'Shaughenessy, T. E., & Swanson, H. L. (1998). Do immediate memory deficits in students with learning disabilities in reading reflect a developmental lag or deficit? *Learning Disability Quarterly, 21,* 123–148.

Overton, T. (1992). *Assessment in special education: An applied approach.* Upper Saddle River, NJ: Merrill.

Overton, T. (1996). *Assessment in special education: An applied approach* (2nd ed.). Upper Saddle River, NJ: Merrill.

Palincsar, A. S., & Brown, A. L. (1986). Interactive teaching to promote independent learning from text. *Reading Teacher, 39,* 771–777.

Palincsar, A. S., & Brown, A. (1987). Enhancing instructional time through attention to metacognition. *Journal of Learning Disabilities, 20*(2), 66–75.

Paulson, E. L., Paulson, P. R., & Meyer, C. A. (1991). What makes a portfolio a portfolio? *Educational Leadership, 48*(5), 60–63.

Paulu, N. (1995). *Helping your child with homework.* Washington, DC: U.S.G.P.O. Available at www.ed.gov/pubs/parents/Homework/title.html.

Pennington, B. (1990). Annotation: The genetics of dyslexia. *Journal of Child Psychology and Child Psychiatry, 31*(2), 193–201.

Pierangelo, R., (2004). *Special educator's survival guide* (2nd ed.). San Francisco: Jossey Bass.

Pierangelo, R., & Giuliani, G. (2001). *Positive restructuring: Creating confident children in the classroom.* Chicago, IL: Research Press.

Pierangelo, R., & Giuliani, G. (2002). *Assessment in special education: A practical approach.* Boston: Allyn & Bacon.

Pierangelo, R. & Giuliani, G. (2004). *Transition services in special education: A practical approach.* Boston: Allyn & Bacon.

Pierangelo, R., & Giuliani, G. (2005). *Assessment in special education: A practical approach* (2nd ed.). Boston: Allyn & Bacon.

Pikulski, J. (1990, March). Informal reading inventories (Assessment). *Reading Teacher, 43*(7), 314–316.

Polloway, E. A., & Patton, J. R. (1993). *Strategies for teaching learners with special needs* (5th ed.). NY: Merrill.

Polloway, E. A., Patton, J. R., & Serna, L. (2001). *Strategies for teaching learners with special needs* (7th ed.). Columbus, OH: Merrill.

President's Commission on Excellence in Special Education. (2002). Retrieved on May 19, 2005, from: www.schwablearning.org/on_the_web.asp?siteid=http://www.ed.gov/inits/commissionsboards/whspecialeducation/index.html%20&popref=http%3A//www.schwablearning.org/articles.asp%3Fg%3D1%26r%3D627.

Pressinger, R. (1999). *Prescription drug exposure during pregnancy.* University of South Florida, Special Education Department. Retrieved on May 19, 2005, from www.chemtox.com/pregnancy/prescription.htm.

Pressley, M., Brown, R., El-Dinary, P. B., & Afflerbach, P. (1995). The comprehension instruction that students need. *Learning Disabilities Research and Practice, 10*(4), 215–224.

Pressley, M., El-Dinary, P. B., Gaskins, I., Schuder, J., Bergman, J. L., Almasi, J., & Brown, R.

(1992). Beyond direct explanation: Transactional instruction of reading comprehension strategies. *Elementary School Journal, 92,* 511–554.

Pressley, M., Symons, S., Snyder, B. L., & Cariglia-Bull, T. (1989). Strategy instruction research comes of age. *Learning Disabilities Quarterly, 12,* 16–30.

Project Choices. (2004). *A LRE initiative of the Illinois State Board of Education.* Retrieved May 19, 2005, from www.projectchoices.org/faqPlace.aspx.

Raskind, W. W. (2001). Current understanding of the genetic basis of reading and spelling differences. *Learning Disability Quarterly, 24,* 141–157.

Reid, D. K., & Hresko, W. P. (1981). *A cognitive approach to learning disabilities.* New York: McGraw-Hill.

Richards, R. G. *The source for dyslexia and dysgraphia.* East Moline, IL: LinguiSystems, 800/PRO-IDEA.

Richards, R. G. (1999). *When writing's a problem.* Riverside, CA: RET Center Press, www.retctrpress.com.

Richards, T. L. (2001). Functional magnetic resonance imaging and spectroscopic imaging of the brain: Application of FMRI and fMRS to reading disabilities and education. *Learning Disabilities Quarterly, 24*(3), 189–203.

Rief, S. F. (1997). *The ADD/ADHD checklist: An easy reference for parents and teachers.* Reston, VA: Council for Exceptional Children.

Rivera, D. (1997). Mathematics education and students with learning disabilities: Introduction to special series. *Journal of Learning Disabilities, 30*(1), 2–19, 68.

Robelia, B. (1997). Tips for working with ADHD students of all ages. *Journal of Experimental Education, 20*(1), 51–53.

Robinson, C. S., Manchetti, B. M., & Torgeson, J. K. (2002). Toward a two-factor theory of one type of mathematics disability. *Learning Disabilities Research and Practice, 17,* 81–89.

Roderiques, A. B. (2002). A comparison of ability-achievement discrepancy models for identifying learning disabilities. *Dissertation Abstracts International Section A: Humanities and Social Sciences, 62*(8-A), 2683.

Roper Starch Poll (1995): *Measuring Progress in Public and Parental Understanding of Learning Disabilities.* Roper Starch Worldwide, Inc.

Rose, D., & Meyer, A. (2000). Universal design for individual differences. *Educational Leadership, 58*(3), 39–43.

Rosenshine, B., & Stevens, R. (1986). The use of scaffolds for teaching higher-level cognitive strategies. *Educational Leadership, 49,* 26–33.

Roth-Smith, C. (1991). *Learning disabilities: The interaction of learner, task, and setting.* Boston: Allyn & Bacon.

Roy, T. S. (1994). Nicotine damages brain cell quality. *Neurotoxicology and Teratology, 16*(4), 1.

Rudner, L. M. (1991). Assessing civics education. College Park, MD: ERIC Clearinghouse on Assessment and Evaluation. (ERIC No. ED 338698).

Sabornie, E. J., & Kauffman, J. M. (1986). Social acceptance of learning disabled adolescents. *Learning Disabilities Quarterly, 9,* 55–60.

Salend, S. J. (1994). *Effective mainstreaming: Creating inclusive classrooms* (2nd ed.). NY: MacMillan.

Salend, S., & Garrick Duhaney, L.(2002, February). Grading students in inclusive settings. *Teaching Exceptional Children, 15,* Retrieved May 19, 2005, from: http://journals.sped.org/EC/Archive_Articles/VOL.34NO.3JANFEB 2002_TEC_Article1.pdf.

Salvia, J., & Ysseldyke, J. E. (1998). *Assessment* (8th ed.). Boston: Houghton Mifflin.

Samango-Sprouse, C. (1999). The hidden disability: Sex chromosome variations (SCV). *American Association for Home-Based Early Interventionists, 4*(4), 1.

Scanlon, D., & Melland, D. F. (2002). Academic and participant profiles of school-age drop outs with and without disabilities. *Exceptional Children, 68,* 239–258.

Schiller, E. (1996). Educating children with attention deficit disorder. *Our Children, 22*(2), 32–33.

Schulte-Korne, G., Deimel, W., Muller, K., Gutenbrunner, C., & Remschmidt, H. (1996). Familial aggregation of spelling disability. *Journal of Child Psychiatry, 37,* 817–822.

Schumaker, J., Deshler, D., Alley, G., Warner, M., & Denton, P. (1984). Mulltipass: A learning strategy for improving reading comprehension. *Learning Disability Quarterly, 5,* 295–304.

Schunk, D. H., & Rice, J. M. (1989). Learning goals and children's reading comprehension. *Journal of Reading Behavior, 21*(3), 279–293.

Schwab Learning. (2004). *LD fast facts.* Retrieved May 19, 2005, from www.schwablearning .org/articles.asp?g=1&r=627.

Scruggs, T. E., & Mastropieri, M. A. (2000). The effectiveness of mnemonic instruction for students with learning and behavior problems: An update and research synthesis. *Journal of Behavioral Education, 10* (2–3), 163–173.

Seligman, M. (1992). *Helplessness: On depression, development and death.* San Francisco: W. H. Freeman.

Sexton, M., Harris, K. R., & Graham, S. (1998). Self-regulated strategy development and the writing process: Effects on essay writing and attributions. *Exceptional Children, 64,* 295–311.

Shalaway, L. (2004). *Planning for parent conferences.* Retrieved May 19, 2005, from http://teacher.scholastic.com/products/instructor/planning_parent_conf.htm.

Shannon, T. R., & Polloway, E. A. (1993). Promoting error monitoring in middle school students with LD. *Intervention in School and Clinic, 28,* 160–164.

Shapiro, E. S. (1989). *Academic skills problems: Direct assessment and intervention.* New York: Guilford.

Shaw, S., Scott, S., & McGuire, J. (2001, November). Teaching college students with learning disabilities. *ERIC EC Digest #E618.* Washington, DC: Author.

Shaywitz, S. (1998). Dyslexia. *New England Journal of Medicine, 338,* 307–312.

Silver, L. B. (1998). *The misunderstood child* (3rd ed.). New York: Times Books.

Silver, L. B. (1999). *Attention deficit hyperactivity disorder: A clinical guide to diagnosis and treatment for health and mental health.* Washington, DC: American Psychiatric Press.

Silver, L. B. (2001, November). *What are learning disabilities?* Retrieved May 19, 2005, from http://ldonline.org/ld_indepth.

Simos, P. J., Breier, J. I., Fletcher, J. M., Bergman, E., & Papanicolaou, A. C. (2000). Cerebral mechanisms involved in word reading in dyslexic children: A magnetic source imaging approach. *Cerebral Cortex, 10,* 809–816.

Sindelar, P. T., Espin, C., Smith, M., & Harriman, N. (1990). A comparison of more and less effective special education teachers in elementary level programs. *Teacher Education and Special Education, 13,* 9–16.

Slavin, R. E. (2002). *Education psychology: Theory into practice.* Boston: Allyn & Bacon.

Smith, C. R. (1994). *Learning disabilities: The interaction of learner, task, and setting* (3rd ed.). Boston: Allyn & Bacon.

Smith, S. (1979). *No easy answers.* Cambridge, MA: Winthrop.

Smith, T. E., Pollaway, E., Patton, J. R., & Dowdy, C. A. (2004). *Teaching students with special needs in inclusive settings.* Boston: Allyn & Bacon.

Snow, C. E., Burns, S., & Griffin, P. (Eds.). (1998). *Preventing reading difficulties in young children.* Washington, DC: National Academy Press. Available at www.nap.edu/catalog/6023.html.

Special education for handicapped children: First Annual Report of the National Advisory Committee on Handicapped Children. (1968). Office of Education, Department of Health, Education, and Welfare. Washington, DC: Author.

Spector, J. E. (1995). Phonemic awareness training: Application of principles of direct instruction. *Reading and Writing Quarterly: Overcoming Learning Difficulties, 11*(1), 37–52.

Spivak, M. (1986). Advocacy and legislative action for head-injured children and their families. *Journal of Head Trauma Rehabilitation, 1,* 41–47.

Sridhar, D., & Vaughn, S. (2001). Bibliotherapy for all: Enhancing reading comprehension, self-concept, and behavior. *Teaching Exceptional Children, 33*(2), 74–82.

Stanovich, K. E. (1982). Individual differences in the cognitive processes in reading: Word decoding. *Journal of Learning Disabilities, 15,* 485–493.

Stanovich, K. E. (1993). Romance and reality. *The Reading Teacher, 47,* 280–291.

Stanovich, K. E., & Siegel, L. S. (1994). The phenotypic performance profile of reading disabled children: A regression-based test of the phonological-core variable-difference model. *Journal of Educational Psychology, 86,* 24–53.

Stevens, S. H. (1997). *Classroom success for the LD and ADHD child.* Winston-Salem, NC: John F. Blair.

Stone, L. (2000). *Readability level analyses for selected documents.* Retrieved May 19, 2005, from www.home.earthlink.net/~lastone2/home.html.

Strauss, A. A., & Lehtinen, L. (1947). *Psychopathology of the brain-injured child,* New York: Grune & Stratton.

Sutton, S. (1998). *Beyond homework help: Guiding our children to lasting math success.*

Swanson, H. L. (1994). Short-term memory and working memory: Do both contribute to our understanding of academic achievement in children and adults with learning disabilities? *Journal of Learning Disabilities, 27,* 34–50.

Swanson, H. L. (1998). Instructional components that predict treatment outcomes for students with learning disabilities: Support for a combined strategy and direct instruction model. *Learning Disabilities Research and Practice, 14,* 129–140.

Swanson, H. L., & Hoskyn, M. (1998). Experimental intervention research for students with learning disabilities: A meta-analysis of treatment outcomes. *Review of Educational Research, 68,* 277–321.

Swanson, H. C., & Watson, B. L. (1989). *Educational and psychological assessment of exceptional children* (2nd ed.). Columbus, OH: Merrill.

Sweetland, R. C., & Keyser, D. J. (Eds.). (1991). *Tests: A comprehensive reference for assessments in psychology, education, and business* (3rd ed.). Austin, TX: PRO-ED.

Taylor, R. (1997). *Assessment of exceptional students: Educational and psychological procedures* (5th ed.). Boston: Allyn & Bacon.

Taylor, R. L. (1991). Bias in cognitive assessment: Issues, implications, and future directions. *Diagnostique, 17*(1), 3–5.

Terrell, S. L. (Ed.). (1983, June). Nonbiased assessment of language differences [Special issue]. *Topics in Language Disorders, 3*(3).

The Education for All Handicapped Children's Act. (1975). Federal Register, 42, 42474-42518.

The International Dyslexia Association. (2005). *Fact sheets about dyslexia and related learning disabilities.* Retrieved May 19, 2005, from www.interdys.org/servlet/compose?section_id=5&page_id=79.

Todd, A. W., Horner, R. H., Sugai, G., & Sprague, J. R. (1999). Effective behavior support: Strengthening school-wide systems through a team-based approach. *Effective School Practices, 17*(4), 23–37.

Torgeson, J. K. (1977). The role of nonspecific factors in the task performance of learning disabled children: A theoretical assessment. *Journal of Learning Disabilities, 10,* 27–34.

Torgeson, J. K. (1988). Studies of children with learning disabilities who perform poorly on memory span tasks. *Journal of Learning Disabilities, 21,* 605–612.

Torgeson, J. K. (1988). The cognitive and behavioral characteristics of children with learning disabilities: An overview. *Journal of Learning Disabilities, 21,* 587–589.

Torgeson, J. K., & Wagner, R. K. (1998). Alternative diagnostic approaches for specific developmental reading disabilities. *Learning Disabilities Research and Practice, 13,* 220–232.

Turnbull, R., Turnbull, A., Shank, M., & Smith, S. J. (2004). *Exceptional lives: Special education in today's schools* (4th ed.). Upper Saddle River, NJ: Merrill/Prentice Hall.

U.S. Department of Education, Office of Special Education and Rehabilitative Services, Office of Special Education Programs. (2004). *Teaching Children with Attention Deficit Hyperactivity Disorder: Instructional Strategies and Practices,* Washington, DC: Author.

U.S. Department of Education. (2000). *Twenty-second annual report to Congress on the implementation of the Individuals with Disabilities Education Act.* Washington, DC: U.S. Government Printing Office.

U.S. Department of Education. (2002). *Twenty-fourth annual report to Congress on the implementation of the Individuals with Disabilities Education Act.* Washington, DC: Author.

U.S. Department of Education. (2003). *Twenty-fifth annual report to Congress on the implementation of the Individuals with Disabilities Education Act.* Washington, DC: Author.

U.S. Department of Labor (2004). *Bureau of Labor Statistics.* Washington, DC: Author.

U.S. Interagency Committee on Learning Disabilities. (1987). As cited in Kavanagh, J. F., &

Truss, T. J. (1988). *Learning disabilities: Proceedings of the national conference* (pp. 550–551). Parkton, MD: York.

U.S. Office of Education. (1968). *First annual report of National Advisory Committee on Handicapped Children.* Washington, DC: U.S. Department of Health, Education and Welfare.

U.S. Office of Education. (1977). *Guide to helping your child understand mathematics.* Boston: Houghton Mifflin.

University of Illinois. (2004). *Urban Programs Resource Network.* Retrieved on May 19, 2005, from www.urbanext.uiuc.edu/index.html-homepage.

Vacca, J., Vacca, R., & Grove, M. (1986). *Reading and learning to read.* Boston: Little, Brown.

Vaughn, S., McIntosh, R., Schumm, J. S., Haager, D., & Callwood, D. (1993). Social status, peer acceptance, and reciprocal friendships revisited. *Learning Disabilities Research and Practice, 8,* 82–88.

Vellutino, F. R. (1979). *Dyslexia: Theory and research.* Cambridge, MA: MIT Press.

Vellutino, F. (1987, March). Dyslexia. *Scientific American, 256,* 3.

Venn, J. (2000). *Assessing students with special needs* (2nd ed.). Upper Saddle River, NJ: Merrill.

Wagner, M., & Blackorby, J. (2002). *Disability profiles of elementary and middle school students with disabilities.* Menlo Park, CA: SRI International.

Wallace, G., Larsen, S. C., & Elksnin, L. K. (1992). *Educational assessment of learning problems: Testing for teaching.* Boston: Allyn & Bacon.

Wallert, T., & Puffer, T. (1995). *A systematic approach for assisting students with learning disabilities in postsecondary education.* Retrieved May 19, 2005, from www.ldonline.org/ld_indepth/postsecondary/ncld_prism.html.

Waterman, B. (1994). Assessing children for the presence of a disability. *NICHCY News Digest, 4*(1), 1–15.

Webb, G. M. (1992, February 19). Needless battles on dyslexia. *Education Week,* 32.

Wechsler, D. (1958). *The measurement and appraisal of adult intelligence* (4th ed.). Baltimore: Williams & Wilkins.

Wehmeyer, M. L., & Schwartz, M. (1997). Self-determination and positive adult outcomes: A follow-up study of youth with mental retardation or learning disabilities. *Exceptional Children, 63,* 245–255.

Wiederhold, J. L., Hammill, D. D., & Brown, V. L. (1978). *The resource teacher.* Boston: Allyn & Bacon.

Wills, L. J. (2000, April). *What works in special education and why.* Vancouver, BC: Council for Exceptional Children.

Wissich, C., & Gardner, J. (2000). Multimedia or not multimedia. *Teaching Exceptional Children, 32*(4), 34–43.

Wodrich, D. L., & Joy, J. E. (1986). *Multidisciplinary assessment of children with learning disabilities and mental retardation.* Baltimore, MD: Paul H. Brookes.

Wong, B. Y. L., Butler, D. L., Ficzere, S. A., & Kuperis, S. (1996). Teaching low achievers and students with learning disabilities to plan, write, and revise opinion essays. *Journal of Learning Disabilities, 20,* 197–212.

Wong, B. Y. L., Butler, D. L., Ficzere, S. A., & Kuperis, S. (1997). Teaching adolescents with learning disabilities and low achievers to plan, write, and revise compare-and-contrast essays. *Learning Disabilities Research & Practice, 12*(1), 2–15.

Wong, B. Y. L., & Jones, W. (1982). Increasing metacomprehension in learning disabled and normally achieving students through self-questioning training. *Learning Disability Quarterly, 5,* 409–414.

Wood, D., Rosenburg, M., & Carran, D. (1993). The effects of tape-recorded self-instruction cues on the mathematics performance of students with learning disabilities. *Journal of Learning Disabilities, 26*(4), 250–258, 269.

Wood, J. W. (1992). *Adapting instruction for mainstreamed and at risk students* (2nd ed.). NY: Merrill.

Worling, D. E., Humphries, T., & Tannock, R. (1999). Spatial and emotional aspects of language inferencing in nonverbal learning disabilities. *Brain and Language, 70,* 220–239.

Wright-Strawderman, C., & Watson, B. L. (1992). The prevalence of depressive symptoms in children with learning disabilities. *Journal of Learning Disabilities, 25,* 258–264.

Yopp, H. (1992). Developing phonemic awareness in young children. *The Reading Teacher, 45,* 696–703.

Name Index

Subject Index